# Spymistress

Also by William Stevenson

*The Bormann Brotherhood*
*A Man Called Intrepid*
*90 Minutes at Entebbe*
*Intrepid's Last Case*
*Kiss the Boys Goodbye*
*The Revolutionary King*

# *Spymistress*

## THE LIFE OF VERA ATKINS,
## THE GREATEST FEMALE SECRET AGENT OF WORLD WAR II

# WILLIAM STEVENSON

ARCADE PUBLISHING • NEW YORK

FIRST EDITION

*Library of Congress Cataloging-in-Publication Data*

Stevenson, William, 1925–
  Spymistress : the life of Vera Atkins, the greatest female secret agent of World War II / by William Stevenson. —1st ed.
    p. cm.
  Includes bibliographical references.
  ISBN 978-1-55970-763-3 (hc)
  ISBN 978-1-55970-886-9 (pb)
  1. Atkins, Vera, 1908–2000. 2. Spies — Great Britain — Biography. 3. World War, 1939–1945 — Secret service — Great Britain. 4. Great Britain. Special Operations Executive — History. I. Title.

  UB271.G7S74 2005
  940.54'8641'092—dc22                                         2004023458
  [B]

Published in the United States by Arcade Publishing, Inc., New York
Distributed by Hachette Book Group USA

Visit our Web site at www.arcadepub.com

10  9  8  7  6  5  4  3  2

Designed by API

EB

PRINTED IN THE UNITED STATES OF AMERICA

# Contents

# Preface

Vera Atkins was the brilliant, highly effective leader of a select group who fought in secrecy against the Nazis in occupied Europe after the fall of France in 1940. These brave young men and women had volunteered for Special Operations Executive (SOE), improvised at this time of greatest peril by Winston Churchill, the last hope of a country whose leaders he had tried for years to awaken to the growing danger of Nazi Germany. Long out of office, he suddenly—"almost too late," he remarked—became prime minister on May 10, 1940, at which point he had to confront those in Whitehall who sought to appease Hitler and make a separate peace. Even loyal staff officers in the War Office of Churchill's government resented the secrecy surrounding SOE and feared that its agents' violent actions against the enemy were incompatible with democratic traditions, "offending international law and the concept of habeas corpus." To these niceties, the utterly pragmatic Churchill responded by instructing the British chiefs of staff "to develop a reign of terror to make the lives of German occupiers an eternal torment." That message also gave Vera Atkins's SOE a license to conduct her campaign in occupied France as her extraordinary mind and steely resolve dictated.

Churchill's hope after he became prime minister was that, sooner or later, America would join England in opposing the formidable Nazi war machine, for despite his indomitable public figure and ringing statements, he was far from sure England could win alone. His relations with President Roosevelt were good, but as the 1940 election neared, Roosevelt warned his friend that antiwar sentiment in the States was high, even overwhelming, which he could not ignore. In that election year Roosevelt—and the American people—were also far from convinced England would win the war. To get a better picture, FDR sent his trusted confidant William J. Donovan, the future head of OSS, to London to assess the situation. There Donovan was put in contact with Vera Atkins. She so impressed him that he reported back to the president his strong impression of her, and Britain's, courage and his conviction that the tide would be turned. Thus it is fair to say that, in addition to her accomplishments as Britain's Spymistress, she was also a key factor in convincing the Roosevelt administration of the Allies' ultimate success.

SOE was Churchill's desperate attempt to demonstrate that there was life in the old lion yet and, indeed, to make life "an eternal torment" for the Nazis, who after their blitzkrieg attacks across continental Europe were preparing to carry out Hitler's Directive 16 and invade England. SOE's mandate from the start was to sabotage, burn, harass, and kill the enemy, "to set the continent ablaze." Its numbers were strikingly few. Of 480 agents in the French Section, 130 were tortured, and many were executed in shocking circumstances. Despite their heavy losses, these men and women, over the four long years of German occupation, wreaked havoc on the Nazis throughout the country. With the growing help of the French Resistance, they cut phone lines to force the Germans to communicate by wireless (so Bletchley could intercept), blew up bridges and tunnels, and derailed military trains. As this book shows, at the time of the Normandy invasion on June 6, 1944, they were so effective in harassing the German divisions rushing from the south of France and the Eastern Front to reinforce Normandy that they slowed down their arrival long enough, perhaps, to have turned the tide of the war.

In prewar Europe, Vera had already been working against this ruthless enemy. She was aided in this clandestine effort by William Stephenson (Intrepid), a Canadian businessman who, together with some other imported North Americans, had early sensed the dangers inherent in Hitler's rise to power, and formed in New York the British Security Coordination (BSC) office. Meeting Vera first in Bucharest and later in London, Stephenson was so impressed by her mind, her mastery of several languages, her dedication, and her fierce anti-Nazi stance that he sent her on fact-finding missions to several European countries, secretly reporting her findings to a few trusted souls in Britain. Together they supplied Churchill, then in his political wilderness, with facts about the growing Nazi threat and the sorry neglect of UK defenses. These facts were ignored by most members of Parliament before the outbreak of World War II on September 1, 1939, when the first German blitz quickly subjugated Poland. A fierce Polish anti-Nazi resistance arose from the ashes to inspire similar resistance movements in other German-occupied countries. Vera immediately saw that France, just across the English Channel, would soon be fertile ground for her agents.

Despite her very British name and demeanor, Vera was actually Romanian Jewish, born Vera Maria Rosenberg in Bucharest. In England, this put her at constant risk from the Alien Act of 1793 and the Official Secrets Act, which criminalizes the publication—even the republication—of certain kinds of information deemed to be a security risk. She took the name Vera Atkins, derived from her mother's maiden name, Etkin, to avoid detention as an enemy alien. Into her old age, she would dance and make merry with SOE survivors who knew her only as Miss Atkins, who honored her for superior qualities of intellect and loyalty, and who never talked of their wartime work until SOE came under attack by postwar critics.

Colonel Maurice Buckmaster, who had worked alongside Vera, was thunderstruck when in October 1958 a book entitled *Double Webs* was published. Its author, Jean Overton Fuller, claimed that SOE's air movements officer in France, Henri Dericourt, had actually been a double agent and that SOE agents were deliberately sacrificed "to draw the Gestapo away from still more secret operations." On November 13, 1958, Dame Irene Ward, a member of Parliament, proposed to table a motion calling for an Official Secrecy Act Inquiry into these and other allegations of SOE incompetence. She was persuaded not to proceed by then prime minister Harold Macmillan, who said an official history would be commissioned. This appeared eight years later, in 1966, written by M. R. D. Foot, with details approved by the government and published by Her Majesty's Stationery Office.

Buckmaster released a public statement that said in part: "The events which took place more than twenty years ago have left their mark on many people who would be glad to have left the dead to sleep in peace (allowing the results of their bravery to speak for themselves). ... We have been called amateurs. It is true that SOE was an ad hoc organization for which no blueprints existed before the war.... The most appalling accusation made against us is that we DELIBERATELY sent out agents into the hands of the Gestapo" to be tortured into disclosing misleading information. "I flatly deny such monstrous and intolerable accusations.... The French Resistance, in the words of

General Eisenhower, 'shortened the war by many months.' The world owes to the men and women of the French Section [of SOE] a debt which can never be fully discharged."

All her life, Vera had fought running battles with bureaucrats and military chiefs who disapproved of SOE "skullduggery." She had scuffled continuously with the SIS, whose European networks had been compromised by the German kidnapping of SIS agents. Some SIS mandarins were actually dedicated to the destruction of SOE. After the war Vera held her tongue, even more conscious of her vulnerability in the Cold War hunt for Soviet-run agents with Jewish and foreign backgrounds.

During her lifetime Vera was publicly silent. She had bitter memories of the SIS effort from 1940 through 1945 to shut down SOE while her agents fought valiantly abroad. Immediately after World War II, SOE's domestic enemies finally succeeded in shutting it down. Then, early in 1946 a mysterious fire gutted the top floor of SOE's Baker Street headquarters, destroying most of its records. According to Angus Fyffe, a veteran of SOE and its record keeper, those records contained political time bombs waiting to explode. Vera and her colleagues had fought doggedly during the war to maintain their independence from the War Office and official bureaucracy. Once the war was over, Vera withdrew to her home in Winchelsea where she lived quietly — and silently — for the next half century.

Vera lived long enough to see Churchill's foresight vindicated yet again. It justified her silence. Why give away secrets to satisfy short-term public curiosity, secrets about underground operations and improvised explosives and weapons that a new enemy could adopt? She still had reservations about the potential power of secrecy laws, but she never believed, as many did when the Cold War ended, that we had reached the end of history. Churchill's book *The River War*, published in 1899 — and her own needless difficulties in fighting domestic enemies — convinced her that secrecy laws could be held in reserve to deal with exceptional danger. She knew that parliamentary procedures could go hand in hand with secrecy, as her hitherto untold story here reveals.

# Introduction

The police sergeant handed me a scrap of paper. "Here's the address. Some secret new ministry. Ask for Atkins. An air-raid warden. Or something." He shifted uneasily. "Okay, on your bike, double-quick!"

The bombing of London was at its peak in the summer of 1940. I bicycled messages between East Ham police station and emergency posts if phone lines were cut. My Boy Scout uniform opened a way through cordoned streets where rescue workers dug for survivors. Hitler's war machine had destroyed France and was poised to cross the English Channel. I had seen from the sergeant's procommunist *Daily Worker* that the chairman of the U.S. Senate Foreign Relations Committee, Key Pittman, said Great Britain faced certain defeat and "must capitulate." The sergeant never read the popular papers, insisting, "They're run by pro-Nazi press barons."

The address was in London's West End. Piccadilly, Marble Arch, and Buckingham Palace had been hit in the night, as well as the Park Lane mansion of the Marquess of Londonderry, a former air minister who wanted an alliance with the Nazis. Of this, I knew little. I was a last-resort means of communication: a small, bare-headed, bare-kneed boy, bicycling past overturned electric trams and their drooping power cables still spitting blue sparks between mangled metal tracks. Drivers of red double-deck buses bravely tried to keep to their peacetime schedules, and some nosedived into pits that yawned suddenly when time bombs exploded. In one crater, the bus to Ladbroke Grove creaked and groaned like a dying dinosaur.

The ministry had taken over a venerable old building, sand-bagged against bomb blasts, windows crisscrossed with strips of paper to limit the shattering of glass. The uniformed porter made me wait in the gallery of shadowed portraits, rows of richly cloaked gentry, rubicund faces plump with self-satisfaction. I imagined the police sergeant gloating, Those smiles'll be wiped off their faces by the bashing we're getting. The toffs had backed the wrong horse in Hitler, hoping his Nazis would build a barrier against Bolsheviks and Soviets. That's what most East Enders said, anyway.

"I'm Atkins." The girlish voice startled me. I had not expected Atkins to be a pretty young woman. She took me to a man wearing a pinstriped suit. He had the accents of a toff. "You're a King's Scout?"

"Yes."

"Then you can be trusted?"

"Yes."

"Your father's safe. He'll be out of France soon. Tell your mum. But if she or you tell anyone else, he'll be dead."

France? I thought my father was in America. Questions froze on my lips. The man had given me the obligatory lesson on the high price of breaking secrecy, and had turned to larger matters. The young woman steered me through dark corridors, up and down broad and barren stone steps, back to the street. She was trim-waisted and light-footed. She watched me swing a leg over my bicycle saddle and shift the gas mask at my back. I braced one foot against the curbstone and looked up. "Miss Atkins?"

She nodded. Smoky eyes pierced into me. She must be reading my mind, with its dirty little schoolboy secrets, its cowardice, its disrespect for silly rules. I was terrified.

Then she unbuttoned her tunic, as if escaping officialdom's stuffy rules. She had long legs that vanished high up into a short skirt. The stockings were silk, and the skirt was far from regulation length. I breathed easier. She was a rebel like me. She bent over the handlebars of my bike, and I became aware of her breasts pressing against a lavender silk shirt that hadn't been purchased with ration coupons.

"Where's your helmet?" she asked.

"My head's too small. And a Scout hat blows off."

She laughed, a rich chuckle, not the tut-tut of disapproving adults. She said something about my brothers and sister. Our mother had decreed that none of us were to be evacuated to the countryside, making it sound like Outer Mongolia: "Father won't know where to look for us when he comes back." Mother was French. It dawned on me that this might be why he was in France and not in Boston. That was where, long ago, he found Christian Science. Ever since then, Mother had read aloud at breakfast each day's lesson from Mary Baker

Eddy and *Science and Health, with Key to the Scriptures*. The ritual validated Father's absences abroad. I had the feeling that Miss Atkins knew about this. We watched each other in the failing light. Then the news sank in: Father was coming home!

How did the man upstairs know? Anticipating the question, she shook her head, as if to say, Don't ask, and offered a cigarette. It was nice to be treated like an adult, but I knew I would only choke on it. "No thanks, Miss!"

She lit her own. The flare of a match seemed like another act of defiance: German bomber pilots were reputed to have superhuman vision, and the wail of air-raid sirens had started up again. I saw, close up, the delicate bone structure of Greta Garbo's face in a movie about Emile Zola, a face promising nothing and offering all. She bent closer, and I sensed her warm body and smelled her bare skin. She said, "You're in the front lines, aren't you, running messages? Dangerous, isn't it, on a bike?"

"Only way to get through all the muck, Miss. And quickest."

"Reliable, too." She was turning things over in her mind. "You don't have wireless at your police stations?"

"Not where I live."

She smiled. A sad sort of smile. Her hand lightly stroked my cheek. It was a surprisingly strong hand. She said something that ended with "all is love." She sounded like Mary Baker Eddy.

"Tell your mother. She'll understand." Miss Atkins tucked a cardboard token into my shirt pocket. "If things get rough, you can contact me. Some public phone boxes sometimes work."

I repeated the words to my mother. She said, "That confirms your father is safe," as if Mary Baker Eddy and Miss Atkins were clairvoyants delivering a coded message.

I asked the police sergeant the next day about the mysterious building. "Who's in charge?"

He countered, "What were you told?"

I said I was sworn to secrecy.

He shrugged. "There you are, then. Nuffink but secrets." He hesitated. "It's some bunch of funnies. Ministry of Economic Warfare. Don't mean much. We can't even fight a regular war."

Soon I would circumnavigate new bomb craters. Each courier run was the whiff of a potent drug: danger. I consulted the cardboard token from the woman with long silken legs: Air-Raid Warden Vera Atkins. A very English name. A very posh English accent. Yet under the cool clipped speech of the English upper class was a trace of my mother's Continental warmth. This was not the only contradiction about Miss Atkins I noticed. How did she get silk stockings in a time of severe rationing? Did she honor the spirit of wartime rules by wearing woolen bloomers, just out of sight? Such a woman, stepping out of the deferential role of peacetime drudgery, aroused a wild surmise. Beside her name on the token was a telephone number. "Never 'eard of it," said the police sergeant when I wanted to dial the number from an outside phone booth, but it rang, and I did get Vera on the line.

My father was flown out of France in an antique Lysander. The pinstriped man who seemed Vera's superior was Dr. Hugh Dalton, dressed up as economic warfare minister, an old Etonian with upper-crust credentials who had long planned a working-class revolution against the Nazis. The Lysander was an army spotter plane, obsolete, but agile enough to ferry agents behind enemy lines.

My reunited family moved to 109 Bletchley Road, Bletchley, home of the ULTRA code breakers who sat in cold wooden huts, struggling daily to solve the ever-changing conundrums in encrypted Enigma signals. The townsfolk never breathed a word. I had to wait until 2001 to be told by a cousin, Jacques Deleporte, how his family in France were shocked when Father returned before D-day. Germans surrounded the house, which sheltered a Jewish family. Father was in uniform as insurance against being shot as a spy. He never spoke of this. Nor did my mother. It was Jacques who finally told me how my mother taught raw agents to mangle their classroom French, if they wanted to survive in Occupied Europe.

In the years leading up to World War II, Vera had provided Winston Churchill with information on Germany's secret preparations for a blitzkrieg when he was in the political wilderness, maligned as a drink-sodden warmonger. In mid-1940 he was suddenly in charge of a war that seemed already lost. In response, Churchill officially founded the Special Operations Executive (SOE), an intelligence agency that specialized in nontraditional methods. Vera became one of its most valuable assets, a spymistress. SOE's structure was so fluid that if she chose to wear the modest uniform of a pilot-officer, she could still give orders to a major general.

With a deliberate lack of secrecy, Churchill proclaimed SOE's directives: Set Europe ablaze! Make Hitler's life an eternal torment! Hit and run! Butcher and bolt! The rhetoric was meant to make Hitler rethink his invasion plans and show Americans their help would not be wasted. After that, SOE became practically invisible, except when Vera was authorized to show an influential American, OSS director William J. Donovan, on his first secret mission for President Franklin D. Roosevelt, the preparations for what she called "closework": the close engagement of a physically superior foe by clandestine armies supplied with hurriedly invented weapons that could be quickly assembled in the field for sabotage, assassination, and hand-to-hand combat.

Vera recruited her agents carefully, trained them until they dropped from exhaustion, constantly tested them, then personally packed them off on missions. Her clandestine army went deep behind enemy lines, linked up with resistance fighters, destroyed vital targets, helped Allied pilots escape capture, and radioed information back to London. Her agents and saboteurs were not armed with aerial fighting machines. If they chose to die to evade capture, they crunched on lethal cyanide pills. They were willing to do everything to liberate Europe from the Nazis.

Before SOE's official birth, Vera worked with impoverished prewar secret agencies and the obscure Industrial Intelligence Centre of the Committee of Imperial Defence (IICCID), which had been formed "to discover and report plans for manufacture of armaments and war stores in foreign countries." The IICCID languished during years of neglect, and its chief, Desmond Morton, conveyed information to Churchill from anti-Nazis like Vera and from active servicemen who risked prosecution under the Official Secrets Act. They disclosed information because they felt their armed forces were betrayed by poor leadership and a lack of vision, or worse. Lord Londonderry, the air minister who presided over the decline of the Royal Air Force (RAF), sent a letter on the eve of war to the German air force chief, Hermann Göring. It began: "Dear General der Flieger and Minister President (though I would prefer to call you 'Siegfried' as you are my conception of a Siegfried of modern times)." It was not only the British Union of Fascists who admired Hitler: the evidence was buried in secret files until now.

Those of Hitler's admirers who were already known among the political and social elite of England in the false peace of the 1920s and 1930s were called Guilty Men, against whom an underground war was fought by a group of self-styled Mutual Friends who combined their special knowledge to warn of Britain's terrifying vulnerability before the open conflict with Germany began. Vera's ideas about covert warfare stemmed from her part in this underground war.

When SOE was born, Vera Atkins's true identity as a Jew of Romanian extraction could have gotten her interned as a wartime "enemy alien." She was uniquely vulnerable to the application of old secrecy laws. Later, as a naval fighter pilot who flew spy planes and was drawn into intelligence gathering, I was bound by the same oath of secrecy that sealed Vera's lips.

Vera acquired a "sterile identity"; personal data would lead only to blank spaces in official registers. In the public domain are 1945–47 postwar reports on how she hunted down those who tortured and killed 118 of her agents who never returned from behind enemy lines, and pursued some of their tormentors into Stalinist territory. Other accounts of her heroic career come from Mutual Friends in the intelligence world, some of whom need to remain anonymous. Some SOE survivors took the risk of talking about the shabby reasons behind the pitiless termination of SOE and the destruction of its records after World War II. They told me their stories of the woman they had greatly admired until her death in 2000. I recorded the authoritative recollections of many who knew Vera, and read notes kept by Sir William Stephenson — the man called Intrepid, who ran British Security Coordination (BSC) out of New York — and his wife, Lady Mary. Stephenson was Canadian; Mary was from Tennessee. Neither had to swear a British oath of secrecy, and so they were valuable sources of information. Their discussions with Vera began in prewar Bucharest, and continued in Britain. Vera's close friend SOE agent Sonia "Tony" d'Artois provided or corroborated much of the personal information. She and her husband, Guy, parachuted behind the lines, fought with distinction, and said they always felt safe in the hands of the formidably efficient Miss Atkins. Sonia described Vera to me as the liveliest of fun-loving companions, when free from professional cares. Another source was SOE's director of operations, Major General Colin "Gubby" Gubbins, who was on a secret mission with Vera in Poland in

1939 when Hitler unleashed the first blitzkrieg. Her unique knowledge of the terrain enabled them to escape with Polish code breakers and copies of the German Enigma coding machines.

In France, I found many records unavailable in London. Other foreign archives are far less restricted. The Swiss Intelligence Agency (SIA) keeps files that were readily opened for me; a director-general of the SIA pointed out that his small country survived on superb foreign intelligence. Americans, often accused of being obsessed with secrecy, gladly allowed me to examine the records of the wartime Office of Strategic Studies (OSS), precursor to the CIA. Bill Colby, a wartime agent and later a CIA chief, shared with me his memories of Vera. Bill Donovan, who launched the OSS, was first shown SOE's improvisations by Vera, before Pearl Harbor, when she convinced him that Britain was not as ramshackle as it looked and was worth U.S. support.

Ian Fleming, who was himself a spy, used Vera as the model for Miss Moneypenny, the secretary to his fictional James Bond, and said, "In the real world of spies, Vera Atkins was the boss." She received no public recognition until 1995, when French president François Mitterrand astounded everyone by making her a Commandant of the Légion d'Honneur. Pete Lee, one of her former agents, said, "Now that her gallantry has been recognized at last, a number of us take great pleasure in lobbying for Queen Elizabeth II to make her a Companion of the British Empire." The Victoria Cross, the highest decoration for courage, was for men only.

This book is my tribute to the incomparable Vera Atkins and all the courageous men and women of SOE.

# Terms and Abbreviations

Abwehr
: German military intelligence.

Arisaig:
: Perfect for training nighttime forces, this is a wild and desolate part of Scotland, ranging from Fort William to the Isle of Skye. SOE's main school was Arisaig House, where agents underwent tough training in hand-to-hand combat, telegraphy, and sabotage. They planted bogus explosives on the area's single winding railroad, had to find notional targets among gale-swept islands, hidden coves, and freezing lochs, and snuck across scrub-covered hills and bogs undetected. A small plaque commemorates the training ground at Arisaig House, now an exclusive hotel.

BCRA
: Bureau Central de Renseignements et d'Action. De Gaulle's intelligence service when he arrived in London, which became Direction Générale des Services Spéciaux from 1940 to 1944.

Black Chamber
: Facility for code breaking and interception of correspondence and communications.

Bombe
: Device linking several captured or replica Enigma machines in an effort to break codes generated by German operators. A later British adaptation was called a *bomba*.

Brûlé
: "Burned." Said of a French network or agent that is exposed or "blown."

BSC
: British Security Coordination. Run from New York by William Stephenson.

C
: Britain's secret service, SIS. Its chief was also traditionally known only as "C."

Circuit
: Loosely, a network, group of agents or guerrilla forces.

| | |
|---|---|
| Deuxième Bureau | Intelligence section of French general staff. |
| D/F | Direction-finding. German D/F vans were used to pinpoint sources of clandestine radio transmissions. |
| DMI | Director of Military Intelligence (British). |
| DNI | Director of Naval Intelligence (British). |
| Enigma | German coding machine. Berlin Cipher Office thought it impossible to crack. |
| FANY | First Aid Nursing Yeomanry. Membership in this British women's auxiliary was sometimes accorded to women agents in the faint hope that, if captured, they would be treated as prisoners of war. |
| FFI | Forces Françaises de l'Intérieur. Free French forces of General de Gaulle. |
| F Section | SOE section dealing with France. |
| FTP | Francs-Tireurs et Partisans. Resistance movement originating with pro-Soviet agents in France. |
| Gadgets | SOE workshops supplied catalogs from which Resistance armies and SOE agents could order special devices by airmail. Q Gadgets included incendiary bricks, limpet mines, tire bursters, silenced weapons, daggers, magnets, rope ladders, railroad charges, underwater gear, dehydrated rations, double-sided briefcases, pedal generators, a one-man submarine, whiskey flasks, folding shovels, watersuits, and explosives disguised as wine bottles, driftwood, plastic fruit and flowers, rusty bolts, stone lanterns, bicycle pumps and even a German flashlight that detonated when switched on. By 1945, the catalog of secret gadgetry filled two hundred pages. |
| GCCS | Government Code and Cipher School. Bletchley code breakers. |
| Gestapo | Geheime Staatspolizei. German secret state police. |
| IICCID | Industrial Intelligence Centre of the Committee of Imperial Defence (British). |
| Jedburghs | Small teams of American and British agents with |

|  | French liaison officers, parachuted behind enemy lines during D-day period to help coordinate closework with Allied invaders. |
|---|---|
| Kripo | Kriminalpolizei. German criminal police. |
| Maquis | French resistance forces, named for the Mediterranean underbrush in which they often took refuge. Originally made up of those evading German forced labor in France. Later, French resisters in general. They were armed and trained by SOE and the OSS and worked with other underground fighters in occupied Europe, sending London vital intelligence from inside German industrial, military, and transport bases. By D-day, Maquis units were so well organized that they sabotaged or fought crack German military units pouring in to encircle Allied landing areas and helped turn the tide when the Allies seemed unable to break out from the Normandy beachheads. |
| MI | Military Intelligence. The organizations to which the designation is applied are not always strictly military. |
| MI5 | Internal security service, or counterintelligence (British). |
| MI6 | Secret Intelligence Service (SIS) (British). |
| MI9 | Escape-and-evasion section of British War Office, charged with running lines for escapees and training military personnel in escape techniques. |
| Milice | Widely feared paramilitary police run by the pro-Nazi Vichy government, infiltrated by pro-Allied Frenchmen later in the war. |
| One-Time Pad | A set of encryption algorithms to be used only once. The wireless operator or sender composes a message and enciphers it by adding to each character the corresponding "key" from a sheet of the one-time pad. The number of the sheet used is included with the message, and the sheet is then destroyed. The recipient, who has a copy of the same pad, deciphers the message using the matching |

sheet, which is in turn destroyed. The one-off nature of the exchange should guarantee that any message sent this way cannot be broken. The original Russian one-time pad usually had fifty pages. Leo Marks at SOE produced an advanced version, using "silks" divided into numbered squares.

OSS
Office of Strategic Services, precursor to the CIA. "The club" included men of enough power to help Vera in wartime—men who later served as presidential advisers (Arthur Schlesinger Jr. and Walt Rostow), UN ambassador (Arthur Goldberg), treasury secretary (Douglas Dillon), and CIA director (Allen Dulles and Richard Helms). Former OSS officers became U.S. ambassadors in a score of countries. David Bruce, who commanded OSS in the European Theater, was ambassador successively to England, France, Germany, and NATO and to Vietnam peace talks in Paris. Bruce was outspoken about the "smug self-satisfaction" of OSS enemies in the State Department.

OWI
Office of War Information (USA).

Pianist
Wireless operator, in SOE and Russian intelligence slang.

PWE
Political Warfare Executive. British agency producing "black" propaganda and misleading information, often through fake German radio stations.

Réseau
Network. In France, a circuit of underground fighters.

RF Section
SOE French section cooperating with General de Gaulle's "independent" F section, originally outside SOE's jurisdiction. Vera worked to bring together six SOE sections that started out operating separately for similar political reasons, a situation she eventually resolved.

Rote Kappelle:
Red Orchestra, a cryptonym coined by the RSHA for Soviet espionage networks. In France after 1940, it used funds salvaged from other occupied

countries and investments sent by the Soviet Union for controlled export firms like SIMEX in Paris. Moscow agents controlled seven circuits in France; each network operated independently and reported only to the "Grand Chef." These Soviet operations were highly skilled in spycraft and caused mutual suspicions between exile governments and especially between de Gaulle and SOE's own French section. At the end of the war, de Gaulle remained deeply worried about the potential power of the Rote Kappelle to seize control in France, although by 1945 it had become difficult to distinguish between dedicated communists and French resisters who simply joined the nearest available anti-Nazi operation.

RSHA — Reichssicherheitshauptamt. German central security office, which included the SD and Sipo.

SAS — Special Air Service (British). Colonel David Stirling founded SAS during World War II to send small mobile teams behind enemy lines to make daring raids. "He destroyed more enemy aircraft on the ground than the RAF did in the air," said Vera, arguing that "butcher-and-bolt" tactics needed to be given more support. The SAS reinforced French resistance armies, parachuting men trained in unconventional SOE-style warfare.

SD — Sicherheitsdienst. Nazi Party security service under Himmler, fiercely competitive with the Abwehr in acting against closework resisters.

Secret Army — Armée Secrète. Amalgamated military forces of the French resistance.

Section D — Sabotage branch of UK War Office. Later morphed into SOE.

Silk — Material, more compact than paper, easy to burn, easy to conceal, and favored by SOE for one-time pads (q.v.). Also, such a "pad."

Sipo — Sicherheitspolizei. German security police. Executive organ of Gestapo and Kripo.

SIS — Secret Intelligence Service (British). Sometimes referred to as "C," as was its chief. Also identified as MI6.

SOE — Special Operations Executive. Secrecy about its existence was so tight that, inside the armed forces, even those at the top were not always aware that SO(1), SO(2), the Inter-Services Research Bureau, Special Training Schools Headquarters, NID(Q), MO1(SP) at the War Office, and A1 10 at the Air Ministry were all cover names for SOE.

SR — Service de Renseignements, run by the Deuxième Bureau and responsible for running agents, tapping telephones, and analyzing media reports and counterintelligence.

SS — Schutzstaffel. Blackshirt elite guard of the Nazi Party. Later evolved into units of special police under the Gestapo and SD.

STS — Special Training School.

Sûreté — French Special Branch, similar to the FBI or Scotland Yard.

Vichy France — Southern zone, unoccupied by Germans until November 1942 but subject to pro-Nazi policing and administration under a Third Republic set up by Marshal Pétain at the health spa of Vichy.

WAAF — Women's Auxiliary Air Force. Officially, Vera Atkins was a flying officer and later squadron leader in the WAAF.

Woburn Abbey — Estate of the Duke of Bedford, near Bletchley. Used as a country retreat by propagandists from London Control of PWE, who called the place CHQ.

# Spymistress

# 1

# Max's Daughter

*At night you feel strange things stirring in the darkness.*
—D. H. Lawrence

Vera Maria Rosenberg seems to have been an enigma from the day she was born. This was in 1908, on June 2 by the Romanian calendar or June 15 by the Western calendar.

She was the only daughter of Max Rosenberg, who had read in the *Oxford English Dictionary* that an enigmatic person was "mysterious, baffling as to character, sentiments, identity, or history." He told Vera: "There's safety in conjecture." She saw her father as an enigma too, sticking to his Jewish name among anti-Semites in Romania, the land of her actual birth, when he could legitimately have claimed to be German. She took his advice and became known as tight-lipped, outspoken, kind, ruthless, beautiful, dowdy, a social butterfly, a scholar, proudly Jewish, more English than a vicar's daughter, forever falling in love with men or only interested in women. Such contradictions cloaked her secret wartime operations. She sought no medals. In her extreme old age, the French awarded her the highest rank in the Legion of Honor, and shamed the British into finally matching this long overdue recognition.

When she died, the libel laws could no longer silence her enemies. Some said she was a communist agent. Others said German intelligence had controlled her. She was not alone in being calumniated. In the latter part of his life, her friend Victor, 3rd Baron Rothschild, heir to the Jewish banking dynasty, who had been awarded the George Cross created in the 1940 bombing of London for "acts of the greatest heroism," had to fight false accusations that he had been an enemy spy.[1]

Max once told Vera, "Names there be which have no memorial. They perish as though they had never been." He quoted a London Cockney's rule: "Sign nothing and they can prove nothing."[2] So upon moving to Britain, she signed no papers. She invented her own cover names to carry out peacetime missions for an obscure intelligence branch of the British Committee of Imperial Defence. In the 1940 German bombing of London, she wore an air-raid warden's armband. When Hitler forecast the invasion of an almost defenseless Britain, Special Operations Executive was hastily improvised to sabotage the enemy. SOE agents joined women's auxiliaries or the armed forces in the hope of being treated as prisoners of war if caught, rather than tortured and executed, as most were. SOE directors had misleadingly modest titles. Vera took a middling air force rank. In 1946 SOE was abruptly shut down. Its files were lost in a fire at Vera's office on Baker Street, home of Sherlock Holmes. Bombs, it was said, destroyed her family papers.

I had promised her not to disclose certain personal affairs. But in 2006 classified files were released to Britain's national archives, making it clear that not all files had been burned and that Vera's life had not been a closed book.[3] She had been investigated by MI5 — the internal security agency, successor to a little-known Secret Service Bureau — that trawled through national census returns.[4] In 1940 Europeans Jews who had fled to Britain from Nazi persecution were put into camps for "enemy aliens." Vera had signed nothing at the successor to the Alien Office when she entered England years before, and she was questioned in 1941 when Romania fell under German rule. Surely Max would have relished this new set of contradictions, but he had died in 1932 when Vera was twenty-four.[5]

Vera's mother was Hilda Atkins, daughter of Heinrich Etkins, who had fled from the Russian anti-Semitic pogroms and settled in 1874 in South Africa, where he shed his Jewish name and called himself Henry Atkins. His daughter registered herself as Hilda Atkins in 1902 at a London synagogue to become the wife of Max Rosenberg. Max joked wryly that he had "no country of origin." He might be Polish, or Russian, or Westphalian. History taught him to be vague about such matters. He had gone to South Africa, and later joined relatives who went into business in Romania.[6]

The British in Bucharest had taken an interest in Vera from the late 1920s. "Her mother's great grand-father, Yehuda Etkins, or Jehuda Etins, was born in Russia in 1766, and detained in settlements for Jews," reported a British intelligence officer.[7] "Yehuda's descendant, Heinrich Etkins, as Henry Atkins in South Africa was joined by Max Rosenberg, an architect-agronomist from Germany. When South Africa's economy collapsed in 1902, he salvaged some money from diamond mining, and moved to Romania to invest in the fur trade, timber, and Danube riverboats."

A curious gap appeared in British records on Vera between 1914 and 1918, the years of World War I. During those war years, Max lived without wife and children in a mansion beside the Danube. The river represented immense commercial opportunities. Its drainage basin extended across east and central Europe, almost to France, and the river wound from Germany to Romania's ports on the Black Sea. Max saw its potential. In Bohemia he had a cousin who later escaped from Auschwitz with drawings of gas chambers and ovens. The cousin used the name Rudolf Vrba to hide his Jewish origins and was active in Zionist movements that saw only one way to fight anti-Semitism: a return to the land of their fathers, Eretz Israel.[8]

In the years since 1867, Romania had passed 196 laws that denied Jews rights. Throughout the region, Jews were repeatedly uprooted by despots who forced weaker neighbors to cede territory and shift borders. Drifters, Gypsies, and higglers were allowed to work for slave wages, but not Jews. The 1919 peace talks after World War I redrew the maps once more. Millions of Jews again had "no country of origin" and were penned within new borders. Anti-Semitism was widely seen as patriotic, with spiritual backing from the Roman Catholic Church and communist backing from Russia.[9]

Vera grew closer to Max when she and her mother rejoined him after the war. Hilda admired Marie, a granddaughter of Queen Victoria who had re-created an English Victorian court in Bucharest after marrying Romania's king Ferdinand in 1893. Hilda encouraged Max to advise the Romanian royal family on investments. King Carol II was quite happy to consult wealthy Jewish businessmen. Max was memorably quoted as saying, "If a Jew makes money for a king, he is welcome at court. If he makes a mistake, he no longer exists."

"Nonexistence" was useful for Jews who traveled in the Zionist cause as itinerant workers under non-Jewish names. A down-at-heel peasant was not worth the attention of Romanian border guards, who pandered to the upper classes. They saw Max as rich and therefore respectable, and let him steer the poor barrow-pushing peasants through border formalities. Vera was in her midteens when she first began to accompany her father to help the barrow-pushers who were Zionist agents. Max drove a Mercedes-Benz with a throaty compressor that trumpeted the exciting new age of motoring. No man of mischief would advertise himself in this way. Vera learned that boldness favored the brave.

"Follow the Jesus strategy," Max told Vera. "Jesus built his power by showing love for the poorest among us." She was always astonished by his breadth of vision. She said later, "He saw Jesus as a military strategist when monarchists ruled from the top down. Jesus put the poor at the top. His followers grew from a handful to a billion, drawn by his call for self-sacrifice. Only the poor made up armies equipped to fight evil." At the time, Vera saw this evil as local history.

"At the turn of the century, Bucharest boasted it was the Paris of the East. Count Dracula represented Romania's bloodsuckers," I was told by Robert Mendelsohn, who later helped Jewish survivors of death camps reach Israel through Romanian ports. "Nothing changed in the thirties. The Paris of the East worshipped money, which was the real obsession."[10]

Max hired the best horsemen to teach Vera to ride, the best marksmen to teach her to use a gun, and the best dance teachers. He sent her to a secretarial college in London and employed her part-time at an office in Bucharest. She learned that Romania's oil was needed by Britain's empire, worried by Russian rearmament of Germany. Global corporations, diplomats, and spies eavesdropped upon each other. "Sex was still Bucharest's chief preoccupation," wrote Vera's later colleague Ian Fleming. "Sexual intrigue was part of the shenanigans. Sex went with treachery, tangle within tangle, agent and double-agent, gold and steel, the bomb, the dagger, and the firing party."[11]

Max was of good cheer. "Nobody liked Jews," I was told by an Egyptian tycoon in Bucharest. "But Max Rosenberg had a mansion and lots of land in what was once part of the Austro-Hungarian Empire. He paved roads to isolated villages and built himself a popular rural base. His wife had the style of an English gentlewoman. She knew being Jewish raised doubts about loyalty."

At the kitchen table, Vera saw Max weep over the Book of Lamentations and the centuries of Jewish suffering: betrayal, tribulation, expulsion, forced conversion, burnings at the stake, massacres, pogroms. He recited: "The Lord is like an enemy. . . . Look O Lord, and consider: whom have you ever treated like this?"

In Romania men of the Iron Guard movement endorsed the ancient hatred of Jews. Hilda spoke of safety in England, "where any problem can be solved over a nice cup of tea." Max said any problem was best solved with a shot of vodka. His wife wanted to live among Englishmen who wore bowler hats and kept a stiff upper lip. Max shrugged: opportunism was a way of life for Romanians. He said that having declared war against Germany while the Allies were winning World War I, Romania had been rewarded by the Allies with Transylvania. When the tide turned and Germany clawed back half of that territory, Romania canceled its declaration of war and so managed to keep what was left. Then Germany faced defeat, and Romania redeclared war to reoccupy other lost territory.[12]

Romanian skill in abandoning and reviving alliances drew foreign observers to Bucharest. Which way would Romania jump next time? Zionists said nobody would help Jews scattered by redefined landscapes. Max only wanted to give Vera the sophisticated air that got upper-class people through all borders. She went to finishing schools in France and Switzerland — which later led to friendship with the widowed mother of two schoolboys destined to become kings.[13] They had ideas about using the magic of an ancient monarchy to change society. "Not in Romania," Vera told them with a tight smile. "Romanian royalty is reinvented by wearers of turbans and red caftans who claim descent from Roman legionnaires. Men of lesser rank wear blue caftans and are castrated after they sire two children." The royal widow recalled Vera's words for me, years later.

Vera's mother moved into a house in Winchelsea, one of the ancient Cinque Ports on the English Channel. Vera liked Winchelsea, but returned alone to the apartment Max had given her in Bucharest. She felt she had work to do. Virulent anti-Semitism was reviving in Vienna. Masses of Jews were again transported along the Trans-Siberian Railroad. Civilized countries shrugged off Hitler's anti-Jewish diatribes. In Whitehall, the staid center of England's civil and secret services, there was much hostility to Zionists. In Romania, the fascist

Iron Guard leader Octavian Goga echoed Hitler's claim that the 1919 peace talks were a Jewish conspiracy to rearrange the map of Europe.

Vera saw that what plagued Jews today would hurt all future dissenters of any faith. She read English spy thrillers whose heroes pitted their wits against what Rudyard Kipling damned as "Teutonic war parties." Espionage required a knowledge of world affairs beyond the small-mindedness described by the Irish writer Walter Starkie: "Bucharest is the town of one street, one church and one idea . . . sex." For Vera, life in Bucharest was made more exciting by a Canadian businessman, William Stephenson, and his American wife Mary, whom he teased as Mary from Tennessee. Vera met them first with Gardyne de Chastelain, representing Phoenix Oil of London, from where Stephenson ran his growing industrial empire. He had laid the groundwork of a small fortune by mass-producing a can opener stolen while escaping from a German prisoner-of-war camp: a perfectly good way to get back at the Germans after being gassed in trench warfare. Thinking that this had poisoned his lungs, and that high flight would repair them, he became an ace fighter pilot. By 1931, already a scientist and inventor, he was expanding into movies and investing abroad in steel, aviation, and mining.

Stephenson was a small man with narrow, piercing blue eyes. He watched Vera's face while he filled in the gap in the story of her family. During World War I, Vera and her mother and both her brothers had lived in Germany. That was why Max had lived alone in his Danube-side mansion.

Vera told the man she called Bill Stephenson about this strange period. In 1914, aged six, she was on a summer trip with her mother and a younger brother, Wilfred. On the way to England, they were trapped in Berlin when war broke out in August. Vera's older brother, studying in England under the name Ralph Atkins, had joined them, and they took refuge in Cologne with the family of Max's brother, who was in the German army. Vera lived in a household split between pro-German and pro-English factions. Reunited with her father in 1919, she saw why Max had kept a low profile during World War I. He was a German Jew.

Stephenson now served voluntarily in the Industrial Intelligence Centre, an almost forgotten British agency within the Committee of Imperial Defence. He had learned about Vera through Sir Vernon Kell, who had fished for traitors in the national census that presented a picture of life in Britain. Kell's security service cast a shadow over Vera, but Stephenson saw her German experience as an advantage. He came often to Bucharest. Behind a screen of commercial activity, he weighed Romania's place in the next world war, which he told Vera was "inevitable as a resumption of the last one." He was interested in the German ambassador to Romania, Count Friedrich Werner von der Schulenburg, a tall, elegant, silver-haired Saxon in his midfifties, manifestly bored by Bucharest small talk. Pretty women brought him to life.

Stephenson saw Schulenburg as loyal to the Reich president, Field Marshal Paul von Hindenburg, a decent man who did not take Nazism seriously. Stephenson had earned the name Boxing Billy as a lightweight champion boxer in the Allied forces, and was light on his feet. He opposed those in England who sided with Germany as a victim of unfair peace terms dictated by the victors in the last war. He did agree that the German foreign office upheld the highest standards of diplomacy, and at a routine embassy party he introduced Vera to Count von der Schulenburg.

Predictably, the ambassador came to life. Beauty and brains were an intoxicating brew. He spoke of a cultural renaissance in Berlin. Vera asked how this could last, if the Nazis built power among unemployed war veterans and appealed to primitive racism. He dismissed the Nazis as *ignobile vulgus* led by a madman who talked wildly about a Gothic empire and about shipping purebred Germans through Romanian ports to "living space" in the Crimea. He damned Hitler as a political spy who infiltrated the military command during the 1918 Spartacus Revolt, betrayed the German Workers' Party to his conservative paymasters, and renamed it the National Socialist, or Nazi, Party.

Vera got her chance to size up Schulenburg at a winter ball at Peles Castle. She told him the castle was ridiculed for its overwhelming display of bad taste. Passengers from Paris on the 1883 inaugural journey of the Orient Express to Bucharest had arrived just as King Carol I ceremoniously put the last brick in place to celebrate the castle's completion. The foreigners, Vera said, had scoffed at this as just another attempt to ape the English royal court. Schulenburg laughed.

She danced all night with the ambassador. She could not have imagined the part he was to play in secret missions, nor the role of the

Orient Express. The count liked her gift for witty responses and her use of epigrams worthy of the Byzantine Greeks. The friendship blossomed. He took her to little restaurants, away from tiresome chatterboxes, and confessed his love for her. She encouraged the infatuation of this man who was thirty-three years older than she. Vera was just twenty-three.

Reporting back to Bill Stephenson, she said the reason Schulenburg put up with the boredom of this Bucharest backwater was because he saw it as a window into Russia. He was obsessed with the warning sounded by his hero, Otto von Bismarck: "Avoid war with Russia at all costs." Bismarck had attacked the Catholic Church for demonizing Jews. He said Jewish-driven culture made Germany the heart of intellectual achievement, and this would end the evil years following 1743 when Jews could enter Berlin only through a gate reserved for themselves and cows. When she heard this, Vera bristled. She pointed out to Schulenburg that Bismarck had founded a Prussian nationalist newspaper in 1848, the same year Karl Marx had founded his propagandist newspaper on the German Rhine. Now German nationalism called for order, and the Soviet Union sought world power.

When she next saw the ambassador, he said that Stalin had no real military power.

"Is that why Stalin is rearming Germany?" asked Vera.

Stephenson recalled later that Vera began to jerk the ambassador out of his smug self-satisfaction. He called Vera his English June rose. She let him think her mother came from Sussex innkeepers. It was true that her mother had left Max, who was in very poor health, to live in Sussex. Schulenburg, assuming she was essentially English, argued that good order was needed in England, as in Germany, to curb Stalin. Bolsheviks wanted order without moderation; Bismarck had wanted an empire to impose order with moderation.

"Was Bismarck's imperial order any different from Stalin's ambitions?"

"Yes!" the ambassador replied. "Bismarck wished to impose a benign pan-German order upon the lesser breeds of Europe."

Impose order? Lesser breeds? The words set off alarm bells. Vera wondered if this orderly racism truly impressed this ambassador, who said he disagreed with Nazi racism. He was her window into Berlin today, just as Bucharest was his window into Moscow. Did he know this? Was he feeding her information, expecting that it would get back to others in England?

Two years before Count von der Schulenburg was transferred to Moscow, she spoke of her misgivings to Gardyne de Chastelain, who was then considering how Romanian oil supplies to Germany might be sabotaged if war broke out again. He watched rivals jockeying for control over oilfields run by his British company, Phoenix Oil. It was early 1932. Ten years later, Gardyne and his wife Marion would be working for Stephenson's World War II intelligence network. Gardyne would parachute back into Romania, while Marion served in Stephenson's New York headquarters.

Stephenson spoke to Vera of German funding of Romanian fascists to ensure future war supplies of oil. Germany had once been the biggest industrial power in Europe, because it had big reserves of coal to fuel steam engines. A new, illegal German arsenal of modern weapons needed oil. He had no doubt that "Romanian oil will reignite world war."

He spoke of Steiny, or Charles Proteus Steinmetz, a German-Jewish engineer who had helped with Bill Stephenson's early inventions. Steiny had met Max Rosenberg while doing research at the Romanian oil institute, which was secretly funded from Berlin. Steiny had heard that Max was "put away" in an isolated medical institution. Vera was not prepared to discuss her father. Anything she said might get back to Max's enemies, anti-Zionists who would kill him.

Mary Stephenson, Bill's dainty wife, accompanied him on his Bucharest visits. She had a disconcerting way of reading the innermost thoughts of others, and knew a Zionist representative, Hélène Allatini, whom she introduced to Vera as a visitor from Paris. Hélène said the Nazis were making Jews flee through Romanian ports to join a secret army fighting the British who held the League of Nations mandate in Palestine. This gave a new dimension to the presence of such a high-ranking German ambassador to Bucharest. Hélène had come here to warn Max. But Vera had left Max on his deathbed. There was nothing that could be done to keep him alive, and those who shared his love for the Zionist cause were staying away to prevent the local fascists from guessing at Max's connections. He was now in a deep coma, with a severe respiratory infection, and had insisted that all visitors be kept away.

Vera understood her father too well. He was a hard man underneath all his bonhomie: hard because there was no other way of survival. He advised her not to let her love for him distract her. She too must have privacy. Trysts with Schulenburg in central Bucharest would get her labeled a whore. Pregnant courtesans were still victims of "honor killings" to save the reputations of rich lovers. Vera's Jewish background made her even more vulnerable. Vera later recalled: "Couples motored into the countryside — it was permitted to fuck if it didn't frighten the horses." Only the upper class had cars. Schulenburg drove an embassy car without a chauffeur, and told his staff he wished to avoid attention while inspecting the borders. He picked up Vera at places specified by penciled numbers to indicate time, date, and location. The codes were scribbled on scraps of paper hidden at the jockey club, where they were both members. The ambassador took Vera on long trips through narrow winding lanes while she continued to ask him about Nazi influence. He blamed rabble-rousers appealing to the despair of Germany's unemployed soldiers: they should enlist help from General Paul von Lettow-Vorbeck. He had been at school with the ambassador, and during World War I he ran a guerrilla war in German East Africa. He was a hero both in Germany and in Britain, where he would win genuine sympathy for German veterans trying to correct awful conditions: in Germany 20 percent of babies were born dead and 40 percent died within a month because requests for basic foods and medicines were denied by the victors. Lettow-Vorbeck was admired by Winston Churchill, who had firsthand experience of guerrilla warfare in Africa and knew Lettow-Vorbeck had actually won his war at the moment Germany surrendered in Europe. Now Hitler promised such veterans "a people's war." Schulenburg quoted a famous memo by Churchill when he became secretary of state for war in 1919: "The wars of peoples will be more terrible than the wars of kings."

Vera discussed all this with Stephenson, who said Churchill, though holding no government office, wanted Lettow-Vorbeck to become ambassador in London to help avert another war. Stephenson wrote down a private London address to which Vera could post information. He said mail was a safe means of communication. The British legation sent routine reports by diplomatic bag chained to a King's Messenger. Sensitive information went by telegram to CX, for the Secret Intelligence Service chief, or to CXG for lesser SIS officers: the traffic was intercepted by the Berlin Cipher Office. Open code in chatty letters was the best way to convey sensitive information. Schulenburg could write like this if Vera moved to London, where Stephenson wanted her to work in his St. James's office.

Bill Stephenson, born in 1896, was twelve years older than Vera. He and Mary had no children, and they treated her like a daughter. They judged her to be trustworthy: she knew that the fate of Jews depended upon preserving all humanity from the new dictatorships. In Berlin, diplomats, who met mostly at cocktail parties, seldom collected useful information. Schulenburg was an exceptional source. Vera should delay any permanent move to London. Bill, as Vera now called him, passed along a bit of gossip: "Britain's royal family sees Stalin as the devil, and thinks Hitler is the man to oppose him."

Vera repeated this the next time she was in the embassy car, and Schulenburg fell into a troubled silence. She sat motionless, a trick she never lost, while he appeared to mull over the story. Then he laughed. So many ironies! He had been troubled because he was being recalled to Berlin for a briefing on talks he might have to conduct with Stalin's men in Moscow.

It was harvest time. There was an unusual poignancy in driving along the rough dirt roads between fields of ripening grain, past wooden cottages where fruit and vegetables hung from overhanging roofs, and Gypsies sold sparrows and Turkish carpets. The winter of 1932–33 approached. Vera remembered her father's private moments with her as a child at this season, and said impulsively that she used to think adults were mostly too old to govern wisely. The devilish energies of grown men should be poured into totally exhausting activities that left them with no time to fight wars.

He stopped the car to savor the smell of fallen wet leaves in the sweet autumnal rain, and said sadly that he'd also had a boyish dream of stopping grown-ups from meddling with people's lives. He longed to return to the child he had been.

"You'll always remain a child at heart," she told him, laughing.

"It will be the death of me," he said.

After a week in Berlin, he came back looking as if he already felt the hangman's noose around his neck. He had expected to discuss his Moscow assignment. First, though, he was questioned about a Jewess named Rosenberg by agents from an almost forgotten department,

Referat Deutschland, originally set up to keep politicians informed about foreign policy. It was run by a junior officer, who initially refused a Nazi demand that he spy on colleagues. Thugs took the young man away, and he came back cured of any old-fashioned ideas about loyalty to friends. The Nazi enforcers occupied new quarters run by Joachim von Ribbentrop, a pretentious wine merchant who had added the honorific "von" to his name. He was not ready to challenge head-on the old aristocrats at the foreign office, but he plotted to become Hitler's foreign affairs adviser. He would do this by taking credit for the greatest of diplomatic coups, a Nazi-Soviet peace pact, to be engineered by Schulenburg.

Vera was puzzled by the ambassador's apparent unhappiness. Wasn't peace with Russia what Schulenburg wanted? At which point, Schulenburg dropped a bombshell: Stalin, he said, was making weapons for Germany forbidden under the Treaty of Versailles. The Soviet Union's own military was far from ready for any large-scale war, but it was providing Germany with secret facilities: a tank school, a flying school, laboratories for chemical warfare, a dive-bomber factory, all to build a Nazi bastion against America and Britain. This was the kind of peace that foreshadowed war.

Vera said there were men in London who would help Schulenburg and other true German patriots thwart this. The count knew she was right: he had his own London sources, including the German ambassador, Otto von Bismarck, the great man's grandson. The younger Bismarck had secretly spoken with Churchill about saving the post-1919 democratic parliament of the Weimar Republic. But Hitler denounced it as a Jewish republic, and Churchill no longer felt there was any worthwhile anti-Nazi opposition. Bismarck pleaded that Hitler was still only the leader of a mob. Churchill wearily responded with lines by Rudyard Kipling: "This is the sorrowful story / Told when the twilight fails / And the monkeys walk together / Holding their neighbours' tails."

Schulenburg recalled for Vera the French prime minister, Georges Clemenceau, commenting presciently at the end of the 1919 Versailles peace talks: "I seem to hear a child weeping." Twenty years later, in 1939, the child would be old enough to fight in another war.

Vera asked, Why could good Germans not act on their own?

The count said Berliners were asking, "Why does Britain take so long to help us?" German industrialists and bankers were scared of the Red working classes and financed Hitler's mobs to attack Willi Münzenberg, the Red Millionaire of Berlin, the flack for International Communism. Hadn't Vera told him the same fear of the Red Menace in Britain influenced royalty? Churchill had been booed in Parliament when he quoted from the Hebrew Bible: "Behold, there ariseth a little cloud out of the sea, like a man's hand."

True Berliners, said the ambassador, admired English nobility, and wore monocles and white ties and tails while toasting the Kaiser in exile. The toast went like this: "To His Majesty—hurrah! Shush! Hurrah! No, softly—hurrah!" Caution muffled their voices after Edward, Prince of Wales and future king-emperor, said the Versailles peace treaty rearranged frontiers so that German settlements fell under the rule of "barbaric Slavs" and a Russian tyranny stretching from the Baltic to the Pacific.

The ambassador encouraged Vera to move to England. She was the one person he could trust on the other side of the widening Anglo-German rift. Perhaps she could later visit Berlin, now that it had revived as an international center? He gave her the names and addresses of friends he trusted. Some were Russian nobles exiled from Moscow and working in obscure corners of Berlin's city government. She should talk with one of Schulenburg's colleagues who had looked into Hitler's postwar records. As a twenty-nine-year-old corporal in an army hospital, Hitler had screamed that the report of Germany's surrender was "the vicious gossip of sexually depraved Jewish youths in a clap hospital." A military psychiatrist wrote in a confidential note that the cause of Hitler's blindness was hysteria, but to calm the corporal, he assured him that he was a superman and would see again. Hitler's sight returned. He took this as a sign that he was the great leader destined to fulfil the old Teutonic Knights' dream of imposing order from the Baltic to the Black Sea.

During one of their last motoring expeditions, Schulenburg said he wanted Vera's friends in London to understand why many like himself were loyal Germans. The victors in the last war had served their own interests. Britain's Balfour Declaration promised Jews a national home in Palestine to win Jewish backing in wartime, but with a proviso: "Nothing shall be done which may prejudice the civil and religious rights of existing non-Jewish communities in Palestine." Such trapdoors were everywhere. Hitler had shown a mad genius for identifying them. "Hitler," said Schulenburg, "preaches a religion of pure Aryan hatred for subhumans. Germany needs outside help or this maniac will lead us all down into hell."

In January 1933, Hitler was nominated as Reich chancellor after much maneuvering. The German republic was handed over to the man determined to destroy it, although a foolish politician who turned opportunism into a fine art, Franz von Papen, had declared, "We have him [Hitler] framed in." Hitler's mole in foreign affairs, Ribbentrop, prepared for Schulenburg's mission to Moscow by having him withdrawn from Bucharest.

Through Schulenburg, Vera had learned to evaluate possible enemies, memorize details, and detach herself from personal feelings. Her voice never quivered when she later told Mary Stephenson: "The ambassador had hopes of saving whatever he could of the country he loved as a young man."

Embassy cars abroad were ordered to fly Nazi pennants. Before Vera's final frantic motoring trip with Schulenburg, she said she could never travel with such insignia.

"When you ride with me, no swastikas fly!" replied Schulenburg.

These seemed fated to be the last words he would ever speak to her, apart from endearments that she kept to herself. "At least, I thought they were the last words," she said later. "How wrong I was!"

Late in 1933, at the urging of Billy Stephenson, she moved to London. While inspecting German steel mills for his Pressed Steel Company, he was alarmed by what he saw as accelerating preparations for war, and he wanted Vera out of harm's way. She received a yellowing clip from London's New Statesman. In it, the novelist D. H. Lawrence had written from Germany in October 1924: "Influences come invisibly out of Germany's flow away from civilized Christian Europe, back to the savage polarity of Tartary.... At night you feel strange things stirring in the darkness."

# 2

# Mutual Friends vs. Guilty Men

"Secret services fix reports to fit policy," Max Rosenberg had warned Vera before he died. He knew the methods of intelligence agencies in every century, in every country. "Lies about you can fester in hidden files."

He had helped British agents with information on the fascist Iron Guard, but he distrusted the spy chiefs in Whitehall. There was no way to correct their files on a private citizen. He had advised Vera: "Become an English churchgoer and a Bright Young Thing."

In London, Romanian bankers expressed surprise at "the secretive disposal" of Max's ashes. Some said his wife had abandoned him to live in Sussex under her former name Hilda Atkins. Bill Stephenson advised Vera never to speak of her Rosenberg roots. In Romania, Iron Guard interrogators pretended to know everything about a prisoner, and to escape further torture, a prisoner might drop Vera's family name. The Iron Guard worked closely with the German compilers of dossiers on Jews.

Stephenson was mentally prepared for the next round of warfare with Germany. Meanwhile, he fought a covert war against British policy makers anxious to appease Hitler. He called them Guilty Men. "This is their bastion," he told Vera on a summer's day in 1934, walking her through that part of central London known as Whitehall.

They strolled from Westminster Abbey to the Mall, from Buckingham Palace to Admiral Nelson's statue in Trafalgar Square, and past the duck ponds in St. James's Park. He showed her White's Club, the haunt of the intelligence community, "where Jews are never welcome." He said, "As a woman, you may look at these clubs from outside. Only men are allowed in. Women are for pushing tea trolleys and tapping typewriters. This is the Establishment, the ruling class. King George V denied refuge to his cousin, the Russian tsar, because it might bring the revolution here, and left the tsar to be executed by the Bolsheviks. Fear of Bolshies dominates the ruling class. The Prince of Wales sees a rearmed Germany as the barrier against Stalin, and Nazi racism akin to attitudes toward inferior breeds in British colonies."

Stephenson introduced her to "Our Mutual Friends." Risking arrest under draconian secrecy laws, the Mutual Friends aired facts about the neglect of British defenses through Churchill, who was a political outcast but still made himself heard. Some of the Mutual Friends had known Vera in Bucharest.

Max had invested what was left of his capital in "the City," London's center of finance and global information. His money kept Vera's mother in comfort. None of the neighbors knew she was Jewish when Vera went to see her in Winchelsea. The coastal town's layout remained as in the days of the Norman conquerors. Memorials spoke of past centuries, when the Channel was crossed by waves of invaders from the Continent. The townsfolk, indifferent to events in Europe, said it would never happen again.

But among Our Mutual Friends, Vera heard plenty of concern about Germany's one-party system. By 1934 Hitler had the power to open prison camps for the Gestapo to fill. In Hamburg, Red agents spoke on the phone with Hitler's Brownshirts to plan the next day's street fighting. Each side hoped to win power through the breakdown of civic order. Winchelsea was minutes by air from Hamburg on the North Sea, but remained blissfully unaware of these events. London newspapers cut most foreign news to a few lines in the back pages, and gave space to Japanese and British armed cooperation against Chinese trade unions and striking workers in Shanghai.

In high society, Vera flattered young men with questions about themselves and smoothly turned aside their questions about her. She had been noted for her flaxen hair in childhood. Now it was black. "It stayed forever glossy black," recalled the prominent London artist Elena Gaussen Marks, who later painted Vera's portrait. "Such a change is natural in some girls as they grow older. The transition from blonde to brunette was fortuitous as cover for her future work."[1]

Vera, now in her midtwenties, was drawn by Mary Stephenson into West End society. Debutantes partied wildly while waiting to be presented at court, oblivious to the burning in Germany of books written by Jews and non-Nazis, and of later atrocities. "This indifference shocked Vera," recalled Mary. "Ze'ev Jabotinsky was urging Jews to evacuate Europe. England was seen as the one viable base for an underground resistance to tyranny. But the necessary public outrage was missing."

The London Season for a small and privileged class lasted from early May until the end of July. The partying was endless: a dance four times during the week; another dance on Friday night. Young men and eighteen-year-old debutantes tore off at weekends to country houses. Stockings were silk in London and lisle in the country. Dresses came from Molyneux in Paris, hats from Madame Rita in Berkeley Square, and elbow-length white kid gloves from Bond Street. Inclusion on the top invitation lists was the highest goal for many of these bright young things.

Mary watched with the curiosity of an American taught to value hard work. The family fortune came from the tobacco fields of Tennessee. She met Bill Stephenson on a transatlantic liner, and soon after, on August 31, 1924, the Sunday edition of the *New York Times* ran the couple's photograph with the caption AMERICAN GIRLS WEDS CANADIAN SCIENTIST. A decade later the Stephensons were lending Vera one of their London flats, to which letters from Berlin were sent by Count Friedrich Werner von der Schulenburg, cautiously signing himself "Old Fritz." The envelopes were addressed to Miss French Simmons, Mary's unmarried name. One letter told of Hitler prancing on the stage of the Potsdam Garrison Church, symbol of the Prussian officer corps. Hitler was seeking favor with the army, the only organized segment of society still resisting Nazification. Senior staff officers who opposed Hitler still looked to Britain for support. Some were seduced by offers of quick promotion. A wartime flying ace, Hermann Göring, as Prussian prime minister, sold his loyalty for a share of the huge royalties from Hitler's New Order writings.

Schulenburg was appointed German ambassador to the Soviet Union late in 1934, with instructions to convince Stalin that there was nothing personal about Nazi propaganda labeling the German opposition as communist: it was merely local party politics. Vera decided the Big Lie was already a weapon in foreign affairs, but suited Schulenburg's need to avoid a Russo-German war. His letters from Moscow were forwarded to No. 5 Kensington Palace Gardens Terrace, now given as Vera's latest residence, a cover. The ambassador wrote in open code. Vera's replies revealed little. Her old lover might be under the control of German intelligence.

She became a secretary-translator in Stephenson's company Pressed Steel, which made nine out of ten bodies for British automobiles. This gave Stephenson his excuse for inspecting German steel mills. He controlled twenty other companies throughout Europe, allowing him to dig out intelligence useful to Churchill. He was known in Germany for an aircraft made in one of his factories, which won the King's Cup air race in 1934. Berlin's curiosity showed itself in the friendliness of German aviators. Stephenson found this ironic, since the British air ministry displayed no interest at all. He had experimented with wireless telegraphy, and as early as 1924, he invented a device to transmit pictures by wireless at the same time Germany put on the market a commercial coding machine that later became the Berlin Cipher Office's top-secret Enigma, taxing the best brains among British ULTRA code breakers. Frank Whittle, a Royal Air Force officer, getting no RAF backing for his invention of the jet engine, turned to Stephenson. "He knew how to hook things up to make them work in unexpected ways," said Whittle. "He'd give a leg up to chaps whose working-class accent stopped them getting past the snobs of Whitehall."[2]

Vera met those who believed in the right of hereditary grandees to rule. If Hitler ruled the Continent, they argued, Britain would be free in the Mideast and Asia to guard its colonies against communism. Lord Londonderry held this view. Appointed Britain's air minister in 1933, at the same time Hitler became Reich chancellor, Londonderry also saw commercial advantages to close relations with Nazi leaders. He put Vera in mind of the German financiers who flew Hitler to party rallies in a plane trailing a banner, HITLER OVER GERMANY. Vera thought Londonderry would gladly fly another banner, HITLER OVER BRITAIN.[3] The British press had ignored Hitler's assumption of total power on January 30, 1933, with one exception. The *Daily Express* ran a banner headline that got the news horribly wrong: HITLER BAULKED OF POWER. Editors didn't seem to care, one way or the other.

Vera learned a rule she would later instill in agents: "You may prepare for surprises in another country, but you'll still be taken by surprise when you get there." At the British legation in Bucharest, she had scanned well-informed situation reports that never prepared her for the London newspaper proprietors, who ignored their own Berlin correspondents' stories of the legalized murder of less-than-perfect babies, the tests for purebred white Aryans, and the labeling of the rest as "subhuman." The growth of concentration camps was not worth a mention.

Stephenson explained: "Newspaper proprietors lust for seats in the House of Lords and oblige a government that wants to read nothing nasty about the Nazis." She still had a lot to learn, but he was impressed by her phenomenal memory, her grasp of many languages, her gift for making others talk. Best of all, she saw the need for unconventional action.

He sent her to explore an England that seemed afraid of another war, and afraid to prevent it. "The leaders sit in the path of the monster and twiddle their thumbs," he said, "like rabbits frozen in the headlights of a truck, flapping their ears instead of running." There was nowhere to run for the poor in London's East End, who got their news through the migrant grapevines. Survivors of pogroms against Russian Jews speculated about the bombers assembled in Russia for the German air force that would later target the East End docklands: "the docks" handled overseas cargoes, without which Britain would starve. Underpaid East Enders were less easily deceived than City merchants. Handicapped veterans of the last war begged for food, their medals already sold. Trade unions were under scrutiny by the internal security service, MI5, on suspicion of communist sympathies. The *Daily Worker* called Soviet Russia the one ray of hope for workers living in East End squalor.

East Enders, on the whole, sensed a coming resumption of what they called the Great War of 1914–18, the War to End All Wars. But many fiercely opposed warmongering. Vera related this antiwar feeling to that of German workers, tricked into believing law and order would end the dreadful poverty that followed the last conflict. The Workers' Education Association in its East End evening classes taught how imperial lunacies led to conflict. One textbook began: "Austria declared war on Serbia on July 28, 1914. Four days later, Germany declared war on Russia, and an Eastern Front stretched from the Baltic to the Black Sea. On August 4, Germany declared war on France and Britain. The

Western Front became a stalemate of muddy trenches from the North Sea to the Alps. Nine and a half million men became battle casualties." Vera came away admiring these tough East Enders. Some were burglars who took pride in using inventiveness rather than brutality. Others were humble inspectors of insurance claims, and knew the weak points in factories whose owners set fires to stave off bankruptcy. Many East Enders spoke Continental languages. Their communities were woven into the fabric of street life. They would make a reservoir of talent for any anti-Nazi resistance operations. They were natural street fighters, schooled in a world of the lower class.

The West End was utterly upper class. Vera heard of its delayed reaction to the massacre in August 1929 of twenty-three Jews in Palestine by Arabs armed with axes. "I can't think why the Jews make such a fuss over a few dozen of their people," Beatrice, the wife of the British colonial secretary, Sidney Webb, Lord Passfield, was quoted as saying by Chaim Weizmann, future first president of Israel. Living in England, he protested against "its insensitivity, its indifference and hostility."

Vera found young men who were not insensitive, though they turned up at posh parties. One was a flier in the Royal Navy whose nickname was Stringbag, also the nickname for the Fairey Swordfish, an antiquated torpedo-bomber with four wings that folded back for stowage on carriers. He said it was held together by string, like a housewife's shopping bag. "Hence," he told Vera, "the name Stringbag."

They met at a West End dinner party in 1935. Her dress was in the latest neo-Victorian fashion: leg-of-mutton sleeves and yards of seams, gores, and flares. The complicated-looking toilette could be swiftly removed thanks to new-fangled zip fasteners and decorative buttons that covered press-studs. Her hair was cut short and brushed forward in a swirl, plastered to her forehead and cheeks in ragged edges, in imitation of the popular Paris-style windswept coiffure.

Mary Stephenson wangled the invitation for Vera because the dinner, at Lady Mountbatten's Brook House in Park Lane, would include Mutual Friends. Edwina Mountbatten was half Jewish. She had not invited her anti-Semitic father, Wilfred Ashley (Baron Mount Temple of Lee), who applauded the Nazi Party for imposing order. "In the next war," he declared in public, "we must fight shoulder to shoulder with Germany."

His distortions of history were so outrageous as to seem comical. Vera asked why the press printed them. Were columnists paid to invent comic scandals? Edwina looked up with a myopic stare. She had just been the target of a gossip columnist: SOCIETY SHAKEN BY TERRIBLE SCANDAL. Her husband, young Louis Mountbatten, was serving on a warship at sea. A columnist reported that she was "caught in compromising circumstances with a colored man." This was Paul Robeson, the actor-singer who left America to escape anti-Negro prejudice. The libel was trumpeted by the *People*, a popular Sunday paper, and was later retracted.

"Columnists writing comedy as history?" echoed Edwina. "Winston Churchill writes about things far from comic, and he's ridiculed for it. But admirers print his columns."

Desmond Morton, who still carried a German bullet in his heart from World War I, added that Churchill had fought Boer farmers in Africa and seen them beat the mighty British imperial armies by irregular methods. "He'll train irregulars if war is forced on us before we get modern arms." Morton was director of the Industrial Intelligence Centre of the Committee of Imperial Defence (IICCID), dismissed by the current government as a warmonger's tool. Senior civil servants sent reports on British defense failings to Morton, knowing his only customer was Churchill.

Stringbag walked Vera home. An early dawn streaked the sky. The streets were silent, the air divine. "He was a bit drunk and lyrical," she told Mary later. "He said he was lucky to be able to fly above a filthy world. I was smitten, perhaps by him, perhaps by his airplanes."

She asked about Morton's remarks about Boers and irregular warfare. Stringbag replied: "The world's most powerful empire in the 1880s was beaten by the Boers without modern weapons. Nothing looked more formidable than our armored trains. Nothing was more vulnerable. Our juggernauts were derailed by blowing up bridges with a couple of sticks of dynamite. We'll have to use Boer methods against Hitler."

Stringbag was fed up with staff generals who refused to modernize. General Sir Archibald Montgomery-Massingberd, chief of the Imperial General Staff, updated a cavalry training manual with a brief addendum on the use of armored cars that he called "mechanized cavalry." His manual's addendum was called "Cavalry (mechanized) and the well-bred horse." Stringbag said the Well-Bred Horse Brigade could only be led by someone with a name like Archibald Montgomery-Massingberd.

On his next leave, the pilot took Vera to Simpson's on the Strand. Before lunch he ordered Pimm's Number One, confessing it was regarded in the navy as the quickest way to seduce a girl. "I drank him pretty much under the table," she told Stephenson, who recalled, "She made Stringbag an exception to her rule against close entanglements. He was spilling the goods on antisubmarine defenses at Scapa Flow, so neglected that the anchorage was vulnerable to U-boats that Germany was secretly building."

Stringbag had a graveyard sense of humor. He sang a lugubrious wardroom song: "They say in the air force / A landing's okay / If the pilot gets out and then walks away. / But in the fleet air arm / The prospects are grim / If the landing is bad and the pilot can't swim." This dim outlook for young pilots, he said, was the fault of admirals who did not believe in aircraft carriers. Naval intelligence had gone to sleep. The Secret Intelligence Service, under the Foreign Office, had a Secret Fund for private citizens who did not seek personal gain when collecting information abroad but who might need money to pursue an investigation. The fund was subject to a secret committee vote to maintain the facade of correct parliamentary procedure. There were no benefits for a volunteer agent with Non-Official Cover. Any NOC agent who got caught was disowned.

How did Stringbag know this? His father was an executive in the Marconi Company. Its radio officers were available in wartime to the Naval Intelligence Directorate. NID seemed unmoved by Germany's production of warships and submarines. He added, "Americans are just as blind. They launched their first carrier, the *Ranger*, and now Washington lawmakers want to scrap it because it costs too much to run."

He recalled the Greek physician Hippocrates: "'A desperate disease requires a dangerous remedy.' These are desperate times. The remedy is dangerous. Right now, it means fighting the Guilty Men."

And he quoted Churchill: "These appeasers feed the crocodile in the hope of being the last to get eaten."[4]

# Kill Hitler?

Would the assassination of Hitler solve anything? Vera thought it would certainly save some of the 600,000 Jews now terrorized by Hitler.

Stringbag said nobody within the ruling class in Britain cared much about Jews. Whitehall mandarins were impressed by Germany's new orderliness, and they would be outraged by any hint of an assassination attempt, because Germany would be thrown back into chaos. Hitler was a welcome phenomenon, according to the influential cabinet secretary Sir Maurice Hankey. He had asked as early as October 1933: "Are we still dealing with the Hitler of *Mein Kampf*? Or is it a new Hitler who has discovered the burden of responsible office?" This was at the time of the *Einzelaktion* order to launch the systematic persecution of all Jews.

Two years later Ramsey MacDonald, then Britain's prime minister, claimed the Royal Air Force was far ahead of Germany, only to be dramatically contradicted by Sir John Simon, the British foreign secretary, who returned from "a goodwill visit" to Berlin to report that Hitler told him the German air force was as powerful as the RAF. Simon the Impeccable, as he was dubbed by critics, said publicly, "Germany is doing splendidly in building its defenses against Soviet Russian expansionism."

Hitler aimed his boast at those in Simon's circle who wanted Germany to build strong defenses against Stalin. On June 18, 1935, in violation of the Versailles peace treaty, Britain signed a naval agreement with Germany providing that Germany would have a fleet equal to 35 percent of Britain's surface craft and 45 percent of its submarines.

The move signaled to other Versailles treaty signatories that London approved of German rearmament.[1]

"We'll end up dead or speaking German," Vera told Stringbag. She had thought some more about this question of assassinating Hitler, and concluded, "High-level assassinations in Europe always lead to massive and unpredictable upheavals." Bill Stephenson, part of the speculation, recalled that "the possibility of assassination was left hanging." But disposing of Hitler by any democratic process was impossible.

Frustrated, Stringbag said to Vera, "Let's get above all this shit!"

He drove her to his aero-club and, under the name Tom Benson, booked a Gypsy Moth biplane, whose fabric wings were held together by wooden struts and wires. She sat in an open front cockpit. He took control in the rear cockpit. She heard his muffled voice through rubber Gosford tubes as he climbed through the muck of chimney smoke and layers of black cloud and broke into dazzling blue skies. "You've got her!" he shouted.

In the mirror above, Vera saw him lift up both his gloved hands. She grabbed the control column and put her feet on the rudder pedals. The aircraft was flying smoothly, straight and level. She followed his instructions: left hand on throttle, right hand on the stick, feet on the rudder pedals. She tried a turn, keeping the nose on the horizon. "Loop the loop!" he yelled, and she sensed his light touch on the controls while he talked her into the dive, and pulled out into a steep climb. When the plane was upside down, they headed down again. "Try another!" he shouted above the roar of the slipstream and the banging of the single engine. She did. He took her through spins. His disembodied voice and the sense of an unseen guardianship was a bond, a promise of unqualified support.

"I really flew it," she told Stephenson later.

"The Moth is as fragile as the torpedo-bombers your friend will fly in battle," he remarked soberly. She suddenly saw the Moth, like its namesake, fluttering on currents of air, vulnerable, easily crushed. That would be Stringbag, in the war she knew must come.

He was based at a stone frigate, a naval air station near Portsmouth. He got away most weekends to give her more flying lessons.

"Better than sex!" she laughed after an afternoon of spins and rolls and inverted loops.

"We'll see about that," he responded. They stopped for a drink in the public bar of a roadhouse. He took a room overlooking a motorway clogged with traffic. He rightly took her comment as a challenge. Their lovemaking had the essential ingredient of danger she relished with Count von der Schulenburg, but in aerobatics she felt a more intensively shared danger, and concealment added to the excitement. She'd return from an afternoon above the clouds, change, and bump into him again at some cocktail party. Poker-faced, he'd be in the company of men with the closed look of civil servants. He explained later. "Mutual Friends don't talk more than they have to."[2]

The enemies of democracy were free to bellow treason. He took her to Hyde Park to watch a rally of Blackshirts led by Sir Oswald Mosley and his British Union of Fascists. It was a warm summer's afternoon in 1935. The Anglo-German naval treaty had provoked Churchill to protest that "the League of Nations has been weakened by our action, the principle of collective security has been impaired. German treaty-breaking has been condoned and even extolled."

At the rally, Stringbag ran into a newspaper friend. He told the reporter: "Germany's got a bigger navy than you dare report."

"'Try me,' said the friend, and wrote in his notebook what Stringbag knew about the secret numbers of German U-boats under construction, and a good deal more that the British government did not want people to hear.

The Blackshirt rally turned nasty. Vera found herself listening to anti-Jewish verbal filth straight from Hitler's *Mein Kampf*. Some people in the crowd yelled protests. Blackshirt knuckle-dusters silenced them. Blackshirt thugs menaced children in the park playgrounds, and cowed their parents. Childhood notions that Vera once shared with the German ambassador about diverting the evil energies of adults now looked hopelessly idealistic. She vowed never to become vulnerable by having children of her own, at the risk of putting their welfare first, at the cost of her beliefs.

If Stringbag had been in his naval uniform, the Blackshirts would have savaged him as a symbol of everything they hated. They had switched from the Labour (socialist) Party to fascism. "The police leave them alone because the alternative is communism," said a man who joined Stringbag and Vera. "If you're unemployed, you go to extremes. Hitler's genius is to give the hungry something to sink their teeth into. Jews."

The newcomer was Israel (later Lord) Sieff. Vera had been a guest at his turreted family house, Cleeve Lodge, by Hyde Park Gate. His wife's father, Michael Marks, had started out like her father, wandering across the anti-Semitic landscape of Eastern Europe. But oppressors could not chase Michael Marks over land borders shouting "You have no country of origin!" because England had no land borders. In 1882 Michael, the peddler of trifles, was free to build his penny bazaar into the giant retailer Marks & Spencer, whose Baker Street headquarters would later shelter Vera's secret operations. Israel had been curious about Sir Oswald Mosley and invited him to speak at a Cleeve Lodge dinner. Mosley said a new political party like his needed "a hate plank" in its platform and "the best hate plank is the Jews."

"Sir Oswald is leaving," said Israel, summoning a butler.

Stringbag heard the story from his father, one of a group of London industrialists and economists at the dinner. None had heard Mosley voice his anti-Semitic views. Most thought vaguely, if they thought at all about the British Union, that Mosley ran a fiercely patriotic movement to free his country from trade unions and striking workers.

"You should be having fun, Miss Atkins," said Israel, taking the lovers home for an impromptu supper. But the fun evening turned into deadly serious discussions. Stringbag believed young Jewish refugees could be trained to resist the Nazis. Whitehall feared antagonizing the Arabs by teaching Jews to fight in Palestine. Yet a professional Scottish soldier, Orde Wingate, was training Jewish fighters in irregular warfare in Palestine. This had Churchill's approval. In 1899, with remarkable self-confidence for a very young survivor of British wars, Churchill foresaw in his book *The River War* that civilization might fall to Muslims whose religion paralyzed their social development. "No more retrograde force exists in the world," wrote Churchill. As First Lord of the Admiralty in 1913, he urged the government to go into the oil business to protect supplies during the radical switch from coal-fired warships to oil. At the Colonial Office in 1921, he chose the emir Faisal as a client king in Mesopotamia (Iraq) to ensure British control between the Tigris and the Euphrates. Out of office in 1923, Churchill tried to merge Royal Dutch Shell and Burma Oil with the Anglo-Persian Oil Company, in which the British government owned most of the voting shares. Vera now understood the link between Gardyne de Chastelain and Persian Oil, and why Gardyne in Bucharest criticized T. E. Shaw, aka Lawrence of Arabia, for training Arabs in irregular "closework" combat.

Orde Wingate trained Jewish fighters in closework, even though this enraged the Arabs. Mollifying Arabs while supporting Jews was a tricky balancing act. Churchill believed the Jews could fight persecution only from a homeland. Millions of Jews were being driven by Hitler through Romanian ports to Palestine to stoke up Arab rage against the British. As a result, Churchill's views met with ferocious opposition in Whitehall.[3]

Vera felt she would never fully absorb the complications of British conflicts of interest, and the magnitude of the task facing those determined to stop Hitler. Her father had emphasized a passage in the Talmud: "Pray for the welfare of government. Without it, men swallow each other alive." This meant a government concerned for the welfare of the people, said Hélène Allatini, the Parisian Vera had first met in Bucharest and who was now staying in London. Hélène said few governments gave guidance in this time when heartrending decisions were made. A relative, Robert Rothschild, was told in Paris not to help the Irgun, the independent secret Jewish army, because the French government could hurt Rothschild businesses. Prominent Jews thought they should stay put, even though Europe's exit doors were closing and future entry into the free democracies was not certain.[4]

"Vera dug up unexpected sources," Bill Stephenson recalled. "I wanted her to travel in Europe. The Secret Intelligence Service was inefficient and suffered from tight budgets after the 1929 crash on Wall Street. SIS officers were still expected to have independent incomes. This meant recruiting among the privileged upper class. Churchill's loss of office in the general election of 1929 had deprived him of authority to press for anything better. Desmond Morton of the Industrial Intelligence Centre was shouldered aside by Whitehall. In secret, he planned for closework."

Because Major Desmond Morton carried in his heart the bullet that had hit him in the 1914–18 Great War, many wondered how he could still be alive and if he was ready for any work. As secretary of state for war in 1919, Churchill had asked Morton to collate intelligence on Russia. Morton took a cottage in Kent. From there, he could now stride unseen across the fields to Churchill's country house, Chartwell, and deliver intelligence on defense inadequacies. Parliamentary privilege supposedly protected Churchill against charges of giving away secrets. Yet his son-in-law, Duncan Sandys, had to hire lawyers after he was threatened with prosecution for telling Parliament about the same defense weaknesses.

Vera heard from Schulenburg that he would like to see her in Berlin while he took a break from his Moscow posting. She asked Bill Stephenson if she should go, and later told Mary: "I used to be scared before going in to see your husband, his look is so penetrating."

"And now?"

"It's the wide peripheral vision he had as a fighter pilot."

"He was called Machine-Gun Billy," said Mary. "As a champion boxer in the armed forces, he used breadth of vision to anticipate an opponent by seeming not to face the opponent head on. You have the same style!"

Bill told Vera to keep the Berlin rendezvous. Germany was still astonishingly open. This was confirmed by aviators who made use of Stringbag's aero-club on flights to Berlin. One pilot had cameras mounted in his private plane. Another was a one-man RAF intelligence service, but without clients among the RAF's top brass. These were bizarre times.[5]

While Vera waited to hear more of Schulenburg's plans, she moved into a small cottage in Winchelsea. Her mother was always glad to see Vera, but an invisible screen separated them. Hilda Atkins could not understand her daughter's preoccupations in London, and Vera could not make Hilda "semi-conscious," in the jargon the Mutual Friends had adopted from the official secret agencies. Hilda Atkins was afraid that her life in Germany during the last war, and her origins as a Russian Jew, might well arouse suspicion if another conflict erupted. Winchelsea had confronted invaders since 1350, when King Edward III set forth from this coastal haven to disperse the Spanish Armada. The townsfolk now ignored upheavals across the Channel. They had turned back wave after wave of invaders, and kept their powder dry, rather than talk about future tactics.

Vera obeyed an impulse to pray in Winchelsea's seven-hundred-year-old church, dedicated to St. Thomas à Becket, the martyr of Canterbury murdered by barons, who mistook the wishes of their king.

Current events cried out for divine intervention, but not in the way suggested by the present archbishop of Canterbury, Cosmo Gordon Lang, chaplain to the nation, whose musings carried weight. He asked if war could be justified. The House of Bishops responded that there were absolutely no grounds for fighting Nazism.

So Vera prayed in this ancient church named after the martyr. She expected no divine intervention to curb the folly of clerics, but she found a calmness of spirit within herself. She sensed no conflict with her Jewish upbringing, but felt close to the many graveyards of English yeomen who had fought for freedom. One of her favorite poems was Thomas Gray's "Elegy in a Country Churchyard." A vision of war inspired a pilot, Geoffrey Wellum, to compose in the style of Gray's elegy, "The fire will come . . . and thou shalt lift thine eyes . . . to watch a long drawn battle in the skies."

The words were prophetic. Soon enough, Winchelsea folk would lift their eyes to watch the Battle of Britain fought in the skies above them.

In London, the Blackshirts accused Churchill of taking Jewish money to champion the cause of an Israeli state. When Dr. Chaim Weizmann had earlier lost the Zionist movement's presidency, Churchill protested: "I don't believe the Jewish people are so stupid." The origin of the Balfour Declaration for a Jewish national home was a 1906 meeting between Arthur Balfour and Weizmann, at the time a lecturer on organic chemistry at Manchester University, who convinced Balfour of the need for a Jewish homeland. Now there was a tenfold increase in migration to Palestine's unoccupied deserts. The Mannheim Jewish Study Institute called upon Jews to prepare for terrible trials to come. The British government responded by cutting Jewish immigration to the level of Palestine's "absorptive capacity."

Israel Sieff and Simon Marks backed a Fund for German Jewry, and brought Vera together with Victor, 3rd Baron Rothschild. He was two years younger, and she found him handsome and self-effacing. In 1935 he was elected to a prize fellowship at Trinity College, Cambridge, but was more concerned about the electrical properties of frogs' eggs. He often dined with King George V, who would boom out, "Ah, Rothschild, don't take any frog's eggs into the bank with you, ha-ha!"[6] Victor de Rothschild had his own natural history museum above the financial base in the City of N. M. Rothschild & Sons. He "found no point in moving money from where it is to where it was needed." The family made him put in time at the bank's subsidiary, the Royal Mint Refinery. There, in another laboratory, he investigated the nature of fertilization in small creatures and searched for clues to the origins of life. His inventive curiosity was to test his courage and powers of concentration when war came. He recounted to Vera the racial slurs from which he had suffered in his schooldays. He recalled the headwaiter at a restaurant asking if he was Jewish and, when he said this was pretty obvious, being asked to leave. He was the youngest ever to receive the Trinity fellowship, and fellow students said he got it because he was "filthy rich" and the college was low on funds and needed Jewish money. These experiences toughened him. He had set out to excel in sports and to challenge much older men in many branches of scientific research. Some of his closest contemporaries at university were later exposed as Soviet spies, but he never considered that their political activities were any of his business. This turned out to be a tragic mistake, but in the decade after he met Vera in 1935, their friendship reinforced her own resolve. He received heartrending letters telling of child victims of Nazi racism, and in a public plea for Jewish refugees he said, "It is difficult for me to believe that I shall ever become the rather carefree and happy scientist I was before all this began."

A close relative of Victor was destined to die as an agent. Another future agent, the author Malcolm Muggeridge, wrote of Victor that "somewhere between White's Club and the Ark of the Covenant, between the Old and the New Testament, between the Kremlin and the House of Lords, [Victor] lost his way. This Socialist millionaire, this rabbinical skeptic, this epicurean ascetic, this Wise Man followed the wrong star and found his way to the wrong manger — one complete with chef, central heating and a lift."

Vera understood his inner conflicts. By 1936, public opposition to appeasement was slowly rising. The regular intelligence services suffered from a form of snobbery reflected in an old copy of the *Naval and Military Record*, republished in 1933: "We should view with grave apprehension any attempt to make officers out of men of humble birth." The original publication was dated June 22, 1910. Stringbag borrowed it to show Vera, because this attitude persisted, whereas modern Germany recruited among the poor, and educated them and trained them hard to become part of a modern war machine.

Shifts in public opinion led Vernon Bartlett, a popular English writer and commentator, to drop his opposition to defense preparations. He now produced a book, *Nazi Germany Explained.* He was to become chief of intelligence in psychological warfare. Vera had congratulated him on his about-face, and he invited her to lunch and swamped her with stories about Oxford and Cambridge universities, inhabited by homosexuals driven underground by the law. Bartlett said some learned from this experience to hide their pro-Soviet activities, and these would have dire consequences.

The "seedy level" of English life at this time was noted by novelist Graham Greene, another future agent. Arthur Calder-Marshall, also a well-known author, wrote that Greene had returned to find an England where the rich Jew was despised by aristocrats; where army majors in hotels ordered up "a pig in a poke" from the brothels. This was a land "inglorious . . . vicious" and made up of sadists, masochists, incestuous sex fiends, and cowards.

Such reactions did little to shake the self-satisfaction of those who never saw England from outside. There were elements of farce, apparent to outsiders. The chief of the SIS was known to the public only as C. He directed the secret service, also called C. Each was a state secret, protected by custom and laws that made it impossible to judge how well C the man, or C the organization, performed. Stringbag, temporarily posted to a naval intelligence office, said to Vera: "The general opinion is that SIS reports are unadulterated fiction. Any porter can point out C's residence in Queen Anne's Gate or himself on a morning stroll, maybe to check if Buckingham Palace has fallen down, or maybe taking a turn through St. James's Park to admire the dome of the India Office and the towers of Whitehall, appropriately wrapped in fog."

Beverley Nichols, a popular antiwar journalist, protested in his book *Cry Havoc!* against "Blowing up babies in Baghdad by pressing a button in Birmingham." He matched the pacifist mood on both sides of the Atlantic. President Franklin D. Roosevelt had to accept the U.S. Neutrality Act to pacify New Dealers opposed to intervention in another war.

Vera learned about such maneuvers when, in 1935, she met for the first time William J. Donovan, an American hero of World War I. On private business as a Wall Street lawyer, he called in at

Stephenson's office. Vera was there and heard Donovan say that Roosevelt had to play the political game and, if he failed to retain power, could do nothing about the Nazi menace. FDR got independent intelligence from a New York group of business magnates, who would be perfectly willing to direct a dark and dirty underground war from which orthodox military men would shrink.[7]

Like those across the Atlantic, Stephenson looked for unconventional talent. Such businessmen looked for weaknesses in the potential enemy. Swedish iron ore was vital to the German arms industry, for instance, and Bill already had tentative plans to sabotage supplies, for he knew a great deal about explosives, too.

So did Victor de Rothschild. He studied the use of miniature explosives in examining natural phenomena. Vera could leave messages for him at New Court, off St. Swithin's Lane, where he oversaw the Fund for German Jewry. One wealthy German Jew, Eugen Spier, picked up the bills for FOCUS, a luncheon club at the Hotel Victoria on Northumberland Avenue. It brought together those worried about Hitler even if they were at opposite ends of the political spectrum. One was a noisy member of Parliament, Dr. Hugh Dalton, a radical product of King's College, Cambridge, who loudly mocked his own Labour Party's pacifist stance. Dalton was one of a few who could bridge left- and right-wing tribalism. He knew trade unionists in Europe who could organize anti-Nazi uprisings. He bellowed his rage at Labour's denunciations of "Churchill the Warmonger."[8]

Vera, still needing to fill in the blanks in her knowledge of this England of contradictions, found in her research that Churchill himself had gone through a passionate antiwar phase. In notes made as secretary of state for war, he recorded, after the end of the Great War, that German atrocities were "followed step by step by the desperate and ultimately avenging nations. Every outrage against humanity or international law was repaid by reprisals . . . The wounded died between the lines; the dead mouldered into the soil. Merchant ships and neutral ships and hospital ships were sunk on the seas and all on board left to their fate, or killed as they swam. Cities and monuments were smashed by artillery. Bombs from the air were cast down indiscriminately. Poison gas in many forms stifled or seared the soldiers. Liquid fire was projected upon their bodies. Men fell from the air in flames. . . . When all was over, torture and Cannibalism were the only two expedients that the civilized, scientific, Christian States had been able to deny themselves: and they were of doubtful utility."

Vera shivered. These were not the words of a warmonger. They were those of a man who feared the insanity of war, and who would do all he could to prevent another. But the words seemed prescient. Churchill would never yield to an enemy who launched another conflict.[9]

# Return to Berlin

On November 5, 1935, street urchins pushed paper-stuffed dummies in old prams and cried, "Penny for the guy!" Guy Fawkes had tried to blow up Parliament some 330 years before. Taking a potshot at Hitler seemed less unsporting to Vera on this day of bonfires saluting Guy and his plan to roll barrels of gunpowder under politicians. A member of Parliament, Harold Nicolson, said, "The feeling is terribly pro-German." Most parliamentarians agreed with King George V, who insisted "we can do business" with Hitler.[1]

Vera ran into the reporter who had made notes from Stringbag's account of the expansion of Germany's secret navy.

"I got fired," the newsman told her. "The paper wouldn't publish the facts. A Blackshirt told my editor that he saw me with my source and I should go to prison for trying to air 'false secrets.' The British Union of Fascists has more clout than your navy friend."

Vera was on her way to the Marylebone Ladies' Rifle Club to pay the annual fee of two pounds, one shilling, sixpence. The club in ritzy Devonshire Place gave her the opportunity to sharpen skills first honed while hunting in the Romanian timberlands. Meanwhile, Bill Stephenson had purchased from a gunsmith on St. James's Street a rifle that he told Vera was perfectly balanced and equipped for a sharpshooter, and inevitably her mind returned to the question of assassination. He had details of Hitler's routine. "The Führer will tighten security soon," said Bill. "But right now, he loves his public appearances." An assassin would have the choice of Hitler as a moving target, in his six-wheeled open Mercedes tourer, or a stationary Hitler waving his arms on a public platform.

One bullet cost a penny at the Ladies' Rifle Club. Hitler cost the lives of those he hated. The equation intrigued Vera. "She'd been moved by Churchill's fear of descending to Torture and Cannibalism," recalled Mary Stephenson. "But he wrote this a year after the Great War ended in 1918, shell-shocked and sick of war. Now, only war would stop Hitler, unless he was assassinated. The only question was: would killing Hitler make him a martyr in Germany, or would it kill Nazism? Bill asked Vera to go to Berlin and judge the mood."

With Count von der Schulenburg hoping to see Vera in Berlin, the moment seemed opportune. Bill Stephenson conjured up papers identifying Vera as a representative of Johnny Walker Scotch Whisky. Its sole agent in Germany was Joachim von Ribbentrop, the representative for Henkell champagne.[2]

German postal services were still swift. Within days, Schulenburg had arranged for her to stay at the Tiergartenstrasse mansion of his wealthy colleague Friedrich "Freddie" Horstmann, head of the British desk at the German foreign ministry and one of the older diplomats who opposed Hitler. The parents of Horstmann's wife Lali were Jewish. Her father, an honorary British consul, was one of the few foreigners to wear Britain's Order of the Garter. Lali arranged for Schulenburg to share a room with Vera in the Horstmann household, widely known for lavish hospitality and many guests. Vera's presence would not seem out of place. The ex-lovers' reunion in December 1935 had been delayed more than two years and yet she felt the old "zoots-zoots," her private term for sexual magic. But for most of the time they talked. There was so much to say. The ambassador was now fully aware of Ribbentrop's influence: Hitler considered him an expert on British nobility, and a future ambassador who would appeal to those in London who admired the Nazi program.

Schulenburg said two million Nazi Party members could not tell seventy million Germans what to do. British diplomats listened to Nazi bigwigs at cocktail parties, instead of venturing into street bars where ordinary Germans asked openly when the British would help overthrow the Nazis. He was concerned that Vera might land on the new and secret "wanted" list, the *Sonderpfändungsliste*: persons to be arrested in countries to be occupied by Germany.

He spent long hours at the foreign ministry and talked feverishly with her through the nights. He had appeared like a ghost from the past, reviving bittersweet memories, and now, two weeks later, he dissolved again. He had proposed a new way to communicate with Vera from Moscow. He kept the odd quality of gentlemanly innocence that first attracted her. She thought it made him the perfect cat's-paw in Hitler's game of placating Stalin until ready to attack the Soviet Union.

As an Englishwoman who spoke good German, Vera saw the two Berlins that kept Count von der Schulenburg in a state of uncertainty. One was the Berlin of the Horstmanns, who clung to a rich cultural past. Freddy Horstmann remembered that after the first anti-Jewish boycott on April 1, 1933, von Ribbentrop invited Jewish friends to a "reassurance" lunch where he advised them not to take Hitler's anti-Semitic talk too seriously: it was aimed at eastern Jews, not German Jews. The lunch had come one day after storm troopers bludgeoned "white Aryans" who tried to shop in Berlin's Jewish stores. Now Ribbentrop inched his way into the self-deluded company of old-style German diplomats. Right across from the established German foreign ministry quarters at Wilhelmstrasse 74–76 was a fledgling bureau in the old Bismarck Palace where Ribbentrop, known as "Champagne Charlie," aped the aristocratic English style and curried favor in foreign capitals. When he visited the French foreign ministry, its puzzled bureaucrats asked Berlin, Who is this parvenu? Hitler dictated a delicate reply: "He is an old party member traveling abroad to clarify the position of the German government." Ribbentrop was getting what he wanted: recognition as foreign adviser to Hitler.[3]

Vera learned of another pretender lurking in Berlin's southwest suburb of Zehlendorf, with a greater appetite for the slaughterhouse. Reinhard Heydrich listened to Mozart, was adored by the police chief, SS Reichsführer Heinrich Himmler, and directed the SD or Sicherheitsdienst, the Nazi Party's intelligence service. On the same block was his potential opponent, Admiral Wilhelm Franz Canaris, who ran the Abwehr, the clandestine warfare section of the armed forces, where opposition to Hitler ran deep. Professional officers who first believed Hitler's "national revolution" meant a return to the old traditions now bitterly resented party thugs who lorded it over the soldiers.

Vera heard Berliners in restaurants and bars voice fear of the party's usurpation of power. They asked questions like "When are the British coming?" Local British diplomats seemed deaf to such appeals. Joseph Goebbels, in charge of Public Enlightenment, sat opposite the

British consulate where the Secret Intelligence Service representative, Frank Foley, was besieged by Jews seeking visas. The daily queue of Jews delighted Goebbels. Foley used the title Passport Officer as cover for the SIS. Paperwork swamped SIS officers using the same cover throughout Europe. They complained that Jewish visa applicants left them no time to pursue their real duties.

Vera learned about the overworked SIS from Ralph Wigram, Churchill's loyal friend in Whitehall, when she returned home in early 1936. Wigram backed her opinion that British diplomats in Berlin were too busy entertaining English personages dazzled by "thrilling Nazi-land." They raved about the blond blue-eyed young Nazis in "utterly smashing uniforms" who escorted them to Hitler's rallies. Vera said: "Great harm is done by visiting the Mayfair hostesses. These admirers of Hitler give an impression that pro-Nazi policy is fashioned in London drawing rooms, and discourage Berliners, afraid to act without British support." Wigram was close to the permanent undersecretary at the British Foreign Office, Sir (later 1st Baron) Robert Vansittart, who was accused by his replacement, Sir Alexander Cadogan, of "dancing literary hornpipes" in assessing the fascist threat.[4]

A colorful Texan engineer-diplomat, Sam Edison Woods, acted as U.S. commercial attaché in Prague. Woods regularly traveled to Berlin on the personal instructions of President Roosevelt to report on German technology under cover of trade talks. He confirmed Vera's observation that the Berlin Cipher Office had reengineered the commercial coding machine first built in 1924 by Cipher Machines of Steglitzerstrasse 2, one of which Stephenson had purchased. Ralph Wigram's superiors refused to confirm Sam Woods's figures on German arms superiority. "Grave and terrible facts," Wigram confided to Vera. He risked prosecution by disclosing these facts to Churchill.

Then she heard that poor Horstmann, her generous Berlin host, the great diplomat and connoisseur of art, had been forced out of the foreign service and out of his mansion on Tiergartenstrasse. The price of integrity and of being Jewish was high, both in Berlin and in London.

# 5

# Crown or Commoner:
# Where Lies the Treachery?

Ribbentrop was appointed ambassador extraordinary of the German Reich, on special mission to the 1935 Silver Jubilee of King George V and Queen Mary. Forty stripe-trousered Germans in penguin suits stood in rows at the extraordinary ambassador's post on the Mall. As King George V came abreast, they gave the stiff-armed Hitler salute in perfect unison.

On Tuesday, January 21, 1936, King George V officially died. He had actually died just before midnight on the day before, having requested a lethal injection of cocaine and morphine, timed to make the august pages of the voice of authority, the morning *Times*, not the trashy afternoon papers.

His successor, Edward VIII, met that same Tuesday with the well-known Nazi, the Duke of Coburg. This was reported by the press spokesman in the German embassy, Iona von Ustinov, father of the future playwright and actor Peter Ustinov. Count von der Schulenburg's foreign office friends in Berlin had arranged for Vera to meet the quietly anti-Nazi Ustinov. Iona repeated to her a dispatch dictated to him by the Duke of Coburg after meeting the new king. "For the eyes only of the Führer and Party Member von Ribbentrop," it reported that Edward VIII told the duke "a British-German alliance was an urgent necessity and a guiding principle for British foreign policy." Edward approved of Deputy Führer Rudolf Hess and hoped he might come to visit. The new king also thought the current German ambassador, the old fashioned Leopold von Hoesch, should be replaced by Ribbentrop.

King Edward's subsequent phone call to Ambassador von Hoesch was recorded by Fritz Hesse, the secretly anti-Nazi reporter for the official German news agency, stationed at the embassy. In this call, the king said rumors of an alliance with Germany caused alarm in Parliament, adding: "I sent for the prime minister [by then Stanley Baldwin] and gave him a piece of my mind. I told the old so-and-so I would abdicate if he made war. There was a frightful scene. But you needn't worry. There won't be war."

Upon receiving a transcript, Hitler was reported to have shouted: "At last! The King of England will not intervene. He is keeping his promise. That means that it can all go well."[1]

Vera saw that the new English king's warm welcome for Hitler's henchmen would have a devastating impact on anti-Nazi Germans hoping for British backup. Without this, how many Germans, for the sake of a principle, would risk losing their wives and children or their jobs?

King Carol II of Romania, in London for the state funeral for George V, was intimidated by Hitler in the same way. His hopes for British support had been dashed so far. "The Führer's boasts cowed the Romanian king," wrote an astute Associated Press reporter, William Russell, who became a young U.S. diplomat in Berlin. Russell had been the first to tell Vera, "Go listen to what people in the streets of Germany really think about Nazism." He was outspoken in his contempt for the diplomatic circuit in Berlin. Stanley Baldwin took absolutely no interest in foreign affairs and provided no guidelines to British diplomats in Berlin, who were thus happy to join in the Nazi-promoted merry-go-round of parties bountifully blessed with rich food and buckets of alcohol. Russell had, in common with other American correspondents, greater powers of independent observation. He later became an American-run agent, whose warm relationship with Vera worked to their mutual advantage. He persistently reminded American readers that Germans longed for outside help to overthrow Hitler.

Hermann Göring was to represent Germany at King George V's funeral, until warned by the embassy in London that his safety could not be guaranteed "because of Jewish refugees." Ustinov reported this to Vera, adding that Ambassador von Hoesch warned Göring about powerful Jewish families like the Rothschilds, who could damage the monarchy's financial affairs, so great was their influence.

She asked Ustinov if this was true. He had a Jewish background. His post at the German embassy was a means to securing a home in England, which he had come to love. He laughed at the idea of rich Jews influencing the Crown. How many rich Jews were there? He himself had little money but stacks of books. His was one of the brilliant minds that once flourished in Berlin's brief cultural revival. Now he lived in a shabby part of London, his books balanced on broken furniture. "Defection is not a profitable pastime," he said mournfully when she helped him move into slightly better quarters. He told her that Ambassador von Hoesch discouraged Göring from appearing at the state funeral in order to prove his loyalty, while he quietly opposed Hitler and worked with trusted English friends.

There was an enormous English muddle at the funeral. The crowds showed violent hostility to Mosley's Blackshirts when they staged an anti-Jewish march. King Carol II was almost lost in the clutter of foreign dignitaries and representatives from the British Empire who came to pay homage. Vera was cheered by the chaos. It was the opposite of the mechanized society lampooned by London-born Charlie Chaplin in his movie *Modern Times*, although the press carried eccentricity too far in portraying King Carol's Romania as a Ruritanian fantasy.

Vera felt a pang of pity for Carol. His flame-haired mistress, Magda Lupescu, was not in evidence at the funeral. Presuming upon old friendship, Vera left a note at his hotel, the Savoy. He received her there while having a massage. "Lying naked on his tummy," she told Mary later, "the poor man worried about Russia, which had a plan of attack through Romania to invade Germany, and about Germany, which had a plan to attack Russia through Romania. If he lost his throne, he would need a nest egg somewhere. But where? I told him his best friends were British businessmen who had developed his kingdom's resources." His fears had been inflated earlier, when he was one of many foreign potentates to visit Hitler's alpine retreat at Berchtesgaden. Most visitors meekly listened to Hitler's arguments, tailored to fit anyone he was receiving that day. He wooed Carol with a reasoned argument for securing Germany *Lebensraum*, or living space, in parts of Europe where the German people were in the majority. Hitler had seemed diffident and humble, but his cold eyes and queer voice scared Carol witless.

After Vera's brief reunion with King Carol, an odd thing happened to His Highness. His masseur got lost in the funeral crowds around Westminster and he wound up in the Abbey with lesser mourners. His picture scattered among newspapers identified him as "King Carol of Transylvania." In the late spring of 1936, a London cartoonist portrayed him as Count Dracula. One who noted the jibes and journalistic errors was an American businessman, Wallace B. Phillips, who lived in London but was linked to a group of influential businessmen in New York who met regularly in a small apartment at 34 East 62nd Street, dubbed The Room. Phillips met Vera at one of the Stephensons' private dinners that summer. Forewarned of Vera's passionate anti-Nazi stance, Phillips told her that he and his American friends were as appalled as she was by Hitler's ability to con foreign statesmen. They had constituted themselves as an informal, self-appointed intelligence mission, in the disturbing absence of any central American secret service. Most Americans shared the British sense of fair play, he said, which made them easy marks when Hitler turned on the charm. The Room was a sort of secret society of elitists. It counted among its members Kermit, son of Theodore Roosevelt, and Vincent Astor, the wealthy property developer and publisher, who treasured his links with England and was close to President Franklin D. Roosevelt. FDR was in a political straitjacket. He sensed the inevitability of war, needed all the information he could get on the Nazi threat, but knew that any overt measures he took might lose him another election.

Wally Phillips's like-minded friends included the American Red Cross representative in London, David Bruce, who would play a key role in a future U.S. Office of Strategic Services (OSS), the predecessor to the Central Intelligence Agency. Phillips's "secret society" reflected Vera's own ideas about closework. David Bruce commented later: "Vera could access people from hall porters to captains of industry." He was among the very few American Mutual Friends who knew her travels in the late 1930s were for the purpose of gathering information. He wrote later: "There was an exciting whiff of danger about Miss Atkins."[2]

Bruce agreed with Vera that if the democracies continued to be deceived by Hitler's declarations of peaceful intent, and turned a blind eye to his actual moves during 1936 — the occupation of the

Rhineland, the proclamation of a Berlin-Rome axis, the German Anti-Comintern Pact with Japan—there would be nobody left to stand up to Germany when, not if, full-scale war broke out. Vera said the only cracks in Germany's armor would be in the factories. Spies could point out the weak spots to trained saboteurs, who could wreak more havoc, at less cost and with more precision, than aerial bombers. She paraphrased Sherlock Holmes: "Now in the building of tanks, I tell you what / There is always somewhere a weakest spot."

The finding of an enemy's weak spots occupied the fertile mind of a veteran of unconventional wars, Colin McVean "Gubby" Gubbins, who had been alarmed by a War Office financial secretary's report saying, "The more I study military affairs, the more I am impressed by the importance of cavalry in modern warfare." In 1936, Gubby was a forty-year-old brigade major in Military Intelligence, stunned by the army's preoccupation with cavalry when Hitler had specific plans for blitz-krieg or "lightning war" tactics, using close coordination between air-borne artillery and mechanized land units, radiophoning orders instead of using the slow dots and dashes of Morse code. Most countries had new methods of encryption and new ways of transmitting Morse. But spoken orders made for swift movement on a narrow battlefront.

Vera and Gubby were fated to escape from Poland together during Germany's first blitzkrieg at the start of World War II in August 1939. From the start, in 1936, their relationship was fraught with danger. Gubby could not hide details of his personal life, because army officers had few private secrets. She saw him as the last of the young adventurers who fought in the Great Game between Britain and Russia to gain dominance along the Himalayas. On the Northwest Frontier (today Afghanistan), Gubby had been with British military intelligence, eavesdropping on Russian wireless signals that linked Moscow with Far Eastern bases as far away as Shanghai. He joked about local tribal warfare as "Afghans bashing Russians, the British raj, and each other."

Gubby was descended from a captain of dragoons who campaigned for Oliver Cromwell in Ireland in the 1600s. His great-grandfather served in outposts of the British empire. His grandfather joined the Bengal Civil Service, and got into hot water for his outspoken criticism of the British raj. In 1863 he was sent back to England where, humiliated and jobless, he killed himself. Gubby's father served in Japan for thirty years under seven British secretaries of state. The son, from the age of seven, never saw his parents for years at a stretch. On the windswept Isle of Mull in the Western Hebrides, he ran wild in the heather or swam in the ice-cold sea.

Vera was five years old when, in September 1913, Gentleman Cadet Gubbins entered the Royal Military Academy at Woolwich, near the East End docklands. The following summer, aged eighteen, he was sent to Heidelberg University for German studies. A local widow rented a room to the boy, who looked like any other impoverished foreign student in patched clothing. On August 1, 1914, Gubby saw notices on lampposts announcing "Germany at war with Russia." His kindly German landlady said he had better leave. She packed his trunk and promised to forward it to him, so he would not attract hostile attention on the train. At Cologne an unflappable Englishman pressed a gold sovereign into his hand, which paid for a third-class railway ticket to Brussels. German border guards inspected the papers of other travelers. Gubby was not even questioned because "I looked too boyish and underdeveloped to be of any use in war to anyone." He reported to the academy on the day Britain declared war, at the same moment that Vera and her mother and two brothers abandoned their own journey to England and took refuge with Max Rosenberg's relatives in Cologne. Three of Gubby's fellow cadets in Germany were caught and spent the war in prison. His trunk arrived three months later with large white letters painted on the lid by his German landlady: AMERICAN CITIZEN'S LUGGAGE. He never forgot the existence of "good" Germans.

Second Lieutenant Gubbins fought on the Western Front until March 14, 1917, when he was sent to Buckingham Palace to receive from King George V the Military Cross for conspicuous gallantry. The boy was back in France next day. Early in 1917, the Bolshevik Revolution broke out, and Russia made a separate peace with Germany. Three months after the Great War's end, Gubby was with the Archangel Expeditionary Force fighting the Bolsheviks, and discovering the caprices of guerrilla warfare. Some White Russians joined the Bolsheviks, and guerrilla forces fought sometimes together and sometimes against each other. Gubby became a red-capped staff officer with General Edmund (later Field Marshal Lord) Ironside, but detested the job and returned to sort out the complexities in the field.

For three years Gubby had to outwit a different kind of guerrilla: the Irish nationalists. Their civilian army was free to choose time, place, and target. He was "shot at from behind hedges by gentlemen in trilby hats and mackintoshes." In the legendary Northwest Frontier and Afghanistan, he analyzed Russian signals intercepted by Y, the most secret of British secret agencies. Later, while he was at the Soviet section of the Military Intelligence Directorate in London, the Russians adopted one-time coding pads. Each page had its own unique key, and was burned after use. Frustrated, he was reduced to examining Soviet publications that gave away nothing. His Afghan experience seemed wasted, and the cost of training an officer for conventional warfare was absurd if the officer was killed by a penny bullet from an Afghan tribesman's musket, the jezail. He spoke of this to Vera, who recognized Rudyard Kipling's "Arithmetic of the Frontier" and quoted:

> A scrimmage in a border station —
> A canter down some dark defile —
> Two thousand pounds of education
> Drops to a ten-rupee jezail.

Gubby's regard for Vera was heightened by the pleasure he got from her appetite for learning and her memory. She had not forgotten the penny price of a bullet at the Ladies' Rifle Club. If Hitler's assassination was out of question, homemade and cheaply produced weapons offered another way to derail Hitler's juggernaut. In Afghanistan, the way tribal ingenuity outdid massive conventional forces taught a lesson to Gubby and his comrades. These included Bill (John Hessell) Tiltman, master cryptographer, and Nick (Frederick William) Nicholls, who set up outstations around the globe to intercept the signals of potential enemies — signals analyzed by the Government Code and Cipher School in shabby quarters near St. James's Street tube station, the cradle of ULTRA code breakers. Nicholls would eventually connect with agents in the tribal rags of European civilians.

Gubby wrote manuals like *The Art of Guerrilla Warfare*. His book *Housewife's ABC of Home-Made Explosives* described how to cook up big bangs for Germans who might invade English homes. *The Partisan Leader's Handbook* told how to deal with informers: "kill them quickly but only after squeezing them dry of information." He said there was not a single book on irregular warfare to be found in Whitehall or anywhere else in the country.

Gubby was a hard-faced Scot with a boisterous sense of humor. He questioned the wisdom of the top brass after he had seen Allied troops mangled in World War I. As a regular serving officer, his record qualified him for a knighthood and general's rank, but these would come later. He was now drawn to Bill Stephenson "like other professionals, by invisible threads, as if to the oracle at Delphi," he said later. He met regularly with Vera, not lunching at swank restaurants but taking tea at a Lyons Corner house in Charing Cross. He asked how she knew so much about German military advances. She said Jewish scientists, escaping persecution, knew a great deal. He agreed that anti-Semitism in Britain stood in the way of training an underground Jewish army recruited from young refugees. Chaim Weizmann, himself a refugee, had perfected a new process for making acetone during a critical shortage of British explosives in World War I, contributing to the Allied victory. Now Hitler was driving out those who knew most about weaponry, a drain that would ultimately cost him dearly.

Gubbins was not hampered by the narrow focus of the SIS and the diplomats in Moscow. With the advantage of his time in Russia and analyzing Soviet military books and signals, he was interested in Ambassador Schulenburg's task of laying the groundwork for a Nazi-Soviet peace pact. The count's letters were now going through a Swedish consular friend, and Vera's replies went via a Stockholm box number. Gubby cautioned her that Schulenburg might not always outwit the Nazis. Gubby remembered Germans who had saved him from prolonged incarceration in 1914, but he feared today's "good" Germans might be used to entrap Vera.

"She doesn't need my warnings," he told Stephenson. "She's got a deep understanding of Berlin. She's a beauty and a killer, you know." A Scot with a touch of the second sight, and a soldier inclined to be biblical, he quoted from Proverbs: "For the lips of a strange woman drip as an honeycomb, and the mouth is smoother than oil. But her end is bitter as wormwood, sharp as a two-edged sword. Her feet go down to death; her steps take hold on hell."

It was a strange, and prophetic, utterance. Gubby's blue eyes drilled into hers when he talked of such matters. Yet at regimental parties he donned his kilt and danced a reel on the table, his laughter booming above the drone of bagpipes.

He had encouraged Orde Wingate to train Jews to fight Arabs in Palestine, even while Whitehall stopped the flow of Jewish settlers into the same territory. How did this contradiction come about? wondered Vera.

Gubby said there were political opportunists and there were those who followed their conscience. Policy was run by those who wavered between opportunism and morality, and these, if dumped in a cannibal's cooking pot, would see the cannibal's point of view. The Jews of Europe offered the biggest pool of talent: they had the incentive to become single-minded closework fighters. Vera said hostility and red tape was alienating many. Britain now would admit only refugees who proved they had permission to go on to the United States. "It's not our finest hour," said Gubby.

From London, the Central Fund for German Jewry in 1936 advised the Haganah's Jewish irregulars on Palestinian soil to practice *havlagah* (restraint) in the spirit of Gandhi's nonviolence. But this was taken as a sign of weakness by the Arabs and strengthened the tough breakaway group Irgun Zvai Leumi (National Military Organization), led by Ze'ev Jabotinsky, whose earlier warnings to Jews to leave Europe had failed.

Orde Wingate had told his trainees, "We are building an Army of Zion." He was asked if he had read anything about Zionism. "Yes, in the only important book on the subject: the Bible," replied Wingate. He was by now regarded as slightly mad by the War Office top brass, but Mutual Friends protected him much the way they covered Section D, a shadowy group of three army intelligence officers whose files were plastered with secrecy labels to foil Whitehall snoopers.

Gubby filled regular army posts. Too many, in fact. He told his wife, Norah, he was tired of military tasks "all over the place." In one period of eight years, he'd had only five months of leave. His working days required him to keep rooms in London, and he visited Norah when he could in the countryside, which she much preferred to city life.

One of the extra tasks loaded upon Gubby was training reservists in air defense. He found no equipment for antiaircraft regiments, despite Churchill's public warnings that the Germans would bomb London: "The heart of our Empire, and a target that cannot be moved."

The Air Ministry retorted that the RAF was fully prepared. Lord Trenchard, the former air marshal, had left the RAF short of planes and pilots. He was now commissioner of London's Metropolitan Police, and introduced an Incitement to Disaffection Act that allowed searches for "seditious literature." If he decided Our Mutual Friends were guilty of sedition and conspiring against the government, it could prove awkward. The law was denounced by the National Council for Civil Liberties as copying "German Gestapo secret-police methods." Trenchard created gentlemen-bobbies, an elitist version of the constables popularly known as "bobbies." He said his gentlemen-bobbies had "superior qualifications." At his new Metropolitan Police College, cadets wore dinner jackets and were waited upon by lowly ex-servicemen in white aprons. The pro-German *Times* lauded the upper-class policeman: "The ideals he cherishes will be those of the people from whose ranks he comes."

Vera's singular background exposed her to the risk of investigation. Luckily, the common sense of gentlemen-bobbies overrode Lord Trenchard's suspicion of Jews and foreigners. But "sedition" meant treason against the Crown, and behind Lord Trenchard were royals whose real influence was profound. Our Mutual Friends, to avoid accusations of secretly plotting against authority, spoke learnedly of the Fourth Dimension of Warfare, presented as an academic study, and proposed working-class uprisings as a means to confront any Nazi occupation. Hugh Dalton was called a traitor to his class for espousing these aims. The pro-Nazi Duke of Westminster said Dalton plotted communist uprisings. Churchill, as a political outcast, mentally earmarked Dalton to become a government minister who would parry questions about irregular operations once the pendulum swung in Churchill's favor.

Vera's birth sign, Gemini, was characterized in Romania with these words, similar to those in England for Gubby's birth sign of Cancer: "Passionate sense of justice. Deep insight into the character of others. Integrity, courage, generosity and compassion are all-important." Both she and Gubby possessed these qualities.

High society giggled over the doggerel "All abide by one old-fashioned rule: / That gentlemen and ladies never tell / Of laughter and frivolity / And abandoned frocks and loosened curls." Vera's friendship with Gubby might have given rise to speculation that they were among the gentlemen and ladies that never told. The Stephensons stopped any such notions by arranging dinner parties with Mutual Friends, where the two could talk as they also did in obscure tearooms. The pair simply held the same beliefs. He could let off steam, for example, about foolish Whitehall policies that allowed Germany to profit from Anglo-Arab tensions in Palestine. A crate labeled CEMENT had fallen from a vessel unloading at Jaffa, scattering ammunition destined for Jewish defense forces. Germany's ally, the Grand Mufti of Jerusalem, Haj Amin, whipped up anti-British hatred by alleging that the cargo was secretly dispatched from London for a secret Jewish army. The vessel had departed, in fact, from a Romanian port, and was part of the Nazi scheme to send Jews to Palestine as one way to inflame Arabs against the British mandate there. An Arab Higher Committee announced a general strike until the British stopped all Jewish immigration to Palestine. The notorious Syrian guerrilla leader Fawzi el-Kaukji cut British rail, road, and telephone communications throughout the region. The crisis could have been avoided, said Gubby, if Whitehall were willing to take advice from well-informed Jews on the spot.

Vera's Zionist friends might argue for a British-backed Jewish Brigade, but the only prominent champion was Churchill, and he was still ridiculed in London by those in power. A Jewish Brigade remained a dream. Gubby and Stephenson thought it would materialize in time. For now, the lack of forward thinking in the defense establishment was scrutinized in that tiny cell of military rebels called Section D. They called in Gubby, who later described how he was rescued from plodding through mind-numbing Soviet treatises at his War Office desk.

> A cold hand took me literally by the back of my neck and a voice said, "What are you doing for lunch today?" I whipped round — it was Jo Holland. I replied I was going to my regimental races. . . . I was told I was having lunch instead with Jo. . . . We adjourned to St. Ermin's Hotel where we met my real host, head of this definitely non-regimental Section D.[3]

Section D for Destruction, as it became known among the few, was in a position to assess the ideas of Vera's like-minded civilian friends. These, at Marks & Spencer, had proposals for a future Jewish Brigade. Simon Marks's favorite historical character was King Alfred, who single-mindedly struggled for a national identity. "I'm proud to be British," Simon told Vera, "but Nazi cowards destroyed the brave Jews who fought for Germany in their thousands during the Great War. We need a government to speak for us." He arranged, through the Fund for German Jewry, to train young German-Jewish men at a camp in Kent. Edmund de Rothschild, a reserve officer in the Bucks Yeomanry, would prepare them for the only branch that recruited from "aliens" in the British armed forces, the Pioneer Corps.

On March 12, 1938, German troops marched into Austria, greeted by civilians who were said to welcome Anschluss, the "reunification of the Germanic peoples." Hitler drove into his childhood home of Linz to celebrate "completion of my mission to restore my dear homeland to the German Reich." Vast and immensely useful industrial and natural resources were incorporated into his domain, along with nine million Austrians; their army became part of the Wehrmacht, the German armed forces, and units were sent at once to Germany. Zionist headquarters in Vienna were attacked by Nazis. The persecution of Jews began. Austria was now a province in the New Order. Britain accepted the Anschluss as a done deal. The former Liberal prime minister, David Lloyd George, one of the most remarkable figures in twentieth-century politics, told Parliament that Hitler was "a great man." One observer wrote, "Lloyd George may not actually tell a lie, but he will lead you to believe what he considers will induce you to do what he wants." He used his persuasive Welsh charm to convince others, like Labour Party leader George Lansbury, that Hitler would do anything to avoid war. Hitler's interpreter, Paul Schmidt, later said that Lord Londonderry, the former air minister, was among many who were emboldened by Lloyd George's oratory to trust the Führer's "wooing of the coy Britannia." The German ambassador in Washington cabled Berlin, "It was striking that Congress took no stand on the German action."[4]

"Fear paralyzed the democracies," Vera said later. "And more British serving officers rebelled against London's inaction," she recalled. "Freddie Winterbotham had the title of 'chief of air intelligence,' but it was a one-man show. He had been a lumberjack in

Stephenson's homeland of Canada. Acting alone, he joined the Paris-based Aeronautical Research and Sales Corporation in a joint venture with French intelligence rebels. Without authority, the French air force was photo-mapping German military installations. Winterbotham and an Australian businessman pilot, Sidney Cotton, made regular flights to Berlin to exploit the comradeship of pilots who had been enemies in the Great War, thus gathering information on the new Luftwaffe. Cotton had his own twin-engine Lockheed aircraft, with Leica cameras concealed in the wings to photograph German installations. Winterbotham pretended to be pro-Nazi to wangle private audiences with Hitler, who told him, 'The only hope for an ordered world is that it should be ruled by three superpowers — the British Empire, the Greater Americas, and the new German Reich.'"

When Winterbotham reported in London that Hitler believed his New Order was endorsed by England's royals, the pilot was told to remain silent. He had sworn the oath that empowers the Director of Public Prosecutions to proceed against those who break the Official Secrets Act. "I'm just a commoner, an ordinary bloke," he said to Vera. "Between Crown and commoner, where lies the treachery?"

# 6

# "England Cut Off"

Vera ventured through Europe into regions where the common man might rise up against oppression. It was obvious that Hitler needed to launch his new army-support warplanes against Poland before the poorly equipped Polish air force took delivery of RAF Hawker Hurricane fighters. Delivery by sea was to be delayed for months while the British Exchequer argued about whether it or the Poles should pay the shipping costs. Stringbag flew mock mine-laying operations in the Baltic, anticipating the use by German warships of Polish ports if war broke out. Vera had to decide where to concentrate guerrillas, using local resources, since tightfisted Whitehall suffered from what the journalist-historian Paul Johnson bluntly called "simple, old-fashioned fear; a dash of cowardice, indeed."[1]

Freddie Winterbotham reported that Poland had a military version of a German "secret writing mechanism." Gubby knew an Englishman resident in Poland, General Adrian Carton de Wiart, who had lost an arm and an eye in the Great War and had won the highest military award for gallantry, the Victoria Cross. Gubby considered a secret mission to join the one-eyed general. Vera knew how to cross the border from Romania, a route least likely to draw German attention. The mission would discuss stay-behind resistance groups, and look for a specimen of the "secret writing machine" that would become the Enigma challenging ULTRA wartime code breakers.[2]

Gubby avoided the SIS. He could not risk being identified with the mythology crafted into a Nazi book for general circulation, *Secret Service: England's Darkest Power*. This claimed to disclose "business secrets of the London murder center." The book's purpose was to spread mutual suspicion among civilians, further encouraging them to report on each other to the Gestapo.

Poland had incorporated the first of Hitler's "lost lands" after the 1919 Versailles peace talks. Hitler said the losses would not have been in vain if Jews were forced to submit to poison gas.

Vera could never talk about such concerns to the Mayfair set, which was in general cynical and cruelly witty, dripping acid on Jews and kings alike. There were those who held this behavior in contempt. One was the Earl of Cardigan, whose ancestor led the cavalry in the tragic Charge of the Light Brigade and reputedly groaned, "Ah, well, here goes the last of the Cardigans," when he saw disaster ahead. "He was wrong, of course," the present earl told Vera. "For here I am." He deplored snobbery and said, "The British Empire is winding down, but too many colonial administrators still equate *Burke's Colonial Gentry* with *Burke's Peerage and Landed Gentry*." He regarded as a metaphor for the country's insularity the headline frequently scrawled on newspaper vendors' billboards: FOG IN CHANNEL — CONTINENT CUT OFF. "It never crosses our minds that it's England that is cut off," said Cardigan, meaning a political fog that hid European events. He was interested in improvising an anti-Nazi resistance and reminded Vera that, in other wars, escapees had often brought back useful intelligence about their former captors. Cardigan was to become an escapee himself. He understood the definition of closework as meaning to get close enough to the enemy to use improvised weapons. He kept notes as a prisoner of the Germans, published after the war as *I Walked Alone.*[3]

Major General Alan Brooke, later Field Marshal Viscount Alanbrooke, would help get badly needed "silent-killer" weapons for closework. Gubby, who had been his personal staff officer, told Vera that "Brookie" haunted an antique bookstore, later made famous by Helene Hanff of New York in her book *84, Charing Cross Road.* Brookie was a dedicated bird-watcher and searched for secondhand books on the subject. Vera caught him between bookshelves. An unassuming man, he was intrigued by her familiarity with the esoteric details of birdlife in Transylvania. They later met at nearby tea shops, where he quizzed her about Romania. He wanted Churchill in power, but he was also blunt and so outspoken that, when his wish came true, he would blast Churchill as a warlord who was pigheadedly proposing some impossible action. Churchill later moaned, "Brookie must hate me." The general commented, "I don't hate him, I love him; but when the day comes that I tell him he is right when I believe him to be wrong, it will be time for him to get rid of me."

By a most extraordinary coincidence, the Charing Cross Road bookshop was owned by one Benjamin Marks, who had invented a simple code that he penciled on the flyleaf to give assistants the lowest acceptable price in bargaining with buyers. His son Leo broke his dad's code at the age of ten, and would become the boyish chief cryptographer devoted to Vera in special operations. He was a baby-faced genius, first rejected as a Jew at the supersecret Bletchley center of ULTRA code breakers.

Gubby knew Vera's acquaintance Edmund de Rothschild in his role as a reserve officer in the Bucks Yeomanry. One of Gubby's duties was to train part-time soldiers of the East Anglia Artillery. East Anglia had no artillery, and he treated the job as a practice run for crudely improvised home defense tactics against German invaders. It gave him a chance to talk to Edmund de Rothschild about a future Jewish Brigade.

For the sake of appearances at the anti-Semitic War Office, Gubby kept an arm's-length relationship with the Fund for German Jewry. One of the fund's five joint presidents was the Marquess of Reading, son of a former viceroy of India. Another was Nahum Sokolow, president of the World Zionist Organization. Zionism alarmed monarchs, who used Jewish financial advisers but dropped them if they did anything to cause a public scandal. At the N. M. Rothschild bank a Fixing Room displayed portraits of the many monarchs it had subsidized. One unlikely borrower was the king of Prussia. Another portrait, of the Empress of All the Russias, hung there because the tsar refused to have his own exhibited in a Jewish bank.

Vera continued reading in London newspaper libraries about earlier years. England was still, in many respects, a mystery. She found, in its recent chronicles, reasons for the initial hesitation among Jews here to see the dangers brewing in Germany. Back in 1935, even Churchill had once seemed to waver. King George V still reigned, and expressed no concern. There were then six major dailies and two evening newspapers, whose proprietors took their cue from the Crown. Churchill wrote in the *Daily Express*: "History is replete with examples of men who have risen to power by employing stern, grim, and even frightful methods, but who, nevertheless, when their life is revealed as a whole, have been regarded as great figures whose lives have enriched the story of mankind. So may it be with Hitler."[4]

Three years later, Vera questioned the young diplomat Ralph Wigram, who was now risking so much to inform Churchill of such views governing the Foreign Office. Why, Vera asked, had Churchill portrayed Hitler in such a way? Wigram said Churchill profoundly regretted it. He had tried to see Hitler as many Germans saw him: a leader who ended their humiliation. In 1935, it had angered some young civil servants enough that they sided with the fiercely anti-German permanent secretary in the Foreign Office, Robert Vansittart. For a time, Vansittart had considered Churchill to be as unbalanced and unpredictable as King George said he was.

"The external persecution to which the Germans have been subjected since the war" was offered as an excuse for Hitler's rise to power by Lord Lothian, one of the architects of the punitive Treaty of Versailles and an opponent of rearmament. He said the murder of Jews was simply "a reaction to this external persecution."

Vera saw Lord Lothian's dismissal of the fate of Jews as pandering to royalty and to those in Whitehall who found it easier to remain blind to the approach of another world war. Churchill in 1935 wanted to broaden his appeal to the center-left of politics by representing himself as a reasonable man, defying Lothian's portrayal of him as a "whiskey-besotted warmonger." Churchill abandoned his brief pretence. Vera was advised to avoid any overt contacts with Churchill that might expose her to the curiosity of internal security officers. She never mentioned in her lifetime the occasions noted by others when she was later consulted by him.[5]

By the late 1930s, Our Mutual Friends had formed an anti-Nazi secret service loosely linked to Section D and working with patriotic businessmen like Stephenson, who assigned Vera to intelligence missions. These informal agents were known as NOCs: Non-Official Cover. She cultivated Ward Price, a senior *Daily Mail* foreign correspondent who had interviewed Hitler and his fellow dictator Mussolini, and wrote approvingly of both. He changed his views later, and became an NOC. Another of her journalist friends, Sefton Delmer, was born and educated in Germany and had been chief of the *Daily Express* bureau in Berlin until 1933. By the age of twenty-six he had walked and talked with Hitler and was now covering the Spanish

Civil War, but he returned frequently to London. He arranged for Vera to become "an assistant, a sort of junior reporter." This gave her further accreditation on foreign travels. Delmer's genius later shone in the Orwellian wartime London Deception Center.

In the Fleet Street press world, correspondents gathered in the local pubs during a break from foreign postings. Vera formed a long-lasting friendship with George Millar, who found newspaper work satisfied only part of his addiction to danger. Geoffrey Cox (later knighted), a Paris correspondent for the *Daily Express*, was a tough New Zealander. "The trouble is," he told her one evening, "most Englishmen agree with King George: Abroad is bloody awful!"

She would eventually make use of all this talent. They were savvy men of the world, as Ian Fleming later called them. "They learned the rough edges because they were not tied to desks."[6]

Cox and Vera would talk until closing time in the Wig and Pen, he recalled, "and then she'd follow a well-established route, Number 11 bus along the Strand, down sleeping Whitehall, past Victoria, Sloane Square and the King's Road to a basement apartment on Cheyne Walk, rented to establish her credentials as a young woman trying to make her own living."[7]

Cox felt that France, if occupied by Germany, was the most promising field for behind-the-lines operations. It was close to England, where coastal residents heard the sound of German guns that first told them of the outbreak of the 1914–18 war. Cox deplored France's reluctance to believe Hitler was a serious threat, but said it was a result of the trauma suffered after the country's emasculation in that war: a tenth of the entire male population killed; almost as many Frenchmen permanently disabled; 673,000 peasants slaughtered and another half million injured. France was eclipsed by the solid German block, producing far more than twice her number of military males each year, towering up grim and grisly. It was the vengeful women of France who would have to fill gaps in any resistance armies.

Paris was where the British SIS kept its largest contingent abroad. Through Mutual Friends, Vera met officers in the French intelligence services, the Deuxième Bureau and the Service de Renseignements, who said nothing was being done to contain Nazi Germany. France was under pressure from London to cut its army by half because large armies would provoke Hitler to retaliate! The absurdity caused one Frenchman to choke on his aperitif. He had an informant in the Berlin Cipher Office who said the only thing to stop Hitler would be the certainty that large armies would *oppose* him.

By 1938 Vera knew that the French secret services had obtained photographs of the Berlin Cipher Office's coding machine. The French quoted the SIS station chief in Paris, "Biffy" Dunderdale, as saying British cryptographers thought it a waste of time to try and solve the puzzle.

Returning to London from Paris in October 1938, Vera felt she had a fresh perspective on English-French historical differences. The French Revolution's guillotines disposed of royals. An Instrument of Abdication had disposed of King Edward VIII on December 10, 1936: "I Edward the Eighth of Great Britain, Ireland and the British Dominions beyond the seas, King, Emperor of India, do hereby declare my irrevocable decision to renounce the Throne." Instead of losing his head to those who disapproved, he had signed away crown and empire to continue living with his American mistress, Mrs. Wallis Simpson.

Iona von Ustinov told Vera of apprehension in the German embassy because the ex-king took the title Duke of Windsor. The House of Windsor was once the House of Saxe-Coburg-Gotha, which changed its German name to avoid public animosity in the 1914–18 war. How long would it take the duke's former subjects to worry about the German connection? Lady Emerald Cunard, an American, who had served up Ribbentrop at her dinner parties as a real live Nazi, had introduced Wallis Simpson to Edward. When Mrs. Simpson learned she would never be Her Royal Highness, she moved to France with her ex-king. Did Wallis Simpson see Hitler as her husband's route back to kingship? She had made a public display of being impressed whenever she was with Hitler. The Duke of Windsor had made no secret, while king, of his approval of the Führer. He had written compromising letters to Hitler that, after World War II, were spirited out of the American zone of Germany by two British agents. The royal family feared that the letters, hidden and so far undiscovered by American occupation forces, might eventually fall into the hands of U.S. publishers. The agents were rewarded with knighthoods. One, Sir Anthony Blunt, got the post of Surveyor of the Queen's Pictures until it became impossible to hide his long history of spying for Moscow. A traitor had prevented the exposure in Britain of an ex-king's dealings with the Nazis, but had leaked the facts to Stalin.

Blunt's betrayal was unnecessary. Ambassador von der Schulenburg wrote Vera from Moscow at the end of 1938 that Stalin knew about British royalty's warm feelings for the Nazis. The count wrote that the Soviet Union's armed forces were in disarray, their leadership purged, and Jews expelled from public service. In Berlin, Ribbentrop achieved his ambition to become foreign minister. Over the years, Ribbentrop had courted friends of influence like Lord Rothermere, proprietor of the *Daily Mail*. A chummy letter to the press baron from Hitler did not surface until the rival *Daily Express* on May 10, 2001, published it with a report attacking Rothermere under the headline HE BELIEVED HITLER HAD THE RIGHT POLICIES FOR BRITAIN. The *Daily Express* reprinted the letter to discredit its competitor in the ferocious circulation wars of the twenty-first century.

During these months before Germany's invasion of Poland marked the beginning of World War II, Ribbentrop and his acolytes had been busy buying the services of British journalists. One, an otherwise obscure newsman and would-be author, James Murphy, translated *Mein Kampf* into English and was rewarded with a job in the Nazi propaganda ministry in Berlin. A well-known writer, Gordon Bolitho, dismissed reports of German Jews being deprived of all rights. "The reason we hear the Jews first is that they wail more loudly," he wrote. The historian Nesta Webster declared that Bolshevism was the creation of Jews. The *Aeroplane*, the gospel within the aviation industry, avidly read by service airmen, published a theory that was eccentrically outside its normal professional concerns, claiming Jews exercised a communist influence on Welsh miners! The Imperialist Fascist League's Arnold Leese, a British army war veteran and surgeon, advocated gas chambers as the most efficient solution to the Jewish problem. All this was emanating not from Nazi Germany but from England itself!

These attacks strengthened the view among Jewish underground fighters in Palestine that England was their enemy. The English were befogged and cut off from reality in more troubling ways than headlines. These strident and eccentric anti-Semitic voices did not speak for the majority, but Vera had been warned that an internal security chief was already associating Jews with communist plots against England. She was firmly entrenched as Vera Atkins in most minds, but it was time to make sure she was thoroughly rid of any trace of Jewish roots. It placed upon her a heavy emotional burden, but it would free her to serve both the causes in which she believed: her Jewish heritage, and this funny old country whose people were ultimately to die for freedom of belief.

# Connections

"Successful spy thrillers use a simple formula," Vera told an American guest of the Stephensons in London. "You take three things a long way apart: An old blind woman spinning in the Western Highlands, a barn in Norway, a little curiosity shop in London kept by a Jew with a beard. Not much connection between the three? You make a connection." She was paraphrasing John Buchan (Lord Tweedsmuir) in his novel *The Three Hostages*.

Her many connections were poles apart in their views on Hitler. The American architect Philip Johnson was a friend of London's social diarist Sir Henry "Chips" Channon. Both adored the male eroticism of Nazi rallies.

"All those dear blond boys in black leather," Johnson exclaimed. Vera and Mary Stephenson exchanged covert smiles.

John Buchan wrote spy thrillers while engaged in high diplomacy. He suggested that Vera should be wary of local pro-Nazis like an adviser to Prime Minister Chamberlain, Sir Joseph Ball, who had an internal security MI5 background and was the Conservative Party's research director and a moving force behind profascists of the Anglo-American Fellowship. "Jews are the demons who created Stalin," Ball had said publicly. What if he were to discover Vera was not quite the purebred English gentlewoman she seemed?

Her travels made unusual connections that might have aroused curiosity if London society were not so indifferent. A neighbor, the expatriate American journalist Martha Gellhorn, wife of Ernest Hemingway, described it: "I can go away, spend six months in the jungle, come back and walk into a room, and people won't ask a single question about where I've been or what I've been doing. They'll just say, 'Lovely to see you. Have a drink.' It is the privacy of absolute indifference."

Ralph Wigram had come home to this same indifference from a posting at the British embassy in Paris. "A bright and steady flame burning in a broken lamp," Churchill called him, knowing that Wigram must die soon from infantile paralysis. "He guided us towards safety and honor." Wigram wrote to his wife, Ava, that he had not been able to make people in Whitehall understand the Nazi threat. "Winston has always, always understood."

To Vera, Wigram was a hero for obeying his conscience in defiance of his pro-German superior, Sir John Simon, who oversaw SIS matters. Wigram withdrew documents from Whitehall, diplomatic reports on the substantial evidence of Hitler's war preparations that Sir John chose to ignore. Wigram passed such papers to Churchill's close scientific adviser, Professor Frederick Lindemann (later Viscount Cherwell), who would drive along winding country roads to Oxford University to photograph them, then motor back through the night to return the originals the next day with nobody else the wiser. Lindemann was born in Germany, and reputedly answered any scientific question from Churchill with such brevity and accuracy that he became known as Prof. Neither Prof nor Wigram could claim immunity from the Official Secrets Act.

"The danger was even greater for Vera. If her activities and origins were known, Ball would get her deported," John Buchan recalled. Wigram arranged work for Vera as a part-time secretary in Whitehall, where she scouted for gifted young people. One of these was Nadya Letteney, who made lists for Vera of other talented linguists among Jewish refugees.

"Wigram was shy and always courteous, clutching his papers, head painfully bent, hand gripping a cane to steady himself while he opened a door for me," Nadya said later. "Hitler would have put him into his euthanasia program. Wigram died a natural death in 1937."[1]

Vera had consulted Wigram about another unlikely connection: Baroness Irene Isabella Margarete Paulina Caecilia von Meyendorff ex den Hause Uxkuell, called Irina, heiress to vast Baltic estates conferred by Catherine the Great. Irina's mother, forced by the revolution to flee Russia, made a fortune in Berlin by investing in highly profitable vending machines. At eighteen, Irina was a classic blond beauty when she was first hired by Universum-Film Aktiengesellschaft (UFA), the largest German film studio. She took the lead in the 1936 movie *Die Letzten Vier von Santa Cruz* and became famous as Die Meyendorff. She was spotted by Vera during a visit to Berlin as one of a circle of anti-Nazis among highborn Russians in key positions. Die Meyendorff bravely refused to give a gloss to UFA's Nazi movie propaganda. Her husband, Dr. Heinz Zahler, was personal physician to her boss at UFA, propaganda minister Joseph Goebbels, and supplied Goebbels with drugs to suppress his cocaine addiction. Irina suggested killing Goebbels with an overdose. Nobody would suspect foul play, she argued, but this went against Dr. Zahler's code of ethics. Later he set aside his scruples to join the July 1944 plot to assassinate Hitler. The plotters were named in British "black" propaganda broadcasts, causing speculation among survivors that British intelligence deliberately exposed them. Dr. Zahler was believed to be among the hundreds hanged on Hitler's orders, many of them named in the British broadcasts.

Questions about this were to be raised in postwar England both by Irina and by Marie "Missie" Vassiltchikov. The daughter of Russian prince Illarion and princess Lydia Vassiltchikov, who had been victims of the revolution, Missie was employed by the British Legation in Berlin, where there was a shortage of Russian linguists. In her diaries, she wrote that British authorities denied any knowledge of such broadcasts naming the plotters. A five-hundred-page government report of the Political Warfare Executive, which was responsible for the broadcasts, remained classified until the late 1990s. This official history made no mention of PWE's broadcasts that named those in Germany involved in the plot to overthrow Hitler and replace him with a pro-Allied government in which Count von der Schulenburg was to be foreign minister. Pro-Soviet members of PWE were later said to have inspired the betrayal of the plotters. Hints of their treachery emerged during the postwar exposure of Soviet agents, Englishmen who served in the British intelligence establishment and who feared that the overthrow of Hitler and the creation of a German government friendly to the Allies would endanger the Soviet Union. By war's end Irina, in self-imposed exile in Bavaria, was penniless after refusing to serve Nazi propaganda. In 1961 she was to meet James Robertson Justice, the

Scottish actor, naturalist, musician, and poet. She lived with him in Scotland, where they flew falcons and built up a circle of friends including a Bolivian ballet dancer, an Icelandic lepidopterist, an Arab ruler, Gaelic scholars, the Duke of Edinburgh, and the Prince of Wales. Irina became a British citizen in 1967. Justice, after a second term as rector of Edinburgh University, suffered strokes that reduced them both to penury. He died in 1975. Keith Bromley, a naturalist and philanthropist, later married Irina.[2]

As the descent to war quickened, Vera in London felt she was watching a Shakespearean drama, a clash between two fierce opponents: Churchill, still hoping for moral leadership from the Crown, and Chamberlain, the ex–Birmingham metallurgist, dull, ascetic, sniffing his disapproval of Churchill's "noisy, voluptuous, flamboyant style." Chamberlain was afraid of tossing out the German ambassador, Ribbentrop, who had rented his house in Eaton Square while Chamberlain occupied the prime minister's official residence at No. 10 Downing Street. The prime minister also took his cue from ex-king Edward, now the Duke of Windsor, who had written to Hitler "as one ex-serviceman to another" to establish a friendly relationship. This note, found in Edward's correspondence, was extracted by Charles (Dick) Ellis, an Australian colonel who survived trench warfare in World War I and later became a British army intelligence officer in Russian Central Asia. His more recent cover included that of a newspaper correspondent in Europe. Ellis cultivated both White Russian and German contacts. He assured Vera that letters were still the best way to convey information. Tens of thousands of foreign citizens living in Germany brought out messages. Germany was not hermetically sealed. Embassies of many countries routinely forwarded mail. Sweden had fifty-three local consular offices in Germany that acted as mailboxes. A Jewish German-language teacher to the Royal Siam Embassy vanished, and the news reached the Central British Fund through Bangkok. The mayor of Leipzig, Carl Goerdeler, broke with the Nazis in 1936 because of anti-Semitism, and worked his way to England. On the advice of Count von der Schulenburg, he met with Vera and returned to Germany. (Goerdeler was to have been chancellor, with Schulenburg as foreign minister, in the new anti-Hitler regime. Both were caught and sentenced to be hanged by the Nazi People's Court on September 8, 1944.[3])

From childhood Vera knew how her father's people always discovered paths of entry and exit. Jews found ways to reach Palestine, where Wingate showed how an oppressor could be undermined with grit and imagination. A Jewish organization, small in numbers but of great complexity, was rescuing thousands of victims of Nazi persecution. Its name in the 1930s was kept secret, but it gave Vera news of fiercely anti-Nazi women working in Poland to bring out Jews and prepare for an expected German onslaught.[4]

Colonel Ellis saw Poland as the target for a first Nazi-run military invasion and shared his notes with Vera. "The seizure of power in Russia by Bolsheviks in October 1917," Ellis wrote, "opened the way for German penetration of the Caucasus and an advance to Persia and Central Asia." He later expanded his notes for a book, *The Transcaspian Episode*, which was kept from publication by British intelligence mandarins until 1963. Bill Stephenson made Ellis his deputy in wartime covert action, and later denounced "attempts to punish Ellis for airing matters that a government obsessed with secrecy wants to conceal for ever. There are many ways to punish free spirited secret servants of the Crown."[5]

By the winter of 1938–39, Vera had made what John Buchan called "connections" with a variety of highly individualistic characters on either side of the great divide between pro- and anti-Nazis. Rudolf Schmidt was a German army officer swiftly promoted by Hitler. His brother Hans-Thilo Schmidt worked at the Berlin Cipher Office, and sold photographs of the Enigma coding machine to the French secret service. Vera knew about Hans-Thilo from Gustave Bertrand, the Paris coding expert, because Bertrand had shared with Ralph Wigram the frustration of dealing with lazy-minded military chiefs. Mutual Friends in the armed services formed one-man covert-warfare intelligence units with official-sounding titles to avoid scrutiny by the top brass. Military Intelligence (Research), MIR, for example, consisted of Gubbins, instructed by a shadow colleague: "Prepare for guerrilla warfare, establish contacts in future occupied countries, foment insurrections, and develop destructive devices." Such planning "lacked coherence and clear purpose," wrote the first government-approved recorder of these activities, William Mackenzie, in an overview kept secret until the twenty-first century. "The planning looked incoherent," Vera recalled. "Units were unknown to one another for the sake of self-preservation." Young rebels inside Whitehall taught her to pen instructions on borrowed stationery, sign a memo as coming from one department, and receive the same memo in the department to which it was addressed. With duly processed but fake authorization in hand, she could obtain facilities for Mutual Friends who enjoyed outwitting Chief of Staff General Sir Archibald Montgomery-Massingberd, that champion of "the well-bred horse" as the chief ally of the infantryman. He had written that "mechanization of the army at the expense of the cavalry is unnecessary and dangerous."

This Well-Bred Horse Brigade mentality was challenged by a new war minister, Leslie Hore-Belisha, a Jew, who demanded mobile mechanized divisions, not cavalry. He was derided as "notoriously Jewish" by upper-class fascists at Stonor Park, Oxfordshire, the family estate presided over by pillars of the Anglo-German federation. Five major-generals who supported Hore-Belisha's reforms were suddenly "without further employment." One victim, General Sir Philip Chetwode, said "the problem in the War Office is complete brain slackness."

Vera expected "brain slackness" in the City, headquarters of global companies upon whose factories, mines, and markets the sun never set, which were stuffed with nephews and brothers and cousins of the privileged upper crust. She was invited to parties that began in a privately chartered train with one carriage for gambling and another for dancing while it sped to distant resorts for a weekend. The national character was masked by an apparent refusal to take anything seriously. But under the cloak of "toffee-nosed little darlings" and "gorgeous glamour boys" she detected a quality defined by the opponent of Count Lettow-Vorbeck in Africa, the notorious British intelligence officer Richard "Dirty Dick" Meinertzhagen, about whom Lawrence of Arabia said: "His hot immoral hatred of the enemy expressed itself in trickery as in violence. [He] took as blithe a pleasure in deceiving his enemy or his friend by some unscrupulous jest as in spattering the brains of a cornered mob of Germans with his African knobkerrie."

The little darlings might make adequate street fighters if they shed their "Smug Pratt" costumes. Meanwhile, their high society patrons finally got rid of Hore-Belisha after he proposed to promote non-commissioned officers. "The Officers' Mess did not wish to be invaded by men who ate peas with their knives," she heard General Chetwode complain publicly. "Few officers of the Army allow much play to their imagination. It would almost seem a crime to be one inch outside the sealed pattern of regulations."

The one-man operation known as Section D kept out of the sealed pattern by hiding in cobwebby quarters at 2 Caxton Street, Westminster. D's chief, Major Laurence Douglas Grand, made up the entire staff under a cover title: Statistical Research. His detractors said he stalked the streets wearing a black homburg and dark glasses, and flourishing a tapered cigarette holder and a swank swordstick from Swaine Adeney. His schemes for subverting the enemy, Gubby recalled, "were pretty wild."

Reckless innovators appealed to Churchill's own distaste for spit and polish. "Loyalty to the State must come before loyalty to the Service," he advised one officer, Torr Anderson, who first confided his concerns to Vera. She sent him to Churchill's secretary, Violet Pearman, who met him in a tea shop. He asked what he should do with secret information about frightening weaknesses in the Royal Air Force. Mrs. Pearman said softly, "Go to Mister Churchill." Regular meetings continued until the outbreak of war in 1939.

Vera knew the risk of prosecution. It depended on how patriotism was interpreted. Y was the single letter used to cover an accepted secret organization that tapped into, and analyzed, foreign diplomatic, military, naval, and other radio traffic "of interest" to British intelligence. Y's chief was anonymous. Y's intercepts, proving the rapid growth of a German military machine, were dismissed, mislaid, or put in bottom drawers. Y's interception of high-speed Russian traffic was conducted from bases in remote parts of the world; Gubbins, for a while, had conducted intercepts of Shanghai-Moscow traffic from a vantage point in Afghanistan.

Unfortunately, access to Y's reports was closely held by powerful men who shared Lord Halifax's wish to avoid nasty confrontations. Halifax voiced no criticism of Hitler's claim that "the German race represents the highest evolution of the human species. It is unthinkable that eighty-five million German Aryans should be compressed within tight borders dictated by others. The Third Reich must expand into more living space."

Halifax saw it as his patriotic duty to thwart Soviet Russian ambitions, with German help. His attempts to get rid of Y's chief, who was enraged by Halifax's efforts to appease Hitler, were challenged through secret parliamentary investigations monitored by Hugh Dalton, the Labour Party chairman of the Anti-Nazi Council. Dalton asked Vera to see a socialist comrade, Léon Blum, the French prime minister who had resigned in 1937 and now wanted to explain reasons for his distrust of British wisdom. For one thing, French intelligence had counted twelve planes in each German air force squadron. The British had wrongly counted only nine, underestimated German first-line air strength, and said "three hundred and thirty German military aircraft with crews are in training." Blum said French intelligence reported that Germany had in service fifteen hundred operational planes of advanced design, some battle-trained in Spain's Civil War.

"Facts," said Vera to Ian Fleming, "are what officialdom wants them to be."

Fleming was one of the City stockbrokers she had first dismissed as "Smug Pratts." Her mind was changed when Admiral John Godfrey transferred from his battleship *Repulse* early in 1939 to become director of Naval Intelligence. Ian Fleming's recruitment began when Admiral Godfrey was lunching at the Carlton Grill with the governor of the Bank of England, Montagu Norman, who made a seemingly offhand remark: "Good chap, Fleming. Old Etonian. Stockbroker, but bored. Covered the Russian show trials of those British engineers for some newspaper." And so Fleming took up position in Room 39 of NID. Fleming's father, Valentine, was a close friend of Churchill's who in the last war had been killed in action. This created a powerful bond, and Ian could convey to Churchill further troubling naval realities. Vera's friend, Stringbag, confirmed for Ian that the Royal Navy clung to certain old traditions that failed to confront modern realities. "A navy pilot is treated as a coxswain, his airplane just a version of the longboat. My navigator has command, and as the Observer. Commissioned observers cannot fly with noncommissioned pilots, who, as petty officers, also cannot sit in at flight briefings in the wardroom."

Vera saw Hugh Dalton as a voice in Parliament who did not submit to Labour Party tribalism. She spent an uproarious evening with him and Rex Leeper, head of the Foreign Office news service, who proposed to flood Europe with anti-Nazi propaganda. He had been a 1914–18 wartime spy, and said it was basically "boot-leather detective work." They were joined by Terence Horsley, a journalist who would later work with actors Laurence Olivier and Ralph Richardson in covert use of the twenty-year-old Swordfish biplanes, the aerial equivalent of "the well-bred cavalry horse."

Vera finished off a pub meal of sausages and mashed potatoes, laced with liberal quantities of ale, and wove her way back to the Cheyne Walk apartment with Dalton, thinking light-headedly of how she might deflect the increasing curiosity of powerful profascists like Sir Joseph Ball. She extracted a bottle of Polish vodka from the larder. "I'm getting into the swing of Polish life," Dalton remembered her saying as she spilled radishes on the kitchen counter. "You take a radish, scrape butter on a knife, slice the radish, leave a filling of butter, sprinkle salt, and knock back the vodka."

"What about the radish?" he asked.

"I suppose," she hiccuped, "you eat it. I haven't got that far in my studies yet. I want to get to Poland before it's too late."

# 8

## Spattering Brains with a Knobkerrie

Hugh Dalton recalled that he would have liked to live inside Vera's head. He said later, "It would be a comforting place full of good things, tidy rooms with fresh flowers and home cooking and fine Scotch whiskey in cut-glass tumblers. And a cellar full of vodka and radishes with a sign on the door: Forget the sentimentality — Kill the bastards!" He understood her duality precisely.

At her Winchelsea retreat, he saw what the sea winds did to sculpt her prominent cheekbones, high forehead, and glorious black hair. He told Mary Stephenson: "Within sight of the French coast, she walked with the measured deliberation of a general, then curled up on a sofa like a kitten."

She scorned "champagne socialists" who pontificated about peaceful solutions, and how there are "no just wars."

Dalton assured her: "In my political constituency are northern coalminers who would never think twice about jabbing a broken bottle in the face of a German or kicking him in the groin." Mary recalled warning Vera that "Dalton's enthusiasm for the unconventional offends many diehards."

Dalton loved it when Vera endorsed Meinertzhagen's philosophy of "spattering brains with a knobkerrie." He never forgot her impassioned words: "We know very bad men plan very bad things. We must find out who they are and kill them. It's not your Christian approach. It's not your English fair play. It means forgetting the freedoms of Germans. They lost their freedom when they voted Hitler into power. Whitehall says we mustn't blow up German factories. Yet the RAF dropped bombs on Arabs when pious Lord Londonderry was air minister."

Vera's explosion followed a conference of thirty-two nations in

July 1938 that dashed all hopes for the rescue of Jews. It assembled at the French resort of Évian-les-Bains near the Swiss border. The American Federation of Labor stipulated that entry to the United States be barred to Jews who might compete for jobs. Hitler rejoiced: "The world agrees that Jews are parasites."

After this, the Jewish revisionist Irgun and the Jewish Agency's more moderate military arm, Haganah, hastened the improvisation of underground railroads for refugees. "Évian," said Ruth Klueger, who later served with Vera, "gave the official signal from the civilized world, telling Hitler to go ahead and kill the Jews."

Earlier in 1938, on Friday, March 11, Prime Minister Neville Chamberlain gave a farewell lunch for Ribbentrop, who had finally gotten what he wanted from Hitler: appointment as Nazi Germany's foreign minister. Ribbentrop had spent two years in London as ambassador. The Churchills were uncomfortable guests at the lunch. News was discreetly conveyed to Chamberlain that German troops were moving into Austria to make it part of the Greater German Reich. Chamberlain said nothing. Frau Ribbentrop lectured Churchill for being "so naughty" in opposing Anglo-Germany unity. Joseph P. Kennedy said Chamberlain was "the greatest man after the Pope."

Kennedy was U.S. ambassador to London. President Roosevelt had concluded that Kennedy in Washington was "too dangerous to have around here." Cordell Hull, U.S. secretary of state, and assistant secretary Sumner Welles opposed any British toughening of policy that could reignite world war and approved Ambassador Kennedy's dispatches, in which he portrayed himself as standing at the heart of the decision-making process leading Chamberlain to appease Hitler.[1]

Kennedy had spoken to the queen mother about Mrs. Wallis Simpson's wish to become a duchess. "I will never allow my wife to curtsey to a tart," said Kennedy. The queen mother "roared with approving laughter," according to Hugh Dalton, who glumly reported to Vera that Kennedy "has another royal supporter."

Poland had a larger proportion of Jews than any other European country. The Jewish underground's transport of refugees through Romania and the Black Sea required increasing funds and voluntary help. An Irgun agent described to Vera how he came home from school as a child in Romania to see his mother hanging from a tree and thought she had improvised some kind of swing until he found she was dead. It was a terrible paradox that in Palestine, Arab marauders harassed a modern Jewish community. From London, Edmund de Rothschild was dispatched to look for other places where Jews might be settled, but the choices were miserable: Madagascar, Ecuador, British Guiana.

Vera thought a sniper should act now, while Hitler continued to appear in public. Assassination was rejected by the Foreign Office as immoral. Did Hitler ever plan to appear outside his borders? Bill Stephenson asked her to revisit the Balkans and form an opinion. Count von der Schulenburg had written to say he was to be in Romania. Would Hitler appear there? In Serbia, Bill owned the Trepca Mine, a source of zinc and lead vital to German industry. From Belgrade, Vera reported that Hitler had commercial agents who would try to gain control of the mines. In Bucharest she learned that the government of Premier Armand Calinescu was under pressure from the British government to stop the migration of Jewish refugees to Palestine. Schulenburg arrived, but the reunion was brief and sad. He said Stalin, influenced by what he knew of Kennedy's defeatist reports, feared Chamberlain wanted peace with Hitler to let Germany gather strength for an eventual attack on the Soviet Union.

Schulenburg reported to Berlin a British demand that Romania block the borders against Jews from Poland trying to join the exodus to Palestine. He wondered why London wasted time on such issues just when a show of British resolve to stand firm against Hitler would avert war. Colonel Hans Oster, deputy to Wilhelm Canaris, head of the Abwehr intelligence section of the military high command, opposed Hitler's plans to seize the German Sudetenland from Czechoslovakia, and sought British support. But everyone knew about Prime Minister Neville Chamberlain's promise to Kennedy that neither Britain nor France would come to Czechoslovakia's aid. Yet the German armed forces were not capable of overcoming the powerful Czech defenses. Schulenburg wanted Churchill to say publicly that Britain would certainly go to war in support of the Czechs. Vera reminded Schulenburg that Churchill had no power. "Well," said Old Fritz, "Churchill is the only man who terrifies Hitler. There must be some way to strengthen his hand through our friends in Berlin."

Our Mutual Friends were active among such Berlin personalities as the German spy chief Canaris, who said Hitler planned the invasion of Czechoslovakia for the end of September. Canaris had sent a note to a British military attaché: "By firm action abroad, Hitler can be forced at the eleventh hour to renounce his present intentions. If it comes to war, immediate intervention by France and England will bring about the downfall of the regime." Oster, Canaris's deputy, asked Ewald von Kleist-Schmenzin, a scion of Prussian nobility and one of the Nazis' fiercest opponents, to fly to London. He arrived on August 18, 1938, with a simple message: "If England is willing to fight, we shall end this regime." Cold-shouldered by the Foreign Office, von Kleist-Schmenzin went to Churchill, who gave him the letter that Prime Minister Chamberlain should have written: "The crossing of the frontier of Czechoslovakia by German armies or aviation in force will bring about renewal of the World War. Do not, I pray you, be misled upon this point."[2]

In August the London *Times*, viewed by Hitler as the voice of Britain, editorialized on the advantages the Czechs would gain by giving up the Sudeten German borderland. On September 10 Hermann Göring publicly condemned "this miserable pygmy race [the Czechs] for oppressing a cultured people [the Germans]. Behind it all is the eternal mask of the Jew devil."

Vera thought Hitler would never be caught off home ground, and Bill Stephenson wondered if a German-Jewish patriot might help in an assassination plot. Vera risked drawing the attention of Sir Barry Domville's fascist agency, Link, by appealing to a reconstituted Council for Jewry in London to publicize statistics about Jewish patriotism: "The percentage of German-Jewish soldiers who died in the 1914–18 war is greater than that of German Christians. Twelve percent of the total Jewish population was killed in action. Eighty thousand German Jews fought in the trenches. Twenty-five thousand got field promotions."

Before Vera could further explore with Stephenson the ways in which Hitler might be assassinated, the Führer demonstrated just how well guarded he now was. Chamberlain, associated in the public mind with his furled black umbrella, which earned him a derogatory nickname the Umbrella Man as the symbol of appeasement, was invited to the fortified Eagle's Nest to talk with Hitler. Before dawn on September 15, 1938, at the age of sixty-nine, Chamberlain made his first flight in an airplane. He landed seven hours later at Munich, not far from the concentration camp publicly identified by Churchill as Dachau. Deafened by the piston engines and dizzy from an unpressurized cabin, Chamberlain finished his journey by rail. Past him rumbled showcase trains, designedly crammed with armed troops and artillery. The Führer made him climb in pouring rain the many steps to the Berghof and gave his unsteady guest a single message: The territory of three million Germans in Czechoslovakia would be brought into the Reich, even if it meant world war. Britain must be reasonable. Chamberlain returned home to announce: "Hitler is a man who can be relied upon when he has given his word."

Vera heard from Mutual Friends in Berlin that Hitler had been on the verge of a nervous breakdown before Chamberlain's arrival. The German military machine was nowhere near ready to pierce the heavily reinforced Czech defenses. When his bluff worked, Hitler did an about-turn and became a loudmouthed bully again. Only the German army could overthrow him.

Chamberlain went back for more talks at the Hotel Dreesen in the small Rhine town of Bad Godesberg. Hitler had occupied a suite there to direct the barbaric Blood Purge of June 29–30, 1934, when he had party rivals murdered. Now, some four years later, on September 24, Chamberlain sat in the same suite and laid out his "solution." The Sudetenland could be turned over without a plebiscite; international guarantees would ensure Czech neutrality. Hitler pushed his luck. The problem, he said, would be completely solved only by a full German occupation by October 1 — the very same date Schulenburg had predicted to Vera.

Chamberlain, as if Hitler's puppet, called on the Czechs to withdraw from the Sudetenland. All military installations in evacuated areas were to be left intact. Rolling stock and vehicles were to be handed over to the Germans undamaged. Hundreds of thousands of Czechs were to leave behind everything: foodstuffs, raw materials, household goods, even the family cow. When the Czechs objected, Chamberlain apologized to Hitler for their obduracy. Hitler screamed, "The Germans are being treated like niggers!" On September 26 he had troops parade through central Berlin to arouse enthusiasm for war. But Berliners scuttled into side streets. "They are dead set against war," reported the American correspondent William L. Shirer.

The parade's commanding panzer general was Rudolf Schmidt, the brother of Hans-Thilo Schmidt in the Berlin Cipher Office. Rudolf sympathized with the scuttling Berliners.[3]

In London, Vera heard Chamberlain tell Parliament on Wednesday, September 28, 1938: "Hitler invites me to meet him at Munich tomorrow morning." She recalled, "Members cheered and threw sheets of paper into the air in celebration. Jan Masaryk, the Czech minister, son of the founding father of the Czech Republic, asked Chamberlain if his country was to be invited to the Munich talks. No, said Chamberlain, Hitler would not stand for it. Masaryk said, 'If you have sacrificed my nation to preserve the peace of the world, I will be the first to applaud you. But if not, then God help your souls!'"

At their final meeting, Chamberlain begged Hitler to sign a joint declaration saying, "We are resolved that the method of consultation shall be the method adopted to assure the peace of Europe." Hitler jumped to sign. Secretly, he had just entered into an agreement with Italy against Great Britain. Chamberlain appeared on the balcony of Buckingham Palace, flanked by King George VI and his queen, beaming down at the cheering crowds. The *Times* of London declared: "No conqueror returning from a victory on the battlefield has come adorned with nobler laurels."

Vera sat in the public gallery when Churchill protested in Parliament: "We have sustained a total, unmitigated defeat." The rest was lost in jeers. She stopped at Bill Stephenson's office. "Winston just stood there, head bowed, while the boos shook the rafters," she said. "The German army will back any leader who gets all these gifts without a fight: Czech coal, textile, iron, steel, electric power, timber. Five years ago, Germany was bankrupt."

On October 5 Churchill made a speech warning that the road through Romania to the Black Sea was now open. The speech was deplored by King George VI. Vera lived to see the *Sunday Telegraph*, owned by a royalist, Lord Black, run a feature on December 8, 1996, with the headline: FORGET THE DUKE OF WINDSOR. A WORSE EXAMPLE WAS SET BY GEORGE VI THE KING OF APPEASERS. The *Telegraph* quoted the

English historian John Charmley, in his book *The End of Glory*, offering "hitherto suppressed details of how George VI supported Chamberlain."

Victor de Rothschild decided it was time to tell the Earl Baldwin Fund for Refugees: "I have interviewed people who have escaped from concentration camps, and I can tell you that their experiences make the many horrors we read about nowadays seem like nursery games. . . . The slow murder of six hundred thousand people is an act which has rarely happened in history. It is an act you can prevent."

In Vera's homeland, Ruth Klueger was the agent for Mossad le Aliyah Bet, the Institute of Illegal Immigration. Ruth Klueger was a twenty-five-year-old redhead when she joined the Mossad, the name that was later given to Israel's central intelligence service. In 1938 she was warned, "If you're caught, you'll be harshly treated. Every government in the world considers you illegal." She was born in Russia and moved as a child to an Austrian border town, and then to Romania. She was the kind of experienced connection Vera needed. Ruth had tried to make a Greek shipping magnate reduce his exorbitant charges for transporting Jews to Palestine. After many fruitless negotiations with the magnate, she told him this story: A Jew had gone to the U.S. embassy for a visa. He was told to come back in the year 2003. "In the morning," asked the Jew, "or the afternoon?" The Greek fell off his chair laughing, and cut his price by two-thirds.

Vera felt that with allies like Ruth, she could manage without official Whitehall endorsement or U.S. aid. In Europe, ordinary civilians organized Ruth's kind of special operations with few tangible assets. Jewish settlers in Palestine could be enlisted when war came. Commando courses for three thousand Jewish youths were provided at an estate owned by Maude Russell, a relative of the Duke of Bedford. Maude's maternal grandfather had been Master of the Mint in Germany. Maude backed Vera's plans for using the young Jews in clandestine warfare, and perhaps even a Jewish Brigade. Vera kept in the background. She still had to dodge the curiosity of Sir Joseph Ball, the former internal security chief who now advised Prime Minister Chamberlain on intelligence matters. Ball's protégé was Guy Burgess, whose love of Nazi youth rallies was colored by his liking for homosexuals. Ball's anti-Soviet obsessions made it easy for Burgess to sell himself as a decent English patriot even while he was being directed by the Soviet KGB to "activate Lord Rothschild of SIS." Burgess was not sure which Rothschild the Russians were talking about. Victor de Roth-schild was the suspect most obvious to British security. He was cleared only after Burgess was exposed in the spy scandals of the 1950s as one of the traitors inside British intelligence run by the Soviets.[4]

# Poland Breaks the First Enigma

Vera knew time was short. The danger signs were dismissed by the SIS and its newly appointed ministerial face, the former viceroy of India, Lord Privy Seal, and Lord President of the Council, now foreign secretary, Lord Halifax. The Polish Cipher Bureau had been secretive about its research into German coding machines, but after seven years of frustration it sought help from Alastair Denniston of the British Government Code and Cipher School (GCCS).

Hugh Dalton had spoken of a Fourth Arm to fight the Nazis, a resistance organization. He told Stephenson that Vera's air of authority, when she cared to use it, would impress Poland's mastermind in code breaking, Maksymilian Ciezki, who worked in the basement of a Poznan army command post with the best of his cryptology students.

Vera felt the urgency to help any local Jewish underground in an uprising. Poland had persecuted generations of Jews. The old Anglo-Zionist relationship of 1917 had collapsed. Two British army divisions were now fighting a full-blown Arab rebellion against Jewish immigration into Palestine. In February 1939 Colonial Secretary Malcolm MacDonald told Jewish delegates at St. James's Palace that if war broke out, British priority must be lines of communication with the East, the Suez Canal, oil, and the naval base at Alexandria. Britain did not feel under further obligation to help develop a Jewish homeland. Dr. Chaim Weizmann said this was like a surrender to Arab terrorism. MacDonald retorted, "Jews have made many mistakes in the past."

"Certainly," said Weizmann. "Our chief mistake is that we exist at all."[1]

On the eve of Hitler's invasion of Poland, forcing Chamberlain to declare war on Germany, a new Military Intelligence Research unit was hastily created in London under the cryptic title of Military Mission No. 4 to Poland. It would attempt to bring back Polish-held Enigma coding machines, and prepare Poles to fight an underground war. The small team included Gubbins and of course Vera, whose knowledge of Romania and fluency in local languages would help the team escape from any sudden world German onslaught.

The mission was disguised as an Investigation of Guerrilla Activities by the few army officers assembled in secret on August 24, 1939, to discuss what would later be described officially as "a flying visit to Poland, Romania and the Baltic States" and "a second visit to Warsaw and Polish Intelligence" and "some evidence of a secret visit to Belgrade" and mustering of "elements for missions for Poland and Roumania." The papers were labeled Report No. 8 to give the enterprise the appearance of War Office top-brass approval. It was later described as involving units "interlocked in a confusing way." The confusion was calculated to bemuse the enemy in Whitehall. The official historian, W. J. M. Mackenzie, played no part in the mission and remained bemused after researching official documents after 1945. His *Secret History of SOE: Special Operations Executive, 1940–1945* was not declassified until sixty-one years after the mission, and after Vera had died.

In 1939 Vera could use the role of a translator-secretary for Stephenson's Pressed Steel as cover in a mission forced to follow a tortuous path to Poland. It was impossible to fly by way of the Baltic on RAF aircraft. There were none available that would not require refueling in regions under German observation. Spain was sealed off now that General Franco had won his war against the Left with considerable Nazi German help, and Spain reverted to the old tormenting of Jews. Spain's Civil War death toll gave Vera a glimpse of the carnage to come: ninety thousand Nationalists killed in action, one hundred and ten thousand Republican soldiers dead, 130,000 persons murdered, half a million citizens forced to flee the country. She had hoped for a neutral Spain with no German border guards to block the travels of British-run agents in an occupied Europe, already foreshadowed by Hitler's placement of bits of Romania and Slovakia "under German protection." Mussolini had sent troops into Albania. "No government has the guts to resist," Vera agreed with Dalton.

Stringbag, briefly home from flying duties, gave Vera a frightening glimpse of secrecy employed to hide uncomfortable realities. The First Lord of the Admiralty, Lord Stanhope, had announced that the crew of the aircraft carrier *Ark Royal* were at action stations. This was kept out of the newspapers by a D Notice, supposedly to protect the state against reports that might imperil the defense of the realm. The *Daily Sketch* editors saw this as a device to silence the press, and phrased its objections to avoid prosecution by telling readers it was demanding clear explanations, but without actually printing the speech. Other newspapers then reported the *Daily Sketch* demand. Readers could only scratch their heads in puzzlement. The navy was demoralized.

Vera made one hurried journey to Poland earlier in that 1939 summer. On her own, as a mild office worker, she could travel directly through Germany. She made a quick reconnaissance of Lithuania, where Hitler annexed the Memel region.

Vera went on to Warsaw. She had been told she could trust a gorgeous young part-Jewish Polish aristocrat, Countess Krystyna Gyziska Skarbek, who was home on leave from her East African plantation in Kenya. She was already thinking ahead about underground resistance, and introduced Vera to an engineer who was also a Polish air force pilot, Jan "Zura" Zurakowski, reputed to be among the best Polish pilots and engaged to marry a seventeen-year-old student friend of Krystyna. "When Hitler breaks his nonaggression pact with Poland and his armed forces attack us," he told Vera, "I have to fight in a high-winged, fixed-undercarriage P.11 that is eight years old and moves at half the speed of German warplanes. We need modern fighters. For God's sake, tell London to spare us a few, but quickly."

Krystyna's mother was Jewish, one of three million Jews still in Poland. From the new German protectorates of Bohemia and Moravia came news that racial laws already applied, that Adolf Eichmann was running a Reich Central Office for Jewish Immigration in Prague, and that a women-only camp was being set up near Berlin. It was called Ravensbrück.

Vera confirmed that a brilliant Jewish mathematician had worked with other code breakers on an Enigma machine shipped to the German embassy in Warsaw. Before it was delivered, they had taken it apart overnight. Since then they had worked out Enigma settings that constantly changed in a highly secret version, and constructed a cyclometer that linked two Enigmas, and another device they called a bombe to handle six interconnected Enigmas. They were willing to part with replicas if the worst happened. Vera left Warsaw, concerned that this vital information had been so long withheld, and traveled first to consult a friend, the French secret-service chief of codes and ciphers, Colonel Louis Rivet of the Service de Renseignements. She asked him about French use of Hans-Thilo Schmidt in the Berlin Cipher Office. Rivet said Hans-Thilo's first dealings had been with a French secret service agent on the German-Belgian border back in 1931. Hans-Thilo had offered manuals for a coding machine. He was then in his midforties and had financial worries. The later risks he took in supplying updates on Enigma's changing procedures suggested that money was not the motive. His grandmother was English, his mother a baroness, his father a professor of history. His brother Rudolf, a general who headed the panzer parade in Berlin, had been chief executive at the Cipher Office from 1925 to 1928, and brought in Hans-Thilo, who soon had access to ciphers for the armed forces and the complex coding machine Enigma. Hans-Thilo had been a relatively young businessman when Germany suffered the raging inflation that saw the value of money sink daily. He had abandoned the illusion, shared by millions, that Hitler was a genius who could solve the country's penury. His initial contact used the alias Rodolphe Lemoine and served the French secret service under the code name Rex. Vera asked Colonel Rivet how the French were exploiting Hans-Thilo. The intelligence chief gave a hollow laugh. "Enigma is not seen as important. Our generals waste resources on training intelligence officers in old methods used in the last war, to get the same old answers to the same old questions."

Vera returned to London to hear Chamberlain promise that Britain would guarantee Poland's independence. Then he went off to tramp the Yorkshire moors. The British empire's chiefs of staff were on their summer holidays. Two weeks before Poland was invaded, Lord Halifax went fishing in Scotland. He sent salmon packed in ice to his Foreign Office underlings.

Vera heard an eye-witness account of Churchill's encounter with the Duke of Westminster. "Churchill had been dining at the Savoy Grill and looked tired and old," Bill Stephenson told her. "All his warnings were proving sound. But it all seemed too late." The duke was with friends. "Someone called Churchill a Jew-lover who conspired against Germany. Churchill stood with head bowed and said, 'We're a family with the wrong members in control.'"

More young officers risked careers to disclose infirmities within the Chamberlain government. A secret intelligence service officer, Anthony Cavendish, said later that the SIS chief "'deplored the violation of decent moral conduct!' The prudery was breathtakingly hypocritical. It condemned the very same things that were his stock-in-trade. We lie from the first day in the service. Our cover makes us liars. SIS puts a man in other government departments. The borders become blurred between private conscience and public duty. The secret agent becomes expert at blackmail. You betray friends, break confidences. Official versions of events are doctored. Weeders hide documents, not to defend national security but to protect careers. It is dangerous for a private citizen to antagonize the SIS. It has character assassination down to a fine art."[2]

Vera became doubly cautious. Sir Vernon Kell, who had run MI5, the internal security service, since its inception in 1909, was saying Soviet spy networks were 90 percent Jewish. This was repeated one evening by a senior MI5 man who was Vera's dinner partner and took her to be a well-behaved Christian. He said: "Jews have no loyalty to the countries in which they live."

Hugh Dalton, as parliamentary undersecretary to the Foreign Office in the Labour government of 1929–31, had overseen the SIS and told Vera that Kell had been "prepared to destroy every file, rather than let records fall into the hands of Jews and Russian agents in the socialist party." Rudyard Kipling summed it up: "You would credit anything about Russia's designs but a little bit of sober fact is more than you can stand."

Dalton was earmarking young men who took risks, bankers or bank robbers, anyone willing to serve what was called the Left Wing, the secret teams he was already sending abroad.

She asked him, "Why the term Left Wing?"

"It applies to ancillary units attached to secret missions that the War Office can disown," he said. "They call us Left Wingers. Yet we're private enterprisers, like the privateers whose letters of marque from Queen Elizabeth made them pirates in her secret service. She let them hang if they got caught."

Selected "pirates" now were sent abroad, their expenses met from the Secret Fund or out of their own pocket. George Taylor, a thick-skinned Australian, disliked being treated as a colonial and rejoiced in helping the planners of closework. He provided a country house near Hatfield in Hertfordshire for training agents, beyond the control of the SIS.

Skepticism about any Nazi threat had been reflected in an entry for Wednesday, March 29, 1939, in the diary of a Foreign Office permanent undersecretary, Sir Alexander Cadogan: "Ian Colvin [reporter for the *News Chronicle*] came and saw H [Lord Halifax] and me and Rex [Sir Reginald Leeper, head of the Foreign Office news department] and gave hair-raising details of imminent German thrust against Poland. I was not entirely convinced. I am getting used to these stories." Ian Colvin was one of many young foreign correspondents who had difficulty persuading editors to print their accounts of Nazi intentions.[3]

Vera had a pool of talent among newsmen like Colvin. One was the *Manchester Guardian's* Frederick Voigt. Through his bank account, Vera sent payments to Krystyna Skarbek. Such reporters believed that information belonged in their newspapers, not whispered into the ear of a civil servant. Colvin, back on his Berlin beat, learned that the German financial secretary, Schwerin von Krosigk, had told British diplomats that Churchill must be given a ministerial post because there was no other way to convince Hitler that Britain really would fight if pushed too hard.

In June 1939, Gubby and Vera had traveled to Poland to talk with its intelligence experts. They were back in July. In Warsaw they visited an Englishman, small, sparrowlike, with bright blue eyes, identified only by the initials AGD. He was a veteran of Admiral Blinker Hall's Room 40 in the 1914–18 war. Room 40 had pioneered the decoding of enemy messages.

At meetings with Poland's military chiefs, Gubby promised, "If the Germans overrun you, I will take responsibility for providing every possible aid to a Polish guerrilla army." Gubby staked his personal honor upon support for what they spoke of as the Home Army.[4]

Others in London would break Gubby's heart by betraying the promise. "The betrayal haunted him all his life," said Vera.

# Betrayals All Around

On the night of July 24–25, 1939, the Poles had unveiled for a secret team of English experts the computer-like mechanism they called a bombe, better able to run through Enigma permutations than the first cyclometers. For years before their bombe, they could read only bits of coded traffic, and were left far behind when Enigma began to develop a capacity that would eventually produce 10.5 quadrillion permutations. Enigma was an electric machine that looked like a large typewriter. The simplest explanation given Vera was that it could be set up in a million different ways. The operator typed out a plain-language sentence and Enigma converted this to a jumble for transmission by wireless. To get the jumble back to plain text, the recipient had to have a machine exactly like that of the sender, whose Enigmas encoded through a combination of rotors and plugboards with key settings that were frequently changed. Outsiders trying to make sense of the jumble had to look for clues and giveaway repetitions. German senders were issued new settings at least once a day.

Vera had to look ahead. The accrued experience of the Poles was almost impossible to pass along through a third party. It would be necessary to smuggle into England the best Polish cryptanalyst at the University of Poznan, Marian Rejewski. His small team had been breaking codes, only to have to start again when the Germans modified their machines. The German defense ministry's Berlin Cipher Office thought the system defied penetration. But the Polish bombes offered a way into orders sent by wireless to Germany's armed forces.

If breaking Enigma codes was essential to Britain's survival, none of the code breakers, nor Hans-Thilo Schmidt, must be caught. He was a member of the Nazi Party, #738736, which made her uneasy. His history unraveled at a meeting outside Warsaw with code breakers and representatives of Britain's Government Code and Cipher School. Now Vera knew who AGD was: Commander Alastair G. Denniston, acting head of GCCS. And for the first time she understood why Louis Rivet in Paris had been so cagey. The Poles had pulled off a coup, and Rivet's French secret service chiefs had issued strict instructions to disclose nothing.

For Vera, Hans-Thilo came into tighter focus. He had trained as a chemist. His mathematical skills led to his compilation of new field codes with a short working life, destroyed after use. He distributed the codes himself, and he was authorized to sign his own travel warrants. After French intelligence contacted him, Hans-Thilo delivered two documents that caught the attention of Gustave Bertrand, head of the Deciphering Section of the Service de Renseignements. Hans-Thilo's manuals referred to the Enigma machine used by the German army.

Back in 1929, the early commercial version of Enigma had arrived for the German embassy in Warsaw. There followed a hectic weekend while two engineers, Ludomir Danilewicz and Antoni Palluth, proprietors of the small Warsaw communications company AVA, drew details of the machine before forwarding it to the embassy. The chief of the German section of Poland's cipher bureau, Maksymilian Ciezki, picked out three bright students, Henryk Zygalski, Jerzy Rozycki, and Marian Rejewski. They worked with the cipher bureau's chief, Gwido Langer, to replicate the wiring inside the Enigma. This was finally completed in 1932, with help from Hans-Thilo's documents. The Poles read German military messages until stumped by Enigma's infinity of variations.

Vera foresaw the need to keep track of the Polish cryptographers, if they had to make a run for it through Nazi-dominated European countries. Then the Enigma secret would be in jeopardy. There had already been one narrow squeak. In Berlin, Hans-Thilo Schmidt's routine was to phone a French journalist and say, "Uncle Kurt has died," if he had anything to report. This prefaced meetings at Charlottenburg railway station. Hans-Thilo would then give the Frenchman new information. On November 6, 1937, documents were delivered by the journalist to the French embassy. But Ambassador André François-Poncet disregarded a warning that diplomatic codes were routinely broken by the Germans. He telegraphed to Paris a summary of Hans-Thilo's latest haul: Hitler's outline for his generals of a timetable for the conquest of Western Europe.

The French telegram was intercepted by the Germans. Wilhelm Canaris, head of the Abwehr, the army intelligence service, was told to investigate. His inquiry was lackadaisical. Vera believed Canaris wanted the British and French to learn of the timetable, and spark Anglo-French action to stop Hitler. Hans-Thilo Schmidt was a liaison officer between the Berlin Cipher Office and Germany's Air Ministry Research Bureau. Canaris cleared him of suspicion and sent him to Switzerland in January 1938 to give British intelligence a copy of the report on Canaris's investigation into the leak![1]

The Poles, the French, and the British knew Hans-Thilo Schmidt under different code names. There were also differences in the definition of "code breakers." The word "code" did not refer to the replacement of plain-language text by Enigma's scrambled letters, for which the proper term was cipher-text. Many who later worked on Enigma at Bletchley Park spoke of code breakers and code for simplicity's sake. Gordon Welchman, at Bletchley, later described to Vera how it came about that different secret agencies offered different accounts of these events because of separate definitions and paths to the same solutions.

For example, Vera heard from the Poles about their cardboard perforation sheets. The sheets were stacked on top of each other over a light, and the places where the light shone through gave clues to current Enigma settings. At Bletchley the first working computer, Colossus, replaced these perforation sheets. "Prior to Colossus, each time the Germans introduced more wheels or connected more plugboard sockets, our work with the cardboard sheets began all over again," said Welchman.[2]

After this summer "look around" in Poland, Vera left Warsaw on her own and traveled by train across the Polish-Romanian border, looking for future overland escape routes. In Bucharest, at the British legation, she read the text of a prophetic broadcast by Churchill on August 8, 1939: "Holiday time, ladies and gentlemen. Holiday time, my friends across the Atlantic! Holiday time, when the summer calls the toilers of all countries for an all too brief spell." Churchill asked, "How had the world spent its summer holidays when the 1914 war broke out? Why!" he exclaimed. "Those were the very days when the

German advance guards were breaking into Belgium and trampling down its people on their march towards Paris! Today, there is a hush all over Europe. Listen! No, listen carefully. I think I hear something. Yes, there it was, quite clear. Don't you hear it? It is the tramp of two million German soldiers and more than a million Italians 'going on maneuvers' . . . yes, only on maneuvers. After all, the dictators must train their soldiers. They could scarcely do less in common prudence, when the Danes, the Dutch, the Swiss, the Albanians — and of course the Jews — may leap out upon them at any moment."

Two weeks later the German-Soviet Nonaggression Pact was signed by Joachim von Ribbentrop in Moscow. Count von der Schulenburg should have rejoiced. The dream he had shared with Vera, the prevention of war between Germany and Russia, seemed to have come true. Yet he was not as happy as he should have been.

In a letter to Vera before the pact, Schulenburg described Ribbentrop assuring Vyacheslav Molotov, commissar for Soviet foreign affairs, there was no appetite for war anywhere in Britain. This neutralized Stalin's scheme to make a pact with France and Britain *against* Germany.

Stalin had reversed his scheme. Why? Vera learned that at the time of Churchill's inflammatory broadcast, Admiral Sir Reginald Plunkett-Ernle-Erle-Drax had sailed on a slow cargo-ship from England to negotiate a pact with the Soviet Union. He disembarked in Leningrad, stretching out his journey, and reached Moscow on August 11, 1939. Then he announced that he had forgotten to bring along his written authority. Irate Russian generals broke off the talks. Stalin believed England's priority was to start a war between the Nazis and Russia and that Sir Reginald's amnesia was a hoax.

"Churchill's broadcast was interpreted as hot air," Billy Stephenson speculated when Vera got back to London. "The dictators figured we had no intention of fighting against anyone. The Plunkett-Ernle-Erle-Drax fiasco led to this pact, but history won't record it."

The German-Soviet pact included secret protocols allowing Russia to seize half of Poland. Schulenburg wrote to Vera that Soviet intelligence had copies of letters from Hitler to the Duke of Windsor expressing a fervent wish to avoid war and hoping the duke would act as a friend of the Third Reich, which in return would help him to recover his throne.[3]

SIS officers in Moscow had given London no warning of the Nazi-Soviet pact. Vera recalled that "a former Rhodes scholar, Baron Adam von Trott zu Solz, a dedicated anti-Nazi, got around London a lot and told me about upper-class English families whose pro-Nazi stance discouraged those in Berlin who needed support against Hitler. One fascist-minded family regularly entertained Queen Mary to tea, and had a son, Anthony Blunt, in our secret services, who reinforced Germany's impression we'd stay neutral." Mary Stephenson commented, when Blunt was finally exposed as a Soviet spy, that Blunt had been given his postwar sinecure as Keeper of the Queen's Pictures only to guarantee his silence on the incriminating letters written by British royals to Hitler that Blunt had rescued from a castle in the American zone soon after Nazi Germany collapsed.

Vera, in this tense year of 1939, aware of some betrayals and sensitive to the likelihood of more, wondered if Chamberlain was going to dump Poland and remain neutral, after promising to declare war once Germany marched into Poland on some trumped-up excuse about Polish aggression.

# 11

## Vera's First Mission in an Open War

Vera left for Poland again six days before its invasion. A Left Wing team was hastily put together by Gubby, equipped with secret service communications gear and self-invented as Military Mission No. 4 (MM-4) to prevent interference from the Well-Bred Horse Brigade, led by a prime minister still worried about provoking Hitler. Young army officers squashed their uniforms into suitcases and wore business suits. "They looked like traveling salesmen," Vera recalled. "I had no clothing problems. I was just a humble secretary-translator."

MM-4 could not cut directly through Europe, nor go through Scandinavia. It had no official existence. If exposed, it would be plausibly denied. Gubby had been told to "inspire confidence among the Polish General Staff" even while Britain's Committee of Imperial Defence was instructed by the chiefs of staff that "no priority is to be given to relieving pressure on Poland." It looked to Vera as if exponents of irregular warfare were intended to be discredited by the failure of this impossible mission. The chiefs of staff were on record as lamenting "underhand methods" that challenged their highly conservative authority.

Waiting in Warsaw was the intransigent one-eyed, one-armed General Sir Adrian Carton de Wiart. He had spent years in Poland and had formed a nucleus of war emergency "stay-behind parties" made up of locally based British businessmen and British embassy specialists. All that MM-4 had to do was find a way to reach him.

On August 24, 1939, Vera joined the MM-4 team in Paris to board a regular passenger train for Marseilles, where a British warship was waiting for them. Five on the team came from a Polish military mission already in London. Traveling through France, Vera saw it was on a war footing, in startling contrast to the unruffled calm in England. Emergency French troop trains took priority over other rail traffic. This meant that Vera's train was sidetracked so often that it reached Marseilles thirty-six hours late. The captain of the waiting British cruiser HMS *Shropshire* had been told nothing about this scruffy little band of thirty civilians except that they must be deposited in Egypt. For the captain, it was more important to get his bigger cargo of colonial officials, plus wives, to British India. He came close to sailing without the mission. MM-4's quarters were so cramped that only Vera and two senior officers had cabins. The others slept on deck. The Poles huddled with secret papers in an open lifeboat, looking glum.

In this last week of peace, Sidney Cotton flew for the bogus company set up in Paris, and waited on the runway at Berlin's Tempelhof airport, the two engines of his Lockheed Electra running. He had been told that Air Marshal Hermann Göring was joining him to fly to London and discuss peace with Chamberlain. Suddenly a car screamed alongside and Luftwaffe officers jumped out and waggled the plane's wing flaps to catch the pilot's attention. Cotton opened a side door. A Luftwaffe pilot, who knew that Cotton, though in civilian clothes, was also in the RAF, shouted a fraternal warning. Göring was not coming. The secret police were. Cotton took straight off without bothering to turn into the wind. Göring had never intended to fly to London. His peace mission was another trick to deceive the British. Dirty tricks set the tone of Hitler's foreign policy, and dirty tricks were to launch the war with a deception the Nazis code-named Canned Goods. It was anticipated by Elizabeth Wiskemann, a British journalist in Berlin, but her warning was not taken seriously in London. She would later serve as an agent in Switzerland.

Hitler telegraphed the Duke of Windsor, now in Paris: "It depends on Britain whether my wishes for the future development of German-British relations can be realized." The duke wired Hitler on Sunday, August 27, assuring him of Britain's peaceful intent.

On Friday, September 1, 1939, Churchill, out of office and out of favor, got a call from Gubby's friend the Polish ambassador in London, Count Raczynski. The Germans had invaded Poland.

Rebels against Prime Minister Chamberlain now included some

within his own cabinet, who burst into 10 Downing Street during a violent thunderstorm on the evening of September 2 and announced that they would not leave until Chamberlain swore to abandon all thought of negotiating with Hitler. It was midnight before the rebels, numbering seven or eight, got the Umbrella Man to see things their way.

Nine hours later, Chamberlain's ultimatum was sent to Berlin: If Germany did not halt its attack on Poland by noon, London time, Britain would be at war. The Germans gave no reply. Chamberlain broadcast a somber message that a state of war existed. Air-raid sirens sounded. It was a Sunday, and the 25th East Ham Boy Scout Troop was on church parade in the narrow streets of terraced housing that would suffer heavily from the German bombing to come. The young sister of a future Royal Navy fighter pilot, Kenneth Boardman, would find her thick black hair turned white when others in the family were killed. Boardman, one of the boys in that Sunday parade, would tell Vera later: "All us kids had known for a year that war was unavoidable. I felt relief and a sort of serenity."

In Morpeth Mansion, Churchill had an apartment. He had to be coaxed to walk down to an open basement "not even sand bagged," where he stood in the doorway and imagined "ruin and carnage and vast explosions." When he spoke in Parliament later that day, he still had to fight a powerful group hoping to stumble out of the war they had just stumbled into. He grasped the weapon on which he could count: the Royal Navy, through which swept the signal "Winston is back!" He was again, after more than thirty years, First Lord of the Admiralty. His friends in naval intelligence, who had arranged the warship carrying Vera's companions to Cairo, confided that Washington's naval establishment had passed along serious intelligence leaks from SIS cipher traffic. "Awful revelations" wrote Alexander Felix Cadogan at the British Foreign Office, in his diary entry for September 21, 1939, underscoring the word "awful." The normally unflappable Cadogan continued: "The whole Department [SIS] apparently recruited by haphazard methods, must be reorganized." This was the first hint of a massive collapse of SIS networks, and the future internecine warfare between SIS and Gubbins's unorthodox secret organization.[1]

The warning came too late to save MM-4, which was dependent on the SIS signals system now compromised, although the mission knew nothing of this. Members were trying desperately to get out of Alexandria naval base on August 31 after being dumped on the quay-side by *Shropshire*. The cruiser had sped off with its colonial adminis-trators. Gubby's appeals for assistance to "the MI(R) element" impressed none of the local British administration, which ran Egypt like a colony, nor army officers in conflict with Jewish settlers next door in Palestine.

Vera got her first taste of special operations in an open war, not the domestic skirmishes between Mutual Friends and appeasers. Boats that were to take the mission to the Romanian port of Constanţa in the Danube estuary had been requisitioned by British authorities. Vera went with Gubby to see what could be scrounged. There was no way to fly directly to Poland without clipping German-controlled airspace. Gubby had a few gold sovereigns provided by the Secret Fund for emergencies. One gold sovereign yielded a large wad of local currency from the money changers. Vera bundled into a broken-down Egyptian taxi that sputtered through the crowded streets to the British Imperial Airways office. The local manager examined in some wonderment this woman who appeared to have taken a wrong turn on her way to fash-ionable Piccadilly. There was absolutely no reason, she said in her best clipped accent, why he could not find a flying boat for charter immedi-ately, and waved the wad of notes for emphasis.

Gubby guardedly disclosed to the local RAF commander the na-ture of his mission. RAF pilots could not care less about forms and reg-ulations. Two Sunderland flying boats were "liberated" to fly MM-4 to Athens. Under Vera's spell, the Imperial Airways manager came through with a third flying boat. All three aircraft landed to refuel at Piraeus.

But once there, the RAF crews were recalled to Egypt, where Poland's invasion meant "the balloon's gone up." The Imperial Air-ways captain was a reserve RAF officer and, with the best will in the world, could not see himself swiftly ferrying back and forth between Greece and Romania with split loads of bags, eighteen large cases packed with secret signaling gear, and many more passengers than he could carry in less than a dozen runs.

At the Polish legation in Athens, Gubby discovered pilots of LOT, the Polish airline. Their two Lockheed Electras were grounded. Normally, one staged through Bucharest, the other through Haifa.

Unarmed civilian aircraft heading for Warsaw were certain to be shot down. The Polish crews agreed to fly to Romania after being told their passengers were "British secret service." But there was no room for the mission's packing cases. This precious cargo had to be shipped by sea to Constanţa. A Greek shipowner agreed, dazzled by a gold sovereign or two, to dispatch an old tub with the cargo at top speed to the Romanian port.

At Tatoi airport, the LOT pilots started up their engines. The MM-4 team short-circuited immigration, pushed aside Greek officials, and ran with personal bags across the hot tarmac to jump into the two Lockheeds. As soon as they were off the ground, the planes banked sharply to dodge gunfire, ignoring urgent radioed orders to complete departure formalities and report their destination. They refueled in Salonika, the pilots having gambled on Tatoi air controllers not sending warnings ahead. The LOT crews were not sure where Greece stood in relation to Germany. With nothing to lose, they shot back into the air the moment their fuel tanks were topped up.

In Bucharest, Vera was in her element. Max's surviving Jewish friends had every reason to help and confide information. She learned of Whitehall's pressure to stop traffic through Romania to Palestine "by the Jewish Revisionists for political reasons and for the sake of profits to be made from the heavy fares charged." The memo to the British legation, from a Whitehall functionary named A. W. G. Randall, had been recovered by Mossad. "I think we need not be too scrupulous about our treatment of this traffic in human beings," Randall concluded.[2]

Vera saw that the real priority in the minds of those who controlled SIS in Eastern Europe was not Poland but preventing Jewish migration to Palestine. The lightning attack on Poland had pulverized Warsaw. The American architect Philip Johnson, once the darling of London's high society and now a press correspondent with the German forces, described the destruction of the Polish capital as "a stirring spectacle" in his dispatch to the U.S. publication *Social Justice*, whose pro-Nazi reports were distributed to British diplomatic posts.[3]

Vera learned from Mossad agents that Adolf Eichmann's Reich Central Office for Jewish Immigration in Prague was forcing Jews to flee through Romania to Palestine as part of a plan to deepen Arab hostility toward the mandate exercised by Britain, so its army divisions would be pinned down by Arab guerrillas. She also learned that in Poland the German SS had started to kill Jews, and the Gestapo was rounding up other Jews to be sent to Dachau. She spent two days at Bucharest's Athénée Palace Hotel, planning with MM-4 the next move. Polish airfields were in German hands. The shipped baggage was miraculously delivered to the hotel from the railway station, and a smiling Jewish boy told Vera, "No charge. Just do what you can for us." What he knew, and who he really worked for, she did not ask. She found the drivers of nine rickety taxis who agreed to drive to the border to meet a Polish train to Lwów. Gubby was in radio contact with General Carton de Wiart. Polish army liaison would assist them with trains from Lwów to Lublin and on to Warsaw, unless the lines were already bombed.

Vera's convoy drove through the heartrendingly brilliant summer scene of oxcarts bringing in a golden harvest, with sun-yellow clusters of ripe corn hanging from the balconies of farmhouses. It was painful to share this interlude of peace in a countryside unaffected by war, and where she had spent so many pleasurable hours with Old Fritz. The roads were in bad shape now. Motoring was slow. At the border, Vera talked her way past Romanian guards, only to find MM-4 had missed its train. On the other side of the river Dniester was chaos. Polish members of the mission assured their compatriots on the border that these English civilians, claiming to be tourists, were not German secret agents.

How was the team to keep the rendezvous with their man in Lwów? Vera and her companions stumbled over a jumble of railway sidings until they came across a coach that looked as if it had been sitting idle since the collapse of the Austro-Hungarian Empire. Someone found a hammer and tapped the wheels and pronounced the wagon railworthy. They rolled it within striking distance of a local freight train. The Polish driver was enchanted to do Vera the small favor of hauling this imperial leftover through the night to Lwów. On the Polish side of the border, homes were in darkness, and young reservists looked for rides to military posts. The team sank into what had been plush upholstery. Vera remarked that the expedition and its frantic improvisations were useful preparation for special operations. Privately, she hoped it would not turn into black comedy.

Next morning in Lwów, the promised liaison officer commandeered a bus to the next connection at Lublin. By the time the team arrived, news had broken of Britain's entry into the war. Gubby's men threw off their civilian disguise. The sight of British uniforms raised spirits. The townsfolk showered the mission with flowers and kisses. A Scots member of the team, Hugh Curteis, donned a tartan kilt and was revealed in all his glory as a brawny bare-legged Highlander, hugged and kissed by an enormous Pole whose huge black beard tickled Curteis until he collapsed in laughter. The tourists were now soldiers, with Vera a camp follower.

The Lublin-Warsaw train rattled through the suburbs of Warsaw. Everyone became suddenly sober. German bombs and shells had flattened the area in advance of the panzer divisions. Gubbins reported to General Carton de Wiart. Hasty consultations were held with the Polish General Staff, unimpressed by MM-4's considerable feat of scrambling here within days. Marshal Smigly-Rydz, the balding Polish commander in chief, needed more. Chamberlain's declaration of war had come days after the German attack, and was broadcast by the BBC only once. Then the BBC resumed the weekend cricket results.

Gubbins dictated a scorching signal to the War Office. What the hell was going on? Englishmen played cricket while Poles suffered far heavier losses than the War Office had prepared for. He had given his word to the Polish general staff that Britain would help Poland fight back. Now there could be no hope if the War Office were to stick its head in the sand again. Vera feared that the Well-Bred Horse Brigade would carefully enter Gubby's protest into his personal file for use against him later.

Whitehall's reply was read out to grim-faced Polish senior staff officers. The War Office wished it to be known that "every week is of value to us in increasing our reserves [and] improving the security of the base from which our offensive operations will ultimately be launched." In short, the Poles should carry on as best they could.

The Polish general staff regrouped at Luków, fifty miles southeast of Warsaw. Gubby sent back to London a personal courier, Tommy Davies, who escaped through the Baltic ports with a memorized account of devastating Polish losses. Without air defense, its arms factories destroyed, Polish cavalry riding against German tanks, the country could not "carry on" in the manner prescribed. Gold sovereigns were rescued from a cache at the British embassy to pay for two American

Studebakers and a five-ton truck for Gubby's group to chase after the retreating Polish commanders. The embassy was a shambles, the butler in tears because all the stocks of wine were abandoned. The English wife of the SIS man in Warsaw, Colonel J. P. Shelley, had been killed in a raid on Luków, to which the embassy withdrew.

Ten days after London declared war, on the eve of the Jewish New Year, Rosh Hashanah, the Jewish quarter of Warsaw was targeted by Stuka dive-bombers.

Marshal Smigly-Rydz was reluctant to disclose his shifting dispositions, because the War Office was now making unreasonable demands for hourly situation reports to be wirelessed in code to London. The Polish commander in chief could not risk confirming for the Germans the full extent of their victory. Military headquarters were moved to the Romanian frontier at Kolomyja, where Vera and MM-4 had crossed two weeks earlier. The remaining gold sovereigns were entrusted to Count Stephan Zamoyski, a friend of General Carton de Wiart. On the count's lawn, for a brief afternoon, Vera took tea while hearing that fifty-five thousand Jews in Vilnius had been rounded up by the Russian Red Army, claiming its half of Poland under the secret protocol with Hitler.

The Soviet Union and Nazi Germany were bizarre bedfellows. Vera tried to find a student friend of Countess Krystyna Skarbek. Vera had no immediate success, but later pieced together the tribulations of the student, Stanley Orlowski. He was captured by Germans on a country road and arrested for being a Boy Scout. He escaped, but then fell into Russian hands and was dragged off to Siberia, where he lingered in slave camps until the Russians were later attacked by Germany. He was freed to go to Persia and fight Germans with Free Pole forces, whose liaison officer was then Sir Harold Mitchell, the parliamentarian industrialist and supporter of Vera as a member of Churchill's FOCUS group.

Krystyna's other young friend, Jan Zurakowski, piloting the venerable P.11 fighter, was among Warsaw's defenders who shot down 125 of the immensely superior German Bf 109s and Bf 110s at the cost of 114 Polish aircraft. Some Polish pilots ran out of ammunition. They flew until, fuel exhausted, they crash-landed in Romania. From there they would find their way to join the RAF in time for the Battle of Britain, flying Hurricanes. As late as August 28, 1939, on the very eve of war, such fighter aircraft were still held up in Denmark while Whitehall argued over who should pay for onward carriage to Poland.[4]

Vera had to think of ways through Romania to supply the Polish underground's Home Army with irregular warfare devices. Some sabotage was already being carried out by Polish regulars. It was hard to convince them of any aid coming from London. Gubbins asked an elderly reserve major commanding an artillery battery where his guns were. "Still in England!" was the wry reply.

The German campaign was over in three weeks. MM-4 groped its way back to the Romanian border. On the Polish side, a guard demanded: "What are you doing in Poland?" Gubby pacified the officer, but said in a bitter aside to Vera: "What *are* we doing here?"

The Polish code breakers had no way out except with the mission. Vera had three: Marian Rejewski, Jerzy Rozycki, and Henryk Zygalski. Jerzy was with his wife, who had been advised along the way to strangle their baby because of German atrocities. She chose to care for the infant and urged Jerzy to go. He would never see his wife or child again. The other two code breakers had been unable to bring their families with them. Their chiefs, Gwido Langer and Maksymilian Ciezki, carried the latest Enigma replicas and bombes, urgently needed in England. They crossed the border, but fell afoul of Romanian soldiers, who insisted on sending them to a refugee camp. Vera got into the camp and told the pair they would have to somehow survive until she could find the means to get them out.

She took the other code breakers by train to Bucharest, where the British legation chief was asked to provide them with visas and arrange shelter and onward transport. He chose to wait for instructions from London. Vera knew what this meant: SIS obstruction. She found a French diplomat, a secret service officer she had known in Paris. Immediately he booked the Poles on the Simplon-Orient Express to Paris. The three cryptologists were to resume work at a French intelligence base, Château de Vignolles, forty miles northeast of Paris.

Gubby's mission assembled on the lawns of the British legation in Bucharest just as news broke of the assassination of Romania's prime minister, Armand Calinescu. German propaganda blamed the British legation, saying it had pressured Calinescu to stop the traffic in Jewish refugees, and further claimed that only the Jewish Question stopped the Chamberlain government from accepting a new German peace offer on September 29, 1939, after Warsaw fell. Goebbels, master of the Big Lie, said a British mission arranged the assassination to sabotage any chance of ending the war. Britain had limited its declaration of war to Poland. That war was over.[5]

Gubby's men on the legation lawn were suddenly aware of how easily they might be portrayed as the assassins. Most shipped out hastily the next day for Egypt. Gubbins and General Carton de Wiart hid inside the British legation to write their reports and make a case for properly arming the Polish resistance. Vera still had influential friends in Bucharest to effect the release of Langer and Ciezki from the refugee camp without drawing attention to their importance in breaking German codes. After Gubby and Carton de Wiart left Romania on the Simplon-Orient Express as civilians, Vera followed. She was back in London six weeks after the launch of the mission. She told Hugh Dalton that her first experience under fire had taught her invaluable lessons. But at the War Office, MM-4's report was read with skepticism by those who saw the Maginot Line, a "Western Front in concrete" along the Franco-German border, as the guarantee that German armies would never reach the English Channel.

There was an unusually long delay — nine months — before MM-4 were awarded a niggardly Mention-in-Dispatches. Nine months was how long it would take Churchill to override those in Whitehall to whom Hitler appealed in another, oddly arrogant peace offer on October 6, 1939.

Hitler knew that although Churchill was back at the Admiralty, he was pitted against powerful figures whose opposition was easily perceived from Berlin. Sir Ernest Benn, a prominent and influential publisher, protested against talk of Churchill becoming prime minister: "I pray that such a catastrophe will be averted."[6] Benn feared a transfer from "the restraint and breeding" of men like Prime Minister Neville Chamberlain to warmongers. After all, the war announced by Chamberlain was now over, wasn't it? Major political figures like Lloyd George issued powerful public arguments for British-German peace talks. Churchill became the target of the worst verbal onslaughts from Berlin and from his fellow parliamentarians.

"Any lessons from Poland," Vera said to Bill Stephenson, "have been trashed." Churchill's Mutual Friend in the Foreign Office, Sir Robert (later Lord) Vansittart, was removed as permanent undersecretary of state despite Churchill's protest that this would be represented "as a victory for the pro-Germans in England." Two months after the fall of Poland, the artist Paul Maze wrote that "the German propaganda spread about is most harmful, especially within Mayfair society."

Churchill fought to have his current director of naval intelligence, John Godfrey, replace Admiral Sir Hugh Sinclair, chief of the SIS, who had died after a long illness. Prime Minister Chamberlain furiously fought this, insisting that Stewart Graham Menzies must become the new SIS chief. Vera asked Stephenson what lay behind this. He said Churchill feared that Menzies, acting in Sinclair's absence, had let the SIS grow slack. Americans, whose clandestine help was vital, were not impressed by "English gentlemen" sharing the goodies among others of the same upper-class origins. Menzies was an old Etonian, a member of the Household Cavalry, and worked in a National Preventive Intelligence Service during the 1914–18 war that focused on the Bolshevik Revolution and the danger of similar uprisings destroying the British Empire. This did not impress anticolonialist Americans, who shared a widespread suspicion that they had been tricked into joining the 1914–18 war by the British secret service.

Menzies had a shadow deputy, Colonel Claude Marjoribanks Dansey. In the 1914–18 war Dansey was a military attaché in Washington, where he was regarded as a man of the lowest cunning. "He sees Bolshies under the bed," continued Stephenson. "He shares this obsession with Hankey." Sir Maurice (later Lord) Hankey was in Chamberlain's current War Cabinet. Two years earlier Hankey, as permanent secretary to the cabinet and the Defence Committee, had "jumped on Churchill for turning over alarming facts about the RAF's utter inferiority." Hankey had expressed shock "that senior officers in the armed forces are in direct communication with a leading Statesman, Churchill, a critic of the departments under whom these officers serve." Such officers, Hankey warned, were "subversive" and should suffer the disastrous consequences. Vera might yet be pounced upon as subversive by Stewart Menzies, who as the acting SIS chief was now in secret contact with Hitler. This partly explained Churchill's resolve to replace him. There was a colossal SIS intelligence failure caused by attempts to pacify Hitler, who was encouraged to think Britain would call off the war tomorrow.

Hitler used tactics that worked in Germany: firing up fears of communists. He said in one speech that pro-German Englishmen saw Bolshevism as the true enemy. His account was surprisingly detailed. He said terrorists had always been associated in London with Bolshevik anarchists. When Admiral Sir Hugh Sinclair was appointed secret service chief in 1923, he moved his private office to a small alley off Kensington High Street. To make sure no terrorists would be led there by his highly visible Lancia Landau, he used the car only to make the club rounds in Pall Mall and St. James's Street. A year later, Sinclair had engineered the downfall of the first socialist government. "So much for political objectivity," said Stephenson.

Hugh Dalton felt Vera should look into an SIS foul-up that yielded the Nazis so much information. Dalton wanted "terrorist acts against traitors and German leaders, not a military job at all . . . explosions, chaos and revolution." This was precisely what the present SIS leaders did not want.[7]

He was not yet in a ministerial position to launch such irregular actions. Vera was the ideal person to look into SIS failures. She was "out of sanction," not beholden to any secret agency. She was back from a dangerous mission without formal Whitehall approval. She knew talented Poles who had escaped and were streaming into Paris to train for guerrilla warfare.

Churchill's inflexible opposition to the confirmation of Stewart Menzies as SIS chief caused prolonged ferment. It became less puzzling in November 1939 when two key British agents were kidnapped on the Dutch-German border by Germans pretending to represent anti-Nazi generals who wanted to make a deal. Between them, the kidnapped men knew pretty much everything about the SIS. Menzies, convinced that "good" Germans sought British allies against communism, had allowed his two agents to walk into a trap. They had wined, dined, and cultivated Nazi intelligence experts who posed as pro-British army officers. Then Hitler narrowly escaped death from a bomb and, in a fury, ordered the snatching of the SIS agents. It was the end of one game, but the start of another for the Gestapo. One of the kidnapped men was identified by Nazi propaganda as chief of SIS in Europe.

The end of Poland was the beginning of a so-called Phony War, during which Hitler's next intended victims began to think they were safe.

# 12

# KBO: Keep Buggering On

Vera felt she had failed a country she helped encourage to resist German occupation. She spoke of this with Stringbag's protégé Nigel Fisher, nicknamed the Fish, who was related to the former First Sea Lord, Admiral "Jackie" Fisher, the charismatic genius revered by Churchill as insidious and ruthless in building the navy that won the 1914–18 war. The Fish was a pilot, yet still schoolboyish in a way that was comforting. He recalled "talking the nights away with Vera. She was hard on herself and upset by the gulf between Warsaw's agony and London's cool detachment. People said, 'Don't you know there's a war on?' to excuse incompetence. But it was a phony war, a false twilight."

The visionary Admiral Fisher, anticipating World War I, had created hunter-killer battle cruisers, fast to attack, quick to escape. He fought endless interdepartmental conflicts. In a moment of exasperation, King George V had once said "he should be hung from the yardarm." Vera felt the equal of an admiral who was a scoundrel to some but whose old brave comradeship braced Churchill for the political battles to come.

Those battles would have to be fought through a democratic process, the outcome dependent upon Churchill's parliamentary skills. Hitler's authority was based on fear, spread through the Reichssicherheitshauptamt (RSHA), the Main Security Office. Vera saw the RSHA as a personal enemy, with powers to spy on the citizenry, to interrogate, to torture, and to execute extending through the Gestapo, the State Security Police, and the SS. In Prague, Adolf Eichmann drew authority from the RSHA. In Warsaw, the RSHA first liquidated those identified as mentally ill or racially inferior, though it actually was aimed at all those opposing German authority. And yet messengers and mail for London still slipped through this apparatus built on blind fear.

Here in London, opponents of Chamberlain could freely challenge his government's wrongheaded authority in early 1940, even with the country at war. Germany's film, radio, and the press were mobilized with unprecedented efficiency to serve up propaganda lies. Vera wondered if the future creation of diabolical counterweapons like London Control, with its specialists in sabotage drawn from ordinary folk, would subvert democracy. London Control was now merely foreshadowed by a central office of information. Winston Churchill, deeply respectful of democratic tradition, could be ruthless in action. "Well," said the Fish, listening to her reflections, "Churchill's got his toehold in Admiralty."

Was Churchill's an adequate toehold from which to fight the appeasers? She had not grown up in the company of Churchill's reputation. She had to piece him together from fragments. In 1934 he was saying, "I'm a ghost, witnessing my own demise." He kept bailiffs at bay by writing prodigiously. His motto was KBO: Keep Buggering On. His enemies said he was a tired old man at the age of sixty-four. Back at his desk in the Admiralty, though, he launched hunter-killer raids against superior fighting ships that Germany had constructed while England slept.

Vera could foresee his hunter-killer instincts emerging in close-work. He had always possessed this kind of ferocity. He was shaping it into a vision for Special Operations Executive from his modest base at the Admiralty. In 1928 Churchill had been at the peak of his career as chancellor of the exchequer. Members of Parliament had crowded the House of Commons to applaud his oratory, and heralded him as the next leader of the Conservative Party. A year later the Conservatives were voted out of office. Churchill quarreled with their leaders on issues he felt were important. In 1931 he was shut out when a national government was formed. He kept his seat in Parliament and, during almost a decade of ridicule, devised his own guerrilla tactics. "Attack! Attack! Attack! Never, never, never give in!" he declared. It underpinned the concept of Special Operations Executive, although his authority to launch it was still a long way off.

The Chamberlain government could do little to stop Churchill from using his position as First Lord of the Admiralty in the War Cabinet to wage irregular war. Churchill seized real executive power within his naval kingdom. He drew upon lessons he had learned as First Lord of the Admiralty from October 1911 to May 1915, when he had been at the same desk where he now sat. Admiral Fisher was then one of his senior advisers. A former assistant to Fisher was Dudley Pound, now Churchill's senior adviser. No wonder Churchill always spoke of "the resumption of World War."

Vera learned from the limited guerrilla warfare that Churchill was able to initiate from the Admiralty. He suffused the Rhine, the main river of German trade and life, with a plague of floating mines. He planned to sabotage iron-ore shipments from Norway and Sweden, exploiting Fritz Thyssen, who had turned against Hitler and was uniquely informed as head of the Thyssen industrial empire. Thyssen said the side that won mastery of iron ores and magnetic iron would be the victor. But Churchill's hands were tied, as he said, by "the awful difficulties which our machinery of war-conduct presents to positive action."

On December 2, 1939, Vera learned that mobile gas chambers were used to murder patients in Poland's mental hospitals. Underground Jewish youth movements in Warsaw were resisting with homemade bombs. Vera listed their needs. At the very top was money. Some of it already came from Jewish organizations. She anticipated a need for the forgery of huge amounts of foreign currency notes. The moralizers in Whitehall would object to counterfeiting money. She would have to break the law so long as Lord Halifax sat in judgment: Churchill called him the Holy Fox for using his High Anglican Church connections. The Holy Fox had an odd sense of ethics: it was he who had approved the decision to deprive Poland of Hurricane fighter planes because it could not pay the cost of shipping them.

In December 1939, Vera had visited Gubby in Paris, where he was in touch with the Polish and Czech general staffs that had withdrawn to France. Stanislaw Gano of Polish Intelligence reunited Vera with Countess Krystyna Skarbek. Krystyna had no idea of the fate of her Jewish mother, Stephanie Goldfeder. She was planning to help with escape lines from Poland to Hungary, and gather arms and explosives for an expanding Polish underground.

Vera also reconnected with Rodolphe Lemoine, the French

secret service officer code-named Rex, who gave her disturbing news. The key Polish code breakers Gwido Langer and Maksymilian Ciezki were still held in the Romanian refugee camp. The French needed them, but if France were to meet the same fate as Poland, some way must be found to stop these Poles from falling into German hands. Lemoine had a transcript from a German propaganda broadcast on Saturday, November 18, 1939, alleging that a Max Rosenberg had taken part in a British-Zionist conspiracy to assassinate the Romanian prime minister. Vera recalled the scene on the British legation lawn. Perhaps the Germans had merely stumbled across someone called Rosenberg? Her father was dead. That same day, nine Czech students had been shot for anti-German activities. "Prague is paralyzed, silent with awe," Gobbels boasted. The so-called conspiracy in Romania was, she decided, an expression of Nazi fear of popular uprisings. The Rosenberg name had been pulled out of a hat to justify brutality by the Iron Guard. As Vera Atkins, she had surely escaped the attention of German security services.

Gubby planned to give her some protection as an officer in the RAF. If she fell into German hands, she could claim prisoner-of-war status under the Geneva Convention. On paper, she worked for an interservice Training Development Centre in the Royal Marine barracks at Portsmouth, which was to raise paramilitary units for Admiral Lord Louis Mountbatten, who was planning combined operations. His outfit fabricated documents, and could wipe out any indication of her origins.

Vera gave Dalton the news that Langer and Ciezki were still virtual prisoners in the Romanian refugee camp. When Churchill was told, he demanded that Chamberlain make Romania account for its "odious behavior" in maltreating those who escaped Nazi brutality. Surprisingly, the demand was relayed. The code breakers were released.

Behind the government's back, Churchill created the new post of Personal Adviser to the First Lord in Scientific Matters, with "a place beside Churchill's Private Office." The adviser was Professor Frederick Lindemann, and the place — a chair beside Churchill's desk — was called the Statistical Office.[1]

Churchill impishly sparked the imaginations of those who would later have to deceive a more vicious enemy than the chiefs of staff. He told Prime Minister Chamberlain that the chiefs were "an obstacle to imaginative debate. The War Cabinet should meet without them when there are matters beyond their competence to be discussed."[2] Lieutenant Colonel Ian Jacob, a War Cabinet observer, wrote that "Winston's mind was so immensely active, he could only be prime minister."[3]

Churchill told Parliament stirring tales of war at sea while Chamberlain sulked. Even followers of Old Umbrella began to whisper, "We have now found our leader." President Roosevelt started a secret correspondence with Churchill, astonishing between the chief of state of a neutral power and an unrecognized foreign leader. Their exchanges were signed "Naval Person" for Churchill and "POTUS" for President of the United States.[4]

Vera had been talent-spotting in Paris in the harsh winter of 1939–40. There was a certain delicacy about relations with the French, who must not get the idea that exiled Polish and Czech military chiefs might be preparing a hurried transfer to England. Vera was a useful foil. Her appearance at the Hotel Régina, where the Polish general staff was based, gave a certain flavor to clandestine meetings with the intelligence chief, Stanislaw Gano. The French saw her as his mistress. Gano needed speedier ways to communicate with Poland's underground army. Vera was asked to bring in mobile wireless gear from London. They needed automatic weapons and transport. The first request, for eight sets of secret wireless equipment, was rejected by the SIS, which controlled all secret communications, on the grounds that nothing was available. As for automatics, the British army had never found much use for them. The Poles could have .38 revolvers, but these only fired rimmed ammunition, which was not available in Central Europe. Besides, the revolvers were too clumsy for skullduggery. Transport was also exclusively in the hands of the SIS, and although Gubby was told, "We can send in wagonsful, dear chap, wagonsful," none appeared.

Krystyna Skarbek, flitting through this frustrating Paris episode, told Vera of the astonishing ingenuity of Poles in escaping to places like British-run Gibraltar. Churchill broadcast a tribute to them: "The soul of Poland is indestructible." Germany and Russia had held it "in bondage for a hundred and fifty years, unable to quench its spirit." The words were regarded as Churchill's promise of help for the Poles if he gained power. To shake off the myth of a phony war, he said Germany still meant to plant itself on the shores of the Black Sea, overrun the Baltic States, and subjugate the Slavonic peoples of southeastern Europe.

Krystyna began work as an agent in the Balkans. She was a self-starter like Vera, and normally would not have taken orders from another woman. Krystyna loved men, and under her spell they would do anything for her. She was very much like Vera, keeping eyes fixed on dangerous objectives. She trekked over mountains through deep snow with messages, arms, and supplies for Poland. She based herself in Budapest. In Prague, Czech underground fighters were already organized. They had lived under Nazi rule, and had no reason to trust British promises. They were smuggling in weapons and equipment on their own.

Paris was full of plotters. The real closework fighters feared the lazy reliance on the Maginot Line. "Our generals and politicians won't heave themselves out of the beds of their mistresses," she was told by Henri Tanguy, a communist introduced by seventeen-year-old medical student Rolande Colas soon after Vera spotted her as a future agent.

Vera was using Paris contacts to pursue inquiries into the carelessness of the SIS. Prime Minister Chamberlain disclosed to the War Cabinet that British intelligence agents had been negotiating with German generals. Churchill's fury can best be gauged from Cadogan's entry in his securely locked diary.[5] "Cabinet told of our contact with Generals." Lord Halifax "mustn't listen too much to Winston on the subject of beating Germany."

Lord Halifax had been first to respond to the overtures made by bogus German generals and had set in motion prewar and wartime meetings with the two luckless British agents. Churchill invented yet another independent resource for waging domestic guerrilla warfare: a Statistical Department run by Hugh Dalton. From this, Vera sourced the raw material for her investigation into the SIS disaster. It turned out that SIS's acting chief, Menzies, had been forced by the fiasco to shut down stations and circuits and to overhaul the organization in London on the assumption that all SIS networks were blown.

# 13

# Your Affectionate Opposition: The Gestapo

Vera reported to Hugh Dalton that the French refused to release the Polish code breakers. Some plan had to be worked out to get them to safety in England. "We can't leave it to the old intelligence queens," he said, and fluttered his hands and rolled his eyes in a manner that was a familiar warning. He settled his large bulk more comfortably in the settee of her Winchelsea home. "I let loose independent scholars to spot how the SIS reports were doctored." He let his head fall back and stared at the ceiling. "Now I need your experience to tell me what really happened. Because those two SIS agents were captured on Hitler's personal orders after he made an approach to Lord Halifax and other appeasers here."

The two British agents had been in secret contact with alleged opposition groups in Germany long before the bomb that almost took Hitler's life on November 9, 1939, in Munich during a commemoration of the beer-hall putsch attempt in 1923. The British agents were kidnapped within hours of the bomb's explosion. Before this, Hitler had silently studied reports on "secret" talks between the SIS agents and Hauptmann Schemmel of the Army Transport Department, whose identity was borrowed by Walter Schellenberg, the ambitious deputy chief of the RSHA foreign intelligence section.

Earlier on the same day of the bomb, Unity Mitford, the Englishwoman rumored to be Hitler's mistress, was comforted by him after she fired a pistol at her head, supposing that a London-Berlin alliance was out of reach. Hitler arranged for her return to her father, Lord Redesdale, to show goodwill, and was encouraged by reports that Neville Chamberlain's principal private secretary, Sir Arthur Rucker, said communism was a greater danger than Nazi Germany.

After surviving the bomb blast, Hitler ordered Walter Schellenberg to lure the British agents, Captain Sigismund Payne Best and Major Richard Stevens, to the German-Dutch border at Venlo, snatch them, and arrange a show trial to discredit the British secret service. Major Stevens was a former Malay police cadet, an ex-lieutenant of the Rajput Rifles, and a translator of Russian wireless signals intercepted on the Northwest Frontier. Captain Best had been selected to take up residence at the Hague by Claude Marjoribanks Dansey, running an agency called Z whose operations in Europe paralleled the SIS. Officers of the two organizations supposedly knew nothing about each other. Best and Stevens discovered each other's existence only when London agreed to the secret negotiations. Dalton was troubled by the actions of Stewart Menzies, still not confirmed in the post of C, the SIS chief. Vera was to review the Best-Stevens negotiations. The agents appeared to act without central coordination.

Vera learned that Hitler had attended a state funeral on Sunday, November 12, for eight people killed by the bomb. Goebbels announced that if the beer-hall celebration had stuck to its announced agenda, the bomb would have killed Hitler, who had started to speak half an hour before schedule and left early. "A miracle," Goebbels said publicly, seizing his propaganda opportunity. "The Führer stands under the protection of the Almighty."

Vera traced Captain Best's connections to heirs of an ancient German dynasty, Princes Philipp and Christopher of Hesse-Kassel, whose grandmother was a daughter of Queen Victoria. The brother princes had joined Nazi organizations in the early 1930s, and were attracted to Nazi elitism and anticommunism. Their names were dropped by Walter Schellenberg in falsely presenting a portrait of pro-British elements. Admiral Canaris and Hans Oster, deputy head of Canaris's intelligence organization and administrative director of the army, were anti-Hitler. Both had supported early appeals for British help in getting rid of Hitler. Best had been in touch with General Ludwig Beck, who resigned as chief of the German general staff after Hitler overrode his warnings against war with Britain. Hitler was reported as saying, "The only general I fear is Beck." Beck's successor, General Franz Halder, wanted to marginalize Hitler, or put him under control of the military chiefs.

The two agents had acted in good faith when Dutch intelligence was asked by the Germans for an introduction to Major Stevens on September 5, 1939. Menzies, while Admiral Sinclair was still SIS chief but already dying, had instructed the BBC to broadcast in its German service the introductory "Hier ist London" twice over to signal that British agents would attend a clandestine meeting on the Dutch-German frontier on October 17. Hitler put off invading the Netherlands after being told that the Chamberlain government wished for German participation in a European League of States against Bolshevism.

Schellenberg had used an English transceiver supplied by Major Stevens, call sign ON 4, to arrange meetings with "the English Secret Service Station." In the Hague, a Dutch company known as NV Handelsdienst voor het Continent was regularly visited by Schellenberg, who knew it was SIS cover, at Nieuwe Uitleg 15. It had a secret phone number, 55 63 31, for use in emergencies. A German secret agent, F. 479, had been in Holland for years and, under orders authorized by Hitler, initiated the talks with Schellenberg or, as he called himself, Hauptmann Schemmel.

When he first met the British agents, Schellenberg wore a monocle in the style of Schemmel, and was taken aback when he saw that Best also wore a monocle. The German spymaster blushed when Best asked: "I say, old boy, why'd you wear a monocle like me?" Schellenberg mumbled that he was shortsighted in one eye. In fact, the monocle was a device for signaling Professor Max de Crinis, director of the psychiatric department of the famous Charity Hospital in Berlin, who came to the secret talks in the role of a key voice of "German opposition." He took cues from Schellenberg, who removed the monocle with his left hand if de Crinis was to stop talking, and removed it with his right hand if he needed de Crinis's support. It all seemed like comic opera to Vera: a top psychiatrist guessing what Hitler's spymaster meant when he fiddled with his monocle in a Dutch restaurant while conning British agents.

On October 30, 1939, Dutch intelligence sent a trusted officer, Dirk Klop, to drive the psychiatrist and the spy chief to Captain Best's Amsterdam office, where it was agreed that peace negotiations would begin upon Hitler's arrest. A protocol was sent to Menzies and solemnly passed along on October 31 to Alexander Cadogan at the Foreign Office, who noted laconically in his diary: "Something is going on in Germany."

Three days later, Admiral Sinclair died. Menzies became tempo-rary SIS chief. Vera now fully understood Churchill's opposition to this becoming a permanent appointment. He suspected the secret ne-gotiations were being run by Menzies for Lord Halifax in his search for peace.

The day before the bomb explosion, the British agents had been in the Dutch town of Venlo, where they asked Schellenberg, in his guise of Schemmel, to produce one of the anti-Nazi generals next day to negotiate terms for peace. The German agreed. But after the at-tempt on his life in Munich, Hitler ordered that Best and Stevens be seized from the neutral Netherlands. Schellenberg waited in Venlo for a teatime rendezvous at the Café Bacchus on Thursday, November 9. The two British agents and their Dutch intelligence colleague, Lieu-tenant Klop, arrived in a large American Buick, crossed the street, and were ambushed by armed SS men in civilian clothes. There was a shootout. Klop was hit. With Best and Stevens, he was bundled into a car and whipped smartly across the border to Düsseldorf, where he died.

Goebbels broadcast the boast, "Our SS nabbed the European head of the [British] Secret Service. Our boys made themselves out to be enemies of the state and so lured this piece of garbage to the border."[1]

Sir Alexander Cadogan, unaware of the coup, wrote in his diary that same day: "Saw Menzies. General did NOT come into Holland today." The general was the German requested by the British agents as proof of the alleged anti-Nazi plot. Next day, Cadogan's diary coldly noted: "Our men who met, or were to have met, Gen[eral] yesterday bumped off." Four days later, Cadogan endorsed a proposal by Lord Halifax and a senior Foreign Office man, Sir Orme Sargent, for an "anti-Comintern pact" that would ally Britain and Germany with Italy, Japan, and Spain against the Communist International.

Later Berlin announced the capture at the Swiss border of "a Dutch bomb maker" named Georg Elser, said to have confessed to working for British intelligence. Best and Stevens were interrogated daily by the Gestapo, and the reports were sent each evening to Hitler. The long interrogation reports were rewritten in three times the nor-mal print size for Hitler, whose eyes were "very weak," according to

Schellenberg's memoirs. Best and Stevens survived, and SIS reports on their activities were embargoed until 2005.[2]

Vera believed Best and Stevens gave the addresses in London of intelligence organizations, and of SIS locations in Europe, plus cover names of commercial enterprises used for espionage, and methods of coding and communication. Intercepted telegrams and analysis of German newspapers flown from Stockholm by a special RAF weekly flight to England yielded German counterintelligence references to "a new sabotage department" preparing for a Special Operations Executive.[3]

On Wednesday, November 22, 1939, Goebbels declared "the English swine" were to be publicly tried for attempted murder and "the British secret service's time-honored method of assassination." Goebbels listed as other typical victims Tsar Nicholas II, King Alexander of Yugoslavia, and Lawrence of Arabia.[4]

The names of British, French, Belgian, and Dutch intelligence officers were announced by Berlin radio. Churchill, infuriated, wrote another powerful plea to have his man, Admiral Godfrey, put in charge of the SIS. Cadogan called it "a tiresome letter" in his diary and expressed the appeasers' widely held opinion that "Churchill ought to have enough to do without butting into other people's business." The confirmation of Stewart Menzies as C was supported by Lord Halifax. The Holy Fox was exploring another "peace channel" through the Italian dictator Mussolini. Opposition to Churchill was orchestrated by that éminence grise of Imperial Defence, Sir Maurice Hankey. Menzies won the day.

A message was sent from Berlin at the end of 1939 over the SIS wireless set given by Major Stevens to Walter Schellenberg for the very purpose of communicating with London. Schellenberg used the free service to boast that there were really no British secrets left. He twisted the dying old lion's tail with a final signal: "Negotiations . . . with silly and conceited people are tedious. A hearty farewell [from] your affectionate German Opposition. The Gestapo."

# 14

# The Phony War Ends

During the ominously grim winter of
1939–40 the only real violence was wind and rain. Vera had won her
spurs but felt lost in the confusion of London politics. She escaped
into "utter irresponsibility," and a sense of removing a heavy load from
her shoulders at her Winchelsea retreat. She was not to learn until
many years later that her visits to the Netherlands had been logged by
the internal security service MI5 as "suspect." Informers claimed she
had paid a large sum of money to German intelligence to secure protection for a relative. The accusation had to be seen in the light of the
SIS fiasco in the Venlo affair, but it lingered.

In high places, similar doubts about Colin Gubbins festered in
the secret alleyways of Whitehall. Gubby in Paris tried to help Czech
and Polish underground armies. He was ordered not to talk to the
Czech intelligence chief, František Moravec, who was exclusively under the wing of the SIS.

Churchill tried to shake off the phony war paralysis. Britain and
France had the power to revive the life of the Poles, Czechs, and Slo-
vaks, he declared in a broadcast on November 12, 1939, warning "bla-
tant, panoplied, clattering Nazi Germany" not to underestimate a
country that might seem hobbled by its adherence to democratic procedures. Parliamentary countries "had to bear with these difficulties."
But there must come an end to shilly-shallying, to nursing vain hopes
of avoiding "the fearful storm about to fall upon the business-like calm
of the masses of our wage-earning folk."

Vera was told by a political opponent of Churchill, Josiah Wedgwood, that the speech moved him immensely. Wedgwood was a
Labour member of Parliament who had fought gallantly in the

1914–18 war and now recognized, as did increasing numbers of wage earners, that Churchill spoke for a constituency that crossed party lines. But Chamberlain took the speech "very badly," according to his staunch supporter at the foreign office, R. A. Butler, who condemned Churchill's words as "vulgar."

Vera came out of hibernation and was seen regularly in both Paris and London. She met Stringbag at Simpson's on the Strand, where they had a lunch of rare roast beef, prefaced with a Pimm's and accompanied by a decent bottle of what Stringbag called "plonk." Good wines could still be found. She asked him to join her again on the coast, for a belated Christmas celebration.

There had been black frosts and snow, gale-force winds and lashing rain on the English Channel. They spent days in bed, sipping the champagne she always brought over from Paris and reading the heroic adventures of Captain Horatio Hornblower, the dashing hero of C. S. Forester's naval sagas. "I felt snug as a bug in a rug," she later told Mary Stephenson. "Life was normal."

There came one of those sudden breaks in the weather that make English winters bearable. A watery sun broke through the clouds. Huddled in duffel coats, they tramped around Winchelsea. The port town had been continuously attacked by French raiders for decades. King Edward I in 1288 left his other domain in Aquitaine to design Winchelsea on the gridiron principle of the French *bastides*. Vera clung tight to Stringbag as they walked along Dead Man's Lane through which, 570 years before, French marauders poured to butcher and rape worshippers at the adjoining church. Winchelsea men had retaliated with barbarous attacks against French coastal ports. The old stories of invasions in both directions had made a deep impression on her, perhaps more than someone English-born, for she had learned the town's history as an adult, whereas children took it all for granted. Stringbag saw the narrow English Channel between his island home and continental Europe as an airman: "Just a hop, skip, and jump from Normandy," he said. "The English and French are better qualified to cross it than Germans." He was laughing. "God, we're so smug in England, aren't we? We live in the past, glorifying our defeats." He added, "Take me, for instance. Promoted from a snotty to an acting temporary sub-lieutenant (Air) in the Royal Navy Reserve. What a title!"

"What's a snotty?" She giggled.

"A midshipman, not old enough to wear a gold stripe round my sleeve. I had brass buttons so I couldn't wipe snot from my nose. In Hornblower's day, midshipmen were snotty-nosed little devils. Too many admirals still live in that other age."

Under the jocularity there were flashes of bitterness. A midshipman friend had been lost aboard the aircraft carrier *Courageous*, sunk by a U-boat in the Bristol Channel. "He was eighteen," said Stringbag. "Whenever he was on leave, if he stayed at London hotels, he'd be mistaken for a boy working the lift. He got fed up and told one snobbish old dowager the lift was out of order. She had to walk up the stairs." Stringbag had been at Scapa Flow, the prime naval anchorage off the northern tip of Scotland, when Churchill had inspected the defenses. Scapa was closer to Norway, a potential hideout for German warships, than it was to London. Churchill had called for an urgent update of antisubmarine nets. Before dawn on October 12, 1939, a German submarine penetrated the Scapa Flow defenses and sank the battleship *Royal Oak*. "She went straight down with an admiral and eight hundred men," said Stringbag. "Bodies are still pinned to the sea bottom by a lash-up of netting so corpses won't wash up and demoralize us." He gave her a straight look, and added, "I'm not supposed to know what you're up to, but get your outfit to pull their fingers out."

Later she recalled his words precisely because she had been angry with herself for blaming the illusion of a phony war on Britain's indifference to tragedies unfolding in Europe. It was easy to forget the deadly war at sea.

She asked Stringbag if the gap in their ages made a difference. He said no. She was looking ahead: maybe she might want his children after this bloody war was finished. But maybe, by then, she'd be past childbearing age. Then she thought: Well, he can't see further than tomorrow. Before he left, he confided that he was to rejoin his squadron on the carrier *Glorious*. "We might be flying Gloster Gladiators." That sounds rather posh, she thought, until he added: "They're biplanes like the Swordfish. Don't worry, they don't sink."

She returned to Paris. There Gubby, now a lieutenant colonel, was briefing an aide about to return to Romania. She stifled a wish to go back, just once, without feeling hagridden with responsibilities. Instead she studied the French countryside as a battleground for secret operations. She was back in Paris at a Russian nightclub when Gubbins gave a Scots Highlander's version of *Stanka razin* and *Ochi chyornye*, delighting his Czech and Polish companions. They were less amused by Gubby's inability to meet their military needs. Poles were getting a thousand kilos a month of supplies through their own clandestine courier service across the Romanian border. Czechs used courier services from Austria through Yugoslavia. Krystyna Skarbek was in Budapest with Andrzej Kowerski, preparing escape lines for both Poles and Czechs seeking training and arms to fight the Nazi occupiers. Kowerski had won the highest Polish military award, for bravery in resisting the German invaders in Poland's only motorized brigade, before he signed up for covert warfare.

French secret service needs had to be correlated with the British. Vera met with Gustave Bertrand of the French Deuxième Bureau, the buyer of Hans-Thilo Schmidt's Enigma manuals. That was almost nine years ago now! Bertrand wanted to keep the Polish code breakers, whose old chiefs, Gwido Langer and Maksymilian Ciezki, had at last rejoined them. Bertrand finally agreed to let what he called "his Poles" cooperate with English experts, provided these came to France, which was awkward.

Enigma messages began to be broken at Bletchley on January 17, 1940, and this could not be disclosed. Alan Turing, Bletchley's codebreaking genius, had to come to Paris. He had built his own electromagnetic improvement on the Polish bombe, which was limited to recognizing the fingerprint of the German sender of an enciphered message. Turing had a pretty good idea of the extreme danger to Britain if Polish code breakers fell into German hands.

The French distrusted Gubbins's efforts to work with representatives of secret armies in Paris. Peter Wilkinson, a twenty-six-year-old Royal Fusilier and a member of MM-4, returned to Central and Eastern Europe and now came back with confirmation that it would be risky to build up resistance forces so long as communications had to go through the SIS. He took charge of a fresh bunch of military aides attached to British embassies, to avoid using communications with London that were under the thumb of the SIS. It was only half a solution.

Gubby returned to London, expecting a lightning German attack that would seize some unsuspecting neutral—probably Norway, because Churchill had used his naval authority to bottle up the Skagerrak as a passage from the Baltic Sea for German warships and to lay mines around Norway. Berlin denounced this as a provocation.

French citizens, not nervous politicians but workers descended from those who had waged the Revolution, with close links to other trade unions in Europe, reported that the monster of the German military was coming out of its winter sleep. Vera again met the young Catholic medical student Rolande Colas. She reminded Vera of her younger self when they talked quietly at a sidewalk café on rue de Varennes, near the Musée Rodin. Rolande said her working-class contacts spoke of "a fool's paradise" among the elite, and of communist-led trade unionists who took the realistic view that France was not equipped, morally or militarily, to withstand the German invasion that their German comrades said was imminent. At the final rendezvous, Vera wrote for Rolande a London address, a small apartment at 5 Rutland Gate in Knightsbridge. "If you ever get to London . . ." said Vera. The look in Rolande's wide blue eyes made further words unnecessary.

Another rebel against French complacency was a student and an acknowledged genius, Wolfgang Döblin. A German Jew, he reminded Vera of her own double life, for he now served in the French army as Private Vincent Doblin, abandoning his name of Wolfgang. He was the youngest doctor of mathematics in the history of the Sorbonne. The Deuxième Bureau's Gustave Bertrand wanted this twenty-three-year-old genius to concentrate on codes instead of serving on the Maginot Line. Bertrand asked Vera to persuade the young man to leave the army; his release was already arranged. Doblin said he must remain at his post, but he agreed to continue his original research into "predicting the outcome of events that are subject to random disturbances." This later became known as probability theory. He was way ahead of his time. He would have been invaluable to Bletchley. Vera felt he would have moved to England to meet "a challenge of highest importance," but French authorities simply refused to part with him.

Vera complained to Gubby that holding back Doblin was criminal misuse of his patriotism. Gubby said: "Same everywhere. Stupidity at the top!" U.S. Ambassador Joseph Kennedy had just proclaimed that "top people" like the English House of Lords still wanted to deal with Germany.

In Paris there was another House of Lords, self-styled, made up of amateurs whose inanities inflamed Noel Coward. He told Vera: "I'm here because I asked Churchill to get me into intelligence. He misheard. He said if you want to use your intelligence, join this outfit. My plan was to use my silly-ass reputation as cover, to gather intelligence during my foreign tours. Instead, I'm stuck among upper-class twits above Schiaparelli's shop, larking about with daft ideas about bombarding Berlin with postage stamps. They carry Himmler's profile to suggest he's getting ready to replace Hitler, and they have sticky bottoms to stick to the pavements, provided it rains!" Noel Coward extracted himself from this Paris House of Lords. It dropped dead carrier pigeons with messages attached to their legs from RAF planes, hoping German counterintelligence would conclude there was a widespread anti-Nazi resistance movement. Several hundred live carrier pigeons were also dropped, but only five flew home, with rude messages from the Germans. Noel Coward said shameful departmental warfare was fed by such wild schemes: "More effort goes into confusing each other than outwitting the enemy," he said. He was later put to work in the improvised intelligence agency run by Bill Stephenson.[1]

By March 1940 Vera truly felt that idiocy ruled. The French wanted to bomb Russia's Baku oilfields to deny supplies to the Germans, but they refused to bomb German installations for fear of stirring up trouble on their western front. On March 23 Gubby was told to prepare for what Churchill called Independent Companies before changing his mind. Not wanting to be accused of interfering in military matters, he redefined the units as amphibious Strike Forces, which put them under his naval authority. The units were hastily thrown together to resist any German invasion of Norway. Veterans of mountain warfare were hastily assembled. Churchill went to his favorite corner of the Admiralty, naval intelligence, from where Commander Ian Fleming got a submarine, *Truant*, to insert the first Strikers into Norway.

The German assault came on April 9, 1940. An enemy air umbrella spread far out to sea, and when *Truant* surfaced near the Norwegian coast, it was hit by German bombers. Peter Fleming, Ian's brother, was dropped into Norway with two Strike Force sergeants "to blow things up." Peter was an adventurer who had walked with his Russian girlfriend across Tibet.

Hitler had a precise timetable for conquering Western Europe. The secret was hardly a secret. He had laid it out at conferences, and details leaked but were treated as part of a war of nerves by the disdainful leaders of untouched democracies. Vera and Mutual Friends, however, saw his Norwegian campaign as the opener, and tried to plan for insurrections. If the Nazis occupied France, a spirit of resistance could be lit. The vast majority of French workers were tillers of the soil. They would take readily to closework. She returned to France, whose leadership was unmoved by the Norway disaster, and motored into unexplored corners, forming plans. Her notes were in shorthand, to be transcribed later. "Doodles," she called them, like: "Domfront. Medieval town on hilltop. Perfect base for operations in Suisse-Normande: original family home of Oliver Cromwell. Locals say: Town of misfortune. Arrive at noon. Hang by one o'clock. May the Hun be the first modern victim."

She foresaw underground roles for Paris friends, some of them young women, some of them newspaper correspondents and businessmen impatient of paperwork, self-reliant, and independent-minded. German occupiers would find it impossible to cover every stretch of the long and open coasts along the English Channel, the Atlantic, and the Mediterranean. Nor could they seal France's two mountainous frontiers with neutral Switzerland and Spain. For secret agents who already knew France, penetration ought to be easy from England. She was to return there one more time before the Germans arrived in June of 1940 — too late, however, to move to England the Polish code breakers still held in France.

She was in time, though, to see the German victories in Western Europe that would sweep Churchill into office as prime minister.

# 15

## "A Gigantic Guerrilla"

Vera wore a London air-raid warden's arm-band, in anticipation of German bombing, when she listened to defeatist talk in Parliament's debate on the loss of Norway. The debate on Wednesday, May 8, 1940, seemed to her to consist of ditherers in the House of Commons until Leo Amery pointed at Prime Minister Chamberlain and echoed Oliver Cromwell's despairing cry in this same place in the seventeenth century: "You have sat too long for any good you have been doing. Depart, I say, and let us have done with you. In the name of God, go!"

Chamberlain went. But Winston Churchill became prime minister amid such hostility that Vera prayed he might last long enough to convince President Roosevelt of Britain's will to resist. Hugh Dalton persuaded the Labour Party to agree to a coalition government at a weekend by the sea in Bournemouth that resembled a beer-guzzling Whitsun holiday until Lloyd George declared, "Britain's prospects are hopeless," and swung opinion against Dalton.

In Parliament on Whitmonday, a tremendous ovation greeted ex–prime minister Neville Chamberlain. Bill Stephenson later groaned to Vera, "Hitler will hear about this through the BBC and figure we're packing it in."

The defeatist undersecretary to Lord Halifax at the Foreign Office, R. A. Butler, proposed "a little publicity committee" to fill the press with letters calling for peace. The BBC scarcely mentioned the news of Churchill's premiership. A week earlier, Colin Gubbins had joined a special group hurriedly put together to fight by any means in Norway. With him was Kermit Roosevelt, a son of President Theodore Roosevelt. Kermit was a long-standing member of The Room at 34

East 62nd Street in New York and its first observer of closework in action. His impressions were tremendously important if Britain was to win support from President Roosevelt.

Vera's informants reported, accurately as it turned out, that King George VI wanted Halifax as prime minister, not Churchill. Wasting no time, Churchill flew back and forth across the Channel in an effort to keep France in the war. "I was appalled to see him arrive at Le Bourget in an unarmed little two-motor Avro Anson," said Vera's French secret service link, Louis Rivet. "The airfield was without defenses."

Churchill's bodyguard, Detective Inspector W. H. Thompson, remembered saying that the task ahead was enormous. "I hope it is not too late," replied Churchill. "I am very much afraid it is." Not knowing how long his premiership would last, he quickly made Hugh Dalton the "minister of economic warfare" to cover for a supersecret Special Operations Executive. Dalton could now unofficially appoint Vera as its spymistress. Both positions were fragile. Vera's role was known to a trusted few. Dalton was excluded from the next War Cabinet meeting when the service chiefs said they had highly secret papers to discuss. Dalton got his hands on the "secret papers." The secrecy consisted of General Henry Pownall's attack on Churchill for acting like a "Super Commander-in-Chief."[1]

Churchill's refusal to behave like a supremo reminded Vera that there was no value in fighting tyranny at the cost of your own values. When the *Daily Mirror* pleaded for the exclusion of appeasers, Churchill replied that appeasers were everywhere. To knock them out would be "a task impossible in the disastrous state in which we find ourselves." He needed to convert them: defeatists, appeasers, pro-Germans, and all.[2]

He kept his temper when called a dictator by Sir Samuel Hoare, First Viscount Templewood, Lord Privy Seal and for the moment secretary for air. On May 25, 1940, the chiefs of staff considered "a certain eventuality," meaning the fall of France. Churchill was quoted as crying out, "God save us!" and he promptly moved Hoare to Spain as ambassador.

Churchill slowly united what he termed his "quarrelsome family" by evoking historical memories of when the country fought with its back to the wall. A precious young man sneered at Churchill's government coalition with socialists and later said, "I spent the day in a bright blue suit from the Fifty-Shilling Tailors, cheap and sensational-looking, appropriate to the new government." John "Jock" Colville had once toasted "the king over the water," the Duke of Windsor in France, still dealing with Hitler. Winston made Colville a secretary, and overnight a Churchillian.[3]

Churchill warned Roosevelt, "You may have a completely subjugated Nazified Europe established with astonishing swiftness, and the weight may be more than we can bear." Such messages went through the U.S. embassy and were leaking to Berlin. On May 17, 1940, a Mutual Friend, Major Jack Dermot O'Reilly, trapped an American code clerk, Tyler Gatewood Kent. He had been passing copies of the secret exchanges to Captain A. H. M. Ramsey, who was distantly related to the royal family. Ramsey confided the material to Anna Wolkoff, a White Russian who blamed the Jews for her family's exile in London. She gave copies to the Italian embassy, which radioed everything to Rome where it was passed through the German ambassador, Hans von Mackensen, to Berlin. "The messages went direct daily to Hitler—priceless information that he read word for word," testified the German spy chief Walter Schellenberg at his postwar trial.

Early one morning, O'Reilly's men burst into a flat at 47 Gloucester Place in central London, arrested Tyler Kent, and retrieved 1,929 U.S. embassy documents from a cabinet plastered with THIS IS A JEW'S WAR.

O'Reilly had been helping Vera prepare for covert action. He knew her contact Nadya Letteney, who now worked alongside Anna Wolkoff's Jewish aunt and examined intercepted foreign radio traffic in a secure section of His Majesty's Prison, Wormwood Scrubs. "The most secret of secret places," Nadya said later. She had charge of translators toiling in cells from which convicts had been expelled. Anna Wolkoff's aunt specialized in sub-Carpathian Ukrainian. She had gone to Finland "for her son's wedding." Finland was invaded by Russia. The aunt escaped to Norway, where she asked the British legation for a British warship to pick her up because of her top-secret work. She was politely told, "The Germans are invading." So she crossed into Sweden and was put on the RAF courier flight to London. Vera was asked to speak with this fast-moving woman. She had been helping

Jews escape from Poland through Lithuania to Palestine. She was cleared of all suspicion. Nadya Letteney had sensed the leaks came from the U.S. embassy.[4]

Vera saw the resolve to follow democratic procedures in wartime as a weapon, not a weakness. The mole, Tyler Kent, was the twenty-nine-year old son of an American diplomat. A clerk in the U.S. embassy code room, he felt FDR and Churchill were betraying Americans. At the time, only 3 percent of Americans wanted to enter the war, according to polls. In January 1940 Anna Wolkoff, whose father had been an admiral in the Russian czarist navy, told Kent that Jews had deposed their family. The mischief began. "A terrible blow!" Breckinridge Long, a U.S. assistant secretary of state, wrote in his diary: "Our every diplomatic maneuver exposed." Ambassador Kennedy prudently phoned President Roosevelt to say that, if the United States had been at war, Kent would have been shot. For once, FDR did not disagree with Kennedy.[5] If the intercepted FDR-Churchill exchanges had been publicized in the United States, they could have destroyed Roosevelt. Laws enacted by Congress were designed to keep America out of European disputes. Churchill needed him to win an unprecedented third term in the 1940 presidential elections. Ambassador Kennedy "came under electronic surveillance," noted Winston's son Randolph Churchill. "We had reached the point of bugging potential traitors and enemies." Randolph later parachuted into Yugoslavia to join Tito's clandestine armies.

Kent was later tried at the Old Bailey in October 1940. A jury took twenty-five minutes to find him guilty, and he was sentenced to seven years. All was done in secrecy. "Catch a spy but never talk about it," Vera learned from counterespionage experts.

From May to June 1940, Gubby's guerrillas had fought as best they could. "Our last battle was covered by all the fighter aircraft that the RAF had to spare — two biplane Gloster Gladiators," he told Vera after he escaped. She was glad to have him back as an ally. They had been working in the close relationship of a loving brother and sister. He was a forty-four-year-old junior colonel whose Strikers fought a vastly superior enemy by blowing up transport facilities. He brought back Norwegians whose work as SOE agents would later destroy material that German scientists regarded as the means for making an atomic bomb. Gubby had proved primitive methods could undermine the most advanced technology, and Kermit Roosevelt admiringly reported this to FDR.

Vera marveled at English eccentricity. Alexander Cadogan at the Foreign Office wrote in his diary: "Situation awful . . . Our [Chiefs of Staff] living in days of the Zulu war." Yet newspapers still advertised holidays on the south coast. The *Evening Star* devoted six of its eight pages to horse races. The *Daily Mail* promoted the Isle of Wight as "peaceful, carefree" until France fell and the "carefree" Isle of Wight requisitioned its holidaymakers' steamers to rescue Allied armies at Dunkirk. In the week ending June 4, 1940, some 861 ships of all shapes and sizes crossed the English Channel to snatch 224,586 British and 112,546 French troops out of the jaws of the enemy. "I feel happier now that we have no more allies to be polite to and pamper," said King George VI. News vendors echoed this new sentiment by scribbling on billboards: ALONE AT LAST!

The swift improvisation of fishermen, small boats, and amateur sailors for that extraordinary armada appeared to Vera to confirm her faith in the improvisations of ordinary folk for closework. Chamberlain's appeasement-minded government had left France with the impression that Britain would prove perfidious in war. Rodolphe Lemoine, who had played such a key role in the Enigma saga, had angrily disappeared back into France, jumping ashore from a Royal Navy rescue ship when its boyish skipper called him just another French deserter. Vera worried that the German-born Lemoine might give away the Polish code breakers still in France, but he was to turn up in difficult circumstances, still loyal to her.

In a prison camp in France, Vera's old friend the Earl of Cardigan wrote in his diary that his German captors boasted of driving the British into the sea. He recalled a *Punch* magazine cartoon from the 1914–18 war: "The Turkish Sultan told the German Kaiser that the British at Gallipoli had been pushed into the sea. Replied the Kaiser: 'You fool! That's their element!'"

"A gigantic guerrilla" was proposed by Churchill, "specially trained troops of the hunter class to develop a reign of terror down these [enemy-held] coasts with at first a 'butcher and bolt' policy, a vigorous, enterprising and ceaseless offensive against the whole German occupied coastline."[6]

But when France sued for peace, there was a silence in Whitehall that Vera described to Bill Stephenson as "sinister." He noted, "Powerful Whitehall influences say it's only Churchill's hatred of Hitler stops us making peace with Germany." To counter this, Stephenson moved to New York to form an organization to reinforce Churchill's reign of terror from that neutral base. Churchill took Lord Halifax's contaminating presence out of Whitehall and parked his "Holy Fox" in Washington as ambassador. Churchill was making the best use of the worst appeasers.

"Bring in the United States, I don't care how," Churchill demanded. The short way was to prove SOE's value. On June 18, he broadcast to Americans: "If Hitler wins and we fall, then the whole world, including the United States, including all that we have known and cared for, will sink into the abyss of a New Dark Age, made more sinister, and perhaps more protracted by the lights of perverted science."

This was a reference to secret German work on an atomic bomb, using heavy water available only in Norway. The French secret service had brought out an existing stock of 185 kilograms in twenty-six cans. Colonel Louis Rivet, who was in England to run French secret armies, said he needed somewhere to hide the cans. Vera looked for space at Wormwood Scrubs, but the old prison was starting to burst with secret agencies. The only totally secure storage site, said Vera, was beneath the throne.

She was remembering the cheeky remark "The safest place to keep a secret is under His Majesty's bottom" uttered by a Dr. Whynant of the Uncommon Languages Group at Wormwood Scrubs, who dealt with intercepted correspondence and came from the Ancient Guild of British Museum Curators.

"What did Dr. Whynant mean?" Vera asked Tony Samuel, the Jewish banker who had met her as a military intelligence corps officer studying the sabotage of Romanian supplies to Germany.

"Windsor Castle!" he replied.

Sure enough, Windsor Castle was the repository of the world's entire stock of heavy water, later used by Tube Alloys, the cover name for British nuclear research, shared with the U.S. to produce the first atomic bomb.

On July 16, 1940, Hitler ordered the invasion of Britain. Dr. Dalton was declared answerable to Parliament for Special Operations Executive. Vera still carried the tin helmet, gas mask, and armband of a volunteer warden while raising "the gigantic guerrilla" in France. Churchill's opponent, Neville Chamberlain, drafted the SOE charter as Lord President of the Council in the War Cabinet. Old Umbrella had wanted peace. German terror bombing made certain he would not capitulate. With tears in his eyes, he gave SOE his blessing, and died soon after.

# 16

## The Lips of a Strange Woman

In an open two-seater 1924 Humber convertible with the coachmaker's plaque implanted in the running boards and a throttle lever on the wooden steering wheel, the bluff multimillionaire Wall Street lawyer William J. Donovan sat beside the pretty young flying officer of the Women's Auxiliary Air Force driving him through the English countryside on his first wartime secret mission. He had been chauffeured around London in sleek limousines. He had called upon King George VI, who stuttered a gracious welcome, had met the dandies who fronted the official secret intelligence services, and had listened to hearty commanders speak of bashing the Hun. He felt more comfortable in this khaki-camouflaged jalopy bouncing along narrow winding lanes during one of the unofficial holes in his official schedule.

His secret forays were made under skies that had never been so blue, perfect weather for streams of German bombers pulverizing the cities. His pretty young driver said a version of a fighter used in the 1914–18 war was in the aerial battles overhead: the Boulton Paul Defiant. From her description, he wondered if she was also a pilot. She said, "The Defiant's only gun turret is behind the cockpit. You can only attack an enemy bomber after you've already passed the bastard."

Donovan was fascinated by Vera Atkins in her trim sky blue uniform and by her underworld of scruffy, baggy-trousered, wild-haired, and unpaid or underpaid amateurs, who fiddled with bits of metal bicycle tubing for guns, faked horse manure to conceal explosives, or wired big radio valves in a colossal decoding machine hidden inside the most hideous of Victorian country mansions. He was getting a different picture from the one painted during splendid dinners in what was left of London's fanciest restaurants. Donovan was more encouraged by this untidy scene than by the stuffed shirts of a crumbling British empire that he detested. And he liked the absence of any bull from his blunt-spoken escort.

On Sunday, July 14, 1940, William Joseph Donovan, WJD, left New York on the *Lisbon Clipper*, a Pan-American flying boat bound for the United Kingdom by way of Portugal. President Roosevelt had been waiting until SOE's charter was signed by ex-premier Chamberlain. The show of British unity was important, even if Chamberlain's part in the charter was kept secret from the public.

Vera had been mining a rich vein of human resources: highly trained airmen escaping from Europe. There were more downed RAF pilots than those still flying. A senior Air Ministry friend described a moment in the cabinet during the Battle of Britain: "The chief of RAF Fighter Command, Hugh Dowding, looked as if he was going to hit Winston. But all he did was hand him a graph. In ten days, Fighter Command would be wiped out."

Squadron leader Bill Simpson, shot down over France, became one of Vera's assets. French farmers had wrapped his badly burned body from head to toe in sheets, allowing maggots to eat away dead flesh. Despite horrendous facial scars, missing nose and ears, eyes bulging from the loss of surrounding lids and skin, shriveled hands bent into birdlike claws, he escaped to England, where he found Vera. His wife, unable to bear the sight of him, left. There was no way to hide his appalling injuries, and instead of returning to France as an agent, as he wished, he became a talent-spotter. He found Virginia Hall, who replaced Tyler Kent at the U.S. embassy. She became an SOE legend. Disguised for a time as a news correspondent in Vichy France, she led a guerrilla army, unhampered by Cuthbert, her name for the wooden prosthetic for her missing lower leg.

Such recruits were law-abiding citizens until a barbaric enemy brought out a taste for mayhem: "Ruse and treachery, the bomb, the dagger, an original and sinister touch which leaves the enemy puzzled." The words were Churchill's. "There are many kinds of maneuver in war, some only of which take place on the battlefield."[1] On July 8, 1940, he told Lord Beaverbrook: "We have no Continental army which can defeat German military power." The one sure path to victory was to "set Europe ablaze."[2]

While walking with Elder Wills through Hyde Park, Vera said, "Women are best at such clandestine work." The two came upon the small brick palace of Kensington, glistening in pale afternoon sunshine through a soft rain. It seemed as if nothing had changed and horse-drawn carriages would come rolling into sight at any moment. Instead, taxicabs were parked along one side of the palace. The black boxlike cabs could turn on a dime in burning streets, and now trailed water pumps. The palace lawns were vegetable allotments. Two little princesses, one the future queen Elizabeth II, were in Brownie and Girl Guide uniforms, peering into the engine of an army truck.

J. Elder Wills, an RAF veteran of World War I, worked among BBC producers, writers, and filmmakers, and was a scenic artist at the Theatre Royal, Drury Lane in London. He invented spy gadgets; his workshops expanded, some in august locations like the Natural History Museum, others in pubs like the Thatched Barn roadhouse. In 1940 he was with the British Expeditionary Force in France when that country surrendered. Wills escaped through Dunkirk and still limped from his wounds. What Vera called his "cussedness" was indicated in his prewar movies, including *Song of Freedom* with Paul Robeson. He now staged deadly deceptions. He agreed about the suitability of women for closework.

"Sex discrimination and class divide this country," she continued. "It hampers full use of the working classes."

He gave her a sideways glance. "Churchill's given the workers a voice in cabinet. But he's never really liked Hugh Dalton."

"Why?"

"Winnie sees him as a socialist who betrayed his upper-class origins."

"Winston's changed his mind," said Vera. "Like he's changed his mind about lady killers." Her face closed up again.

"She never came closer to revealing how high she'd climbed in a world run by men," Elder Wills said later. He never really knew until later who employed his theatrical talents in producing mockups of airfields and military bases to deceive the enemy.

Whatever Vera might say about Churchill's present tolerance of Hugh Dalton, she knew he was still resented by others. Lord Halifax, while foreign secretary, pretended Dalton did not exist as minister of economic warfare, with the real power to oversee secret operations.

Instead, Halifax had dictated hilarious guidelines for hiring spies: "If obliged to recruit local secret agents, His Majesty's representative should consult the following list that defines matters which can be discussed with the authorities of the country concerned . . . and activities which cannot be discussed officially by a more or less legitimate outfit to produce unusual and respectable weapons, the gentlemen concerned all being in uniform and therefore not to be confused with saboteurs." Halifax had insisted that the Secret Fund could not cover the costs of "a cloak and dagger outfit."

What made Vera a woman "bitter as wormwood" were not these past follies, but the news that Stringbag was lost at sea. She blamed senior intelligence officers for ignoring warnings from a twenty-one-year-old Bletchley analyst, Harry Hinsley, who regularly sent information to the Admiralty's Operational Intelligence Centre (OIC) in the Citadel near Trafalgar Square. His disembodied lower-class accents fell upon the deaf ears of pukka naval officers. During the Norwegian campaign, he deduced that German warships were breaking out of the Baltic into the North Sea from listening to enemy wireless instructions that were repeated on other frequencies never before used. The Citadel failed to pass along his conclusions to warships at sea. The German battle cruisers *Gneisenau* and *Scharnhorst* ambushed the British aircraft carrier *Glorious* on the evening of June 8, and quickly sank it. There was not even time to launch its planes.

Vera, not being listed as next of kin, knew few details until Ian Fleming belatedly broke the news that Stringbag was missing. Hinsley had been ignored "as some snotty-nosed kid basing hunches on broadcasts picked up in a hut in the countryside." But his rare ability to reach accurate conclusions from scant details was shared by Churchill, who brought Hinsley into his inner circle. The country bumpkin became a senior intelligence guru.

She received more bad news. Vincent Doblin, the German mathematical genius who joined the French army instead of working on codes, had remained at his Maginot Line post to delay advancing German troops and cover his comrades' withdrawal. The Jewish refugee who might have helped solve Enigma shot himself with his last bullet rather than risk capture as a disposable Jew.

Vera began chain-smoking Passing Cloud cigarettes. Stiff shots of Scotch also helped. She faced problems like those confronting Gubby, who had to plan homeland guerrilla resistance to potential invaders. "I had a blank check, but was there money in the bank to meet it?" he said later. "We had perhaps six weeks before German forces could launch a full-scale invasion."

Vera, too, had a blank check but little visible cash. Stephenson, who had known Bill Donovan since the 1914–18 war and trusted him despite his wish to see the British Empire dismantled, impressed on her SOE's immediate task: win U.S. covert help. She must show Donovan everything about SOE. But what was there to show? Everything seemed jerry-built, except at the old Royal Arsenal in Woolwich, known as The Shop. It produced a time pencil-fuse and yellow soft plastic that a saboteur could drop on a fire or blast with a shotgun. Nothing would happen unless it was properly detonated. Tommy Davies had snatched platinum worth a fortune from under German noses during the rush out of France, and this generated some funds. In and around Bletchley, university undergraduates were paid a pittance while they sweated over German codes.

She sensed that these humble measures impressed Donovan more than the Whitehall grandees who tried to "duchess" him while the wine flowed at private dinners. His legal career had taught him the artfulness of con men. Britain was in a mess now as a result of leaders like Lord Halifax, who, as recently as July 1938, had told Hitler's adjutant, Fritz Wiedemann, that the foreign secretary "would like to see the Führer entering London at the side of the King amid the acclamations of the English people."[3]

# 17

## Sabotage Etcetera Etcetera

$V$era was briefed on SOE's special task by Bill Stephenson between his two secret visits to the United States, the first in March–April 1940, when he was identified as a company director representing the British Ministry of Supply and teamed up again with William J. Donovan, who argued for a coordinated intelligence service during meetings in the Manhattan apartment known as The Room. On his second visit, Stephenson was identified as a British civil servant. His casual Canadian style disarmed those Americans described by the canny Scottish industrialist, Sir Harold Mitchell, as "extremely hostile to Britain." Mitchell was hurrying home through the United States to become military liaison officer with Polish armed forces in England. All the occupied countries now had governments-in-exile along with their own military missions in London, a drab locale but less smug than Paris.

Vera had to win over Donovan, also courted by Stewart Menzies, whose confirmation as C, the SIS chief, had been unsuccessfully opposed by Churchill. Stephenson, an outsider and colonial, was looked down upon by Menzies and his class. Vera hoped they would hide their distaste for Donovan, the Irish-Catholic opponent of British imperialism.[1]

Vera was disclosing to Donovan the hidden world of SOE, while the SIS and its political supporters argued against SOE plans to foment mass uprisings. Steve Mackenzie of the SIS recalled being warned to "stay clear of Stephenson" during a wartime assignment to the United States. The white man's clandestine methods might inspire black, brown, and yellow imitators in Arabia, Africa, and Asia. This fear was evident when SOE's Sir Douglas Dodds-Parker, who ran secret wartime operations in North Africa, had to abandon a postwar lecture tour in South Africa because the white government at the time was afraid black Africans would adopt SOE methods. Dodds-Parker planned to discuss how SOE's black African agents in Ethiopia had defeated white Italians.[2]

Vera memorized Stephenson's thumbnail sketch of Donovan: "Born in Buffalo, N.Y.; destined for priesthood; fought in Mexico with the U.S. cavalry; commanded the 1st Battalion of the 69th Infantry Regiment, the 'Fighting Irish,' in the 1914–18 war; given a Congressional Medal of Honor and the nickname Wild Bill; wants America to lead the world, not retreat into isolationism. Roosevelt is sending him on first 'special intelligence mission' to measure British resolve."[3]

Donovan's known opposition to FDR's domestic policies made him unlikely to draw the attention of German spies monitoring Pan-Am flights. In any case, Hitler wanted his spies to focus on the Duke of Windsor, dithering in neutral Lisbon over promises to restore him to the throne if he would collaborate. Donovan passed through Lisbon unnoticed, and in London slipped away at intervals from the official agenda. He said nothing about what he was looking for, nor why he was really here. There was an unspoken understanding between him and Vera. He liked her steely beauty, her long lustrous black hair tied in a bun, her dark intelligent eyes peering at him from under her RAF cap. The trim blue uniform advertised an athletic figure. He was amused that she had to drive him in a series of old cars, including the snub-nosed Humber of which she said, "It's as old as I am." She was thirty-two, but looked younger.

Donovan saw a countryside enjoying rare sunny weather. Outnumbered RAF fighters scrawled chalk-white contrails across the bluest skies. Some peculiar planes were sent up against the enemy. When Vera talked about them, her understated humor reminded him of others who had faced death with stylish buffoonery. When comrades were lost, RAF aviators gathered around the piano, quaffed beer, and sang this lament:

> So lift up your glasses steady,
> Let's sing in this vale full of woe,
> Let's drink to the dead already,
> And here's to the next one to go.

He surmised that Vera's polite avoidance of personal matters concealed a burning rage. The nation was not fully mobilized. There were not enough uniforms nor guns to go round. Yet the land was as calm on the surface as when Drake played bowls while waiting for the Spanish Armada. Flying Officer Atkins put on a happy face at the edge of the precipice. Not knowing her origins, Donovan supposed the English were not as uptight as he thought.

Vera treated him as part of what Stephenson called "a conspiracy of patriots" in Astor's Room, named after Vincent Astor, a more likely choice for this secret liaison because of his English family connections. After the original deliberations in 1927 the small apartment on East 62nd Street became The Room. Intelligence was collected and compared among well-to-do adventurers: banker Winthrop Aldrich; David K. E. Bruce, later to liaise with SOE; publisher Nelson Doubleday; and Astor himself, who knew how to trace foreign plotters through bank accounts. "Every spy needs money," he told FDR at his 1933 presidential inauguration. By mid-1940, FDR was astonishing intimates like his treasury secretary, Henry Morgenthau, with proposals for blowing up oil wells and blockading Europe by sea, "leaving a small channel open directly to England." Such schemes, Morgenthau recorded in his diary, "left me with my breath taken away."[4]

Roosevelt tacitly approved Stephenson's creation of a coordinated intelligence agency in New York, but wanted his own man to scrutinize SOE, not some notorious Anglophile. Donovan was a critic of the Imperial Preference that hampered U.S. trade with British colonies. FDR's political caution was not always understood. "U.S. aid is not possible," Churchill wrote despondently the previous Christmas Day. "Roosevelt is our best friend, but I suppose he wants to be reelected and U.S. isolationism is the winning ticket." FDR assigned a man thought to be anti-British "to discover if we were worth supporting," recalled Ian Fleming's nominal spy chief, Admiral John Godfrey, in his memoirs. America First isolationists would not suspect Donovan of favoring the British.

Donovan suspected that SOE would take years to be up and running properly, especially in the face of Whitehall opposition. "Delay is the last weapon in the bureaucratic armory," he observed from his own experience in interdepartmental wars. Churchill was half American. Perhaps this accounted for the miracles of improvisation revealed by

Vera. She took initiatives that exceeded her apparently low-level authority. Donovan wondered if the name Vera Atkins was a cover, it was so commonplace.

She drove him along a route taken months earlier by three charabancs loaded with Captain Ridley's Hunting Party, which was the cover for the Government Code and Cipher School (GCCS). The name struck Donovan as hilarious. The route went by way of Marble Arch and some forty-seven miles northward along the old Roman road known as Watling Street, through the villages of Great and Little Brickhill, turning left at Fenny Stratford, then right onto Bletchley Road. He had been here before. Now she wanted him to catch the authentic flavor of the country's largest clandestine operation, in which participants were ordinary folk with no pretensions. She paused for a pub lunch at the Shoulder of Mutton in Old Bletchley and was amused by his reaction to young men in patched tweed jackets and girls who mostly looked just young enough to attend finishing schools. She drove on, beyond an extraordinary muddle of stables and huts where code breakers worked. Donovan was unprepared for off-duty youths in gray flannel trousers who played cricket beside a muddy lake that was overlooked by the mansion called BP for Bletchley Park. BP was strategically located at the intersection of railways running north, south, east, and west, and was easily accessible by train for its Oxford and Cambridge "boffins," many of them long-haired and gaunt, who shambled through BP's barn doors. Old buildings had been converted and muddy lanes paved over by a Mr. Faulkner who turned up in full foxhunting gear on his way to ride with the Whaddon Chase Hunt. Mr. Faulkner had been instructed to take to the grave the secrets he knew. He was developing a priceless property: its core would become known as ULTRA.

Donovan was entrusted with an overview of work that revolved more and more around Enigma. It was clear that U.S. industrial capacity was needed. Even machines as elementary as teletypes, which shift increasingly heavy loads of text at high speed between outlying signal stations and analysts, were unobtainable in sufficient quantity. For starters, GCCS and a network of secret departments required four seven-line and two twelve-line Hellschreiber machines from America. The threat to shipping increased or decreased according to how speedily Bletchley deciphered orders to U-boats. On April 26, 1940, for instance, a German trawler had been targeted so that up-to-date Enigma documents could be seized. A prolonged period in which U-boat signals were not read could be disastrous. U-boats were built and launched faster than the British could sink them. U-boat torpedoes caused a near-fatal drop in supplies to the United Kingdom.

Vera showed Donovan the contrast to the extravagances of his own country, which was far more advanced in the efficient management of production lines. BPers, cloaked in wooden sheds by heavy blackout curtains, made their calculations with pencil stubs and stumbled around in apparent disorder. Ian Fleming devised a scheme to capture a German rescue boat with another naval Enigma on board. A German bomber, gently forced down onto an English field, was restored for flight with a crew of British closework experts disguised in the gear of captured German fliers. The commandos were to crash it in the English Channel. When a German air-sea rescue boat arrived, the operatives were to board it, remove everything to do with the latest Enigma, kill the German rescuers, and make sure Berlin did not detect a ruse. Ian's code name for this was Ruthless. Vera feared even someone nicknamed Wild Bill might see Ruthless as the brainstorm of a crackpot. She redirected Donovan away from Ian Fleming to the less flamboyant Colin McVean Gubbins.

Gubby coolly answered questions about the MM-4 mission in Poland, knowing Donovan might be asked to carry out work abroad for SOE, under cover of U.S. neutrality. Gubby joked that he had learned from Donovan's Irish cousins how to wage guerrilla warfare. This neutrality shrank in significance after Hitler's Anti-Comintern Pact with Japan. Americans were inclined to see the pact as a bulwark against communism. Gubby was happy to be assured that Donovan felt it foreshadowed a global war against the Allies.

Vera had mesmeric powers at her disposal. They were unnecessary in the case of Donovan. The day before his departure, Cadogan, now Churchill's chief adviser, coolly noted, "Quite a good air battle over Dover. C has news that invasion will come. Hope so."

This defiant spirit reinforced Donovan's endorsement of collaboration with SOE when he joined President Roosevelt in the New England countryside on August 10, 1940. He had flown back to New York in a camouflaged British Sunderland flying boat. SOE seemed a model of future coordination for the U.S. navy and the U.S. army, which absurdly hugged their own secrets and took turns—the navy one day, the army the next—submitting decrypts of intercepted signals. Churchill had decreed, "All Secret Service reports about affairs in France or other captive countries are to be shown to Major [Desmond] Morton. [He] is to see everything and submit authentic documents for me in their original form."[5]

Donovan discussed with FDR the inclusion of open-code messages to agents in regular BBC transmissions. Vera had suggested a similar use of FBI shortwave stations and commercial transmitters. For example, the Christian Science radio station WRUL broadcast as far away as the Middle East and the Balkans, regions where Allied agents might soon be needed. Hyphenated Americans born in Europe, with language and other skills, could train in SOE methods on the U.S.-Canada border, at a base to which recruits would travel unhindered from the neutral United States into wartime Canada. FDR quietly approved of these and other proposals, provided they caused him no political embarrassments.

During the last week of Donovan's British tour, "Sabotage Etcetera Etcetera" described the agenda of a War Cabinet attempt to get rid of Hugh Dalton as economic warfare minister. Vera had avoided any mention to Donovan of this maneuver to bring SOE under the influence of the Well-Bred Horse Brigade: he might have lost faith in SOE's future. Even Cadogan was infuriated by the game playing. "This is sloppy," his diary noted. "We want to get someone to take a grip on Sabotage &c. and pull it into shape."

Dalton, nicknamed Doctor Dynamo for his wildly energetic resolve to arm European workers for mass uprisings, rekindled fears of "Bolshie revolutions." He wanted Vera to "take a grip" on sabotage and other imaginative ways of creating mayhem. She did not have to advertise her position in the hierarchy with epaulets of high rank and impressive titles. She was not required to consult Churchill and stride through the corridors of power, as did many who wished to create an illusion of their own importance. In handling Donovan, she succeeded through quiet force of personality in pulling things into shape.

# 18

## A Year Alone

Only Vera could give Donovan an overview of SOE's rapid but seemingly chaotic multicellular growth by the time he returned to London in December 1940. He knew more about her: that she favored brand names in cigarettes and booze, that her aura of a well-brought-up English gentlewoman did not mean she came from a distinguished family nest, that she could escape through hostile borders, that she charmed foreign intelligence chiefs, that she had shot her way out of a pro-Nazi Romanian border trap, that she was compiling a register of potential agents, each of whom she personally vetted even after recruiters questioned them.

"No woman in the history of espionage has exercised such power," Stephenson recalled telling Donovan before they flew together from New York into England's dismal Christmas season. It was the middle of what was later called the Year Alone by the islanders, who felt isolated by the enemy. Stephenson, busy with operational plans to undermine the enemy in the Western Hemisphere, was also worried by Britain's detention of enemy aliens. It would be a disaster if Vera were scooped up along with Jewish refugees, to be shipped to detention camps in Canada. Even if SOE spoke to the right people, it still had powerful enemies at home.

"Document her as your permanent secretary," joked Ian Fleming.

Stephenson wondered later if this marked the moment when Fleming dreamed up James Bond and a secretary named Moneypenny. Bond's alias, 007, was used by British intelligence to denote Germany's diplomatic code in the 1914–18 war.

"Vera kept a lowly position, and avoided the attention of officials rounding up foreigners," Mary Stephenson recalled. Mary had moved to New York by now and was missed by Vera, whose letters were hand-carried by recruits sent to work for Bill, whose cable address was now Intrepid.

Donovan had submitted to Roosevelt a paper titled "The Way the British Government Gathers Intelligence." FDR, safely reelected for a third term, approved of Donovan's unofficial return to inspect SOE's progress.

Vera had widened SOE's scope. Free from spit and polish, scientists and skilled workers beavered away in hurriedly converted shacks, barnyards, stables, country houses, and churches. Assets called each other "chums" and improvised sleeve guns, exploding rats and cow dung, decoy footprints, and false identity cards. Estates like Beaulieu, the family home of Lord Montagu, became bases for training in field-work. SOE, said Donovan, stood for Stately 'Omes of England.

Donovan was fifty-seven and heavily built. Stephenson, forty-four, still looked like the bantamweight boxer he once was. Their support of Vera angered SOE's enemies in Whitehall. The Air Ministry had already refused to "provide planes for assassins." Vera had to point out that agents parachuted behind the lines to organize resistance armies and not to eliminate Nazi leaders.

Vera could now show Donovan a spreading network of secret bases where would-be agents underwent rugged physical training. She took him to the Scottish estate of Sir Harold Mitchell, whose family castle hosted the Polish president in exile, Wladyslaw Rackiewicz, and General Wladyslaw Sikorski, whose soldiers trained there for subversive operations in German-occupied Poland. Mitchell, now in the armed forces, owned coal mines, ships, and railways. One railway conveniently ran through the training grounds.

Donovan watched a nail-biting scene. Tied to the railway tracks was a blindfolded girl, Rolande Colas, who later would be memorialized by U.S. Special Forces at Fort Bragg. She was back from a brief mission in France and was taking special training to deal with dangers she understood firsthand, but for which few trainee agents were fully prepared.

For this exercise, she was told to guard a piece of information with her life. She was told a train would thunder through within five minutes. She still had time to confess. Vera, playing her conducting officer, said to the training sergeant, within the girl's hearing, "Switch the points, Sarge. I hear the train coming!"

"Yes, ma'am. Pass me the lever."

"I gave it to you!"

"You've got it, ma'am!"

"Oh shit! Where is it?"

The noise of the train reverberated. Vera shouted, "Cut the girl free!"

"Too late, ma'am. Jump clear!"

Rolande stayed silent. The train passed on the other track. Donovan had not been let in on the ruse. "If this one becomes known to recruits," Vera said briskly to a somewhat shaken Donovan, "some new level of sadistic testing will have to be invented."

Donovan met with Gubbins, who was preparing for British guerrilla warfare against possible German occupiers while "encouraging and enabling the peoples of the occupied countries to harass the German war effort by sabotage, subversion, and other methods." British defense units, short of everything, were teaching civilians to fight behind the lines at home and abroad. SOE was to deliver personnel and ordinance to occupied territories. Agents had to be parachuted "blind" until reception committees were organized by local resistance groups: there were no underground elements to receive the agent on the dropping ground, no household known to be ready to give shelter, conceal kit, and arrange onward passage.

Rolande Colas, on her first mission, brought the communist organizer Henri Tanguy, "Colonel Rol," into contact with Vera. "Communist networks grew in Europe after Stalin set up the Comintern," Rolande explained. "The best are in France. They're trained in sabotage. It's more efficient than assassination. And covert action is more humane than mass bombing, don't you think?"

Such an ethical question already bothered Ian Fleming's brother, Peter, who was back in Scotland after Norway's collapse. He fostered what he called "a Shetland bus service," shuttling agents between Norway and the islands of Shetland. Vera said a saboteur wreaked more havoc with a single cunningly placed pencil-bomb in a factory than a fleet of bombers.

"What about innocent civilians killed in reprisals?" asked Peter.

"Their numbers won't ever come near the losses of our bomber crews or the masses of civilians killed by aerial bombs," she replied.

She was thinking far ahead. Gubbins had to tackle the immediate task of building from scratch an underground army to torment any German invaders of Britain. "We must raise very small units that will melt away after a battle," he told his old chief, General Sir Edmund Ironside, now commander in chief of Home Forces. "We need an overall title, uninteresting so as not to catch attention, but necessary when filling out forms to get supplies." Getting supplies from the bureaucracy was like squeezing blood from a stone, so Gubby visited police stations to collect weapons taken out of private hands, as required under war emergency powers. He found that other such weapons had been tossed into village duck ponds or dumped in the sea. An interim title was found that impressed the police but meant nothing to the listening enemy: Auxiliary Units.

Peter Fleming described their hideouts in cellars, woodlands, farms, and badger holes as "like the Lost Boys' subterranean home in the second act of *Peter Pan*." In charge of auxiliaries was an officer from the Sixth Rajputana Rifles of India. Veterans were hauled out of retirement and blossomed as instructors and inventors of devices that would fool the enemy. Small units had to communicate without wireless sets and telephones, so "bunny runs" were reamed out between two-man underground posts. Messages in gutted golf balls were rolled through these artificial rabbit channels. Pitchforks and shotguns were shared out among elderly town clerks, lords of the manor, poachers, retired chief constables, and anyone else able to stand on two legs and swear without blushing an oath under the Official Secrets Act that he or she had a clean record.

Laurence Grand put aside his furled umbrella and the daily carnation in his buttonhole and, without visible authority, set up civilian stay-behind teams. He improvised Station XII at Aston House in Hertfordshire, an hour's drive north of London, Station IX at the Fryth Private Hotel in Welwyn Garden City, Station XVII near Hertford, and a decidedly ungodly hit-and-run unit at the Old Rectory in Hertingfordbury. Stations were numbered out of sequence to deceive the enemy. From America came pistols and ammunition. Friends there had asked what would help. Anything, replied Gubby, that goes bang.

Gubby was called a loose cannon by the hard-boiled General Bernard Montgomery, who was to become the leading British soldier of World War II. Having got his men out of France, Monty was trying to replace lost equipment while positioning his tattered 3rd Division to block the expected German invasion. Austere, crabby, and puritanical, he was outraged when an Auxiliary Unit, consisting of one elderly ex-poacher, broke into his headquarters. Monty had boasted to Churchill that the headquarters were impregnable. The old poacher penetrated the impregnable, worked his way around Monty's bedroom in a tumbledown farmhouse, and tossed a homemade Molotov cocktail — gasoline in a beer bottle — at the general's precious peach tree, incinerating it. The poacher vanished into the undergrowth. He could have been a German saboteur. Monty's coastal defenses had just been inspected by Churchill, who saw, despite Monty's claims of efficiency, a lack of troop transport but "large numbers of buses plying for pleasure traffic, up and down the seafront at Brighton." Churchill ordered Monty to commandeer the buses, in the tone of a schoolmaster telling a lazy boy to pull up his socks.

None of this endeared to Monty the concept of "dirty tricks." His opposition could cause problems if, as Donovan hoped, an Anglo-American alliance was to confront Germany. Vera decided she had better tell Donovan all he needed to know. Later she was judged to be worth a score of formal briefing sessions. As U.S. supreme commander, General Dwight Eisenhower was so offended by Montgomery as a field marshal that Ike seriously wondered if he could tell any of his American generals to take orders from him.

Vera frankly confirmed Donovan's impression that, behind the facade orchestrated for his benefit by Whitehall, there was confusion. The German air minister, Hermann Göring, had said publicly during the past summer, "I plan to have this enemy down on his knees so that an occupation of the island can proceed." By Christmas, Göring was bombing open cities.

Vera shared with Donovan the pragmatism of the grizzled old sergeants on the shooting ranges: "Shoot straight by instinct, out of your pocket or backwards between your legs and out of your arse. Unless you're in bed, put all your weight into your feet. If you are surprised in bed, don't waggle your pistol like a flabby cock. The pistol must always be your pointed finger." She added that the instructions had been slightly amended when girls became shooters. She told Donovan how escapees brought home disconnected bits of intelligence that could be assembled to fit changing pictures of conditions behind enemy lines. A simple example was an escapee's story of how he had aroused suspicion because he did not know French workingmen wore hats or berets on their heads all the time. He was lucky that he learned this from friendly Frenchmen in a bistro who guessed he was an escaping British prisoner when he removed his cap at the bar.

Vera drove Donovan to Biggin Hill, the air base near London. They talked with Jan Zurakowski and other Polish pilots who had escaped to join the RAF. Zura always spoke in a soft, almost high-pitched voice. In Warsaw he had told her how he mentally sat outside himself in dicey situations, observing his performance in the cockpit. Zura guessed her role when she said there was a need for pilots to fly solo missions behind enemy lines. He volunteered: "If I'm still alive."

In another intelligence failure, the RAF had been initially unprepared for new German tactics. Zura and his Polish comrades, in combat over England, taught lessons about an enemy who broke the old rules. Young RAF pilots, as university students and reservists, had been taught to fly in neat formations. This past autumn, enemy bombers protected by Messerschmitt 109s and 110s had attacked London as the "brain and nerve center of the British High Command." For ten days, children basked under brilliant sunshine and watched air battles directly overhead. On September 15, Churchill followed one battle from RAF No. 11 Group headquarters at Uxbridge, and asked the group commander, Keith Park, "What other reserves have we?"

"None," was Park's reply.

Every serviceable RAF fighter was airborne. The enemy had been led to believe that other aircraft must be held in reserve, since any sane defender would never commit all weapons to battle. The gamble succeeded. The tattered German air fleets retired. Only by such deceptions — in the air, on the ground, or at sea — could Britain stay afloat.

The vicious Christmas bombings saw Germany expend more quality machines and men. By contrast, Gubbins's ground-defense preparations still resorted to cheap improvisations. Vera called them Gubby's Goon Squads. She showed Donovan their training base in the Vale of the White Horse, near Swindon, on a sprawling West Country property. The stables were converted into classrooms, haylofts became dormitories, and instructors lived in the servants' quarters. "Secret sources provide small quantities of equipment," she told Donovan. "Most secret sources are country squires who should have turned them over to the authorities." Half a million old Springfield rifles from the United States were shared out among clandestine units. The squads became self-contained groups of three or four men, operating from independent underground bases, each with its own cache of arms and stores. "They cost nothing to run," said Gubby, who had joined the two. He described a false alarm after favorable tides for invasion were predicted in the English Channel and the Eastern and Southern Command received the code word "Cromwell!" This was a precautionary warning, unbeknownst to the Vicar of St. Ives in Cornwall, who mistook a fishing fleet for the enemy and ordered his church bells to be rung. The bells set off a chain reaction, comparable to the lighting of beacons from Land's End to John o'Groats in 1588 to warn of the Spanish Armada's approach. Skies were scanned for German parachutists who, it was rumored, wore nuns' habits. Eventually Dad's Army of elderly home guards was told to relax, a pair of innocent nuns was released, and the vicar went red-faced to bed.

Some twenty-five hundred RAF pilots had prevented the invasion. Zura and his fellow Poles accounted for 5 percent of these, and were credited with inflicting 15 percent of German losses. These survivors who escaped from Nazi-occupied Europe proved the essential role of rebels against a German conquest. Near Bletchley, Station XII spent on explosive devices the equivalent of $23,000 in today's money, which seemed a fortune to the impoverished SOE. Secrets were kept by deliberately separating special units and by concocting meaningless titles. It was hard even for Vera to be sure who ran what. This confounded SOE's enemies at home. Malcolm Muggeridge, the writer and a wartime spy, observed that although SOE and the SIS were on the same side, they were more abhorrent to one another than they were to the German intelligence corps, the Abwehr.

Donovan's American egalitarianism made him prefer SOE's use of people from all walks of life. London's *Daily Mirror*, the voice of the workingman, depicted the army as "overburdened by officers drawn from the privileged classes." Gubby was a soldier after Donovan's own heart. When Gubby became Vera's director of operations, he moved into quarters provided by her good relations with the owners of Marks

& Spencer. SOE became known as the Baker Street Irregulars, after the street urchins who spied for Sherlock Holmes. They were lodged on Baker Street, along with the headquarters of the large retail store chain whose chairman, Simon Marks, was SOE's undisclosed patron. Donovan had strong sympathies for the Jewish victims of Nazism and agreed with Vera that they should long ago have been supported in rebellion against Hitler. The Joint Palestine Appeal became the United Jewish Appeal, whose future deputy chairman, Sir Isidore "Jack" Lyons, came from a family long established in York. An ancestral Isidore Lyons and other Jews had been executed, their heads displayed on spikes along the city of York's encircling walls, after refusing to convert to Christianity. Donovan discussed with the current Lyons family the need to get so-called enemy exiles out of the detention camps. Their knowledge of Europe should be exploited. The help expatriate Jews gave SOE was never openly discussed. They were well aware of the anti-Semitism lurking under brass hats. Hugh Dalton told the chiefs of staff, "Covert action is too serious a matter to be left to soldiers. Whenever I try to destroy anything anywhere, I am caught in some diplomatic trip wire."

Vera could not be tripped up. Her authority was hidden. She relied greatly on personal connections. She had coaxed a sympathetic squadron leader to lend her an RAF rescue boat to plant Rolande Colas on her first mission. The girl had made her way from the coast to Paris to discuss the raising of resistance armies, and returned to rendezvous with the boat at a set time. The twelve-day operation netted hard and current facts that otherwise would have been difficult to glean. Vera later parachuted her back in, despite the objections raised by the chief of the air staff, Charles Portal, who thought there was "a vast difference in ethics" between dropping a spy from the air and "this entirely new scheme for dropping what one can only call assassins."[1]

Rolande's mission was an example of the importance of carrying out operations through personal contacts. The War Office preferred the old formula "firepower and overwhelming force." Donovan saw the wisdom of officially keeping Vera at the modest level of a flying officer, free to change uniforms and modest rank or adopt the guise of Miss Waple when screening possible agents in a Wigmore Street apartment. She attracted none of the Whitehall enemy fire that was aimed at Dr. Dalton and architects of the upstart SOE. "The worst thing that can be said against SOE's skullduggery amateurs is that 'they are not one of us,'" commented C. P. Snow, the writer and molecular physicist. He came from the unfashionable Midlands, was educated at an obscure government school, and was part of London's Jewish community. He selected scientific personnel in highly secret work. "Be thankful," he told Vera, "you don't have to leave telltale squiggles on government requisition slips."

This freedom intensified the envy of departmental rivals, who were obliged to submit everything in triplicate. Informality was SOE's grim necessity. "Grim" was not a word Donovan would have used as an old hand at impulsive action, but he understood grim necessity during a visit with Churchill that Christmas. Grim necessity sent secretaries fluttering, scooping up papers. They scuttled to where Churchill was to settle in for a night's work. He had several choices: the old tube station at Down Street in Piccadilly, which Vera called The Burrow, or the former typists' basement room at No. 10 Downing Street, which she called The Barn, or under a corner of the Board of Trade building facing St. James's Park at Storey's Gate in a subterranean War Cabinet room. Few knew beforehand Churchill's imminent whereabouts. He was a moving target. The House of Commons on the Thames was easily spotted by bombers, so Parliament sat in Church House, the Anglican Church headquarters facing Westminster Abbey. And so it seemed to Donovan that perhaps some of the ambiguities, the formlessness of SOE, the disorder and hodgepodge and anarchy surrounding Vera, were well justified.

He left London on New Year's Day 1941. Vera delivered him to an RAF flying boat at Plymouth Sound that set course for Britain's first imperial coaling port and military bastion, Gibraltar. He carried a flask of hot turtle soup, a hamper of fresh lobster, cold pheasant, Stilton cheese, and three bottles of Moselle to celebrate his fifty-eighth birthday. There followed an official silence until Roosevelt received a cable in March 1941 from Churchill: "I must thank you for the magnificent work done by Donovan in his prolonged tour of the Balkans and Middle East. He has carried with him throughout an animating, heartwarming flame."

"America was still neutral with Donovan on our side," Vera would say later. Once he was gone, she discovered, among other things, how to time secret operations by phases of the moon. "I'll come to thee by moonlight, though hell should bar the way." One of the poem-codes used by agents to encrypt messages, that line was from a nineteenth-century poem called "The Highwayman" by Alfred Noyes, which reflected a popular view of masked men robbing the rich to give to the poor. Her agents often had that rogue quality. Their accomplices were captains of small boats, submarines, and aircraft. Pilots perfected techniques for landing agents. Fliers who had to land on small meadows operated the week before and after a full moon. The brighter the moonlight, the better the ability to navigate at low altitude by following railroads and rivers to steal through hostile territory. Insertions by sea were best made when there was no moonlight at all.

# 19

## A Civil War Ends, a Nightmare Begins

"Winston Churchill is trying to end the civil war at home," said Mary Stephenson. Churchill spoke gently of his old enemy on Tuesday, November 12, 1940, when he told Parliament, "History with its flickering lamp stumbles along the trail of the past, trying to reconstruct its scenes, to revive its echoes, and kindle with pale gleams the passion of former days. The only guide to a man is his conscience; the only shield to his memory is the rectitude and sincerity of his actions. It fell to Neville Chamberlain, in one of the supreme crises of the world, to be contradicted by events, to be disappointed in his hopes, and to be deceived and cheated by a wicked man. But what were these hopes in which he was disappointed? What were these wishes in which he was frustrated? What was that faith that was abused? They were surely among the most noble and benevolent instincts of the human heart: the love of peace, the toil for peace, the strife for peace, the pursuit of peace, even at great peril."[1]

"What a week!" Vera commented to Tony Samuel. He was twenty-three, nine years her junior, and consulted her about blowing up barges along a stretch of the Danube that she knew well. In that week, German bombs blew to smithereens the nearby Sloane Street tube station. U-boats sank a record number of cargo ships and threatened to isolate Britain. Germany attacked Greece, and the RAF had one squadron of outdated Gladiator biplanes to defend it. Roosevelt was told Britain could not pay for U.S. munitions. Lord Halifax said to American reporters, "Well, boys, Britain's broke. It's your money we want."

Tony Samuel met Vera for lunch at his family's banking firm, M.

Samuel & Co. She told him that she didn't understand why Churchill was honoring an old enemy.

"Chamberlain tried Churchill's soul," Samuel replied, "but the world must see we preserve the continuities, the centrality of parliamentary and constitutional government. In 1910, Churchill's paper 'The People's Rights' led to pensions, prison reform, national insurance, job security, and the first welfare state. That made him a socialist in Chamberlain's eyes, a turncoat."

Samuel enthused about the spirit of fair play. His Jewish origins put him at risk when he gathered industrial intelligence abroad. He was the youngest son of Viscount Bearsted, and was on the Gestapo list of persons to be arrested after the occupation of Britain. His family business, Shell Petroleum, had a network of commercial agents, some of whom were also collecting information on the enemy. He said Churchill's tribute to Chamberlain would kill stories abroad about English appeasers who still put out peace feelers.

"Do you believe appeasers can still hurt us?" Vera wondered.

"Yes. Some Americans think we competed with them for German business because Chamberlain once said Britain could not survive as outcasts in Europe. Our investments were enormous. Halifax wanted control of European commerce. Winston's speech should end the acrimony. However much one citizen knows about a subject, there's always someone who knows more. He needs all of us to pull together."

Samuel mumbled. It was not what Mutual Friends called "the artful mumble of a spy." He was growing deaf. He limited his operations to the acquisition of confidential files abroad. He was in Budapest when his safe house was raided. He flushed documents down the toilet. The plumbing recycled the papers into a toilet below, where the chief investigator was sitting with his trousers down. "The fool didn't like to pick the papers out of his pooh."

"I prefer our knaves to their fools," said Vera.

"No, no. Our side would never have knaves," he joked. Then he asked her about Bill Stephenson. Mary had returned briefly to London, and she knew Samuel would be joining her husband's intelligence service. He was to be registered as G 202 while operating in Latin America.

Vera walked alone that afternoon through the bombed streets of

Aldgate, part of Worktown, a term used by Mass Observation, an organization founded in 1937 to record all aspects of everyday life. M-O's driving force was a controversial eccentric, Tom Harrisson. As a schoolboy, he organized the first national census of the great crested grebe. He studied the ways of cannibals in the Pacific, and founded M-O to help Whitehall measure the public pulse. Critics said M-O studied the masses as if they practiced alien cults. Its section on the Aspidistra Cult analyzed why potted aspidistras dotted lower-middle-class homes. Aspidistra happened to be the code name for the SOE project to control one of the most powerful transmitters in the world, for which the Radio Corporation of America, RCA, was being cautiously approached. M-O's report on an Aspidistra Cult caused hearts to miss a beat in counterintelligence, until the confusion was cleared up.

Harrisson was to parachute into Japanese-held Borneo, where he led a guerrilla force of headhunters who had an age-old tradition of collecting the heads of strangers. Harrisson ordered them to limit their hobby to Japanese heads. After the Japanese surrender, he thought it only right that the headhunters should keep the heads. For following his own rules, he was banished from Borneo. He was later killed in the crash of a Bangkok tuk-tuk.

In 1940–41, Vera combed through M-O lists for potential agents among streetfolk who scraped a living in imaginative ways. "Circus acrobats to burglars. I don't care how they made a living before the war, provided they're honest villains," she told Harrisson. His rule was that M-O should be totally immersed in the culture under examination. She asked why his snoopers did not inspect the tribes of Whitehall. He replied that Whitehall was too dense a jungle, adding that "SOE is safe from my snoopers because it's impossible to find it has any culture at all."

In the November 1940 week of nightmares, when mighty German planes bombed London, British bombers retaliated by attacking Berlin, where the Soviet foreign minister, Molotov, was pressing Hitler for an answer to just exactly when German forces would invade the British Isles.

"We had heard of the conference beforehand," Churchill told Parliament, "and, although not invited to join in the discussion, did not wish to be entirely left out of the proceedings."

Ambassador von der Schulenburg's letters foreshadowed the Molotov-Hitler meeting. Moscow had accused Germany of violating the Nazi-Soviet Pact. Ribbentrop sent Schulenburg a telegram to hand to Stalin. It proposed to divide the world between Germany, Japan, Italy, and the Soviet Union. Schulenburg waited four days before giving it to Molotov, not Stalin. The ambassador shirked facing Stalin's wrath over Hitler's evasions.

When Molotov went to Berlin to ask when Germany would invade, Hitler said he was waiting for the weather in the English Channel to improve. The Soviet commissar said weather in winter never improved. What were the Nazi leader's real intentions? There was a blistering row. Then Hitler switched moods, painted the British Empire as a worldwide estate in bankruptcy, and purred, "Those who would share the plunder must not quarrel." With British bombs ringing in his ears, Molotov said the empire was evidently not so easily carved up.

Vera's sources claimed that Hitler wanted Romania before Stalin exploited it as a base for subversion throughout the Balkans. One expert observer, now in London, Charles "Dick" Ellis, met her at a rendezvous on the little bridge in St. James's Park. He remembered telling her that Romania was lost. Hitler had dispatched a military mission to Bucharest. "To the world their tasks will be to guide friendly Romanian relations," Hitler told his High Command. "The real tasks will be to protect the oil and protect the southern flank in the coming war with Russia."

King Carol abdicated and moved to Switzerland. Vera thought it useful to talk again with him. She had the excuse of visiting her acquaintance in Lausanne, the widowed mother of young King Ananda of Siam, now Thailand. Ellis advised caution. "The Swiss intelligence service is the best. It needs to be, for a small country bounded by hostile forces. It's a means for us to meet friendly Germans on neutral ground."

Also in November 1940, Gubbins was formally installed at Baker Street. On the twenty-fifth came the first official SOE directive: "to undermine the strength of spirit of the enemy forces, especially those in the Occupied territories." This was one in the eye for the SIS, whose loss of networks had prompted Churchill's anguished cry "I'm cut off from all intelligence out of Europe."[2]

Vera obtained Hitler's directive for Operation Barbarossa, dated December 18, 1940, "to crush Soviet Russia in a quick campaign before the end of the war against England." One version came through her U.S. consulate friend in Berlin, the former Associated Press correspondent William Russell. This was repeated by the U.S. commercial counselor, Sam Woods, who regularly met informants in a Berlin moviehouse. Woods had been in Rome when Mussolini boasted that his mighty navy made the Mediterranean "an Italian lake." British ships would be expelled from the sea lanes to vital Mideast bases.

On the day Churchill honored Chamberlain's memory, twenty Swordfish biplanes crippled Mussolini's battle fleet at its Taranto base. Italian warships were sheltered in the shallow Taranto anchorage, but Swordfish torpedoes ran near the surface, guided by wooden fins jury-rigged by ship's carpenters on the carrier *Illustrious*. This had never been done before. Vera taught SOE trainees the lesson: "Timing, surprise, imagination, and audacity can undermine a more powerful enemy."

The Japanese embassy in Berlin dispatched naval experts to study the operation. Six weeks later, U.S. Ambassador Joseph Grew in Tokyo reported rumors of plans for a surprise attack on Pearl Harbor.

If the Japanese learned from Taranto, so did Vera. The Ruthless plan to capture an Enigma machine had been delayed by lack of independent means of communication. The Swordfish raiders had kept radio silence, but air gunners trailed long wire aerials for telegraphing in Morse code. SOE had no signals system independent of the SIS or the Diplomatic Wireless Service, which retained control of wireless communications. Vera asked Fleming, planner of Ruthless, for help. He found her some coils of aerials used by the navy's ancient Walrus amphibians. Vera prepared her own wireless operators to use such long aerials.

In that dark November, Vera learned of other simple ways to overcome a lack of sophisticated gear. Boy Scouts, and those with special skills who were called King's Scouts, bicycled messages when bombs cut telephone lines. Wearing her air-raid warden's armband, she asked one biker why dummies of Guy Fawkes were still pushed through the streets, just as before the war.

"There are three words you need to know about Guy," was the cryptic response. "Ask old man Marks at 84 Charing Cross Road."

Vera did not find old man Marks but his young son, Leo.

"Ah, yes," said Leo. "Gunpowder, treason, and plot."

"But why push Guy around in the middle of the blitz and bombs?"

"Guy Fawkes reminds us that Hitler can blow up Parliament, betray it, plot against it, but we'll hang, draw, and quarter him for it, just like we did Mister Fawkes," said Leo, the precocious young rebel.

Jews in France were already being registered and warned they would pay for acts of terror. Vera's agents must be invisible, like the paper-stuffed dummies that were part of the London scene. Her operatives must perform in separate cells, in touch only through couriers who disappeared into the scenery. Girls on bicycles. Farmworkers trudging between hedgerows. Home base would have wireless operators in the field, equipped with the kind of aerials trailed behind the outdated Swordfish and Walrus.

Leo Marks's first encounter with Vera preceded his entry into SOE. As chief cryptographer, he dabbled in psychology and wrote one movie script so grim that it was banned by censors. He would ask each girl who wanted to work on codes, "Do you do crosswords?" If they did, they were in. Leo's explanations came later. He was the Jewish genius who invented a safer option to SOE's old coding system. He produced one-time coding pads of finest silk, inserted in the lining of an agent's clothes. Random numbers were printed on the silk; each line of numbers was used for coding one message only, and was then cut off. If the Gestapo closed in, the silk vanished at the touch of a match. His silks gave an agent the chance to live a little longer, rather than swallow a cyanide pill to cheat the torturers. Later, Vera said that the agents worked "between silk and cyanide."[3]

A recurring nightmare haunted Vera during this winter of 1940–41. It reenacted a scene observed by her father, Max Rosenberg: Villagers in a graveyard at midnight, digging up a body. A pitchfork driven through the corpse. The heart removed. Garlic spread over the mutilated corpse before it was laid back in its grave. The heart carried on the pitchfork to a crossroads, where it was burned, the ashes dissolved in water, the solution drunk by children and parents. The villagers, thinking they were chased by a vampire that drank their blood after rising nightly from the grave, had followed a ritual that inspired the 1897 classic *Dracula* by Bram Stoker, a resurrection of the terrifying legends of Transylvania. Such superstitions were being spread again through Europe by Nazi propaganda against the Jews.

Her nightmare left Vera feeling isolated. Within her London circle, nobody had her uncommon insight into the Nazi mind. She had watched Count von der Schulenburg in Bucharest awakening ever so slowly to Berlin's stealthy corrosion. Now she watched Occupied France in a similar stupor. A colonial-style administration was run from Paris by the German military commander. His regional commanders negotiated with local officials. Deals were made, as in prewar Berlin, to humbug honest folk. Mimicking Hitler's early appeal for national resurgence, the authority of the delegate-general of the French government in the Occupied Territories was invoked. France would rise again through work, family, and fatherland. Vera knew people would rebel against the hocus-pocus. But informers would betray resisters. Small businessmen would rat on rivals. Article 19 of the German-French armistice, known as the surrender-on-demand clause, meant in reality that rich Jews would be robbed by those who denounced them.

A German ordinance required a census of Jews. At Tours, the Feldkommandant made Jews carry identity cards stamped "Juif." At Saint-Nazaire, René Ross, who had won medals for outstanding bravery in the 1914–18 war and again in 1939–40, was listed among Jewish hostages to be killed in reprisals. Forgotten was the French Revolution, which had removed the stigma of being called a Jew. Nazis and their sympathizers revived it — slowly at first, but Vera knew the pace would quicken. She would need to watch for little local treacheries that could destroy an SOE network.

To ease the tension that gripped agents on the night they left for hostile territory, she never permitted anyone to see on her face or in her manner anything other than the understated English way she had cultivated of handling threats with humor. She would joke with Moonlight Squadron pilots who had to creep at shallow levels across hostile territory, "Mother always told me to fly low and slow."

# "Specially Employed and Not Paid from Army Funds"

The winter's terror bombing of London for seventy-six consecutive nights in 1940–41 began a twelve-month stretch that ended when Hitler declared war on the United States in December, thinking that Japan had dealt a crippling blow at Pearl Harbor. Instead, Americans mobilized. During the Year Alone, Vera fought for scraps from the bare table of the chiefs of staff: SOE was starved for aircraft and ships until Bill Donovan's men in London, like David Bruce, were empowered openly to lend a hand. Bruce recalled: "Ill-equipped agents gave evidence of solitary courage that Vera found hard to describe except in the words of the French writer François, duc de La Rochefoucauld, 'Perfect courage is to do without witnesses what one would be capable of doing with the world looking on.'"

One agent, Virginia Hall, preferred to quote Tweedledum: "I'm very brave generally . . . only today I happen to have a headache."

Virginia worked undercover first as the *New York Post* correspondent in Vichy France. She cabled her reports like any neutral journalist. After SOE recruited her, she followed the same procedure. There was safety in this. Cable companies did not hand out Press Collect cards to just anyone. Counterespionage watchdogs expected that an agent pretending to be a journalist would have reverse-charge cables rejected at the other end. She relied on legwork and the wooden prosthetic that she called Cuthbert. Her activities became increasingly complex, in step with Vera's needs.

Virginia's prewar life might have aroused German suspicion. After studies at European universities and an intensive French-language course at George Washington University in Washington, D.C., she worked in Poland with the U.S. diplomatic service. A shooting accident in Turkey led to her acquisition of Cuthbert. She traveled through Spain to England and became a coding clerk in the military section of the U.S. embassy, where David Bruce passed her on to SOE. When Paris fell, Virginia was driving ambulances. She escaped to London, and returned after a defeated France was divided. Germans occupied the larger Atlantic-coast and northern zone, nominally governed from Vichy, whose militia did much of the Gestapo's dirty work in the unoccupied zone. Charles de Gaulle, an obscure junior French general, sounded a call to arms from London four days before the armistice, in defiance of what he called "this French state government run from Vichy."

Virginia reported, "The French are stunned by the nightmare of occupation. Acts of resistance begin as small pinpricks. Ninety percent of the population work the land, and a peasant revolution spreads." She later sheltered escaping Allied servicemen, some of whom she called her "carrier pigeons." They transported coded reports that could not be cabled. "Not," she said later, "real pigeons sent into France by the SIS, whose agents were supposed to tie secret messages to the pigeons' legs and send them home."

In February 1941 Vera directed Virginia to Squadron Leader Bill Simpson, who was still undergoing plastic surgery, his hands so badly damaged that he was never again able to write except with a pencil jammed between a mutilated thumb and the stump of the adjoining finger. But, in compensation, "I developed a precise memory!" he told me later. He trained others in memory development. "Not needed by Virginia," he said. "She already had a photographic memory."

On August 23, 1941, armed with an American passport, she took a commercial London-Lisbon flight and then a train to Barcelona. In Spain she acquired a new U.S. passport and accreditation to cover Vichy government affairs. By September 4 she was filing "think pieces" full of valuable insights. She described Vichy as "an infinitesimally small place to accommodate the government of France and the French Empire."

Virginia found that her press reports could deal with small details of everyday life, which were useful for Vera, without alarming Vichy's censors. Much could be read between the lines by SOE. She wrote seemingly harmless observations, conveying vital information: "There are no taxis at the station, only half a dozen buses and a few one-horse shays. I took a bus using gazogene, charcoal instead of gas." She contacted French farmers who had helped Bill Simpson. Some, he had told her, were abreast of Nazi activities. "Abreast is literally true in the case of a brothel keeper and her tarts," she joked later in a coded letter to Vera. She analyzed small-town newspapers that covered local affairs in revealing detail. In November 1941 she relayed an ominous item: "Dutch farmers are being resettled in Poland."

Daily broadcasts from Christian Science Radio on WRUL shortwave from Boston helped her make deductions. She cultivated Vichy officials identified as anti-German in U.S. shortwave broadcasts controlled by the FBI. Its director, J. Edgar Hoover, was collaborating with Stephenson's secret agency based in New York, and proposed the title by which it became known: British Security Coordination, BSC.

So long as America remained neutral, she had access to U.S. consular offices with code rooms through which she could communicate sensitive material. Later Bill Donovan arranged further cover for her as a *Chicago Times* correspondent, paid through the New York branch of the Bank of London–South America, and asked for her transfer to neutral Spain, where she helped Allied escapees deal with local police. After four months, Virginia protested that life in Spain was too boring and returned to France.

In the early days Virginia had about the same freedom of movement as Sam Woods, the Texan in Berlin. She had journalistic cover; he used his consular position to gather intelligence. Unlike Virginia, who concealed Cuthbert with long athletic strides during overland journeys, he was not handicapped. She found the French inventor of special oil burners used on the great ocean liner *Normandie*; he had been under pressure to work for German shipbuilders, escaped, and volunteered his expertise to the British navy.

Virginia had an apartment in Lyons, a safe haven on an escape line along which Allied servicemen who burrowed their way out of prison camps traveled to neutral territories. One downed pilot, Hartley Watlington, later said, "In her kitchen, you could pretty well count on meeting most of your friends passing along the escape route." He recalled her advice: "Say something loud in a bistro, and nobody pays heed. Whisper and a dozen ears tune in."

A Gestapo chief famously said, "I'd give anything to get my hands on that Canadian bitch!" By then she was no longer passing for a foreign correspondent, and had to operate underground among resisters who thought she was French-Canadian. In October 1941 eleven agents were caught in Marseilles, one of her regions. This was a serious blow to resistance networks in southern France. Virginia built up her own fighting units, and called in other British agents, including Peter Churchill.

Wireless transmitters might lead to the entrapment of an entire network, but Virginia conceded the need for them as SOE expanded. Vera needed SOE signal masters to sort out messages from operators in the field. The Germans were refining methods of tracking secret transmitters in France, whose huge industrial capacity was harnessed to the German military machine and needed protection against saboteurs.

Vera missed Bill Stephenson's presence in London, although he came back on short, mysterious visits. He was a priceless source of ideas. After his own escape as a war prisoner in 1918, he had plunged into a golden age of garden-shed invention. His first radio set was built in a cottage cluttered with glass valves, copper wire, and soldering irons. He had progressed to the powerful wireless sets of stamped gray steel that became the bulky means of communicating by telegraphy. His home in New York was the Hotel Dorset, in a penthouse Mary rented from Marion Davies, the widow of William Randolph Hearst. There he could talk openly with Vincent Astor and other intelligence-minded Americans. He foresaw laser-beam technology before the public had even heard the word "laser." In these hard times, he resorted to simple improvisations. If factories and freight trains were blown up, France would resort to what he called a bicycle economy. Agents on bikes would become part of the scenery.

Vera also missed Billy "because he mixed the deadliest martinis. Booth's gin, high and dry, easy on the vermouth, twist of lemon peel, shaken not stirred." Ian Fleming copied the recipe during one of his naval intelligence conferences in the U.S. and used it in his James Bond thrillers.

Vera received word from Algeria that the Polish code breakers had been evacuated there, but were sent back to a code-breaking base in the unoccupied zone. It seemed inevitable that the Enigma secret would be uncovered by the Germans if they took control of all continental France. Hans-Thilo Schmidt, the Enigma spy, had been sighted in Switzerland on a trip from Berlin. Was he now playing a double-agent role?

Count von der Schulenburg was back in Moscow, and in touch with Vera. The idiosyncrasies of diplomatic life allowed officials from one side to bump into those from the other at lavish receptions. This allowed him to pass letters to an intermediary for dispatch in a British diplomatic bag. The dangers of interception were multiplying. But another rich source of essential intelligence had opened up: Imperial Censorship.

This came about through Lord Tweedsmuir, better known to President Roosevelt as John Buchan, the author of spy novels. As governor-general of Canada, Tweedsmuir proposed during the period of U.S. neutrality "to slip down inconspicuously to discuss delicate matters" with FDR, who wrote back, "I am almost literally walking on eggs. I am at the moment saying nothing, seeing nothing, and hearing nothing." Lord Tweedsmuir took a train to New York for "a medical check-up" and met Roosevelt at Hyde Park.

This was the last great espionage adventure for Tweedsmuir. The Scotsman was a committed Zionist, his name later inscribed in Israel's Golden Book. FDR agreed to direct U.S. transatlantic air and sea postal services through Bermuda and Trinidad, colonies under tight British control. Girls sent from Britain had been trained to open and reseal packages without leaving a trace. Tweedsmuir died at the age of sixty-four, at a bad moment in 1940 when his knowledge of covert action was needed in a burgeoning U.S.-U.K. intelligence alliance. The records were never released in Britain, but government archives in Bermuda contain messages exchanged between Stephenson and Imperial Censorship, specifying which letters or cargos from North America to Europe should be scrutinized, leading to an abundance of useful intelligence.

Vera learned of German plans to mobilize slave workers and hitch French factories to the production of weapons and munitions. Time was needed, though, to improve sabotage devices, time to persuade French industrialists to make things easy for SOE demolition experts. Postwar compensation was guaranteed by BBC broadcasts incorporating a phrase of the French manufacturer's own choice. Some occupied French ports built U-boats; this provided swift access to British trade routes, reducing the need for German ocean raiders to follow longer and stormier lanes through the North Sea and around Scotland. SOE battlefields were extended to countries with coasts capable of penetration. Norway was closer to British northern bases than those bases were to London. Norwegian agents were already operating there. Denmark was reached through Sweden. Holland produced Joop Westerweel and Joachim Simon, who sent Jewish escapees through Andorra.

Most urgently, Vera wanted to use the young New York editor she had met in Berlin, Varian Fry. At the age of thirty-two, he moved to France to help Jewish refugees threatened with extradition to Nazi Germany under the infamous surrender-on-demand clause that was agreed upon by Vichy after the French surrender. Nearly four million refugees were squeezed into the unoccupied zone. In Marseilles, Fry began to plan an American Rescue Center, enraged that the French defeat received less press attention in New York than the World's Fair. Vera located Fry through Stephenson's agency in New York. She needed Jewish mathematicians and scientists who could be put to good use. "The Nazis stupidly threw away the very talents needed to develop new weapons," she recalled. Another new agency, MI9, collected intelligence from Allied servicemen trickling home. MI9 escape routes, to remain secure, were kept separate from Fry's organization. Fry had priceless help from a Viennese cartoonist, Bill Freier, who purchased blank identity cards from tobacco shops, inserted an imitation of the rubber stamp of the local prefecture to give the ID cards an official gloss, then wrote in false names and backgrounds. Fry himself learned tricks of the subversive trade, and a new career awaited him when he was finally forced to leave France.

The U.S. embassy in London watched coded correspondence from U.S. legations in Europe that might help Vera. This was arranged by David Bruce, who had backing from those who agreed with the damning conclusion reached by Ian Fleming and Admiral Godfrey after trips to Washington: "There is no U.S. Secret Intelligence Service. When Americans refer to their SIS, they mean the small and uncoordinated force of special agents who travel abroad on behalf of government departments. These agents, are, for the most part, amateurs without special qualifications." Until Donovan got his own spy service, the *New York Times* was, Fleming wrote, "more reliable, faster, and cheaper."

In London, Vera kept small rooms in shabby hotels for some administrative work. Gubby used offices vacated by His Majesty's Prison Commissioners in the Marks & Spencer complex. Outside 64B Baker Street there was now a brass plate labeled Inter-Services Research Bureau. Each occupied country in Europe had its own intelligence group, and their liaison officers dealt with the bureau's country section representatives.

Young Leo Marks joked that he was hired by SOE only because it was thought he was related to Marks & Spencer, and could get the owners to provide SOE with more accommodations. His job description as "specially employed and not paid from army funds" illustrated the difficulty many had in pinning down who came from what department to work where.

Vera had a mental list of "double-rankers," servicemen in civilian clothing. Ben Levy, a prominent playwright, was "specially employed" when he was posted to New York under a false name. He presented himself at BSC as "Mister Charles." A secretary said, "Oh, you must be Ben Levy." After that, he was never confident about security, especially when running agents into Albania by sea.[1] Lord Halifax in Washington knew Bill Stephenson as "Mister Williams." Such precautions caused the sort of muddle that was also useful in shrouding SOE and BSC activities from their enemies at Whitehall. Vera did what she pleased "within the constitutional spirit of SOE, which is to break the rules." Stephenson's main offices in Rockefeller Center were flagrantly shared with Bill Donovan.

Donovan was named coordinator of information in an interoffice memo scribbled by FDR with the request "Please set this up confidentially." Under this shroud, Donovan returned to London. He found Vera in "a broom cupboard" among the cluster of Baker Street offices happily remote from Whitehall. SOE's main switchboard was also designed to mislead, plugged into exchanges geographically wide apart in a public telephone system that all subscribers used, dialing the first three letters, followed by numbers: WELbeck, AMBassador, ABBey. SOE numbers were secret, and unauthorized callers were mystified when sidetracked to some innocent subscriber.

Young officers who fancied joining SOE were informed: "You do not go to Baker Street. You are invited." Vera told Donovan, "It's like a club unlike other clubs. Women can join. The membership commit-

tee looks you over, in an office at the Horse Guards or a room somewhere in central London." She knew Donovan was not fond of clubs
confined to England's ruling class. King George VI's brother-in-law
David Bowes-Lyon and officers of the royal household were members
of SOE, but it was one club open to street hawkers, too. Its administrators were bankers, but it was not accountable to any board of directors.

Enormous financial backing was being mustered for Donovan's
equivalent to SOE. He saw how Vera had to beg for crumbs. She was
anonymous, and unable to state her case for U.S. funding. Yet there
was growing American goodwill as Londoners were seen to emerge
from the 1940–41 aerial bombings with heads unbowed. Money and
arms could have been raised by Mrs. Miniver, a stiff-upper-lip Englishwoman venerated by Americans since the release of a popular movie
whose propaganda value, said Churchill, was worth a battle fleet. She
was sent on North American lecture tours, but could say nothing
about SOE's plight. There was no real Mrs. Miniver. She was played by
a columnist, Jan Struthers, who before the war wrote in the *Times*
about the simple joys of London life, of a country home in Kent, and
nothing more worrisome than flighty parlormaids and a hubby who fell
asleep behind his newspaper after dinner. In wartime, Americans believed her to be Mrs. Miniver, plucky housewife, gallant mom, holding
up against the Hun. The Roosevelts had her stay at the White House,
and Hollywood turned Mrs. Miniver into Greer Garson.

Donovan asked about Ian Fleming's Ruthless. "It was buggered
up," Vera said. "Bletchley needed the latest German navy version of
a three-rotor Enigma. We made the wreck of a twin-engine Heinkel
flyable. We called in Charles Fraser-Smith, who had managed the
Moroccan royal family's farmlands. He was in an English village working on Q gadgets, named after the Q gunships that are disguised as
trawlers to trap U-boats. We robbed an old airship base near Bedford,
forty minutes by motorbike from Bletchley. We took flying gear from
crashed German airmen. Fleming was in Dover to direct the operation. Then it was scrapped. We had no control over SIS wireless signals, and these were monitored by the Germans, who might figure
Ruthless was a decoy to capture one of the latest Enigma machines.
Then the cat would be out of the bag."

The cat, of course, was Bletchley's breaking of Enigma codes, and
the incessant demand for the latest German versions. The dispute

over control of wireless communications came to a head. While SOE's messages were decoded by the SIS before being passed on, the deputy SIS chief, "Uncle Claude" Dansey, could hold back information. Dansey accused SOE of loud bangs that drew enemy attention to his own operations. Vera had yet to believe that any such operations were possible after the SIS debacle. Secrecy protected the bungling of all intelligence agencies from public exposure. Vera needed U.S.-made equipment manufactured to SOE's designs. Fraser-Smith designed new kinds of wireless transmitters and transceivers, but he was hampered by shortages of materials and qualified workers.

It was not easy for Donovan to see behind the security screens. Vera had said her family records were lost in the 1940–41 bombing raids. There was no way to disprove this. Donovan was now used to local customs of discretion and understatement. "Very heavy attack on the city" was all that Alexander Cadogan noted of a raid that almost incinerated St. Paul's Cathedral.

Vera contrasted Cadogan's verbal brevity with his formal title of Permanent Undersecretary and Therefore Principal Official Adviser to the Foreign Secretary. She said, "The Brits hide behind long titles and few words." Cadogan used two words for terror bombers: "Dirty dogs."

The bombing that broke the 1940 Christmas truce brought Donovan firmly on Britain's side. After SOE finally wrested control over its own system of signals, Vera insisted that messages be kept short. Long-windedness gave the enemy time to home in on agents, which almost terminated the Polish countess Krystyna Skarbek, known to Vera as Madame Marchand and later as Christina Granville.

# 21

# "She Could Do Anything with Dynamite Except Eat It"

Poland's agony intensified. Vera turned from the discouraging distractions of interdepartmental warfare to draw strength from the Polish countess's bravery and ingenuity. Krystyna worked alone to bring out surviving Polish servicemen. For an underground army rising from the rubble left by the German onslaught, she smuggled in supplies, using her own resourcefulness. Her reports from inside Poland made painful reading for Gubby, scarred by his inability to keep his word to arm Polish guerrillas. Air drops were planned, but the withholding of suitable RAF planes delayed the missions.

Krystyna Skarbek was born in May 1915 on a large family estate outside Warsaw. She had been a rebel at school. "It was Catholic, and I had a Jewish mother," Krystyna said later. "That was as bad as having divorced parents. I was stigmatized as 'unruly' after I set fire to a nun."

She regularly climbed mountains as a youngster, got to know all the ski instructors at the winter resort of Zakopane, and smuggled cigarettes, tobacco, and Polish vodka across the frontier for fun. The experience was proving more useful now than good marks.

She had first arrived in England in 1940–41, the twenty-five-year-old wife of Jerzy Gizycki, whose ambition to write adventure stories had taken them to East Africa. "I was walking down Pall Mall and got talking with a man I'd known in the East African Rifles," Jerzy said later. "He asked if I was doing anything and I said no, just bored in a publishing house. He said, 'They're looking for dumb asses like you to jump out of airplanes into France.' And he gave me an address. There was a stony-faced woman there, attractive but cold as charity, and that's pretty chilly. I know now that she was Vera Atkins. She listened to me, and when I said I spoke French, she said, 'Well, doesn't everyone?' and I thought she was an idiot because everyone doesn't speak French. I was leaving when she said something in French slang that made me come back. She'd been checking me out. She gave me someone to see at a place that sounded like Bare Arsehole. It was Blair Atholl on this duke's estate. Sergeant majors shouted orders like, 'Kill the bastids!' I saw no sign of parachutes."

Jerzy needed no parachute. He was "specially employed," in the same way as Kavan Elliott, British Agent D/M 97, whose son Geoffrey was unable to document his activities until the twenty-first century. Jerzy took commando training, was sent to Paris as a soap salesman for Lever Brothers, and was told to sit tight.

Krystyna was interviewed by a Major Gielgud. She later discovered that he was the brother of Sir John Gielgud. The major was delighted by the clarity and detail of the reporting from this astonishingly attractive young woman. Krystyna said the Germans behaved like bullies when they moved in packs, but pissed in their pants when separated from their pals, and shat in their pants if attacked singly. She proposed, with great passion, ways to reinforce Polish morale, and to let them know they were not forgotten. Gielgud passed her over to Vera. The two spoke the same language: sabotage, subversion, scare the shit out of the Germans. Krystyna said she was able to return to Poland by skiing over the mountains. She could send back reports through Budapest, where she had friends who were able to travel freely in Hungary, and even Austria.

Vera arranged for Krystyna to be based in Budapest, and to be paid the equivalent in today's money of $10,000 over a six-month period as a news correspondent. Payments would go through the bank account of the *Manchester Guardian* writer Frederick Voigt. The money originated with George Taylor, the thick-skinned and wealthy Australian businessman who helped finance closework.

Krystyna first worked with Andrzej Kowerski, running escape lines for Polish and Czech servicemen on their way to England to resume the fight. Her sexual allure allegedly drove a potential SOE agent to despair when she rejected his advances. He threw himself into the Danube. "Fortunately," Vera noted acidly, "the Danube was frozen."

Krystyna wanted to install a mobile radio news station in Budapest that broadcast in Polish. She understood the importance of getting as much accurate information into the country as possible. She first returned on skis, and gathered details of disorder within the German ranks during five weeks of constant travel. Krystyna scooped up a ragbag of detailed information that contradicted Whitehall's impressions. She reported: the German army and the Gestapo detested one another; there had been a massacre of some ten thousand German soldiers from Bavaria when they had tried to rebel against Berlin's High Command; about one hundred Poles were shot dead every night in Warsaw. The Polish people only needed weapons to rise up against their German oppressors. There existed an estimated 100,000 armed men in eighteen militant resistance groups. Their few arms were either stolen from German depots or gathered from massacred Polish officers. She identified German army units moving eastward to what she had heard called "the Russian front." But the countess failed in the one thing dearest to her heart: she could not persuade her Jewish mother to leave Warsaw.

Her husband, Jerzy, meanwhile sent a message to Vera, whom he knew only as X-3, saying he was fed up, had nothing to do in Paris except dodge the Gestapo, and above all missed Krystyna. He was told to make his own way to Istanbul and report to Gardyne de Chastelain.

Gardyne had first parachuted back into Romania, knowing the ways of Marshal Ion Antonescu, who had declared Romania's Nazi Iron Guard the only recognized political party. Gardyne hoped to mend a two-year break in communications between the Romanian resistance and London, but local police picked up his three-man team. He was released when he said he had come back to make peace with Antonescu and preempt a Russian attack. He left by sea for Istanbul, where he was attached to an intelligence section at the British legation. He knew Krystyna's movements, but was unable to disclose them to Jerzy, who was encouraged to try his hand at some local espionage.

Krystyna made six crossings from Hungary over the mountains to Poland, and another eight crossings through Slovak frontiers. She gave a comprehensive picture of munitions moving eastward on the

German rail systems. She described a wagon that appeared to carry a "gassing chamber." She reported on U-boats under construction in Danzig. On January 24, 1941, the Hungarian police arrested her and delivered her into the hands of the Gestapo. She denied the accusation that she had British friends, and insisted she was a writer and broadcaster. She chewed her own tongue until blood spilled over her clothing when the Gestapo seemed ready to move from rough questioning to torture. Between bouts of coughing, she said she suffered from tuberculosis. A sympathetic Hungarian doctor confirmed this. She was released and, thumbing her nose at the Gestapo thugs who thought she had furtive reasons for knowing the British, went straight to the British legation. The minister, Sir Owen O'Malley, told her to get out of Hungary before worse things happened, and issued her a British passport in the name of Christina Granville. Then he hid her in the trunk of his official car and drove her over the border into Yugoslavia. In Belgrade, she delivered to the British legation the last of the microfilm she regularly collected from Poland, hidden in her ski gloves.

O'Malley said that Krystyna was the bravest person he had ever known. "She could do anything with dynamite except eat it."

Later she was awarded the George Cross, the highest recognition for bravery given to civilians. In her final large-scale action, she led her French maquisards in a spectacular military battle. When the French maquis entangled German reinforcements sent to help repulse the Allies on D-day, other enemy forces were trapped in the Falaise Gap by armed Poles. She called that "a nice poetic touch." This, Vera said later, was uncharacteristically wordy. Krystyna customarily used terse language in her written intelligence summaries.

Krystyna's accomplishments in the year 1941–42 alone proved that closework was not a stopgap, it was absolutely indispensable. Yet Vera could disclose nothing that risked breaching security, and SOE still had to fight for supplies from the regular armed forces. Beaulieu Manor in the New Forest, the family home of Lord Montagu, was loaned to SOE as a finishing school, the last holding center before agents left for the field. There were now nine covert agencies, cloaked in such secrecy that the Political Warfare Executive's official history was classified until the end of the century, and still obscured more than it revealed. Donovan glimpsed some of its work after Vera pointed out that he could "find" U.S. shortwave transmitters to expand PWE's Propaganda in Enemy Countries.

PWE had originated in an unmarked corner of the Foreign Office in the prewar rebellion against appeasement, and was originally quartered in Electra House on Victoria Embankment under the cover of the Imperial Communications Committee. PWE then moved to the Duke of Bedford's sprawling estate at Woburn Abbey, where London Control came on weekends to work out deception schemes within bicycling distance of Bletchley. PWE was designed to work with SOE, but there were fierce battles between the armed forces, security boffins at the Home Office, the Ministry of Economic Warfare, the Foreign Office, the BBC, and the General Post Office. PWE's most controversial boss was Sir Bruce Lockhart, convicted as a British spy in Russia and exchanged for a prominent Soviet prisoner in 1918. Lockhart was an author, journalist, and diplomat, and had also been a rubber planter in Malaya, now Malaysia. He was too much a man of action to suffer fools in the secret agencies, where, he wrote later, "most of the energy which should be directed against the enemy is dissipated in interdepartmental strife and jealousies."

The same wasted energy initially hindered Vera's efforts to cooperate with the Free French secret services, which were a law unto themselves. She needed to know more about her missing Polish code breakers, and she baited her hooks with snippets of information. One useful piece of bait was the Earl of Cardigan, who, as an escaped prisoner of war making an epic six-month overland journey through occupied France, had kept notes that would interest the Free French. The earl had stopped along his way to shelter at Virginia Hall's safehouse in Lyons. Seeing his impoverished state, she sent him to her friend the U.S. consul. There was a magical moment when the earl — in rags, and carrying on his shoulder a *pioche*, a fairly heavy farm-laborer's tool, something between a pickaxe and a hoe — stumbled into a consular cocktail party and confessed he was the Earl of Cardigan. The consul had a special fund for "distressed British subjects" and advanced the earl enough money to continue on his way, over the mountains into Spain.

Cardigan was happy to report that "the working poor in France are the most generous." His observations might seem pedestrian in normal times, but the German occupation made it almost impossible to keep track of the smallest, ever-changing details of French life. "Traveling on bicycles and on foot is best," he advised. "Be careful to fit into the local landscape. Don't tense up among Germans; don't catch their eye. I was in a deep sleep when the Germans came knocking on my door in one hideout. I said, 'Come in!' in English. Luckily, nobody noticed. Their regular soldiers are feeling just as lost as you, and this lot saw me as a poor old sod, down on my luck. If you ask for a *café noir* in a cafe, you get twigged right away. Black coffee disappeared long ago. It's the little things that betray you."

Vera needed similar eyewitness reports from Jews that Varian Fry helped to escape. Those from Germany, on arrival in England, were labeled enemy aliens, the category she had very carefully avoided falling into, and were difficult to question in detention camps. Arthur Koestler escaped French detention only to be told in Lisbon that London refused to issue him a visa. The British consul general, Sir Henry King, slipped Koestler onto a KLM flight to Bristol. But there he was arrested and sent to Pentonville Prison. He was moved to discover that in England, putting a man to death was still treated as a solemn and exceptional event: guards walked on tiptoe and a mighty hush fell over Pentonville whenever a German spy was hanged. Koestler was finally released. He summarized English attitudes as "Be kind to the foreigner, the poor chap can't help it." When he said this to the locals, they nodded in modest agreement. "So few saw the joke that I began to wonder whether it was a joke after all."[1]

Back on another exploratory visit, Bill Donovan saw SOE's explosive devices put together in places like the Thatched Barn, an old coaching inn north of London. There was always someone somewhere who knew how to rig something deadly, using can openers and soldering irons. Vera introduced him to John Godley, later Lord Kilbracken, who hid experience behind an absentminded air. Known as "God-Save-Us" Godley, he piloted Swordfish biplanes catapulted from grain ships and oil tankers in the North Atlantic to look for U-boats. His future lordship, aged twenty-two, explained how he coped without toilet facilities: "I ask the chap in the back cockpit to pass me a dust-marker can. It's not a good idea to throw it over the side when it's full of piss, because the slipstream blows it back in your face. So I hold it between my knees, fly left-handed, warn the crew to hide behind a bulkhead, and then chuck it vertically upwards." It was impossible to

*Vera Atkins during one of her few relaxed moments.*
(Courtesy of Lieutenant General Eugene F. Tighe, Jr.,
U.S. Defense Intelligence Agency)

*The ambassador Count Friedrich Werner von der
Schulenburg; here seen with Marie "Missie"
Vassiltchikov, one of Vera's key agents in SOE.
Vera met Schulenberg in Bucharest in 1931,
where she quickly discovered his strong
anti-Nazi sentiments.*
(From the collection of Marie "Missie" Vassiltchikov)

*William Stephenson, the man called Intrepid, director of British Security Coordination (BSC) in New York.*

(Photograph courtesy of Sir William and Lady Mary Stephenson)

William "Wild Bill" Donovan, chief of the Office of Strategic Services, which later became the Central Intelligence Agency.
(Courtesy of BSC Papers)

*Colin Gubbins.*
(Courtesy of BSC Papers)

*Polish countess Krystyna Skarbek (Christina Granville) in 1939.* (Courtesy of BSC Papers)

*Indian princess Noor Inayat Khan.*
(Courtesy of E-Spread Risk Management, Bermuda)

*Peggy Knight after the war.*
(From the archives of Squadron Leader William Simpson, courtesy of E-Spread and Bermuda National Archives)

*Virginia Hall, "the Canadian," correspondent for the* New York Post.
(Courtesy of Veterans of the OSS)

*Diana Rowden.*
(Courtesy of Jacques Deleporte
and French Special Branch)

*Andrée Borrel, chief assistant to
Major Suttill.* (Courtesy of Commission
d'Enquête Parlementaire sur les Événements
Survenus en France de 1933 à 1945)

*Sonia and her husband, Guy d'Artois, both SOE
agents. Sonia provided or corroborated much
of the personal information on Vera, who
was a close friend.*
(From the collection of Sonia d'Artois)

*Sonia Olschanezky before the war.*
(Courtesy of Sonia d'Artois and Sydney Holland)

Marie "Missie"
Vassiltchikov.
(Courtesy of the Earl
of Cadogan)

Violette Szabo, who rescued the White Rabbit
but was executed at Dachau on the eve
of the Allied victory.
(Courtesy of Karen Newman)

Wing Commander
Forest Frederick Edward Yeo-Thomas,
the "White Rabbit."
(Courtesy of Herbert Rowland, BSC Papers)

*Peter Churchill, thought by the Germans to be Winston's son.*
(Courtesy of E-Spread and BSC Papers)

*Odette Sansom, later Peter Churchill's wife.*
(Courtesy of E-Spread)

*Tom Harrisson, founder of Mass Observation movement, who parachuted behind Japanese lines in Borneo.*
(Courtesy of BSC Papers)

land the Swordfish back on the ship, which had rockets on rails to launch the aircraft but no deck for their return. Pilots ditched in the sea or bailed out, hoping the convoy would see them. Godley became the youngest commander of a navy squadron, covering convoys crossing near the Arctic Circle to supply the Soviet Union after Hitler invaded. He still flew Swordfish with cockpits open to icy blasts.

In Germany, by contrast, scientists were already building prototype jets and flying bombs and missiles designed to drop vertically in space. Polish agents smuggled out pieces of the new rockets. Yet Vera had difficulty explaining to the Ministry of Works why SOE needed cowsheds in a remote hamlet to make gadgets whose purpose could not be disclosed, or why a parachute jump tower was necessary.

Wanborough Manor was a sixteenth-century mansion, surrounded by parkland and ideal for intensive training. It stood on the Hog's Back in Surrey, an address that reinforced Bill Donovan's blurred impression of strange faces in odd places. Vera said, "If we throw out some trainees because they don't measure up, they already know too much, so they're put into other service units, and gagged by the Official Secrets Act." Some recruits had experience in the Afghan hills, fighting warrior tribes. One instructor, old by any standard, maintained his sniper skills. He trained French sharpshooters, and demonstrated in dummy runs how to derail London-bound express trains by laying dynamite charges. He gave the usual crisp advice regarding informers: "Listen to what they have to say, then kill them."

Moral objections to these "gangsterisms" were raised by the chief of air staff, Sir Charles Portal, who did not like "dropping men dressed in civilian clothes for the purpose of attempting to kill members of the opposing forces." Vera had to maneuver around protests wrapped in ethical terms. There was absolute opposition to her proposal that Jews were more useful in SOE instead of in detention camps. When Arthur Koestler did get out, he was full of hard-won advice: "Without a *carte d'identité*," he said, "any agent will be outside the law." His own French identity card went to SOE's counterfeiters to be doctored and used by another agent. Koestler was one of many Jews with the scientific expertise to help modernize Britain's ramshackle defenses. In 1931, as a science editor in Germany, he had looked into the future by contemplating splitting the atom. He had speculated about the chain reactions. German scientists ridiculed him because they had discovered the hydrogen isotope $^2$H, deuterium, and its oxygen compound, called heavy water. This meant, Koestler predicted accurately when he finally got anyone in London to listen, that German atomic bomb research was heading in the wrong direction.

Germans suspected of being spies went to Camp 020, the former military psychiatric hospital at Ham on the southwest outskirts of London. Lieutenant Colonel Robert "Tin Eye" Stephens was its monocled administrator. Information that was potentially useful to SOE was wrung out of Nazi-run agents. That is, if Vera got to them before they were hanged. Two, Josef Waldberg and Karl Meier, landed by dinghy on the Kent coast and were caught and strung up. Others were persuaded to return to Germany as double agents, but were not told their parachutes were never going to open. Dead on arrival, their corpses carried false information to fool the enemy. SS Officer Alfred Naujocks disclosed the German deception preceding the invasion of Poland, under questioning by Tin Eye, who told Vera, "Naujocks said he preserved bodies in Polish uniforms, and riddled them with bullets to trump up the charge of Polish aggression across Germany's sacred borders. He was a Nazi murderer and fixer." By the winter of 1940–41, Tin Eye had hanged fourteen prisoners. He said of an English turncoat spy, "Hanging's too good for him," but hanged him anyway. He was the multilingual keeper of counterintelligence files that eventually grew to the hundred-thousand-card index that enabled the XX (Double Cross) Committee of PWE to manipulate agents who first worked for the Nazis and, in one way or another, could be turned, and sent back with misinformation.

# 22

## The Black Chamber

Vera avoided card files. She kept in card-board boxes the bare essentials, and memorized the rest in what she had called her Black Chamber ever since Mary Stephenson got her a bootleg copy of *The American Black Chamber* by Herbert O. Yardley. The book upheld Bruce Lockhart's argument that energy that should be directed against an enemy was dissipated in interdepartmental strife and jealousies. Yardley's memoir was published in 1931 and was hastily banned. Before the outbreak of the 1914–18 war he was a young tele-graph operator and, through his own brilliance, rose to become chief of the code room, which he named the Black Chamber, in the White House. In 1929 Henry Stimson, as secretary of state, saw deciphered Japanese messages and said, "Gentlemen do not read each other's mail!" He stopped the decoding of foreign embassy cables. "Thousands of documents were destroyed for domestic political reasons to do with internal rivalries," wrote Yardley.

Vera recognized his description of diplomats arguing so loudly about policy in the code room that it was impossible to get any work done. "Jolly, good-natured, smartly dressed pigmies," he called them. One jeered at a warning that codes in use were not safe. Yardley showed how the codes were easily stolen from the vault. Its combina-tion numbers were taken from the phone book on a daily rotation that any fool could work out. He said cipher brains and originality were all that was needed. He demonstrated how America was cheated of "the most tremendous victory in the annals of warfare" through blind trust in old ciphers used in the great offensive of September 12, 1918. Plans were telegraphed across the Atlantic by cable. The contents were re-covered through induction by German submarines using wire laid alongside a stretch of the oceanbed cables. The Germans were prepared and broke the offensive. The Black Chamber had relied on a code easily broken by the submariners.

Vera's Black Chamber, being mostly in her mind or in shoe boxes, reduced the risk of burglary. Yardley's book was delivered by Bill Donovan. Now that he ran the first U.S. foreign intelligence agency, she told him how Harry Hinsley's reliance on memory and distrust of paperwork took him, the son of an unemployed laborer, into Churchill's committee on submarine warfare. Hinsley's mother cleaned other people's houses. Her son did not impress the equivalent "pigmies" in Britain's upper-middle-class network, who had deep roots in the regular armed forces, administration, colonial service, and public life. But he did please nonconformists like Stephenson and Donovan. Both men were relieved to hear that Vera's irregulars were being joined by more and more dissenters, who submerged their personal idiosyncrasies to suffer the tough training required. Most were as capable of independent self-discipline as Churchill, who wanted an end to the carelessness that was causing naval losses, like the one that had cut short the life of Vera's lover.

Hinsley, long-haired and scruffily dressed, marched into the Admiralty Operational Intelligence Center to demand that spit-and-polish officers listen to him. Four years earlier he had made boldness his friend. At eighteen, curious about Germany, he lived there during the last summer of peace. He won a scholarship to study medieval history at Cambridge, where he learned to wrest deductions out of old documents in a way that later would enable him to discern links when analyzing German wireless traffic. He taught himself to spot indications of future enemy activity. He penned a formal letter complaining that the navy's OIC officers worked "in so aimless and inefficient a manner that all their time is taken up in groping at the truth and putting as much of it as is obvious to all on card indexes."[1]

Hinsley improved at making accurate conclusions from fragmented enemy signals. If the navy required the source of some prediction of enemy movements, one answer now sufficed: "Hinsley." He sat at Battle of the Atlantic emergency meetings chaired by Churchill. On the first occasion, Churchill asked, "Who is that boy?" Desmond Morton whispered that Churchill himself had asked for Hinsley's presence at these tense moments. The prime minister muttered, "Yes, yes," and returned to paying close attention to what Hinsley had to say, not to his working-class accent or to his habits of dress.

Moral courage led Vera, too, to shrink from reliance on card indexes. She told Donovan: "Incompetent intelligence analysts feel safer surrounded by fat meaningless files, like babies sucking security blankets." She did not underrate the Camp 020 index system, because it served a different purpose. For her agents, it took courage to fight alone, without the backup of written instructions and performance records. So much depended upon the honesty of colleagues. Vera discussed courage many times with Donovan. There were few others in whom she could confide.

The American's visits to measure SOE's progress gave her an opportunity to relax and amuse him with gossip. She told him the story of Douglas "Tin Legs" Bader, who had lost both legs but was allowed to continue fighting in air battles over England and "collected a gong" from King George VI. The king, who had a stutter, recalled that the German raiders used Fokker aircraft. As he pinned on the medal, he asked, "How many have you shot down of the F-F-Fokkers?" Bader dutifully replied: "Well, sir, five Messerschmitts, two Heinkels, and a Junker, sir."

Donovan liked Vera's story of the Netherlands' Prince Bernhard, in London to represent Dutch resistance. A bomb exploded in the entrance to an apartment block where he had been a dinner guest. Clambering down through the rubble, he murmured, "So kind. Most delightful evening."

In recounting such stories, Vera reflected the surface cheerfulness of the people around her. After the terror bombing of London for seventy-six consecutive nights in 1940–41, her anger was deeply personal. She received reports from Paris of gleeful Germans scooping up champagne, expensive perfumes, and other luxuries. Ernst Udet, director of air armament, had gone on a drunken spree, shouting his contempt for Hermann Göring, who dressed extravagantly in a purple silk blouse with puffy sleeves, high hunting boots, and a long hunting knife shaped like a Germanic sword in his belt, planning what he called the Great Battle to grind down Britain's air defenses before a seaborne invasion.

"Göring's all washed up," said Vera.

"Why?" asked Donovan. "He's next in line to Hitler."

"He's also no longer running his own air force. Udet, who claimed he built the greatest air fleet in history, was found dead, a revolver at his side, after scrawling on a wall: 'Göring sold out to the Jews.'"

Donovan asked why German fliers kept fighting. Courage?

"It's easy to look brave when things go your way," Vera said. "Civilians display true courage by getting on with their daily lives between nights of terror bombing. They do it from a sense of duty. Duty is the mother of courage. Real courage is in facing impossible odds."

She was more animated than he had ever seen her, since she had spoken of a pilot she had known and lost. She said natural courage was not readily apparent, like other aspects of character. It had nothing to do with nationality. Pilots in the Battle of Britain included 147 Poles. Duty drove them, also hatred and often despair.

Some extra quality drove Krystyna, the Polish countess. She had sent word of Jan Nowak, formerly of Poland's horse artillery, whose cavalry had charged German tanks. He was now fighting underground, and was anxious to make a fearfully dangerous journey to London to personally plead with Churchill for help. Krystyna had built a network from Poland to the Turkish legation in Budapest. The network chief, Marcin Lubomirski, was arrested while bringing British prisoners out of Poland and was sent to the Mauthausen concentration camp. Before ending up in the gas chambers there, he escaped. His whereabouts were unknown.

Nowak arrived in London during the cruel winter of 1943–44, bringing material evidence of German experiments with new weapons, together with a touching handwritten tribute to Winston Churchill from Polish resistance fighters. Nowak cooled his heels for weeks before he could deliver this to Churchill, which puzzled Vera. She worried that hostile forces were at work behind the scenes. Gwido Langer, the Polish mastermind who broke the first Enigma code, and all his code breakers should be in England. Direct contact had to be made with closework fighters in Poland, because she was not sure that the government-in-exile in London was entirely free from political bias. She needed to hearten the Poles with drops of arms and supplies, and it took all her tradecraft and charm to "borrow" an old RAF Whitley bomber. The Armstrong Whitworth Whitley's normal range was 630 miles, hardly enough to reach Poland. Its cruising speed was 165 miles an hour, which made it a sitting duck for German fighters. Vera had an auxiliary fuel tank fitted to extend the range and adapted the bomb bays to hold cylinders attached to parachutes. The conversions were designed by an Englishman who had run an engineering factory in southern Poland before the war. He was known as Colonel Harry Perkins when he joined Gubby in Warsaw during Vera's first mission there. Krystyna, who seemed to leave a trail of lovers behind her, called him "Perks Kochay" or "Darling Perks" in letters that reached him at one of the secret SOE "toy shops" in England. Accusations that she was a double agent had been made against her by the Polish government-in-exile. Gubby used his reputation to stop the lies, which again seemed to be politically motivated. Vera gave Krystyna permission to return to France to learn the fate of any Polish code breakers still there.

Flight Lieutenant John Austin was chosen to pilot the Whitley to Poland. The flight would take fourteen hours, through enemy skies. Vera sat with him during practice runs. Austin dispensed with the normal crew of five, replacing them with three Polish parachutists, and loaded the aircraft with fuel for 1,930 miles. The only way to get off the ground with extra fuel and containers was to open the throttles, rush down the runway, heave the Whitley into the air, drop back on the tarmac, and keep bouncing until fully airborne. Vera winced, thinking of her couriers and bicycle brigades and of Krystyna begging for advanced technical apparatus to meet the needs of the secret armies.

The old Whitley bomber, even after the pilot managed to get airborne, did not get far the first time. The oxygen was insufficient for long flights at high altitude; the exactor controls tended to freeze, which prevented the aircraft from climbing; and if the lines leaked, one restored pressure by urinating into the system. It gave a new meaning to being "full of piss and vinegar," Vera recalled. The second time, without gunners in the forward or rear turrets, the pilot had to turn back with engine trouble. On the third try, the stripped-down Whitley lumbered into the air after several sickening plunges and droned through the night skies to Poland at twelve thousand feet, with everyone freezing from the numbing cold. Three Polish couriers parachuted. Resistance leaders in Warsaw were overjoyed. Here was proof of massive, future air support.

Couriers began hair-raising overland journeys from Poland to England with proof of home army successes and with appeals for air support. Among the mandarins of Whitehall, though, there were concerns about the Soviet Union's reaction to a British secret army on Stalin's doorstep. The chief of the air staff, Charles Portal, again raised objections. "My bombing offensive is not a gamble," he insisted. "I cannot divert aircraft from a certainty to a gamble, which may be a goldmine or may be completely worthless." Vera noted waspishly that the bombing force was strained by outlandish improvisations like razzles, transported in milk churns filled with water to avoid spontaneous combustion before being released on flare chutes to set fires on the ground. Razzles also set fire to bombers' tails. Teabags were thrown overboard to prove to the Germans that Britain was not being starved by the U-boat campaign.

# 23

## "She Has to Believe in What She Is Doing or Go Mad"

"Say White Rabbit and Three Blind Mice to Vera and you need say no more," recalled Leo Marks, SOE's boy coding genius. The White Rabbit was the nickname for a thirty-eight-year-old Englishman, F. F. E. Yeo-Thomas, general manager in 1939 of Molyneux, the great Paris fashion house. Three Blind Mice was the poem-code of a suburban London shopgirl, Violette Szabo, who left school at fourteen. Their lives, one genteel and privileged in origin, the other humble, brought them together with Virginia Hall and Rolande Colas, all recruited in Paris when Vera first went there scouting for agents, and all three were brilliant and brave in adversity.

France was still a great power. With a population of 105 million, France was the largest powerhouse to fuel the new German Reich. France had a revolutionary past that made it ripe for resistance against an oppressor, but it was also so highly individualistic that the Free French seemed always in disagreement. The White Rabbit, hopping in and out of this country haunted by local pride and ancient prejudices, negotiated agreements between guerrilla forces with a display of such nerve and moral integrity that he was able to push his way into Churchill's presence with a plea for greater material support. And the agent's reputation was such that Churchill had to listen.

Head and shoulders above the other exiled European government leaders stood General Charles de Gaulle of France. His authority bridged the divisions, but he had no experience in closework. Nick Bodington, a former Reuters news agency man in Paris, began by forming liaisons between resistance cells and moved back and forth to

France with such nonchalance that internal security, MI5, with no experience of the realities of field operations, suspected he was working for both sides.[1]

Vera knew secrecy provided opportunities for character assassination. De Gaulle's Free French in London, competitive and divided among themselves, tried Churchill's patience to the breaking point. Vera understood the peculiarities of their secret-service people on Duke Street, and they in turn were more ready to confide in her than in the SIS, which was distrusted as an arm of the British Foreign Office when Halifax was associated with appeasement.

The French spymaster Jean Moulin advised her, "When tired or upset, or both, *eat*." When in London, he started his day with ham, eggs, sausages, tomatoes, toast, marmalade, and tea. He would consume this un-French breakfast after a long night's work and then telephone a private number, Whitehall 4503, and walk to the Cavendish Hotel on Jermyn Street to be shown into a drawing room where, he claimed, Victorian chorus girls used to hang themselves in despair when pregnant. "Our war," he told Vera, "gives the desperate a reason to live."

Moulin was one of the tragic giants of the French resistance. He observed dryly that the purity of English womanhood was a nineteenth-century concept that influenced the War Office view that "women are 'doing their bit' in factories or noncombatant branches of the armed forces. If they must engage the enemy, they can do it on their backs." A propaganda poster in the Duke Street office of the Free French showed a blond bombshell seductively draped over a daybed, surrounded by uniforms, under the bold warning: KEEP MUM. SHE'S NOT SO DUMB! Moulin said: "English ladies never reveal secrets in the heat of passion. They close their eyes and think of England. I never thought of Vera as English."

Between them there was a shared excitement, tightly controlled. She drew comfort from his intellect. He was teased by her faint air of not quite belonging. "She has a smile that is as remote as it is seraphic," he was quoted as saying. "She must believe in what she is doing or go mad."

Before coming to London in September 1941 to plead for working capital, arms, and supplies, Moulin organized three resistance groups. He saw the untidy structure of SOE as a challenge. "Vera sandpapers egos until most of the secret services in exile work with her, though always with their own political agendas," Moulin wrote in a report to General de Gaulle, who had tried his hand at covert action when he escaped from France in 1940 and launched the Bureau Central de Renseignement et d'Action. In its first closework mission, BCRA lost seven members, decapitated by the Germans. Another six French agents were beheaded later in that January of 1941. Vera gently pointed out that it would be wiser to build upon the growing spirit of spontaneous resistance among citizens, who misdirected Germans on the metro, dropped them off at the wrong bus stops, or sold them faulty goods. To give form and direction to this became Moulin's task.[2]

In London, de Gaulle's secret service planners lacked any experience in such work. Rémy, the code name for Gilbert Renault, ran one network for de Gaulle, while Marie-Madeleine Méric ran another for SOE. Vera did her best to make them speak with a single voice through the BBC, which broadcast prearranged open code messages, such as "Sister Aline wears pink" or "The cat eats fish this morning." The system was suggested by Georges Bégué, the first SOE agent parachuted into France with a wireless transmitter in a suitcase. Back from a difficult mission, he reported that the Germans could jam his transmitter and were using direction-finding vans. He had an ally in Vera, whose rule was "Keep it brief." Short enigmatic phrases were crafted by the initiator, and had meaning only for a particular agent. Bégué became known as Captain Noble to BBC producers, who inserted his terse messages into broadcasts to Europe that began with the opening bars of Beethoven's Fifth Symphony, the heart-stopping *dit-dit-dit-dah*. This was also Morse for the letter "V" — for Victory — a promise of liberation. A V-Committee was formed, but Vera became uneasy about a backlash to its longer, more explicit instructions for amateur sabotage. "'How to make your own bomb' sounds like fun," she objected, "but overenthusiastic French listeners might draw attention to our trained agents in the vicinity."

A former South African farmer, Douglas Ritchie, known as Colonel Britton in the BBC's "London Calling Europe" programs, advised, "When you knock on the door, when you rap the table for a waiter in a restaurant, do it like this." And he would tap out the Morse for V. Transcripts of Colonel Britton's broadcasts were distributed in Britain, prompting MI5 to protest that this would incite communists and trade unionists. Vera already had reservations about psychological warfare experts with no experience in the field. When Colonel Britton prophesied "the greatest battle in the history of the world . . . And you in Europe will attack," foreign governments-in-exile protested that they would prefer to broadcast their own guidance to their secret armies. And so "Colonel Britton" was hooked off stage.

Vera liked de Gaulle for stopping off to say farewell to his dying mother in Brittany before escaping to England. Two days later, he was shaving in the Hyde Park Hotel when Jean Monnet, future "Father of the European Community," and Charles Corbin, the French ambassador, burst into his bathroom to propose a union between the United Kingdom and France, with a federal constitution, one parliament, one government, and common citizenship. De Gaulle flew back to France with the proposal, but it was too late. The government had accepted defeat. De Gaulle escaped again, and went to see Churchill, enjoying an afternoon's sunshine in his garden. The tall, gangling Frenchman brought tears to Churchill's eyes: Britain stood alone, and the only ally was de Gaulle's vision of an "undefeated France."

The ill-feeling between the Free French and the SIS had been aggravated by Lord Halifax, who was still running foreign policy when he tried to stop de Gaulle's broadcast on June 18, 1940. "Any Frenchman who still has weapons has the absolute duty to continue the resistance." Surrender of any piece of French soil was "a crime against the nation." He told all generals in the French Empire to disobey the Germans. "I am France," he declared.

"De Gaulle is like a man skinned alive," declared the American novelist Mary Borden. "The slightest touch, even if meant to be friendly, makes him bite." Mary was the wife of General Sir Edward Louis Spears, who had watched de Gaulle plead with Churchill to send over more aircraft before France fell. Churchill said if Britain had to fight alone, it would need every pilot and plane. De Gaulle had fallen several steps back and, after a silence, said in English, "You are quite right." Churchill wrote later: "Here stood the Constable of France."

Terrible choices were being made. Vera learned to make those choices without dithering. She concluded, "It's faster than if I weigh all the evidence and confuse myself through a long drawn-out process of arriving at a judgment by studying every angle. The longer I dealt

with emergencies, the more I realized my mind had absorbed experience and information that produced snap judgments that I could
trust."

She had learned early, from Churchill's decision to sink part of
the French fleet on July 3, 1940, killing 1,297 French seamen who had
been allies a few days before. A combination of the French and German fleets would eclipse Britain's strained navy. At Mers el-Kébir near
Oran in Algeria, an ultimatum was issued to the French admiral: join
us or we'll take action. At 5:56 P.M. a British bombardment sank
French warships. A Vichy court convicted de Gaulle in absentia to a
term in jail and later condemned him to death as a traitor.

De Gaulle remained emotionally raw. Churchill, remembering
the general was born in Lorraine, groaned in a moment of exasperation, "The biggest cross I have to bear is the Cross of Lorraine." But
that cross was symbol and sword of nonnegotiable French sovereignty.

Vera had to remind herself that an English prime minister,
William Gladstone, having ordered the bombardment of Alexandria
in 1882, still admired France, "tingling as it does to the very finger
ends with vivacity, running over with a thousand kinds of talent." The
Vichy French government brought Germans in contact with diplomats. Vera was in touch with French-Canadians who maintained a
presence in Vichy because the province of Quebec was traditionally
French. Until November 1942, when the Germans occupied the south
of France, Vichy was a place to gather information and deal with silent
anti-Nazi Frenchmen and Germans. The U.S. ambassador to Vichy,
Admiral William D. Leahy, had worked with FDR when Leahy was
chief of naval operations from 1937 to 1939. While France was divided between northern occupied and southern unoccupied zones, his
reports were invaluable. Vera judged that Vichy's usefulness no longer
outweighed the value of destroying resources needed by the German
war machine in both zones.

"You'll have to make tough decisions," Vera told the White Rabbit before he was listed as Wing Commander Forest Frederick Edward
"Tommy" Yeo-Thomas. He had started at the bottom of the RAF lad-
der. He was rejected as a volunteer in 1939 by the British military attaché in Paris. Asked later how he got his White Rabbit nickname, he
replied, "Because I work for a fuckin' Mad Hatter's Tea Party." He
trusted Vera's cool judgment, but was appalled by some SOE foul-ups.

On his last mission, he escaped from German torturers in such wretched physical shape that his father, seeing him on his final return to England, said, "My God, he's become an old man."

The White Rabbit was saved by Violette Szabo, who perished in a German death camp. When he first arrived in London, Violette Szabo worked behind the counter at Woolworth's. She fell in love with a French Foreign Legion captain, Étienne Szabo, during General de Gaulle's emotionally charged parade through London of the Free French on July 14, 1940. Étienne knew the girl as Violette Bushell, whose mother was French. Violette thought it might be nice to give one of these poor French soldiers a decent home-cooked meal. Soon after, they married. Étienne left to fight in North Africa, and Violette volunteered to be trained as an agent. Leo Marks was going through her security checks when he discovered that she had made mistakes with the reserve poem she had chosen for coding her messages. Leo said that sometimes spelling mistakes were made because of an unconscious dislike of the poem chosen. She said she had always disliked knowing only nursery rhymes; the poem was one she had never been able to spell correctly in French as a child. The difficult word was "three." She kept spelling it in French as *troi*, leaving off the final *s*. A simple mistake like this could cost her life. The poem was "Three Blind Mice." Violette was given a poem composed by Leo himself.[3]

From France, Virginia Hall stoically reported that explosives parachuted to resistance groups were stored so badly that plastic showed signs of mold and metal parts were rusting. She could not let trigger-happy maquisards go off half-cocked. De Gaulle wisely wanted to unify opposition to the Germans and create a single solid Resistance, which would husband its strength but rise up when the right moment came, rather than squander resources in separate, small actions that resulted in savage reprisals against innocent civilians. Virginia relied upon her personal reputation to restrain more and more young men who were joining the Francs-Tireurs, Combat, and other independent guerrilla forces hiding in the forests. She was afraid they would provoke reprisals by launching their own ill-prepared actions, and only provide practice for German antiterrorist squads and an excuse for them to burn down nearby villages.

Virginia was creatively using her experience with escaping Allied prisoners. She kept a mental map of couriers and subagents who did not know where newly arriving "bodies" came from, nor where they went. Each courier was sequestered in a public park until nightfall, when he or she was taken to a safehouse. Bodies did not need to know exactly where they were. Safehouses and contacts changed at frequent intervals. These escape lines became a foundation for coordinating SOE work. For example, while Jean Moulin was in France, he operated with one set of false papers in his pockets, with a courier following at a distance with another set of false ID for Moulin in case of emergency.

The "Palestine Express" was Vera's name for a major escape route. One of her early recruits, French businessman Victor Gerson, had proposed that a permanent chain of "helpers" would simplify SOE exits and entrances. In May 1941 Gerson's wife, Giliana Balmaceda, volunteered to reconnoiter such a line. Chilean by birth, Giliana was a beautiful young actress of the Paris stage, whose SOE training sharpened her professional skill of slipping into the skin of another character. She proved unusually adept at distinguishing between those who volunteered to help escapees and those professing to rebel against the Germans while secretly informing their counterintelligence police. Giliana looked for *sédentaires*, often elderly people, who stayed in one place and were willing to use their sedentary habits to provide staging posts along the escape line. These staging posts, or safehouses, were often run by middle-aged ladies, who sheltered escapees in their unobtrusive houses in Paris. Giliana traveled widely, and returned to London along the same route, using her Chilean passport to move through Vichy France and Spain to Gibraltar. By mid-June, she was with Vera to deposit a large haul of intelligence and the names and addresses of those who were willing and could be trusted to help.

Giliana's husband, Victor, took SOE training and met up with Virginia Hall on his second insertion into France by submarine with Peter Churchill. Victor's first arrival by parachute in September 1941 was almost his last. He was dropped into a Marseilles trap set by the Gestapo and barely escaped. Victor put together an escape line running from Amsterdam through Brussels, Paris, and Lyons to the Spanish frontier. All the young couriers, with the exception of the journalist Jacques Mitterrand, were Jewish and sent other Jewish customers on the "Palestine Express" to the Middle East. Their stopover in Lyons was arranged by Virginia Hall: a few hours of rest at a certain Madame Caravelle's modest little *salon de coiffure.*

Jews rescued by the New York editor Varian Fry were prevented from entering Palestine. The Zionist leader David Ben-Gurion said the British barrier "strikes at the very heart of the Jewish national home." The Haganah Jewish defense force made its own grenades and bombs, while still trying to work with the local British administration. In a battle for the British cause, a Haganah officer lost one eye: this was the future Israeli army chief and defense minister Moshe Dayan. Others in Haganah broke away to form groups to fight the British. The opportunity to make more trouble was seized by Adolf Eichmann, the SS officer in charge of implementing the Final Solution: he shipped more Jews in "coffin ships" down the Danube and across the Black Sea and the Mediterranean to Palestine. Anthony Eden, as secretary for foreign affairs, insisted that the exodus be stopped in order to calm the Arabs, whose goodwill was needed while Britain's only military victories were in North Africa. Eichmann, during a prewar fact-finding tour of the territory, had told Hitler that Jews could be ransomed for profit. Now he used them to force the British to choose between turning them away and fanning the flames of anti-British feeling in the Arab states.

*Routiers,* the fiercely independent truck drivers of France, hurtled between transit points with escapees packed tight under tarpaulins. The drivers held German permits as employees of German factories or the Wehrmacht, and among their loads were growing numbers of downed Allied airmen and other servicemen. By the end of 1941, with the U.S. finally at war, Virginia Hall could call for professional American military help. She needed to bring discipline to the volunteers in her partisan armies. Although the early missions had gone well enough for Vera, from the winter of 1941 to the spring of 1942, disaster followed disaster.

# The Flying Visit

Although the end of U.S. neutrality made it easier to tighten and expand clandestine collaboration between SOE, the U.S. president, and Bill Donovan, there was a mystery that Vera had to clear up, because it caused American misgivings about Churchill's ability to continue waging war if appeasers were still trying to make peace deals with Hitler.

Vera had already disclosed a great deal about operational techniques to Bill Donovan. One evening at Winchelsea, she quoted:

> The sea is calm to-night.
> The tide is full, the moon lies fair
> Upon the straits. On the French coast the light
> Gleams and is gone; The cliffs of England stand . . .

The lines are from "Dover Beach" by Matthew Arnold. Moonlight told Vera when operations were possible. At sea when the moon was invisible, in the air when the moon was full.

"A spasm of moonstruck craftiness," she called the moment when Hitler's deputy, Rudolf Hess, landed by moonlight in Britain with a timing that was more calculated than either side admitted publicly.

Ian Fleming's brother Peter had written a novel, *The Flying Visit*, a satire on what would happen if Hitler parachuted into England. Hess turned fantasy to near-truth on that moonlit night when he landed close to the Scottish estate of the Duke of Hamilton. Peter's book, far from being written with foreknowledge, poked fun at English politics. Hess's arrival, though, sparked speculation about a continuing appeasement party in London in this period before the U.S. joined in the war.

Deputy Führer Hess had piloted a specially equipped Messerschmidt 110 along a difficult and indirect route to the duke's home. Hess bailed out and fell into a field, where he gave his name to an open-mouthed farmworker as Alfred Horn, and asked to see the duke, who was a fighter pilot and wing commander in the RAF. Hess carried a list of royals thought to be friendly to Germany and still willing to negotiate.

Vera took Charles Fraser-Smith, the designer of Q gadgets, to a secret location where a uniform was laid out on a trestle table. Fraser-Smith recalled later: "She said she'd given Hess something to ensure he didn't wake up until morning, then said, 'This is his uniform. Make an exact copy. We must have it back to him in four hours.' She didn't tell me Hess was in the Tower of London."

Fraser-Smith often got clandestine help from Courtaulds, the textile experts whose executives worked with Vera, and from Elder Wills, whose main "laboratory" was a carpenters' shop at the Victoria and Albert Museum. His assistants included former wardrobe masters and makeup artists from his Elstree movie studios. Elder Wills also managed a secret factory in Margaret Street near Oxford Circus, employing teams of Jewish seamstresses and tailors who could imitate clothing from almost anywhere. They scouted London synagogues for cast-off refugee clothing from which foreign labels could be detached or foreign shoes fitted with sliding heels to hide microfilms and codes. Now a Courtaulds expert checked the uniform, and announced it was made from high-quality synthetic lightweight gabardine. Elder Wills found a likely substitute. Fraser-Smith compared it with the original. "I took Hess's tunic between forefinger and thumb with a most unaccountable feeling of excitement," he said. "There was something surreal about handling the uniform of a man who helped lead the Germans against us in the bloodiest of all wars. I went through the pockets feeling for hidden compartments. Then I turned to a tailorcutter from Elder Wills' factory and asked for an exact copy."

Fraser-Smith, in the conscientious spirit of his voluntary work as a governor of the British and Foreign Bible Society, said, "I made it my business to stay on the right side of everyone, especially Vera. She drew a curtain of silence around Hess. And so must I."[1]

The deputy führer's dramatic arrival could not be kept out of front-page headlines in the British press, but nothing was published about the list of prominent figures who had been regarded by Hitler as pro-German before the war. In Washington there was concern: had Hitler been encouraged to send a peace envoy while preparing to invade Russia, hoping to enlist the support of well-known anti-Bolshevik personalities? Churchill had to say again that there would be no time squandered on supposedly friendly Germans. He wrote carefully in his postwar memoirs that Hess "came to us of his own free will [with] something of the quality of an envoy." Hess was the only Nazi war criminal kept in jail until his death many years later. He was never permitted to give his side of the story.[2]

Vera wondered if the flying visit was a complicated deception plan. The Nazis were not as expert in this as was the London Control Directorate. LCD now seldom consulted Vera or SOE's sister services, and was later discovered to have been infiltrated by pro-Soviet propaganda specialists. Records were destroyed after the war. Broadcasts dictated by London Control named anti-Nazi Germans for reasons that seemed only to serve the purpose of assisting Soviet interests.

The secrecy was described as "evil" by Air Commodore G. S. Oddie. The highly decorated RAF flier wrote of Hess as a man "guided by his own code of honor" in a foreword to a later anthology of heavily censored letters from Hess to his wife, Ilse. Oddie quoted some significant words from Rudolf Hess: "I had not realized that Churchill had become powerless to prevent the catastrophe enveloping us." The catastrophe was Nazi Germany's invasion of Russia, immediately following the Hess mission.[3]

There had been forewarnings. Krystyna Skarbek had provided eyewitness accounts of German troop movements through Poland to the east. Hitler had disclosed the schedule for invading Russia to the fifty-six-year-old Marshal Ion Antonescu of Romania, who had assumed dictatorial powers. Vera heard from Ambassador von der Schulenburg in Moscow that before the Hess flight, Stalin had put an arm around his shoulder. "We must stay friends," Stalin told Schulenburg. "Do everything to that end." The German ambassador had flown to Berlin, and on April 28 reassured the Führer that there was no possibility of Russia attacking Germany. Schulenburg returned to Moscow, seemingly the victim of a double deception, and sent a note to Vera innocently quoting Hitler's reassurance to Stalin: eight German heavy divisions were being "transferred away from eastern Europe."

On Saturday, June 21, 1941, Schulenburg was instructed to charge the Soviet Union with "sabotaging, terrorizing, and spying against Germany." The next day, at 5:30 A.M., Count Friedrich Werner von der Schulenburg delivered to the commissar known among Russia's elite as "Iron Arse" Molotov the fatal German declaration of war. "It is," Schulenburg told Molotov, "madness."[4]

Vera could judge the reliability of agents by finding collateral intelligence. Her opponents were increasingly clever at planting false information. She was puzzled by conflicting evidence: Schulenburg had said no German troops were preparing to invade. Then he delivered a German declaration of war despite his many claims that he fervently prayed, like Bismarck, for the avoidance of a Russo-German war.

At least it simplified the disputes between the French Communist Party and other underground networks. Communists were now fully at the disposal of the Free French in London and in Vera's F Section. There had always been a degree of guarded cooperation, which had more to do with the French character than with politics. The former metalworker colleague of Rolande Colas' father and leader of the communist Francs-Tireurs (Snipers) et Partisans, Henri Tanguy, had already assisted de Gaulle's Forces Françaises de l'Intérieur, or FFI, as it began to be more widely known.

Vera won the help of two special RAF squadrons. Though poorly equipped, they were assigned to deliver agents, arms, and supplies into France with more regularity. She disclosed SOE's changing requirements to the Scientific Research Department run by Professor Dudley Newitt of the Imperial College in Kensington. A chain of "laboratories" was improvised from odd corners of distant buildings to manufacture special equipment and documentation for agents and invent new devices on a grander scale. The greatest need was to improve communications now that the communist-run circuits were ready to work with de Gaulle's FFI. There were still tensions, but Vera was seeing more French escapees who wanted only to be trained to go back and fight, regardless of politics. She had to oversee the painstaking work of comparing stories, watching for double agents, and looking for contradictions or falsehoods in a flood of intelligence.

By mid-1941, escapees like Diana Hope Rowden had been reaching England in growing numbers. Diana was a twenty-one-year-old tomboy who had lived with her mother in the south of France in the 1920s. When they returned to England, Diana attended the Manor House, a private school in Surrey. In 1932 as a shy teenager she won a scholarship to the Sorbonne. At the outbreak of war, she volunteered for the French Red Cross. After France fell, she stayed behind until mid-1941, when she escaped through Spain. Gubbins's deputy director, Harry Sporborg, saw her file. Multilingual, she became an assistant section officer for RAF Intelligence. Diana was later featured in a postwar *Time* magazine article that asked if she had been used by London Control as a decoy, leading to her execution. This was never given credibility by Squadron Leader Bill Simpson, who considered Diana to be "good material" after meeting her at the southern English resort of Torquay. He could see she was "healthy as a flea," a free spirit, her recklessness under control, her skills honed in prewar days by crewing on yachts instead of going to classes. She knew Brittany and Normandy well. Simpson thought she deserved to spend the rest of her life sailing, which she adored. She went into action with equally ill-fated companions, Cecily Lefort and Noor Inayat Khan.

Vera systematically gathered anecdotal information from sources like Diana, knowing that conditions changed and details needed to be updated. The girl had recalled that the daily baguette was gone. Bread rations were down to twelve ounces per person per day. Those who normally smoked cigarettes now puffed on "tobacco" made from nettle leaves, linden flowers, or Jerusalem artichokes. Taxis were wicker bath-chairs pulled by bicycles like the rickshaws of French Indochina. Paris had become a woman's city, where the whispered question was "Any news of him?" This was usually followed by a quick shake of the head. Men were hired by German factories, but it was clear they were slave workers.

Out of wellsprings of information, Vera drew her own conclusions. Agents in the field should be supplied with huge quantities of French francs, real or counterfeit. She had growing lists of businessmen in France who might advance real money if repayment was guaranteed in BBC broadcasts, with a phrase proposed by the lender inserted upon receipt by Morse transmission from the borrower-agent. Tactics of counterintelligence were changed by the "Gestapo," a term the French applied indiscriminately to all German security services. Admiral Canaris ran army intelligence, and his archrival Himmler ran the SS's Sicherheitsdienst. The army put its routine field police in uniform and its secret field police in civilian clothes. Himmler controlled the Sipo, security police units divided between the Kripo, which dealt with crime, and the true Gestapo, or secret state police. Vera's agents were taught to tell the difference. Their survival after capture might depend on which security branch held them. Vera updated lists of these organizations and the addresses of their headquarters and outstations, noting changes and gleaning what she could of the treatment received by captured agents. The German army sent those who claimed prisoner-of-war status to regular prison camps.

She tracked ever-changing regulations on rationing, travel permits, curfews, and the sentiments of local people. She estimated that nine out of ten French citizens hated the Germans, and "made the best of a bad job" until provided with credible leadership as part of a coherent plan. Vera verified the accuracy of her own information by examining that of the Free French and felt at times as if she was putting flesh on the bones of characters in a spy novel. The conquerors, she wrote, "presently pay for purchases in overvalued German occupation marks. The French call the Germans *doryphores*, potato beetles that devour the leaves so that the plants die. The Germans strip the shops of luxuries by using occupation marks set at an artificial rate, which in effect makes their pocket money worth five times its true value. It was only ten years prior that the four biggest banks in Germany were closed down by a depressed economy that hit rock bottom. Now a new generation of Germans regarded Hitler as a genius for making them feel rich." The German Reichsbank was making huge profits by manipulating currency exchanges wherever Germany ruled. A million French prisoners of war worked in German factories and were joined by French "slave laborers." The Germans were taking sweet revenge for French reparations after the 1914–18 war, but they were spreading hatred that might result in a single-minded resistance.

Diana Hope Rowden was a mine of information. She said most of the ordinary German soldiers she'd seen were straight off the farm, looked a little lost, and "missed their Mums." Some found solace in cheap brothels, but their euphoria at finding that their money went a long way soon wore off. In Paris it was beyond the average German soldier's means to go to Maxim's, which was run by a Berlin restaurateur, Herr Horcher, who licked the boots of top Nazis like Göring. Caviar overflowed at Petrossian's, if you could afford it. Coco Chanel was the expensive mistress of a senior German officer after she reopened her haute couture house on the advice of André Gide: "Come to terms with yesterday's enemy. That is not cowardice but wisdom." The most exclusive brothel, One Two Two, serviced German officials, who ignored an official ban on whorehouses. Maurice Chevalier still sang. Picasso still painted. Jean Cocteau wrote as cynically as ever. Frenchmen who ran the black markets made bigger profits than they ever had as peacetime shopkeepers. But Frenchmen working the land were in the vast majority, and their rage against the oppressor infected the cities.

Diana repeated a lot of gossip, of course, but it was the significant gossip by which an observant young woman could read the people's mood. Her reports were easily checked against later arrivals coming by way of MI9, the escape-and-evasion agency that was causing unease at the top of the SIS. Nothing could stop MI9 as a new and expanding secret service from organizing and training the armed forces on how to break out of enemy prisons and return to England. Its own agents would eventually help some twelve thousand airmen escape captivity, many of whom flew again. By his conquests, Hitler had created horrendous policing problems, and it was impossible to block the dozens of smaller exits out of his Fortress Europe. His expansion of "German" frontiers left a vast population theoretically trapped within that "world of barbed wire" described by the Earl of Cardigan. The very size of the Greater German Reich left gaps and weaknesses. The old Viking sea routes went through the Orkney and Shetland Islands, whose inhabitants were British but Norse by origin. The Shetland Islands had been a Norse colony until the fifteenth century, and were now part of Scapa Flow's Home Fleet outer defenses. The string of flat islands dotted a vast emptiness of ocean across which sudden gales blew. In Kirkwall, the Orkney capital, Vera heard the old joke that one day the wind stopped and everyone fell over. But from here she could float agents in small boats that slipped unobserved past German coastal forts in Norway. Neutral Sweden was closer, too, and a discreet SOE transit point was maintained there by British military attaché Malcolm Munthe, son of the famous author of *The Story of San Michele*, Axel Munthe. Malcolm's services included regular RAF flights to England by Mosquito fighter-bombers that carried agents in their bomb bays and supplied weekly intelligence culled from European newspapers.

The flow of escapees out of France yielded the greatest dividends, and it was important that Vera become deft in dealing with the secret services of de Gaulle and his FFI, to whom many escapees came first. At the end of 1941, her own F Section acquired a nominal boss, Maurice Buckmaster, after internal and near-suicidal departmental bickering. He was an old Etonian and more acceptable to other government departments than SOE ragamuffins from government schools. His prewar job as Ford manager in Paris had earned him a place on the chilling Wanted List France, *Sonderpfändungsliste Fr.* It was lucky that the Gestapo in France called agents and circuits "Buckmasters." It drew attention away from Vera.

Vera still had to argue against Whitehall mandarins, who said SOE put up "smoke screens." They were blind to historical precedents. The SIS liked to claim its roots went back at least as far as Elizabeth I, who had employed "explorators" to subvert the Catholics plotting in France. SOE descended from the deceptively named Alien Office, which had kept the French Revolution from infecting England, directed the assassination of Tsar Paul of Russia in 1790, and funded French resistance to Napoleon. The Lord Halifax school of thought, "on-the-one-hand-this-but-on-the-other-hand-that," was the absolute opposite of the Alien Office's philsophy of quick action.

After Russia became an ally, and with Halifax parked in Washington, the Foreign Office surprised Vera by sending SOE advisers to Moscow. Long after the war, after many attempts to hush up the facts, MI5 counterintelligence disclosed the extent of Soviet infiltration. Peter Wright, a retired assistant MI5 director, forced a constitutional crisis about the conduct and oversight of secret intelligence by defying a ban on his book *Spycatcher*, reporting details of English moles who were protected from prosecution after they confessed to spying for Moscow.[5]

After Pearl Harbor, SOE grew in stature. Donovan appointed officers of considerable standing to his London station, where his deputies, cheerfully accepting the jibe that OSS stood for Oh-So-Social, made very clear their support for Vera. Skirmishing parties, trained by SOE and operating under names like the Small Boat

Squadron, picked away at the outer German battlements of France, using canoes and tools whose very simplicity made them easy to acquire. In countries like Hungary, it was said the Gestapo took off on Friday and resumed work on Monday. In France, they were overstretched by resistance groups united under de Gaulle's man Jean Moulin. Many partisans were, in sentiment, anti-Gaullist. Vera discovered just how brilliantly Moulin could inspire them to overlook differences by his personal example. Resistance leaders saw, as did Vera, the scars on Moulin's throat, inflicted by a razor before he escaped his German jailers.

# 25

# Shattering Laval's "Shield of France"

Vera joined a small Free French celebration in Duke Street into the early hours of New Year's Day 1942. Before the last hoarded bottles of champagne were emptied, Jean Moulin left to parachute back into France. At the age of forty, he had been the country's youngest prefect. He had stayed at his post in Chartres until dismissed by the Vichy government after he refused to sign a German-dictated declaration that French civilians had been burned alive and in other ways slaughtered by the French themselves. Rotting corpses littered the streets, victims of German atrocities. Prefect Moulin refused to arrange a municipal cleanup, insisting that the Germans finish their own dirty work. He was jailed, tried to slit his throat, and was rushed to hospital. "I survived but felt I was on borrowed time, and should give to the cause whatever remains of my life," he told Vera. He had escaped German surveillance, acquired two fake identities, gathered details of anti-Nazi activities in the Rhone valley, and slipped over the border with the help of the U.S. consul in Marseilles. With a fake identity as Professor Jean Joseph Mercier of the International Institute in New York, he crossed overland to Lisbon. The British flew him to Poole, in Dorset, on October 19, 1941.

Moulin was questioned in the London district of Wandsworth by MI5 counterintelligence at a place previously known as the Royal Victoria Patriotic Asylum for Orphan Daughters of Soldiers and Sailors Killed in the Crimean War. He was not so much offended as intrigued, observing that he did not feel like an Orphan Daughter.

Vera salvaged him, curious to learn about his contact with a well-known Soviet agent in Paris, Henri Robinson, who had suggested the Hess mystery was really quite simple. Soviet agents in Berlin reported that the British would join Germany in a war against Russia. Hitler instructed Deputy Führer Hess to reinforce this impression while preparing to launch an invasion. None of this really mattered to Vera. The Russo-German war had brought her a reservoir of agents, previously hesitant about placing their well-organized networks at the disposal of the French underground. Moulin was a symbol of republicanism, to counter accusations that Gaullists planned to impose an authoritarian government once France was free again.

Vera escorted Moulin through an intensive course of training in SOE techniques. He was dropped into Provence on New Year's Day with a microfilmed message from de Gaulle hidden in a matchbox. This empowered Moulin to build conspiratorial cells of no more than seven men and women. Cell leaders would know only their immediate superiors in a chain of command reaching back to London. Moulin was called Rex by Vera. In France he was code-named Max. He was joined by Jean-Pierre Reinach, a young French army officer who had been captured in occupied France, escaped, reached England, and had fallen in love with Naomi, sister of Edmund de Rothschild. They married at the Great Synagogue in London before Reinach and Moulin parachuted back into France.

Jean-Pierre Reinach defended the Free French and FFI for being so obsessively secretive. "Closework is a blueprint for terrorism. It will be used against us by others rising up against white imperialism someday," he said to Vera while being briefed on codes by Leo Marks. Leo had an unusual sensitivity to any pupil's chances of survival. Leo had no credible reason to stop this idealistic young man from dropping to his death.

Moulin's latest reports began to arrive in February 1942. By then, Vera was allied with Admiral Lord Louis Mountbatten, whose Combined Operations launched coastal raids with primitive equipment. Vera and Mountbatten saw eye to eye. The French industrial working class formed a sound basis for mass uprisings. But the Foreign Office and the SIS intervened to complain about the allegedly erratic proceedings of SOE agents. Hugh Dalton was at the point of no return as SOE's parliamentary voice. He was seen as "Communistically inclined." Vera found this laughable: when she was with Ambassador Schulenburg in Bucharest, he had identified Stalin's leading agents, who burrowed out of sight and kept silent. Dalton was anything but invisible or silent. He was loud-mouthed, and poked around the SIS looking for examples of bungling, a threat to the illusion of SIS infallibility. So he was made president of the Board of Trade, where he would cause less friction, since foreign trade was virtually nonexistent. Bletchley decrypts of the U-boat Enigma ciphers had suddenly dried up. Enemy signals were unreadable because the Germans had added a new rotor to their naval Enigma machines. Shipping losses soared in a theater of war Churchill regarded as the one in which Britain might suffer final defeat. In assigning resources, he had to give a lesser priority to swamping Nazified Europe in a wave of terror.

Dalton, while still at SOE, had been infuriated by "a most graceless clodhopping" memo from Cadogan, undersecretary for foreign affairs, alleging that SOE "employed its own jargon to lay down a dense smoke-screen." Dalton was replaced by a supposedly more pliant Viscount Wolmer, the Earl of Selborne. "He's not very inspiring," commented Cadogan. Yet it was Selborne who made the damning accusation later that "SIS would never hesitate to use us to advance their schemes even if that meant the sacrifice of some of our people."

The SIS claimed that its hostility to SOE was justified because Moscow had instructed the French Communist Party to control internal resistance, and to work toward a national insurrection after the liberation of France. Yet Moulin, far from being a Soviet agent, was busy making sure that a French secret army would control the communists. He worked underground for fourteen crucial months, during which Pierre Laval, Vichy's prime minister, declared, "I hope for a German victory," and projected an image of his Vichy regime as the Shield of France. Then he launched a program of "voluntary labor" that turned into mandatory labor. French youths were forced to work in German factories. Thousands took to the hills in what was openly spoken of as Resistance. Seventy or more clandestine newspapers were published regularly, carrying reports of "La France libre" and the Free French. All of the Laval regime's anti-Semitism, including the transportation of Jews to death camps, was advertised in the roundup. Jewish children were carefully separated and dispatched in separate wagons to avoid "scenes of emotion," Moulin reported in helpless disgust and despair.

Moulin was flown back to England in a Westland Lysander. This nimble RAF spy plane was old by the standards of the time, but it had short, rough-field capabilities. It had been designed in the early 1930s, with a high wing behind the pilot, allowing for excellent all-around vision. American experts praised it as revolutionary, to the astonishment of RAF pilots, who were resigned to hearing their machines were obsolete. It had a cruising speed of 180 mph with a single Bristol Mercury engine, but it could reach 300 mph in a dive. All pilots were told to remember "what a tough job agents take on," in guidance notes by Wing Commander H. S. Verity. "Try to get to know [the agents] and give them confidence in pick-up operations," he wrote. "Don't let any [pilots] think they are sort of trick-cycling." Pilots were cramming extra "bodies" into space for three passengers, and bringing home gifts of perfume and champagne from French closework fighters.

What Moulin brought back was a dossier on the Resistance and news that Naomi Rothschild's young husband, Jean-Pierre, had been killed.

Vera had to harden her heart against an emotional attachment to Moulin and distress over Jean-Pierre's death and its validation of Leo Marks's premonition. She was increasingly restrained in her personal feelings, and yet she knew her success came from "getting inside" others, which required a great deal of sympathetic understanding. She feared for Moulin, who returned again to France with Yeo-Thomas, the White Rabbit, to free one of their comrades from German captivity. By then, Moulin estimated, there were some 200,000 partisans ready for a massive uprising. Resistance leaders were heartened by the sight and sound of a middle-aged British officer. Often partisans were forced to share a single weapon among several men. The White Rabbit constantly battled to break down the reluctance of the regular British armed forces to spare a few crumbs for them. He was hampered by secrecy: few knew of his heroic work.

In June 1943, Moulin was captured after an informer told the Germans "a Gaullist is in the neighborhood." He might have escaped, with so much experience in changing his appearance and identity, but he still carried the matchbox in which de Gaulle had inserted the microfilmed authorization for Moulin to speak for the general. The damning evidence was discovered. Fourteen resistance leaders, rounded up with him, were tortured and killed. Vera forced herself to read eyewitness accounts of how he was dismembered by the Gestapo until he died.

Three days before Moulin's horrific end, during the night of June 17–18, 1943, Pierre Raynaud, a French subaltern–sabotage instructor, had been dropped to join Francis Cammaerts, a graduate of the tough commando school at Arisaig in the Scottish Highlands. Raynaud became convinced that he was the victim of betrayal. At the same time, Noor Inayat Khan, often described as an Indian princess and a talented writer of children's stories, parachuted into France and began a long journey to a tragic end that would prompt speculation that she, too, was betrayed.

During the eighteen months since Moulin's New Year farewell party of 1941–42, Vera had seen physically tough young agents become paranoid when things went wrong for quite ordinary reasons. Raynaud believed his landing was observed by Germans who were waiting to follow him to Paris. He came to believe that SOE's F Section deliberately sent inadequately trained agents who, if caught, would break under interrogation and mislead the Germans with information given them by London. Such conspiracy theories were contradicted by one young female wireless operator, Yvonne Cormeau, who parachuted into France later that summer and found herself sitting in front of Francis Cammaerts, Raynaud's contact, on a train to Toulouse. "He looked straight through me," she reported, "and we ignored each other." There was no evidence of inadequate training. What sometimes did happen was that agents forgot safeguards after becoming comfortable in their hostile environment. A sudden encounter with an old friend from training school would lead to sharing a drink together, and then the Gestapo would pounce. Sometimes agents had to arrange a direct meeting to pass messages. Yvonne Cormeau had learned to write such messages on thin paper, tightly rolled and inserted by a needle into a cigarette, which could be partly smoked and then casually dropped. But even she, honored as a craftswoman who transmitted four hundred coded messages in a year, broke a rule that mandated that an agent should keep constantly on the move. She remained in one hideout for six months. The Germans were looking for an English wireless operator in the region, and her hideout was in a village with no running water, which seemed a good reason for not bothering to look there.

"Her reasoning was perfectly sensible," commented Vera. "She could watch from her attic over long distances for any suspicious German movements." Rules were meant to be broken, provided this was not done in a moment of sheer absentmindedness. This kind of reasoning did not satisfy Pierre Raynaud, who became obsessed with the idea that some agents — young, hurriedly trained girls — were given information they would reveal under interrogation and unwittingly deceive the enemy about Allied plans.

Gubbins reviewed SOE's training programs and its mobilization of highly skilled craftsmen, and agreed with Vera that anyone who believed agents were graduated before they were fully trained was suffering from paranoia. Some greenhorns, like Princess Noor and Diana Hope Rowden, although graded by instructors as unfit to go into the field, were sent anyway because their special skills were desperately needed, and they proved to be the toughest and most innovative in resisting interrogation under torture.

To make sure that SOE training was watertight, Vera revisited the rugged terrain at Loch Ailort, twenty-four miles west of Fort William on the coast of Scotland, where young men and women lived in a grim old house with cold granite walls, whipped constantly by high winds, that was hardly ever visible through the thick tall trees reaching higher than the roof. Mist and rain soaked the surrounding hills. The region was gloomy beyond belief, and the high fatality rate among aircrews at a nearby naval air station was almost entirely due to pilots flying into hilltops or losing their way in foul weather and running out of fuel far out to sea. Jack Wilson, formerly deputy police chief in Calcutta, oversaw instruction.

In September 1942 Vera concluded that the training grounds near Fort William were beyond subversion. "The Polish instructors had gone through hell in Soviet labor camps," she recalled. In that Scottish wilderness around Loch Ailort, the Poles recognized that under Jack Wilson's air of toughness was the honest purpose of a benign schoolmaster, who wanted to hammer home the art of surviving even worse challenges than Siberia. He had introduced Kim's Game, based on the Rudyard Kipling tale of a boy required to train his memory in order to live. Wilson had taught boys the mental disciplines that now, at the age of fifty-two, he introduced into Special Training Schools. The STS mushroomed into seventy "schools for danger" around the globe. Wilson's first wartime assignment had been with Gubbins's Independent Companies in Norway. He regarded the experience as a practice run for proper guerrilla warfare and helped Vera plan the insertion of agents to kill one of Hitler's chief instruments in the slaughtering of Jews, General Reinhard Heydrich.

Vera had first gone to the Fort William area with Gubbins and Polish soldiers evacuated through Dunkirk with their commander, General Władysław Sikorski. Gubby had known since boyhood the forbidding hills and the deep lochs of freezing black water. He had first selected it as a redoubt if Germany occupied Britain. Sikorski told Vera that the dismal landscape suited his Polish soul. The viaducts and bridges were perfect for exercises in sabotage. The countryside was bleak and challenging, and offered a foretaste of what an agent might encounter anywhere in Europe.

Vera found quarters for the Polish government-in-exile in the office of *Boy Scout Magazine* editor F. Haydn Dimmock on Buckingham Palace Road. Their role in shattering Laval's Shield of France would prove heroic. Few among Whitehall's regular service officers, and only those with the need to know, had any inkling of what went on behind the inoffensive magazine's blacked-out windows.

# 26

# "We Are in the Presence of a Crime Without a Name"

"Look!" Vera said, proudly waving a piece of soft toilet paper in front of Jan Zurakowski. "No more scraping your bottom in the loo."

Zura was bug-eyed. Many public washrooms had only squares of newspaper hanging from a nail. Vera had emphasized secrecy for this rendezvous. The Polish fighter pilot wondered if she had called him here to boast of this wartime adaptation of gentlemen's disposable handkerchiefs, sold exclusively in Harrods before the war.

Vera had asked him to meet her at SOE's Small Scale Raiding Force (SSRF) canteen near Kensington Palace Gardens Terrace, parallel to Embassy Row, a posh neighborhood of London's most expensive properties, now mostly blitzed. The SSRF canteen was improvised from the remains of a bombed pub on Church Street, just off Kensington High Street. The canteen was open to all servicemen, but in a shabby back room Vera enjoyed total privacy. Zura waited to learn what she really wanted to talk about.

She spoke of new shipping losses in Arctic convoys carrying war supplies to northern Russia. Local Soviet radio lapses were causing horrendous losses among British ships loaded with Russia-bound cargo scraped together to satisfy Stalin, who put constant and heavy pressure on Roosevelt and Churchill to reinforce Russian forces on the Eastern Front. If Stalin lost faith in his Western allies, he might make a separate peace and renew his old alliance with Germany. Vera warned: War on two fronts promised victory over Hitler. War on a single western front meant certain defeat for the Allies. Zura didn't need to be told that Poland's only hope was to be liberated by the West. What he now learned was that in September 1943, PQ18, an Arctic convoy, had been endangered by Russian wireless traffic whose codes were broken by the Germans. The previous convoy, PQ17, had sailed from northern Scotland along the Arctic route to Murmansk and suffered the loss of twenty-two merchant ships with cargo totaling 3,350 tanks and military vehicles, 210 warplanes, and some 100,000 tons of food and ammunition.

Bletchley now knew that the Russians were discovering the dates of convoy departures from northern Scotland and transmitting details to Polyarny, near Murmansk, in ciphers already broken in Berlin. Was this deliberate sabotage, and if so, who was responsible?

Zura was one airman qualified to undertake a mission to confirm or dismiss Vera's suspicions. He was one of her oldest and most trusted allies, their relationship close to a love affair, although both lived by the decent values for which they were fighting. Neither would cross the line between mutual respect and physical intimacy. Vera had promised Zura that everything would be done to get his girlfriend, who was Jewish, out of Poland. The odds were against it, and now it hurt her to ask him to risk his life again after all he had already done.

First she disclosed to him the existence of the only fighting squad whose actions were granted complete immunity from all legal accountability, including the ancient statute imposing criminal penalties for unsanctioned secret operations. She had never provided such disclosure before. Potential agents were first studied from a distance for suitability, introduced gradually into the killing arts, and left to make their own deductions once they were deemed fit for action. The final bit of official business was swearing the secrecy oath. Nothing was said about the technical illegality of their work. SOE specialized in murder and mayhem. Vera had to spell it out for her friend in clipped sentences.

Zura saw an astonishing hardening in her. She wore a short pleated Harris tweed skirt and a simple ivory blouse in place of a uniform, and at first glance appeared demure. Her lush black hair curled just below the square shoulders, sexy but short, as if to remind male admirers that she was likely smarter. Her straight posture declared her authority: her chin lifted just a bit above the norm, not arrogant, but enough to make the elderly waiter rush to please her. It was clear to

Zura that, however old and scruffy, the waiter had the highest level of security clearance. Under his apron, he packed a gun.

This new toughness in Vera's manner followed her recent discovery that while she was herself escaping from Poland into Romania, the German "ghettoization" of Polish Jews had been discussed in Warsaw by Adolf Eichmann, the grocery clerk who ran the Bureau for Jewish Affairs at the Reich Security Headquarters and was known to Vera as a signature on forms circulating through the SS, the Nazi elite. But on October 4, 1943, SS Reichsführer Heinrich Himmler had told his highest-ranking leaders meeting at Poznan, "Most of you probably know what it is to see a hundred corpses, or to see five hundred, or a thousand. To have gone through that and yet . . . to have preserved our decency — this is what has made us hard."

Vera had gotten hold of the text of that speech. "She became harder than any SS executioner," Zura was to tell me many years later. "She felt guilty for not knowing sooner that Eichmann had been in Warsaw while she was there, and *why* he'd been there. God help anyone who got in her way now. She was in a state of fury. She felt she'd let down my Jewish girlfriend. She sounded utterly pitiless when she outlined the SOE skullduggery she believed was the only way to sap the strength of an enemy whose purpose was not conquest but genocide, and to fight those who gave no priority to stopping the genocide."

Other frightful details had now reached her. She knew how deadly facts were ignored in London when so much might have been done to disrupt the Europe-wide network of railroads serving the death camps. When Whitehall appeasers still sought to pacify Hitler, she worried about the machinery for killing millions. Zura said, "She forgot she hardly had time to sleep, preparing covert warfare before Churchill took power . . . I saw a report that even then she was 'fearless but defies officialdom to get her own way.' Now nothing stood in her way. It was not as if the terror was secret. Even before Churchill finally took charge, our Polish couriers were reporting 'gassing machines' run by engines taken from dismantled Russian-built submarines to kill Jews at Auschwitz."

On January 20, 1942, fifteen top bureaucrats involved in the "natural diminution" of Jews met in a villa at 56 am-Grossen-Wannsee. SS Reichsführer Heinrich Himmler told this conference that "emigration" meant extermination. Before the war, Adolf Eichmann was already known to Whitehall, since in 1932 he had been intercepted at the border of Palestine by British Mandate authorities. He had arrived under the cover of a newsman for a well-respected Berlin newspaper and was later identified as "special deputy charged with preparation of the Final Solution." Within weeks of the French surrender, the puppet regime at Vichy took instruction from a General Commission on the Jewish Question, directed by SS Captain Theodor Dannecker, head of the Gestapo's Jewish office in Paris. The first deportations from France to Auschwitz began within months of the French surrender: several thousand children between the ages of two and seventeen were never seen again. All this had been known in Whitehall.

Zura said Vera had rock-solid proof that the German program of "natural diminution" had already begun while he was trying to fly to England and she was trying to escape Romania. She remembered, too, how Czechoslovakia had been betrayed by Chamberlain, who had sneered in public that nobody in England knew or cared about such countries in Eastern Europe. "They cause only chaos and incomprehensible trouble for generations," he was quoted as saying.

Actually, Churchill in a BBC "Broadcast to the World" on August 24, 1941, had attempted to publicize the Nazi terror, saying, "We are in the presence of a crime without a name." His words were printed in leaflets to be dropped by air throughout Europe in 1942, but Vera told Zura that the Air Ministry opposed the waste of warplanes for such pointless missions.

Zura and other Polish pilots were already familiar with the use of secrecy to conceal domestic embarrassments. Polish veterans of the aerial clashes over Warsaw had fought anonymously in RAF Squadron 303, otherwise know as the Kosciuszko Squadron, named after the eighteenth-century Polish hero Tadeusz Kosciuszko. The name was never acknowledged. Air Ministry officials had tried to prevent the use of Polish pilots in the Battle of Britain. Tributes to their skill and heroism came later from regular RAF pilots, who said the battle would have been lost without the intervention of the Poles, who were horrified by the RAF's use of outdated tactics against an enemy whose modern tactics clearly had never been studied.

Historians today record the vital role of the Poles in defeating the

1940 German aerial onslaught, but at the time their role was unknown to the public.[1]

In 1943, Vera told Zura, "You were fighting to liberate your own country when you saved England. When this war's won, Churchill and Roosevelt will let Stalin take Poland." It was clear she had lost all illusions.

After her initial disclosure, Vera invited Zura to a weekend walking through the Sussex countryside around Winchelsea. There she outlined a mission involving dangers that even Zura had never faced. She needed a Polish-speaking pilot to fly solo in the Baltic area and record Russian wireless transmissions. These were not picked up in their entirety at Bletchley, and code breakers were not sure if transmissions originated in the Russian-occupied part of Poland. Zura flew a series of these spy missions, refueling at a secret base on the Finland-Sweden border. He was never told the results. He wrote me later: "The RAF's top brass resented Vera's 'irresponsible, unauthorized efforts to influence policy' and saw her as an interfering woman, uneducated in the traditions and disciplines of a fighting service." But Zura saw Vera was right: Poland would be sacrificed to placate Stalin, and he wanted to take his girlfriend, if she escaped, as far from the Soviets as possible. Meanwhile, he advised Vera on escape lines for downed fliers.

Vera could have seen Zura behind closed doors at the Boy Scout magazine office sheltering the exiled Polish government, but she was wary of eavesdroppers when secrecy was so difficult to preserve among governments-in-exile. Some things must be kept secret; some secrets should be deliberately leaked. She had confided to Mary Stephenson some misgivings upon learning before the war that Eichmann had met several times with Haganah Zionist militants in Berlin. One meeting had been reported in *Der Stuermer*, the radical anti-Jewish periodical; other meetings took place between Zionist agents at the Hotel zur Traube, near the Berlin Zoo. Prewar Haganah representatives needed to test Eichmann's claim that he wanted only to resettle Jews in Palestine. He had gone there in the winter of 1937, traveling by train through Romania and boarding a ship at Constanţa for Palestine, carrying false credentials as a journalist for *Berliner Tageblatt*—a newspaper whose owner and editor in chief, both Jews, were replaced when it was "coordinated" into the Nazi Party. The Soviet Union put its best intelligence resources into finding out if Eichmann meant to use

Jewish refugees to damage British relations with Arabs. One Soviet source was Kim Philby, later exposed as a mole in the British SIS. His father, Harry St. John "Jack" Philby, met with Zionist leaders including Ben-Gurion and Chaim Weizmann in February 1939 and promised that substantial Jewish immigration to Palestine could be purchased by a Jewish "loan" to the House of Saud and Ibn Saud as "boss of bosses" in the Arab world.

After she found that facts had been twisted or ignored, Vera pushed harder than ever to win respect for these Jewish military organizations, still seen as enemies in Whitehall. Nothing had appeared in the British press in November 1940 when the illustrious U.S. correspondent in Berlin, William Shirer, reported that his "spies," as he called informers, discovered why strange death notices appeared in German newspapers, using phrases like "after weeks of uncertainty" a beloved son or daughter had "unbelievably" died in an area around the castle of Grafeneck, which was said to be a "hospital." Shirer found Grafeneck surrounded by "black-coated SS men"; trucks with tarpaulins thundered into the "hospital" all night. He concluded that the Nazis were murdering the mentally ill for "eugenic reasons." An unanswerable form letter was mailed to relatives: the dead son or daughter had been "saved from a lifelong institutional sojourn" and death came as "a merciful release." Euthanasia had been justified, but not a word had appeared in print in the three years since Shirer's first horrified conclusions. After the decision to go to war, the Chamberlain government and newspaper proprietors who toadied to the royal family had either suppressed the reports or dismissed them. Vera had waited three years to learn of the euphemism for genocide. It was clear that not only Jews were the intended victims of a dictatorship intent upon perfecting an Aryan race.

Vera was absolutely sure that the only hope for the Jewish people was to create their own state. Churchill seemed to yield to the American policy of shutting out Jewish immigrants on the theory, Go with the ally best able to serve your interests. Whitehall stepped up attacks on SOE as an out-of-control agency teaching terrorism against international law. Vera continued as fiercely as ever to argue that democratic control was her aim in uniting French guerrilla groups, but she could not talk openly of this without ministerial approval, which had to come from the antagonistic Foreign Office. Its SIS chiefs feared that uprisings fomented by SOE might help French agents recruited by the German Jewish communist who called himself Henri Robinson. He was said to have been instructed by Stalin to make France the Red front of the Soviet Great Patriotic War. In the bowels of the SIS, however, were British-born traitors reporting to Moscow and, because of pro-Soviet sympathies, eager to destroy SOE.

Zura discussed all this with Vera after his clandestine recordings of Russian broadcasts of escort arrangements for the Arctic convoys. Admiral Bill Mott, briefing officer on ULTRA for Roosevelt, would later report Stalin's refusal to agree to the West's airlift of supplies to anti-Nazi underground armies. Mott identified John Cairncross as a Soviet-run spy at Bletchley from 1942 to 1944, betraying ULTRA secrets to Moscow and then becoming a formal SIS officer. ULTRA information was not supposed to be disclosed to the Soviet Union, according to future U.S. Supreme Court Justice Lewis W. Powell. As a wartime U.S. Air Force colonel, he was one of a tiny American group empowered to "accept" ULTRA intelligence from Bletchley to guide General Carl Spaatz's U.S. Strategic Air Force in bombing German industrial centers.[2]

It made no sense to Zura that the Russians would give their German enemy the details of convoys bringing urgently needed supplies. His mystification only deepened after the revelation by Hitler's spy chief that "Russian shortwave transmitters extended over all German-occupied territories, and neutral countries too, from Norway to the Pyrenees, from the Atlantic to the Oder, from the North Sea to the Mediterranean." Walter Schellenberg made the claim when he became a postwar adviser to the Americans on Soviet espionage.[3]

For a long time Vera was to remain in the dark about the reasons for Russian broadcasts using codes already known to be broken by Berlin. She was working exhaustively on SOE operations while trying to understand SIS motives in betraying Zionist guerrillas, in synchronization with Russian propaganda that encouraged anti-British feeling in Arabia. On Friday, March 6, 1942, the London *Daily Mirror* ran a cartoon by the famous Zec. It showed a lone merchant seaman clinging to a life raft, his ship torpedoed, his agony starkly etched against the terrible isolation of an empty ocean. The caption came from an announcement in the House of Commons: THE PRICE OF PETROL HAS BEEN INCREASED BY ONE PENNY—OFFICIAL. Zec's message was that badly underpaid seamen suffered terrible losses to fill the pockets of war profiteers. The *Daily Mirror* was reminded that the Communist Party's *Daily Worker* had been closed down for such "vicious and malignant criticism." Then the *Mirror* columnist William Connor, under his pen name of Cassandra, spoke out against a new British policy of stopping further Jewish immigration to Palestine. He was immediately drafted into military service.

The need to study masses of contradictory information became painfully obvious, but Vera suffered from a lack of qualified analysts. Her sources reported that, while shipping Jews to death camps, Eichmann also increased the flow of refugees to Palestine. She could only guess that the contradiction arose from Nazi calculations that if the British had to intercept the refugee ships, this tied up their warships. Yet if they let in the Jews, they would alienate the Arab world. Churchill did try for an Anglo-American denunciation of "elimination" that masqueraded as emigration. He squeezed a declaration out of ten Allied governments-in-exile on December 17, 1942, deploring Hitler's oft-repeated intention to exterminate the Jewish people. Not one government, including the U.S. and U.K., would put its name to documents setting out the facts. The public was left in ignorance of what the declaration really meant. At this point, Churchill apparently gave up.

"But Vera went for the jugular," said Zura. She got the Archbishop of Canterbury to speak out against the lack of action to save Jews. He said that polls in the United States reported a *rise* in anti-Semitic sentiment, and his warnings led Christian groups, labor unions, and humanitarian activists to demands measures to help surviving Jews. To curb public outcry, Whitehall called a conference on the day the Warsaw ghetto uprising broke out, April 19, 1943. The conference ended as the Warsaw Jews broadcast their final appeal: "The last 35,000 Jews in the ghetto are condemned to execution. Save us."

The conference took place between British cabinet members and a small U.S. delegation in Bermuda. The British territory's "censorettes" intercepted communications between the Western Hemisphere and Europe. Buried in such secrecy, the island was ideal for a conference that was never meant to produce action. The U.S. government issued permits for only five wire-service reporters, who had to rely on handouts. "It was a mutual anticonscience pact," Vera said later. "Americans did not want to compromise their tight immigration policy." The Archbishop of Canterbury condemned the whole affair as disgraceful. Discussions were kept secret on the pretext that Allied security was at stake. A one-page bulletin said concrete recommendations were made but must remain confidential because of "military considerations." Vera knew what this meant, from the report of parliamentary undersecretary Richard Law, later Baron Coleraine: "The feeling in England is widespread against the Jews [but] American public opinion is subjected to extreme pressure from an alliance of Jewish organizations." The conference was pious humbug.

Vera spoke with Chaim Weizmann about this fresh proof that a Jewish Brigade must be formed. Again she saw secrecy used to hide intentions and mistakes. Chaim's son Michael was killed piloting a warplane in a botched operation to stop the German battle cruisers *Scharnhorst* and *Gneisenau* slipping through the English Channel after being bottled up in the French Atlantic port of Brest for months. On the night of February 11–12, 1942, they escaped. A naval board of inquiry suppressed details of what Lord Kilbracken, a navy Swordfish pilot, later called "perhaps the sorriest debacle of the war." Six old Swordfish biplanes were launched against the battlewagons. The RAF's modern aircraft "waited in their hundreds," as Kilbracken put it, on the ground. The German warships, accompanied by the heavy cruiser *Prinz Eugen* and destroyers, left Brest during 198 minutes of darkness and sailed for three hundred miles undetected until they reached the Straits of Dover, while telephone arguments raged between naval and RAF commanders over which service should take responsibility. Thirteen of eighteen Swordfish crewmen were killed. Their commander, Eugene Esmonde, was awarded the highest decoration, the Victoria Cross, but he was dead, too.[4]

Chaim said bitterly, "My son fell in a cause for which the Zionist flag has not yet been unfurled." Another son, Ezer, flew RAF Spitfires and later became chief of the Israeli air force and then the president of Israel.[5]

SOE had no political or racial agenda. Since there was not yet a Jewish Brigade, Vera prepared, with combat training, agents like the Jewish ex-boxer Alec Rabinovich, a wisecracking wireless operator in Peter Churchill's French network. "Wireless operators are SOE's most valuable links in our chain of operations," Vera told the cryptologist Leo Marks. By this time, Operation Lavatory had inspired Elder Wills to design wireless aerials to look like the pull chain above French toilets.

Vera won the fight with SIS for control over SOE communications and now had a signals directorate under Leo Marks with a "harem" to handle coded traffic. The girls' reports were intercepted by the SIS deputy chief, Claude Dansey, by tapping the teleprinter lines to Baker Street. De Gaulle's Free French insisted on using their own secret codes to outwit Dansey. Messages from their agents in the field were passed through their offices in Duke Street.

"So the Free French had one code we knew and another we didn't," Vera told Bill Stephenson. "De Gaulle said his code was locked in a safe. Then one of his agents sent an indecipherable, mutilated by atmospherics or careless coding, and Leo was asked to help." Leo was always trying to prevent "repeats." Each time an agent made a mistake in coding, he produced an "indecipherable" and London had to ask for a repeat. Thus German detection vans were given more time to close in on the agent's location. Leo wanted to reach a stage where original messages would *always* be broken. Sometimes it took 750,000 attempts to break an indecipherable. Leo was slowly building up teams of bright girls who swore there would never again be such a thing as an indecipherable after they heard Leo's graphic account of what happened to agents who were caught while repeating a message.

Leo locked himself in the Free French lavatory to unscramble an indecipherable. Meanwhile, the agent in France blew out his brains when the Germans burst in while he repeated his transmission. "He was afraid they would torture the information out of him," Vera recalled. The agent should never have been asked for a repeat, because Leo was already solving the puzzle while sitting in the Duke Street toilet. After this, he called it Puke Street. "The message was sent in the French code," he said later. "In the loo, I discovered this supersecret French code was the same as ours." De Gaulle's Free French added their own prefixes while working the British code, and the British were not supposed to know. Leo broke the dead agent's indecipherable and sent it to de Gaulle without comment.

Leo Marks was always fearful of losing agents because their messages got unintentionally scrambled. He became alarmed whenever he caught someone like Violette Szabo repeatedly making mistakes that seemed so tiny but could endanger an entire network. He made new agents understand how they might accidentally produce these "indecipherables" while encoding under deadly pressure: cold, hungry, and lonely, trying to recall preselected words from "recognition poems," injecting safety checks, tapping out Morse while enemy radio-locator vans searched for them. The Germans honed their detection skills to shut down power stations in sequence until a sudden suspension of dit-dit-dahs betrayed the agent's location. To counter this, batteries were used for a new batch of wireless sets, and crude ways were devised to crank them up. Independent signaling apparatus had been neglected in the beginning. Yet the Bank of England always had secret telegraphic codes. One SOE executive who knew about these was Geoffrey Courtauld of the international textile merchants. The Courtauld company used codes in its cables abroad, and Vera shamelessly drew on these private business experts for advice.

"She learned it was a good idea to do the *Times* crossword puzzle, to know the *Oxford Dictionary of English Verse*, popular slang, and English music hall songs," Admiral Mott said later.[6] "These were sources for encoding messages and also enabled her to deal with memorized poem-codes that became garbled in transmission. She'd solve an indecipherable by a kind of lightning intuition." The question asked of each bright young female interviewed to handle coded traffic was "Are you good at crossword puzzles?" To answer "Not really" could be decisive. Did she love music? A negative was just as bad. "Terrible at arithmetic?" A despairing and reluctant "Yes" was greeted with a smile that astonished the candidate. Vera knew any damage done by a math teacher at school was easily repaired, but if the puzzled woman had a tin ear and disliked crossword puzzles, she was shunted into some other service.

Leo Marks was in awe of the way Vera found time to help with communications. He was himself capable of immense bouts of intense mental activity. "I supposed it was because we were both Jewish," he said later. "We watched helplessly while the Allies ignored pleas to bomb the death camps or the intricate network bringing from all over Europe the slaves who would be worked until they were no longer useful, then sent to the ovens, and we wanted to end the nightmare despite the Whitehall skeptics who dismissed guerrilla warfare as a means to quickly collapse the enemy infrastructure. We knew what awaited agents caught by the Gestapo."

# 27

# "Thin Red Line"

"I was lucky that secret American support for SOE pre-dated U.S. entry into the war," Vera said later. "Bill Donovan's missions throughout Europe confirmed that 'no country of origin' meant doors were closed against Jews who still got out of Europe."

"It's a vast concentration camp," reported an anti-Nazi German aristocrat, Baron Rüdiger von Etzdorf, working for SOE. "Millions may be sent to places like Russia when the Third Reich collapses."

"Nobody in Whitehall spoke of this," Donovan David Bruce, told his London-based representative of the Office of Coordinator of Information. Bill Stephenson was expanding secret training camps along the unguarded U.S.-Canada border. From Montreal, U.S. collaborators could now fly unobserved to Scotland in modified RAF bombers, avoiding scrutiny of the Pan-Am Clipper routes.

Donovan had his own sources in the Iberian peninsula who reported seeing a German baron with an "English gentleman." Vera reassured Donovan: Baron von Etzdorf was a friend introduced in prewar Berlin by her ex-lover, the ambassador Count von der Schulenburg. Etzdorf had told her that after meeting Hitler, he found "everything about the little Nazi unpleasant." Etzdorf now organized escape routes that led to Lisbon: "The last open gate in the vast European concentration camp."

A brother, Dr. Hasso von Etzdorf, worked in Berlin with the chief of the general staff, Colonel-General Franz Halder, also anti-Nazi, who knew Marie "Missie" Vassiltchikov, the Russian princess. Missie had warned Vera that these influential anti-Nazis would "have trouble forming a united front if Britain doesn't help." Baron von Etzdorf had wangled a diplomatic posting to Madrid, from where he could communicate with Vera. There he met Sir Samuel Hoare, sent to Spain as ambassador because his appeasement reputation might help keep local fascists neutral. Vera viewed Hoare as one of the Old Cronies' Club: aristos who levered each other into top jobs and had pro-Nazi leanings. His pals had advanced him from secretary for India in 1931 to foreign secretary in 1935. He encouraged the then French prime minister Pierre Laval, executed in 1945 for Nazi collaboration, to believe Mussolini should keep his Italian military conquests in Africa. Hoare became secretary for air in early 1940, a serious setback for the RAF until Churchill took power and sent him to Spain so that Hoare's fascist contacts might be discouraged from letting Germany use Spanish coastal bases, the more easily to attack Atlantic convoys. Virtuously citing his ability to keep Spain neutral, Hoare torpedoed SOE's plans for guerrilla warfare there. The advice Vera gave the baron was "squeeze what you can out of the old Hoare by playing on his invincible faith in his moral superiority."[1]

The German baron had helped Jews to escape the surrender-on-demand agreement between Vichy and Germany by working with Varian Fry. Fry was free to work with Vera on his unique connections, for he was now part of Donovan's clandestine office in London's Grosvenor Square. The secret cooperation was described by Desmond Morton, Churchill's old intelligence adviser: "U.S. Security is being run for them at the President's request by the British. A British officer [Stephenson] sits in Washington with Mr. Edgar Hoover and General Bill Donovan for this purpose." Donovan picked Fry's brains to make better use of young Jewish escapees, helping them defeat "enemy alien" rules. Fry, the Harvard-educated classicist who had risked his life inside the enemy camp for fourteen months, knew precisely Vichy's program against 330,000 Jews in France: 168 different decrees forced them, among other things, to shop between 3 and 4 P.M. and banned them from most professions. Many had fled to France to escape German persecution, but were now put into work camps. Fry knew how to exploit divisions within the Vichy-run police, how to locate French anti-Nazi resisters, and how to avoid Gestapo entrapment. Most important, he was sure, by promoting a common aim among quarreling factions, anti-German resistance could be achieved first in France to inspire wider uprisings. An ardent champion of this view was "Tommy" Yeo-Thomas, the White Rabbit.

The Yeo-Thomas family had lived in France since 1855. Tommy was thirty-eight when Britain declared war, and he left his office on rue Royale in Paris to offer his services. The local British military attaché said he wasn't needed. The French Foreign Legion said he was too old. So he gave his car to the British air attaché and was grudgingly accepted into the RAF at the lowest rank, unpaid, to interpret for RAF Bomber Liaison in France until all lines of communication were broken on June 11, 1940, by the German conquest. He got on a cargo boat evacuating some of the last British troops to England.

He shared Vera's graveyard humor. "We're outcasts," he told her, "until the buggers need us to do their dirty work. Me Tommy, you Vera—we're Tommy Vera." He paraphrased Rudyard Kipling: "O it's Tommy this and Vera that, an' both you go away / But it's 'Thin red line of 'eroes' when the drums begin to roll. . . . For it's Tommy this Tommy that, an' 'Chuck 'im out, the brute!' / But it's 'Saviour of 'is country' when the guns begin to shoot."

Tommy glimpsed her grim wit when she left him a note: "Since we're fated to be Tommy-Vera, you should know we're fiction. 'Tommy' was used 128 years ago in a War Office guide for a soldier to apply for 'marching money' at two and a half pence per mile to cover himself, wife, and child. The Duke of Wellington in 1794 found a Grenadier with a bayonet thrust in the chest, a sabre cut across the head and a bullet in his lungs who gasped, 'It's all in a day's work, sir.' *His name was Thomas Vera.*"

Vera noted: "The Grenadier combined loyalty with *'proud insubordination.'*" Yeo-Thomas used this to describe his own refusal to obey imbecilic rules imposed from on high by a swelling bureaucracy that forbade members of different SOE country sections to exchange information. He planted a question in the House of Commons: Why wasn't better use made of civilians with firsthand experience of living among the enemy—like himself?

He joined Vera's F Section in February 1942 and in Baker Street "saw the ghost of Sherlock Holmes passing by in a hansom cab. I'll honor the great detective by applying Holmes's methods in France."

He later said: "Vera terrified me at first. Those cold eyes . . . She's scholarly-smart. She knew all the books used by agents for coding and quoted *Alice in Wonderland*, who said you can make a word mean different things. 'Not so,' said Humpty-Dumpty. 'The question is, which is to be master.' She made herself the master. She won against old SIS codemakers who clung to dangerous old ways of making words mean different things."

Tommy knew how Hitler used his Vichy puppets to exploit the traditional loyalty of police and civil servants to French governments. "Spread word that Vichy is not the legitimate government," she told Tommy when he joined her. "General de Gaulle governs Free France."

The frictions caused when Marshal Philippe Pétain first set up his Vichy government in the so-called free zone typified squabbles within the intelligence comunity in London, which included often mutually hostile foreign elements. Vera needed to override all differences to reach the common goal of defeating Germany. She whipped up anger against Pierre Laval, the Vichy prime minister, by publicizing Laval's words: "The Resistance is financed by Jews so others can do the fighting for them." Any French citizen could see Jews were now being sent by the wagonload to the camps along with French "slaves." Some opportunists seized Jewish businesses at knockdown prices. She planned a day of retribution. It meant overcoming the fact that de Gaulle was not the elected leader of an elected French government.

Vera proposed strategies for SOE's Western Europe Directorate. She had to work with two French sections: F, run by Buckmaster, and RF, working with de Gaulle. RF's chief was known by the code name Colonel Passy, and Whitehall treated him with caution as a de Gaulle "subversive" in an unelected group that could not be registered as a government-in-exile. Passy had no experience in intelligence, and simply believed that de Gaulle as head of a postwar state would wipe out the memory of the corrupt prewar government that let France collapse into moral decrepitude.

Passy had inserted the first Gaullist agent, and later explained that until he understood the departmental war between the SIS and SOE, he saw Vera's people as pursuing activities multiple, secret, and complicated. Tentacles reached into every corner of Whitehall. When he knew more about Vera's motives, Passy backed her department intrigues and drew up a list of closework actions that civilians could take to help the final liberators of France on D-day. He had a personal stake in not wishing to see his own people burned alive in village churches for isolated acts of defiance.[2]

"Passy left wife and children behind," Vera told Yeo-Thomas.

"He's cut off from his own utterly different culture. He wants a maximum of informers to tell him precisely what they see, what they know, but to sit tight. He wants agents as *envoys* to collect this information, put it in context so he can plan the final insurrection. He's afraid of small, premature actions that will push the Germans into organizing frightful techniques of counterterrorism."

Passy proposed that he parachute into France, together with Yeo-Thomas. Vera told Yeo-Thomas of lessons learned from the early insertion of a Free French paratroop battalion to ambush German pilots known to travel by bus from their quarters to their airfield near Vannes in Brittany: it had seemed sensible to kill the pilots on the ground before they could carry out their bomber target-marking missions over England. By December 1940 the Free French had readied Operation Savanna. But the RAF first said Savanna was a despicable act, involving the "assassination of fellow combatants." De Gaulle asked sarcastically if bombing innocent civilians was less despicable. There was a long silence. The fatal consequences of delay were soon to be demonstrated. On the night of March 15, 1941, the RAF released one old bomber and Vera drove out to a secret airfield where Scotland Yard men searched the paratroopers to make sure they carried no incriminating evidence. "I know nothing the Gestapo would find useful," said one parachutist, refusing the offer of a suicide pill if he needed to cheat the torturers. The five were dropped "blind," and nothing more was heard. Three turned up a month later, after being picked up by submarine. Two found their own way out through Spain. The mission failed because the German bomber crews had changed their routine during the RAF's long delay.

Operation Josephine B, which followed soon after, blew up a power station near Bordeaux. Both operations taught that closework must have up-to-date target information. Vera expanded resources for gathering such intelligence. The survivors of these early missions, who had to grope their way back to England, alerted Vera to more espionage possibilities using downed airmen, and to the usefulness of escape routes.

Vera learned more about Passy during intensive predrop training. His real name was André Dewavrin. "My ignorance was total when I became the Free French intelligence chief," he confessed. Even his taking the name Passy from a Paris metro station near home exposed a dangerous innocence. "Now I know pseudonyms should have letters matching your laundry marks. Never adopt a name remotely connected with your previous life."

Passy had been fighting the Germans in Norway at the same time as Colin Gubbins, with a unit drawn from the Foreign Legion and the Chasseurs Alpins. He had been awarded Britain's Distinguished Service Order and Military Cross, and additional Norwegian and French decorations for bravery. After the 1940 defeat, French soldiers like himself had gone through the agony of choosing between repatriation and staying to fight with de Gaulle. On July 1, 1940, Passy had gone to de Gaulle's temporary office near Westminster Bridge at St. Stephen's House, where the general told him to organize Free France's Second and Third Intelligence Bureaus.

Passy scratched together a team of other young Frenchmen, simply because they happened to share a boardinghouse with him on the Cromwell Road. None had the foggiest notions about covert action. Passy learned espionage from someone he called "Uncle Claude," finding it easier than Sir Claude Edward Marjoribanks Dansey. Passy soon divined that Uncle Claude's purpose was to rob SOE of a nascent French intelligence service and keep it for himself at the Secret Intelligence Service.

Vera saw Passy as a handsome man of thirty, not much younger than she. His dreamy manner covered an intensely orderly mind. He was tall, with thinning blond hair and the innocent face of a teenager. His blue eyes were apt to drift away and then suddenly return to drill the person he was addressing.

"He studied fortifications!" Vera once joked to Leo Marks. "That's why he's so good at stonewalling." It was in the early days when Passy's Free French put up walls against shared information and distrusted an ally who had escaped after the French defeat. In August 1940, Passy's first tiny London base consisted of two wooden canteen tables, a chair, and two benches in a cramped three-room suite of Free French headquarters at 4 Carlton Gardens. Within a month, Jacques Mansion returned from a Passy-inspired mission. It showed Vera how fast Passy could work. His staff of amateurs had combed the camps and hospitals that held Frenchmen who had reached England, seeking men they imagined would make good agents. Jacques had landed on the Brittany coast from a small fishing boat and come back with news of German dispositions at Ouistreham, a fishing port adjoining Caen on the Normandy coast. Passy dispatched to the area a Lieutenant Maurice Duclos, trained for artillery, and Jacques Mansion. They were to send back information by carrier pigeon. Vera did not sneer. She had seen French *pigeonniers* rising one hundred feet or more, with spaces for pigeons in holes winding around the interior. The brick towers belonged to a crumbling age of medieval manors and were overlooked by the enemy.

Passy's RF Section subsequently "lived out" at No. 1 Dorset Square, dubbed "the circus of clowns" and previously occupied by the Bertram Mills Circus. Passy's working quarters advanced to a seven-room pavilion at 3 St. James's Square, then settled in at 10 Duke Street, near Selfridge's, with a luxurious substation behind Kensington Palace. His communications improved upon carrier pigeons after Duclos turned up on Christmas Day from Lisbon, followed two weeks later by Mansion, who had escaped through Spain. Both had been helped by Baron Rüdiger von Etzdorf.

To spot more Iberian exits, Passy had chosen a young filmmaker, Gilbert Renault, whose movie on Christopher Columbus made him friends in Spain. Renault made a swift reconnaissance, got back to England, and was given a crash course in new codes before being flown to Lisbon. Soon Passy was getting demands from his moviemaking agent for wireless equipment. Renault did not relish tying messages to the legs of pigeons.

Passy was afraid that a multiplicity of intelligence services in France could cause confusion. He asked Yeo-Thomas to help build a united front. Vera felt a brief stab of pain. Yeo-Thomas might not return, and he was becoming indispensable in confronting her domestic enemies. He was also the only Englishman she knew who could deal with the Free French without provoking a national temper tantrum, and get information in return. One early crisis arose because de Gaulle was told the Free French navy's admiral, Émile Muselier, was to be arrested. MI5 counterintelligence agents had unearthed what appeared to be letters suggesting Muselier sided with Vichy. But the letters were forgeries. MI5's espionage B Branch seemed determined to discredit the Free French. De Gaulle was losing trust in all intelligence services until Churchill apologized for MI5's interrogations of French escapees.

It was an insult, said Passy, that the English should look for pro-Nazi Vichy agents when other secret services did their own vetting.

Yeo-Thomas was itching to get away from this wrangling. Vera would have gladly gone with him. She was, though, the one person able to regularly bridge the gaps. The British wanted to win the war; Vera wanted to keep up the pressure of covert action; the Free French wanted to win the peace and wanted to wait until resisters united behind de Gaulle as a peacetime leader.

Passy was quick to misinterpret incidents. A French recruit, Francis Basin, completed SOE courses in microphotography and invisible inks. He had to make his own way across England and memorize details of an airfield in the wilds of Wales. He passed the test, and was told to go to a clandestine meeting in the Dorchester Hotel's bar. He was cautiously drinking warm Irish beer, which he detested, when a stranger pushed through the noisy crowd and roared at the top of his voice: "Basin, you're a German! You're under arrest!" None of the drinkers showed any interest. The stranger whispered in Basin's ear. Then every head turned. "See," said the stranger. "Behave like a conspirator and everyone suspects you." It was meant to be a jovial SOE lesson in psychology. Passy thought it was another attempt by MI5 to fail his men.

Yeo-Thomas was one of the few who could persuade him to continue with the planned Operation Seahorse, which was to demonstrate Anglo-French mutual trust. Vera took the opportunity to put Passy through a crash SOE training course and took him to Wanborough Manor, the sixteenth-century "school" on the Hog's Back. He saw resources stretched thin to deal with large numbers of recruits, many of whom would never make the grade. He was told, like others, to forget all he had ever been told about firearms. "Get off two rounds quick as light," said Vera. "The ideal murder weapon is the *silencieux* with luminous sights. There are more target points on the body than you'd think. Phosphorus grenades send Germans up in flame, but your body has less attention-grabbing weapons — use your feet, your nails to gouge out eyes, your fingers to choke off the carotid arteries or slash a throat."

Passy asked if Americans were capable of such things — he had heard they had joined forces with "the thin red line of 'eroes." Passy also knew Varian Fry, and learned a lot from the American. "The biggest danger is betrayal," Fry had said. "Avoid arousing jealousy, so don't get involved with women. Greed grips even seemingly reliable contacts. Avoid *any* discussions, religious, political, whatever. Many agents have foreign origins, and they've got to be careful if they run into someone from their homeland. There are Ukrainians and Cossacks used as ancillaries to German counterintelligence. The advantage we have over Germans is their lack of flexibility. The Gestapo uses only black Citroëns, for example."

A surprising number of Americans with extensive prewar business experience in Europe, as well as diplomats like William Russell, the former AP correspondent in Berlin, were gathered in London by Donovan. Gradually the silliness of departmental and national frictions was giving way to the handful of dedicated men and women from all parts of the world and all levels of society whose only aim was to operate behind enemy lines, an invisible and thin red line to undermine the enemy by rebelling against orthodoxy and worn-out rules.

Later, Passy recalled that his only contribution as a newcomer to the spy game had been his telling Vera to stop smoking like a chimney. He found it slowed the reactions.

"It gets me through the life I live," she joked, confirming for him that the real lifeline was a quick sense of humor, even in the worst of times.

# Fully Occupied

Vera turned Tommy Yeo-Thomas into François Yves Thierry, who carried forged papers showing him to be forty years old, formerly with the 34e Bataillon de l'Air, now back as a clerk in Paris, with a *carte d'identité* issued by the Paris Préfecture de Police on April 16, 1941, and a *feuille de démobilisation* from Marseilles dated September 2, 1940. He had a driver's license and a current ration card. Yeo-Thomas was to investigate with Passy the potential for resistance throughout France, discuss a future inter-Allied command with leaders of anti-Nazi movements, and bring back lists of supplies needed: Guns. Explosives. Comunications gear.

Vera told the BBC to send a message in its French service to a schoolteacher Tommy had known, Jose Dupuis. "Tommy à Jose: Nous reboirons bientôt du bon vin de Chignin." He would drink Chignin wine with her again, soon. She would understand.

On the night of February 24, 1943, Vera drove Tommy and Passy to Tempsford, ten miles east of Bedford, not far from Woburn Abbey and a half hour's drive from Bletchley. On a camouflaged airfield, the RAF's 138 Special Duties [Moonlight] Squadron waited. Vera had disturbing news. The Polish Enigma team were at Château des Fouzes, between Montpellier and Avignon. On November 4, 1942, they had heard a prearranged BBC message: "The harvest is good." It heralded the Allied invasion of North Africa four days later. This threatened the Mediterranean coast of France, and the Germans took full control of what had till then been the unoccupied zone. The code breakers quit the château three days before the Germans barged in. It was more important than ever to get them out of France before they tangled with French resisters whose loyalties might waver between political factions.

Operation Seahorse, the insertion of Passy and Yeo-Thomas, was timed to take best advantage of the moon, but it was a filthy night. Tommy said later, "I hadn't a clue where the moon might be, full or empty." Passy concealed his L-for-Lethal pill inside his signet ring and Tommy less theatrically put his pill in his waistcoat pocket. The two agents put on rubber helmets and spine pads, pocketed revolvers and compasses and knives, struggled into their parachute straps, and waddled out to a waiting four-engine Handley-Page Halifax bomber. Vera had seen the availability of aircraft creep up from five in the summer of 1941 to roughly twenty aircraft, the numbers and type varying according to RAF priorities. The planes were scattered between Newmarket Racecourse and a small corner of a fighter base at Tangmere, near Chichester, as well as the Tempsford base. Vera clasped the men's hands, murmured her customary "Merde alors!" for good luck, and boosted them through the small hatch.

Before dawn the agents were back, cold, exhausted, and cross. The pilot had been unable to locate the reception committee's lights. Passy and Yeo-Thomas were confined to dispiritingly shabby rooms in South Kensington, unable even to pop round the corner to the nearest pub. On Friday, February 26, they were taken out again. Another cold winter's night but now a waning moon. Three hours later, cramped from sitting between ghostly great packages, ears hurting from the noise of engines and the lack of pressurization, they wanted very badly to jump when the dispatcher told them to hook up the static lines at 0300 hours. They sat on the edge of the hole and saw lights below. The dispatcher signaled and Passy dropped. Yeo-Thomas followed. There were always a few moments of euphoria after the chute opened. Then the ground came up with a rush.

"C'est vous, Shelley?" A man's large rough hand gripped Tommy, who had no idea who Shelley was. He agreed that he was indeed Shelley, to avoid needless chatter. The packages floated down on parachutes. Shadows escorted Tommy and Passy into a wood.

"Who is Shelley?" Passy asked.

"I thought you'd know," Yeo-Thomas replied.

Back in London, Vera discovered that someone in Duke Street had informed the French reception committee that "Frances Yves

Thierry" was code-named Shelley, but hadn't bothered to tell Yeo-Thomas, sitting in Vera's F Section office.

Foul-ups were common. A psychiatrist kept on tap by SOE repeated: "Stress is not something to cope with like some brave little Girl Guide, Vera. You're letting yourself get stretched too far."

Gubbins was directing operations that now extended across Eastern Europe to the Far East. From India, aerial drops were made by Liberators that flew enormous distances into Japanese-held territories with agents of Force 136 of SOE in cavernous cargo holds, the pilots sometimes unable to find their jungle drop zones and forced to return from aborted missions, the agents battered by sixteen or more hours of nonstop flight. One young Force 136 agent came from Thailand's royal family. As a student in England, he had been branded an enemy alien when the Bangkok government, in the absence of their schoolboy king who was in Lausanne, sided with the Japanese. "I thought Vera Atkins should be locked up as an enemy alien until she told me how to get around the label," Prince Bisadej told me in 1992. "She'd known both my cousins. One was murdered. The other became Ninth Rama.

"She told me to join the Pioneer Corps. Then I'd be a noncombatant. I said, 'I don't want to be a noncombatant.' I wanted to do what another Siamese prince was doing, flying with the RAF. 'He was born here,' she said. 'If you join the Pioneer Corps we can shuffle the papers.' That's how all Siamese got into Force 136. Instructors thought we were small little brown chaps with no muscle. But we'd been brought up on hard exercise, and after I knocked out a sergeant, I was taken more seriously. I was dropped into Burma and walked up into China to Kunming where we had an anti-Japanese representative from Bangkok. I was given tasks, and walked down into Laos and then northern Thailand. It was more fun than lifting potatoes. But it made me an enemy of my established government. Vera was the only person who seemed to understand. She'd had to make choices too."[1]

Vera's priority was building up French networks. Code and teleprinter sections were set up in a mews off Baker Street. Leo Marks christened it "Danseyland," after Uncle Claude of the SIS. "He was totally paranoid about SOE," said Leo. "The army sergeant who first directed me into SOE said, 'It's called SOD or something—some potty outfit for misfits.'"

Vera had to remain in London while Gubbins flew to SOE/Cairo, where Countess Krystyna Skarbek, now Christina Granville, lobbied for another assignment. She was told to break off contact with Polish organizations linked to SOE in the Balkans. One Polish faction had decided that another faction was infiltrated by either fascists or communists. SOE/Cairo seemed "a nest of vipers," said Bickham Sweet-Escott of SOE later. "Nobody could possibly imagine the atmosphere of jealousy, suspicion and intrigue between secret and semi-secret departments. Christina Granville had the courage of a lion and was treated abominably by inferiors."[2]

Lieutenant Colonel Tony Simmonds was in trouble for having brought out of Greece some sixty-five Jews in old caïques without telling anyone. Simmonds had been in Palestine with Orde Wingate, the expert in irregular soldiering. Simmonds's courage and initiative only prompted bureaucratic wails about agents acting on their own. Gubby had to tidy up what was becoming a scandal, and considered sending Krystyna to Hungary to revive her old routes into Poland. This brought protests from one Polish faction in London that she was a Gestapo agent. Krystyna was finally dispatched to France, where she became even more of a legend. But first she had to be freed from Cairo.

"SOE in Cairo is working across, if not against, the war effort," reported Vera's friend the iron-willed Hermione, Countess of Ranfurly. She had gone independently to Cairo in the wake of her husband, Lord Ranfurly. She later reported what the butler said when His Lordship received orders from his yeomanry regiment, the Sherwood Foresters, to report for duty.

Lord Ranfurly asked his butler, Whitaker, "Are you coming too?"

"To the war, my lord?" asked the butler.

"Yes."

"Very good, my lord," said Whitaker.

His Lordship was reported missing in the desert when the Countess of Ranfurly was expelled from Cairo by a vindictive one-eyed brigadier who was, she said, "making a cock-up of SOE finances." She told Anthony Eden that "any amount of money is being wasted by this hush-hush organization which is in chaos." She jumped ship at Cape Town. She was lucky: the ship was torpedoed after she left. She told the local Thomas Cook travel agent she was on a secret mission and got a rare seat on a commercial flight back to Cairo. There, helped by beauty and social connections, she dodged the one-eyed brigadier and infiltrated the higher levels. "It helped that you knew how to write an invitation properly, and how to arrange a bowl of flowers," she remembered. She was said to know more secrets than anyone, and to have taught General George Patton to dance the Boomps-a-Daisy.[3]

From SOE/Cairo, saboteurs were within easier reach of countries like Romania in southeastern Europe, the source of half Germany's cereals and livestock, most of its tin, and a great deal of its aluminum ore, lead, and copper. But there were quarrels between those who said Tito's communist partisans were killing Germans and those who said he was killing right-wing guerrillas. Churchill's son Randolph parachuted into Yugoslavia. His Croatian secretary-translator, Mrdjn Lenka, told me years later that she fell in love with him when he arranged for the RAF to drop her an English/Serbo-Croat dictionary. His father, Winston, took to calling Tito "Marshal," but when the countess met Tito herself, she briskly dismissed him as "short and stocky and dressed to kill."[4]

Vera was improving relations with the SIS, which had an important Turkish station in Istanbul where her old mentor Gardyne de Chastelain ran special operations and employed Krystyna's husband, Jerzy, as a spy. De Chastelain knew Vera's difficulties in handling civilians who had to make decisions behind the lines but got into trouble for not going through the proper channels.

Gardyne de Chastelain was planning to parachute into Romania for SOE to sabotage oil wells and river traffic. For the logistical and other support he would need, he looked to Vera and not to Cairo, scorned as "a nest of spies, all betraying each other."

The turmoil in Cairo worsened. Egypt's pro-German leaders wanted to get rid of the British, who had been campaigning here since Nelson's victory at the Nile in 1798. If Cairo fell, Churchill would have to resign. His successors would make peace with Germany. It had been on June 21, 1942, that Churchill, staying in the White House, received the devastating news that Tobruk had been surrendered by British troops to the Germans: "One of the heaviest blows I can recall during the war."[5]

Tobruk was a garrison of 35,000 British soldiers. The surrender undermined Churchill's efforts to convince the United States that the tide would turn in Europe, and not to devote attention to the Pacific.

The Western Desert had provided the only British land victories in 32 months of war. American newspapers reported the fall of Tobruk as heralding the fall of Churchill. On June 28 a motion of "no confidence" was introduced in the House of Commons. Churchill survived. But this was one of many crises that demonstrated the fragility of democratic leadership, and the danger that another government might make peace, or dismantle SOE.

Vera's friends in the Jewish Agency were realistic. Jews were no longer being smuggled into Palestine through Romania's ports to embarrass the British. Romania had lost Bessarabia and Bukovina to the Soviet Union, and Jews were blamed. Jewish soldiers of the Romanian army were massacred. A death train loaded with some 2,500 Jews had been guarded by Romanian and German troops; dehydration killed 1,400 prisoners in the cattle cars during a five-day journey to the camps. About 100,000 Jews out of three times that number who had been living in Bessarabia and Bukovina were taken by the Soviet authorities and never seen again. Where Vera had once driven in the German ambassador's limousine along wide boulevards, bodies of butchered Jews now hung from the branches of the wonderful old trees that formerly shaded the chic cafés of Bucharest.

Vera faced overwhelming resistance to her making use of the chief victims of terror themselves, the Jews, and involving them in warfare. The chief rabbi of London was concerned that by the time a regular Jewish army brigade could be formed, its soldiers would be embittered by Britain's closure of Palestine's doors and its abandonment of promises implied by the Balfour Declaration. She had support from Lord Louis Mountbatten at Combined Operations for recruitment of those most bent upon revenge. He said the arithmetic overwhelmingly favored covert action. A packet of plastic explosive applied to a strategic point on one power transformer did more harm in an industrial area than costly Allied bombing raids. When the RAF launched a campaign against enemy transport systems, locomotives were singled out for low-level attacks to reduce the rolling stock and overload the repair sheds. Seventy locomotives a month were hit from the air during 1943. "To achieve this, seventy-eight railwaymen have been killed and three hundred seventy-eight wounded," reported Vera's French agent, who was a senior rail engineer. "By contrast—sabotage damaged eight times as many locomotives, with no civilian losses." Confirmation came from pilots on train-busting operations who were shot down and served with the Resistance.[6]

Railway workers favored clandestine operations, as did workers in factories serving the German arms industry and armed forces, and all were asking for leadership and supplies from outside. This was confimed after Vera's team was electrified by a message. "The little white rabbit has returned to his hutch," the BBC announced for French listeners on April 17, 1943.

Tommy Yeo-Thomas shared a Lysander pickup plane with Passy, Commandant Pierre Brossolette, and an American flier named Jim Ryan whose Flying Fortress had been shot down. Tommy had walked openly around Paris among SS men in their black uniforms with skull and crossbones. He had found his friend Jose Dupuis, still teaching at the same girls' school, and she had built him a network. Before his murder, Jean Moulin set the strength of a secret army at 50,000 with a reserve of 100,000. Yeo-Thomas had raised morale by being seen as a British secret-service officer, and he came back with new observations: "The *gazogène*, a wartime utility tractor, and the *remorqueur*, a towpath tractor, are good for transporting concealed weapons. There's a wartime *digestif* made from grape skins, it's white and called *marc*. Bean oil is now used to emulsify the hair. Be careful to tell the difference between *anciens combattants* and the French equivalent of the Hitler Youth, Les Compagnons de France, and watch out for Vichy propaganda that the world is run by the Old Lady of *rue Threadneedle*—which means the City of London, the Rothschilds, and Imperial Chemicals."

In Paris, Tommy had visited his father, who loudly greeted him in French as a stranger and then, once the apartment door was closed, asked, "What the bloody hell have you been doing for the last two years?" The older man had been carrying out small terrorist acts on his own account.

Brossolette, who flew on the same Lysander, had a distinctive white lock in his thick black hair, which had to be dyed to avoid identification. The dye had almost worn off since he had dropped into France, in the same moon period as the White Rabbit and Passy. Vera knew Pierre Brossolette as a prewar broadcaster of foreign news commentaries, dismissed from his job when he spoke out against the Munich "surrender." After Paris fell, he had run a small bookshop near the Lycée Janson de Sailly, whose pupils came to whisper of activities against the Germans rather than to buy books. He had escaped to England in April 1942 and had gone to Passy, who said Brossolette was "the man amongst all I met in life [who] made the greatest impression."

The White Rabbit's return provided Lord Selborne, SOE's political voice, with hard news to report to the chiefs of staff in his campaign for more generous SOE support: "Sabotage is widespread . . . support of a very effective kind can be given to regular military operations." But Vera was afraid Selborne was exhausting himself fighting those who said SOE wasted weapons and supplies. Her best hope was that Donovan's high-level London staff would rubber-stamp an official directive that SOE was the single authority for coordinating covert action and the work of "patriot forces." One agent, Major Ben Cowburn, returned with news of Virginia Hall. The *New York Post* girl had saved his bacon after he was dropped wide of the mark; he had lost contact with the reception committee, and she had to scurry around to find him a wireless operator. Vera decided Virginia should be recalled for training as a telegraphist and provided with one of the new radio transmitters. It was likely that she would become part of Donovan's new OSS. Vera was having to choose Americans over the SIS at home. Cowburn, an oil engineer in peacetime, had carried out four secret missions against oil targets, and later wrote scathingly of the legend "that the Secret Intelligence Service was omniscient." Its members, he said, were "seen only at fashionable Mayfair parties wearing stupid expressions and talking only about horse-riding, grouse shooting, and memories of their days at Oxford or Cambridge."[7]

Donovan's American officers were eager to learn, and they shared with Vera a conviction that unconventional special forces were the way of the future. Cowburn and other Englishmen like him, who came from the real world of hard knocks, said SOE's enemies were staff officers who moved seamlessly into government service straight from the cloisters of the same old establishments — Eton, Harrow, Winchester, Oxford, Cambridge — and were never exposed to the hurlyburly of life on the streets.

After the White Rabbit's reports gave SOE a stronger voice, Vera asked the Polish government-in-exile to appeal to all Poles to hide Jews. The Soviet Union had executed Polish army officers and occupied more than half of Poland. In Warsaw, the final German liquidation of the ghetto had started on April 19, 1943, the eve of Passover. The German attack had been anticipated by the central ghetto's 30,000 Jews, and when the liquidators broke in, they found people had burrowed underground. Gas was pumped into the tunnels in a German *Grossaktion*. Major General Jürgen Stroop broadcast a tally of "56,065 Jews seized, 7,000 perished. After deportation, 6,929 were exterminated, which adds up to 13,929 Jews destroyed."

Jozef Cyrankiewicz, a future communist leader in Poland, ran the Socialist Party's underground at the time and later said: "After seeing cattle wagons loaded up for the death camps, I felt we must mobilize the surviving Jewish communities from the Baltic to the Balkans. I was in Auschwitz when we sent couriers to London. Prisoners asked the Allies to bomb Auschwitz so the Nazis might stop the enormous trans-Europe traffic to death camps."[8]

Vera talked with the Polish National Council in London about the appeals from Auschwitz. Samuel Zygielbojm, a member of the council and of the Jewish Bund, sent a cable to President Roosevelt that was not answered, failed to make his case in London, and finally committed suicide in despair. George Orwell, while making BBC war commentaries, noted that within the British Civil Service there were those who simply did not believe the reports of atrocities. A colonial officer, J. S. Bennett, wrote a memo: "What is disturbing is the apparent readiness of the new Colonial Secretary to take Jewish Agency 'sob-stuff' at face value. As a political maneuver, this will establish a good precedent which the [Jewish] Agency will no doubt exploit."[9] Orwell's misgivings led to his fictional Big Brother and the memory-holes down which unpalatable facts disappeared forever.

Vera mapped routes that SOE agents could follow into Poland, using information from French "guest workers" in German factories. They were bribed to lend their passports, from which details could be copied by Polish agents. Thus Jan Karski got out of Poland with a message for SOE's Lord Selborne: "The unprecedented destruction of the entire Jewish population is not motivated by Germany's military requirements." But Alexander Cadogan complained: "These people with odd initials and numbers puzzle me more than the enemy." Jewish agencies had objectives that disturbed his Foreign Office boss, Anthony Eden. Where would the Jews go if given the means to liberate themselves?

The Polish courier Jan Nowak worked his way to Stockholm and was flown by the RAF to Scotland to report to Churchill on Poles, including Jews, skilled in underground work but in need of airdropped supplies. Nowak had to go through Desmond Morton, whom he described as "the voice of anti-SOE elements." Nowak claimed that Morton misrepresented the original report and forced him to wait three months before Churchill would see him in March 1944. The Polish courier proudly handed over a Home Army brochure inscribed to Churchill by a calligrapher in a secret Warsaw print shop. If it had fallen into the hands of the Gestapo along the way, Nowak wrote later, he would have been hanged. Churchill glanced at it and asked if Nowak could write "all that you want to tell me on one page."

"I shall try," Nowak mumbled.

"If it is longer, my secretary will put it straight into the wastebasket," Churchill told him.

The courier's head was crammed with enough information to fill several hundred pages. Nowak revered Churchill but "the interview lasted only seven of a scheduled ten minutes," he told Vera. He wrote in a bitter memoir later: "The whole effort of Underground Poland, achieved with enormous sacrifice, had been completely out of proportion to the place and importance it occupied in British and American strategic planning. The Allies seemed afraid to offend Stalin who forbade RAF planes to refuel on Soviet bases. Only six hundred tons of weapons were delivered to Poland compared with ten thousand tons to France during one period." He praised Vera's organization, though, as "our most loyal and important ally. She and SOE always fought to give aid to our cause."[10]

Vera saw the treatment he received as disturbing confirmation that Whitehall was now under the thumb of those who put no value on well-armed young Polish and Jewish closework fighters, though they were the most highly motivated of tyranny's victims. The choice was being made: the war would be won by first "area bombing" German cities. It seemed a long time since Churchill wrote in the aftermath of the Great War: "Torture and Cannibalism were the only two expedients that the civilized, scientific, Christian states had been able to deny themselves."

# 29

## Bluff and Counterbluff

Resistance leaders despaired of getting adequate airborne supplies. Vera met Polish underground agents at their hideout, 18 Kensington Palace Gardens, one of the stately old Victorian mansions still standing among the bomb ruins. The Poles confirmed the blocking role played by Desmond Morton. They said that his intelligence work reached back to another era, that he was old and tired, and influenced by Vera's opponents, and that Churchill let Morton decide who and what should reach him from the secret armies.

Vera had Emmanuel d'Astier de La Vigerie airlifted out of France to go directly to Churchill, who knew Astier as a poet. He told the prime minister, "Two Germans are killed for one French resister." Astier later wrote that Churchill's plea to give aid to "brave and desperate men" had been lost in his continuous battles with those who still wanted to throw him out as prime minister. He could not defend SOE in public when he was being accused of being "the warlord of organized terrorism."[1]

Vera was frustrated because, besides Admiral Canaris and several disaffected generals, there was widening detestation of Hitler in Berlin. If the Führer could be killed by agents masquerading as German resisters, the Nazi structure would collapse. Fake German radio stations, Kurzwellensender Atlantik and Soldatensender Calais, spread reports invented by the Political Warfare Executive of German anti-Nazi actions. Resources for this "black propaganda" increased when Bill Donovan sent Robert Sherwood, the dramatist and friend of President Roosevelt, to work on "market research" and provide powerful new U.S. radio transmitters with the secret help of the U.S. Federal Communications Commission.

What was really known about Hitler as a man? Vera flew to Canada to question his former friend and foreign press chief "Putzi" Hanfstaengl, driven out of the Third Reich by the jealousy of Nazi propagandist Joseph Goebbels. Putzi saw Vera at a Canadian army camp holding German POWs: some were being coaxed to switch sides by experts from nearby Camp X, SOE's STS 103. Americans with European backgrounds were trained there beside Lake Ontario between New York State and Canada. This made it easy for U.S. volunteers to avoid border authorities. At Oswego, New York, on the U.S. side, Donovan's OSS built a spy school. Secret transborder crossings were easy. Vera flew with Putzi from the adjacent Service Flying Training School (SFTS) at Kingston, Ontario, landing at Oswego, where Donovan escorted the pair to another protected area, Fort Belvoir, near the U.S. capital. There playwright Clare Boothe Luce, wife of the publisher of *Time* and *Life* magazines, shared information she had gathered on every aspect of Hitler's habits, and confirmed Putzi's view that Hitler had nervous breakdowns that ended when he presided over mass rallies or intimidated personages like Neville Chamberlain. On Vera's return to Camp X, she brought a leading American anthropologist, Carleton Coon, who stayed to gently interrogate Putzi further. With Coon went Aaron Bank, later honored as the Father of U.S. Special Forces. Bank, fluent in German and French, was a U.S. Army lieutenant who later drew up a plan to capture Hitler.

Coon later said of Vera that he had never met a more extraordinary woman, "nor ever met a finer group than her SOE staff — a pleasure to go anywhere or take on any job with them. Unfortunately, I cannot say the same for the Secret Intelligence Service, which holds itself aloof from SOE. The question is whether the worst enemy of SOE is Germany or SIS."

Bank saw that the SOE-SIS conflict would foreshadow his struggle to launch the Green Berets. He wrote after the war: "We trod a tortuous path through army traditionalists, and the Central Intelligence Agency was fearful we'd tread on its charter." He understood why Vera Atkins was never openly acknowledged in her commanding role. "There was deep distrust of women, fears of 'feminine intuition' intervening, and disbelief that women could fight and kill, or win male confidence enough to organize civilians for guerrilla warfare."[2]

Vera needed a dramatic success. It would require very much more time and research to kill Hitler—who, if he survived, would declare, as he had done before, that he was protected by divine providence. Putzi claimed that the Führer would fall apart if a chief lieutenant were killed, however. She selected SS Obergruppenführer Reinhard Heydrich, whose movements were far more predictable. The plan, code-named Anthropoid, was kept within a tight circle. It might be condemned as an act of terror by the U.S. Joint Chiefs of Staff, which was trying to curb Bill Donovan and his new OSS—to the extent that, when Donovan sent more officers to London, the U.S. Passport Office was planning to stamp their passports "OSS" until Donovan stepped in. "It was like stamping I AM A SPY on our backs!" said David Bruce, Donovan's man in London.[3]

Operation Anthropoid was also kept secret from General George Veazey Strong, called "King George" for his autocratic grip on U.S. military intelligence. Strong was afraid that Donovan's OSS would eat into his own budget. Strong might "spill the beans to Lord Halifax, the ambassador in Washington," Vera told Bill Stephenson, who had not forgotten Halifax's dreams of making peace with Hitler. It was agreed: the Holy Fox would again trumpet his moral objections to assassination.

She found two Czech volunteers to drop into Czechoslovakia, where Heydrich was "Protector" and followed a well-known route through Prague to his office. The agents carried handguns, a submachine gun, Mills bombs, antitank grenades, explosives, fuses, detonators, a spigot mortar, and a lethal hypodermic syringe. Vera felt a personal need for revenge. At the notorious conference "regarding the biological destruction of the Jewish race," Heydrich had uttered the words Hitler dared not speak. She had seen IG Farben's dividends double in the first year that its subsidiary sent Zyklon-B to gas death-camp inmates.

Weeks passed without news of Anthropoid. Then Vera got copies of "a German spy's report" to the German intelligence chief on the Eastern Front, General Reinhard Gehlen. It quoted Donovan as saying the Russians had 360 divisions ready for a new counteroffensive against the Germans. Gehlen saw the report on May 24, 1942.

Three days later, the Czech team's long silence was broken with news that Heydrich had been assassinated. Two brave men with limited weapons had shown they could pierce Hitler's armor. But the Führer concluded that he himself had avoided the murderous conspirators and, in delivering the eulogy at Heydrich's funeral, once again boasted that he was untouchable. He rejected Gehlen's theory that the West was trying to undermine German morale with fake breaches of security and other deceptions. Hitler issued instead a so-called Commando Order: "All terror and sabotage troops of the British and their accomplices who do not act like soldiers but instead like bandits will be treated as such."[4]

Heydrich's killers had been dropped from one of a small number of RAF bombers available for all clandestine operations. The operation cost no aircraft. Still, Vera was encountering stubborn opposition. "The war has to be won fair and square," she was told by Sir Arthur Harris, commanding RAF bombers. SOE, Harris said for the record, "is amateurish, ignorant, irresponsible, and mendacious."[5]

A heavy price was paid for Anthropoid. German reprisals caused 5,000–10,000 civilian deaths. The Czech team, with other agents sent from England, died in gun battles. Hitler issued a direct order: all men in the Czech mining village of Lidice were to be killed, the women imprisoned, the children taken away. In October 1942, he ordered the execution of all captured parachutists even if they served in regular military units.

Vera argued that Donovan's unconventional tactic of planting an apparent leak on a "German spy" broke the rules but advanced the cause. He used the same "German spy" to report an impending Allied invasion. The German High Command wondered if this was genuine or another bluff. Operation Anthropoid reprisals cost little, compared with civilian casualties caused by the use of overwheming power. Vera won U.S. support: SOE agents could be dropped by aircraft code-named Carpetbagger, drawn from the 801st/42nd U.S. Bomb Group stationed at Harrington in Northamptonshire. This countered the RAF's reluctance to release planes for Vera, and further tightened her alliance with Donovan.

His best U.S. agent, Allen Dulles in Switzerland, reported what could be bluff on the German side. Colonel General Rudolf Schmidt had vanished from his German panzer command. Did this mean his brother, Hans-Thilo, who first sold Enigma secrets, was under arrest? Admiral Canaris, chief of the Abwehr, the intelligence arm of the High Command of the Armed Forces (OKW), was already leaking information through Switzerland. He reported that Hans-Thilo had been in Gestapo hands since early April 1943. The Berlin Cipher Office thought the new Enigma was secure, because Hans-Thilo's activities had been "disclosed" by his original spymaster, Rodolphe Lemoine, caught in Paris during the previous month. In truth, Lemoine deceived Berlin by saying Hans-Thilo merely sold long ago early Enigma versions that were dismissed by French and British intelligence as outdated commercial machines.

Allen Welsh Dulles was a coconspirator with Stephenson against control by the SIS and U.S. "do-nothings." Born in 1893 and now aged forty-nine, he was a veteran of The Room in New York, a peacetime lawyer and diplomat, who single-mindedly took over as Coordinator of Information in New York, evicting the Guild of Organists and the Rough Diamond and Van Dam Corporations from offices one floor above those of Stephenson operating as the "United Kingdom Commercial Corporation" on the twenty-fourth floor of 30 Rockefeller Plaza. The proximity of the two meant easy and unseen exchanges of information.

Stephenson had arranged for Dulles to consult Vera before he went to Bern as Donovan's chief agent in Europe. Dulles learned that Bletchley and ULTRA code breakers were limited to German signals transmitted by wireless telegraph. The enemy also used landlines and couriers. He worked out other ways to collect gossip, including tapping into international phone calls and cables, which, even from occupied Europe, continued. He met night visitors from over the German borders in his darkened garden apartment at Herrengasse 23 in Bern. In this way, he prepared another anti-Nazi German channel. He had Vera's word for it that Canaris was among those top-level Germans hoping for an Allied victory. Canaris needed to discuss this with a top-level American at some remote venue—not Switzerland, where he would be quickly identified. Vera thought of her friend Gardyne de Chastelain, whose wife Marion now worked for Stephenson in New York. Gardyne was in Istanbul, where he knew another disillusioned German, Paul Leverkuehn, head of the Istanbul branch of the German "War Organization suboffice." Leverkuehn had recently seen Canaris and proposed a secret meeting with the U.S. naval attaché in Turkey, Commander George H. Earle, a former governor of Pennsylvania and a good friend of President Roosevelt. In January 1943 Canaris had asked Commander Earle if Roosevelt would help anti-Nazis overthrow

Hitler. Canaris's proposals were lengthy and sensibly detailed, but eventually Roosevelt rejected them. Canaris, hoping for an armistice that would allow Germany to finish off the war against Russia, then fed information through the Swiss Intelligence Agency to Dulles. The Swiss, Vera had long ago discovered, ran one of the most efficient secret services in the world. "They had to. Nothing else would defend their neutrality," she told Marion. And their best people were anti-Nazi, despite the Swiss-German cantons. Dulles accumulated growing quantities of intelligence. He detested "generals looking over my shoulder," and chose to speak with Vera instead of Whitehall. He believed Admiral Canaris truly did not think the Berlin coding system had been broken. Hans-Thilo was in a Gestapo prison and as yet there had been no trial. More importance seemed to be attached to his brother Rudolf, arrested as one of the Führer's favorite generals. Heydrich's murder had unsettled the Führer, after all. He said Rudolf was "guilty of ungrateful disloyalty."[6]

But was this intended to mislead Hitler's enemies? Bluff and double-bluff created a quagmire of uncertainty. Suppose disinformation were planted in Enigma-coded messages to mislead Bletchley? So far, its code breakers, now including Americans, had recovered nothing from enemy traffic that lacked corroboration from other sources. Vera was worried when "wireless games" between the enemy and SOE grew. More agents fell into German hands and were forced to transmit as if still at liberty. She knew this by instinct and was already making deductions, in addition to instructing her agents how to warn the signalmasters in England if they were sending under enemy control. When this happened, messages from England to the captured agents gave false information to deceive the other side. But frequently the warnings from captured SOE agents were missed, and discovered only when it was too late to save agents' lives.

Vera got some relief from the nerve-wracking intensity of monitoring whispers emerging from the ether when she dealt with aircrews who had been shot down and worked with resistance groups before escaping with hard, indisputable reports of realities. The pilots' discipline in the air was strict. On the ground, they defied uniformity: the top button left undone on their battledress tunics, their caps crumpled and visors bent, their booze-ups at the bar to bury emotions after a comrade was killed. Their breezy style upset uptight senior commanders, but reflected a very special kind of personal initiative. Secrecy for secrecy's sake exasperated pilots dealing with SIS officers. The SIS had built a departmental structure in India, which was beyond Vera's control. Her Australian friend Terence O'Brien, a seasoned pilot, said SIS secrecy imposed needless stress on pilots flying SOE agents under orders from a new Inter-Services Liaison Department (ISLD), which he called "a particularly deceptive title for SIS as an organization renowned for its lack of liaison with anyone or any department." Dangerous misundertandings arose when SIS bureaucrats ruled that pilots must not disclose mission details to the agents they carried.[7]

Vera digested the lessons. In Europe, SOE flights followed sensible guidelines. Wing Commander Verity, by the summer of 1943, celebrated an increase in European operations with a note: WONDERFUL MOONS FOR THE LYSANDERS! The disfigured fighter pilot Bill Simpson admired the way Vera's image as a buttoned-up flying officer concealed the secret authority that alienated the SIS.

She discussed her unease about the narrow line between state-run terrorism and games of deception with Charlie Dunne, the Canadian pilot who survived flying old Gloster Gladiator biplane fighters from small ships at the start of the war to fly Liberators on long flights across the Bay of Bengal, dropping SOE's Force 136 agents. "We live in a new world of terror," he said. "We have to be better at it than the enemy." This was echoed in a moving appeal to Churchill written by Prince Svasti, descended from the Siamese monarch who was the model for the musical *The King and I*, and cousin of the boy king still in Lausanne. The prince wrote, "Buddhists abhor taking life. But we kill the greater evil." After missions in Japanese-occupied territory, he set forth the need for better coordination between regular British armed services and "their poor cousins of SOE."[8]

Coordination improved for Operation Foxley, the code name for killing Hitler, because the plot demanded research from military experts and their intelligence on the current precautions to protect the Führer, on precise details about his hideaways and the arms and uniforms and routine of the highly trained special forces guarding him. From Berlin, Admiral Canaris conveyed a scheme to kill Hitler by anti-Nazi generals, arguing that an enterprise that seemed to be homegrown would win support from German civilians for a new regime.

In Whitehall, the underground armies were still seen as a disorganized rabble. Acknowledging this inescapable reality, the Free French poet Emmanuel d'Astier wrote to Vera: "Churchill is a hero out of the *Iliad*, the lone and jealous governor. It is useless to look to anyone else for help."

Vera knew a rebel able to make Churchill listen, regardless of interference run by Desmond Morton, the intelligence adviser who had been condemned by Nowak as "the voice of anti-SOE elements."

# 30

# The White Rabbit Hops into the "Governor's" Den

The White Rabbit, Tommy Yeo-Thomas, returning to Baker Street after one of his runs into France, agreed that Vera could not bypass Desmond Morton without prompting risky political speculation. She told him: "The civil war goes on . . ."

"Nobody need know if you hop into the Guv's den," suggested SOE's chief cryptographer, Leo Marks. He thought Tommy could slip through the fences erected in Whitehall after all the dangers he had overcome.

Tommy had scrambled out of France in the dead of night on November 15, 1943, with two French girl agents hidden in a hearse. The funeral was organized by Berthe Fraser, arrested in September 1941 while helping British prisoners escape. She survived fifteen months' interrogation by dishing out useless misinformation, and was then released as "a burden on resources" by Admiral Canaris's men in Paris, who "never take their jobs seriously," Canaris's aide Inga Haag told Vera. A Berliner, Inga helped Canaris use his foreign-intelligence position to pick away at Hitler's grip on power. Her diplomat husband was posted to Romania, where Inga helped escaping Jews.[1]

The White Rabbit said Whitehall's departmental warfare reflected the gap between the Gestapo and Canaris's men. Agents were less at risk if questioned by the latter, but Whitehall was deaf to such tips from the old folk in France, the *sédentaires*. Tommy greatly valued their experience. Weighed down by years of toil, they formed *sixaines*, groups of five under an elected "sergeant," and hid homemade Cross of

Lorraine flags to await "the uprising." They wrote information in tiny French script on wafers of paper for Tommy to take to London, where they imagined a well-oiled machine was purring away.

Berthe had buried the White Rabbit under funereal flowers, observing that "Germans think it's traditional to transport a corpse through the night." The local undertaker provided grilled steaks and wine for the cortege winding its way through dark country lanes. A reception committee of armed French farmworkers guarded the makeshift landing field. German antisubversion squads prowled the region. Ten Resistance fighters escorted the trio when a Lysander purred into the meadow. Their leader apologized for France's surrender: a formal little speech from a dignified old man. "It is a great honor for us to guard an English officer," he said. Into the Lysander the French stuffed small comforts they feared were not available in England: calvados, wine, champagne, perfumes, and cheeses of all kinds. And a catalogue of what they desperately needed: benzedrine, daggers, grenades, guns with silencers . . .

The White Rabbit contrasted this with Leo Marks's deskbound struggle against outdated SIS coding systems. Vera said, "Leo suspects some SOE agents are caught and send back deceptive messages dictated by their German captors. When Leo tries to warn Bletchley, he has to go through third parties who don't listen. If incoming messages contain *no* mistakes, he senses trouble. There isn't an agent born who doesn't make mistakes."

SOE now had an executive committee that hesitated to send Tommy back into the field, because he knew too much. Meanwhile he went with Vera to give lectures to girls who turned Morse signals from the field into readable messages to be teletyped to a network of specialists now spread over a large rural area around Bletchley. He praised their persistence in unscrambling "indecipherables" and helped them see that behind the indecipherables were French patriots who took terrible risks. He described a French grandmother croaking the name of a captured agent outside a Gestapo-run prison until she got a response that identified the cell from which his escape might be organized. He spoke of a captured French woman agent who was waiting among deportees to be herded onto wagons at a Paris railroad station; she saw a colleague in a Red Cross food van, grabbed a smock, and handed out sandwiches until they could both suddenly drive off. He told the girls, "The English Channel immunizes you from a world where homes are torn apart by men wearing death's-head patches, searching for our agents. Yet our French friends stick to a rule: 'Save the agent at all costs.'"

The chasm between two worlds hit Tommy when he wore his RAF uniform to receive from General de Gaulle the Croix de Guerre with palm, and was told by the Air Ministry that he could not wear it because de Gaulle had no authority. He got the Military Cross from the British army, and was ordered to give it back. "An army medal cannot be worn on your air force uniform!" said a chairborne air commodore, demanding why Tommy had failed to read the latest Air Ministry Order (AMO) on this important point of etiquette.

"I was in France, sir, where I don't get AMOs," said Tommy.

"Well, don't let it happen again," snapped the air commodore.

A neighbor shoved through his letter-box a white feather pinned on a sheet of paper with one word: COWARD. His secret missions imposed silence on his wife, Barbara, whose only link with him was one-way. Her terse reassurances were broadcast by the BBC and prefaced "du moineau au lapin"—from the sparrow to the rabbit.

In England, Tommy spoke to restless Americans held in quarantined country houses. They included two future CIA directors, and his audiences sensed politics behind the delay in parachuting them into France. He brought them to their feet by shouting: "Great is de Gaulle of the French!" He told Operation Carpetbagger aircrews and RAF special-duty pilots not to quit reception areas too hurriedly if signal lights were delayed. Resistance fighters bicycled for miles in all weathers to the rendezvous and might find substandard batteries were failing, so then bicycled in search of replacement torches. Everything was makeshift. These irregular *francs-tireurs* needed daytime jobs to keep alive, and dodged the pro-German *milice*, the Vichy French paramilitaries who had already helped deport 80,000 suspected resisters to Germany. Resistance was equated with "disorder" by Vichy.

"Disorder seems to be the RAF's interpretation, too," Tommy said when Vera disclosed that their allocation of aircraft had suddenly dwindled. The White Rabbit sounded depressed.

She urged him: "See the man that d'Astier calls 'the governor.'"

So Tommy did. He worked through the inventor of the tank, Major General Sir Ernest Swinton, a friend of Churchill. On a wintry first day of February 1944, the White Rabbit sat with Churchill, painted a vivid picture of legions of French resisters who were starved of weapons, and reminded the prime minister of his vision to turn France into "a gigantic guerrilla" with the order "Set Europe ablaze!" The flames were dying in official channels.

"You short-circuited those official channels," admonished Churchill. "This might make trouble for you." Then he broke into his most cherubic smile. "But I shall see . . . ah . . . that no such thing shall be allowed to happen."

Churchill asked Desmond Morton why he had failed to forward the reports that Tommy said he had written on these matters. Morton stumbled in his responses: doubted the claim that saboteurs caused systematic damage to vital railroads at far less cost than aerial bombings; that "train-busting" air raids against railroads wasted huge resources and were far less effective than a couple of agents trained to halt enemy traffic with dynamite; that RAF bombings more often devastated civilian neighborhoods.

Churchill brought Tommy back and asked how many aircraft he needed. The answer: "At least one hundred, to carry out two hundred fifty sorties within each moon period." Forty-eight hours later, Vera got word that seventy four-engined RAF bombers were available for parachute drops, with additional light planes for pickups. After all the past parsimony, it seemed an armada.

"I don't put much beyond our Tommy if it helps the Free French," Nick Nicholls, SOE's director of signals, told Vera. "But to have gone all the way to the prime minister on his own initiative defies belief. The whole of SOE is in his debt." Still, Nick shivered to think that guerrilla armies were salvaged because one bold man had a back door to Churchill. It underlined Vera's handicap as a woman. Clever and efficient, she could never talk freely to a male-dominated professional intelligence service where she was a nonentity.[2] Even her prewar cooperation with Morton no longer counted.

Bad news followed. Pierre Brossolette, who remained in France with Jean Moulin to coordinate guerrilla operations, had been captured and was held in prison at Rennes, near the coast of Brittany. His telltale lock of white hair must eventually show through the dye. Moulin was already dead. Unification of the many different Resistance elements was again in doubt. Little Kay Moore, a French-speaking

English girl who bridged the gap between SOE and the Free French, told Vera: "The White Rabbit feels he abandoned Brossolette and wants to save him before the dye wears off!"

Vera gulped. She needed Tommy's unquenchable optimism, and the moral support of a man who, far from dismissing women, regarded them, when in the field, as superior in many respects. But she had to let go. His was the lone voice able to assure French resisters that they were not forgotten. Gubbins objected that Tommy knew too much; nobody could hold out indefinitely against skilled torturers. Tommy defied him: "If you can get through the first few minutes, you've got it made. The worst things come at the outset . . . small inconveniences, hair-pulling . . . tiny humiliations."

The White Rabbit went to see Squadron Leader Kenneth Dodkin, listed as an operational RAF pilot by the Germans, who seemed not to know that Dodkin could no longer fly. The White Rabbit spent hours at Dodkin's country home, absorbing his mannerisms and history. He had Dodkin's RAF serial number engraved on identity discs to be flourished if Tommy got arrested. He would then claim prisoner-of-war status as S/L Dodkin.

Tommy was the first English agent to be sent on an operation for the Free French without one of their officers to watch him. He could talk frankly to both the French and SOE without compromising himself, which was why his new code name was Asymptote — a line that approaches but never meets a curve. Vera's Operational Orders betrayed no emotion: "We require for you to report back where action may be expected. . . . 'Lousey' is the code word indicating the target is prepared. . . . You will tell us your further financial needs after you take into the field the sum of five hundred thousand francs."

He sat one night with her in Leo Marks's untidy little Baker Street office to learn about "silks," providing an agent with a way to encode messages from cribs imprinted on silk one-time pads. The White Rabbit proposed to use silks for long important messages, and an old-fashioned poem-code as backup. Leo fretted that SOE agents in Holland were under German control. The top brass rejected his circumstantial evidence. Tommy said he'd bang a few heads together — if he got back. Leo glanced at the White Rabbit's signet ring concealing the death pill, and spent the rest of the night composing the poem-code that his friend could use:

They cannot know
What makes you as you are
Nor can they hear
Those voices from afar
Which whisper to you
You are not alone . . .
They cannot reach
That inner core of you
The long before of you
The child inside
Deep deep inside
Which gives the man his pride . . .
What you are
They can never be
And what they are
Will soon be history.

A day later Leo was grilled by Nick Nicholls, now SOE's director of signals. There was a rule against sending into the field any SOE officer with knowledge of other country sections, agents' codes, security checks, and other conventions. Nick ordered Leo to write down "the whole bloody lot" of what he'd told Tommy. Leo came back with a sheet of paper, blank except for Yeo-Thomas's name. Nick roared: "There's a limit to the torture anyone can take. God knows how many agents we lose if Tommy breaks."

Leo was defiant. They were all in Tommy's debt for chewing out Churchill. Was it fair to stop him rescuing the Frenchman who had so many times saved him? Nick hesitated and then wrote a formal statement to SOE's executive: "Yeo-Thomas only knows stuff overtaken by events."

Twenty-three days after the session with Churchill, Tommy was on his way with Vera to the Tempsford base. He chose to parachute blind rather than wait for a moonlit night, landing at Clermont-Ferrand, some 250 miles south of Paris. There he would reconnect with agents likely to know if Brossolette had been moved, and then Tommy would set about rescuing him.

In mid-March reports reached Vera that Brossolette had been transferred to Gestapo headquarters on avenue Foch in Paris. He had jumped through a window to his death rather than risk breaking under torture. On March 21, 1944, the White Rabbit was picked up by the Gestapo. Churchill asked to be kept informed.

Vera did not rule out the White Rabbit's safe return. She had heard of stranger things from airmen who escaped after being shot down. They pioneered new ways to freedom by learning from local inhabitants how to poke holes in the Western Wall, built to confine millions within Fortress Europe. Allied servicemen who escaped brought back personal observations and insights that were impossible to replicate from a distance, no matter how diligently Vera might analyze reports from the field. Escapees were eyewitnesses of a special sort. They showed her how to achieve a seemingly impossible combination. She needed personal initiative in her agents, streetwise rebels who instinctively defied authority, while she also had to insist upon obedience to lifesaving rules. Agents were freelancers, not drilled to respond to the day-to-day authority of watchful officers in the regular armed forces. Vera had no control once an agent left her sight. The best escapees were downed airmen, schooled in self-preservation. They were natural rebels, highly individualistic, but their profession required them to be constanty alert, completely detached in observing the unexpected, with technical skills that sharpened their ability to assess whatever they saw and experienced after being shot down.

But the White Rabbit was in a tight hole, and Vera worried about how he might escape.

# An Unplanned and Gigantic Spyglass

Hair tucked inside a naval officer's cap, scarf muffling her face, wearing a duffel coat and black uniform trousers tucked into flying boots, Vera saw the early dawn split by fierce blue flames from the racing engines of Hellcats parked near the end of a narrow street whose tumbledown terraced houses were separated from the naval air station by a wire trellis. Four of the U.S. Lend-Lease Hellcats shut down their engines. Two more moved from the verge of this Liverpool slum to a makeshift runway, pointing toward cargo ships for the next Atlantic convoy. But the two Hellcats were not shepherds. They were heading out over occupied Europe, packed with the latest spy cameras.

Vera looked like any other service pilot. She had been brought here by John Godley, the future Lord Kilbracken, after a frank talk in a Covent Garden restaurant, in a discreet room once used long ago by King Edward VII to entertain his mistress Lillie Langtry. The London restaurant was patronized by old-school aristocrats who liked their main courses bloody and well hung. Godley was no longer a roast-beef man. He had the Twitch, the jerking of an arm, the twitch of an eyelid, after too many missions since he first flew antiquated Swordfish biplanes into battle.

They had discussed Vera's need for natural rebels. Her agents were beyond supervision in territories where the Vichy French ran fifteen security agencies and innumerable informers. By 1943 German army divisions in France had risen by 50 percent to thirty-eight because of Resistance activity, whereas a mere twelve divisions held down Norway and Denmark. Hitler had heard Stalin's demands that the West open a second front. And France was the obvious gateway. Inside, traps and traitors threatened agents night and day.

"Stalin forbade communist networks to work with us," said Vera. "Then Germany attacked the Soviet Union. Now we've a shitpile of networks that distrust one another while working more or less with the Free French. I haven't time to lay out all the updates and subtleties for agents, and those who report back operate within limited space and lack an overall view."

Godley always understood. He'd seen Vera bedeviled by service rivalries. The RAF feared being reduced to a supporting role, without a seat at the top table beside the army and navy brass. The numbers game — the number of cities and civilians destroyed, the numbers of U-boats sunk — developed a dynamic of its own. Men in the War Office taunted SOE's male executives: "How many divisions do you have?" Vera had to make do with miserly resources, at most three thousand on her secret lists, including her French aides.

Godley despised unimaginative stuffed shirts. "They've come up with an abortion of a *new* plane," he railed, "to perform fifty-seven varieties of missions. Mostly it kills those who fly it." When he attacked enemy ships in his antique biplane, he judged deflection by lightbulbs strung along its wings. Human ingenuity made up for idiocy at the top. He prompted her to make use of downed airmen, who covered the length and breadth of France, which was how she now came to be standing in rain puddles in the gloom while pilots timed each other's exits from the cockpits of the four silent Hellcats as if trapped upside-down under the sea. They endlessly repeated a tiresome routine: release links to the cockpit, kick off boots, loosen clothing, suck in air trapped in the canopy while the machine sinks into cold black terrors. No panic. Mind separated from body. She thought of her lost lover Stringbag. The loss of such men led to their successors drilling each other in this boring procedure. They lightened it by competing to beat each other's escape timings.

"Downed aviators make good soldier-spies because of this repetitive self-training. They're disciplined to act with complete detachment," Vera told Mary Stephenson, who recalled the self-discipline Billy used to escape in World War I with valuable information. Vera also wrote — though Mary never dared tell Bill — that she had

adopted their "wham-bam-mornin'-ma'am" philosophy. "I can't in-
dulge in long-term emotion," she said. "I'd break down."

Vera had a strictly business date for Sunday, June 27, 1943, with
John Hartley Watlington, one of two airmen whose operations into
Europe she wanted to learn more about. The other was Chuck Yeager,
an American proud of his West Virginia hillbilly origins.

Hartley Watlington flew lone-ranger missions. His skills were in-
herited from a Bermuda ancestry of English swashbucklers. When he
failed to show up for the Sunday date, she guessed he was gone.

"I work by moonlight," Hartley had told her. "I fly very low, follow the silver of a river, hop hedgerows between village churches." He
was piratical in the elegant fashion of the first Queen Elizabeth's buc-
caneers, licensed to roam the high seas and plunder ships of the
monarch's enemies. He roamed the night skies to pounce on German
"tip-and-run" raiders returning from hitting targets in England, when
they were at their most vulnerable, descending and almost out of fuel.
At 0220 hours on June 22 he circled an airfield near Amiens. He saw
no flare paths. The raiders were not yet expected. He switched to his
secondary role as a "train buster" and hovered above one train whose
driver opened the firebox "to illuminate the target for me," said Hartley later. "French railroadmen knew we only attacked troop trains."
He made a low pass to study the wagons when tracer bullets hosed his
Mustang and plugged his radiator. He jettisoned his cockpit canopy
to clear the blinding smoke, and repeated into his microphone a
nonsense rhyme to give time for listening stations in England to fix his
position:

> Little Willie in the best of sashes
> Fell in the fire and got burned to ashes.
> After a while, the room grew chilly.
> Nobody liked to poke poor Willie.

The ground stations took cross-bearings and gave him a course to
steer. The last words he heard were, "Watch yer arse, cobber!" from an
Australian radio watch-keeper. Both knew the aircraft was too far
away to reach home, or ditch in the Channel.

If pilots jumped over the side, Mustangs often hit them with wing
or rudder. Hartley automatically pulled his Mustang's nose up, jammed
the stick forward, and catapulted out, free and clear. "Moonlight lit up

great countryside. I studied it with intense interest from under my parachute canopy," he wrote in a later report for Vera.

He landed on top of a wooded hill and followed the drill, mind free from fearful speculation. He stripped insignia from his uniform, and sliced off the tops of his flying boots to look like walking shoes. He checked his escape kit: silk maps, local currencies and coupons, food tablets, pills to purify water, benzedrine, milk concentrate, chewing gum, and a rubber hot-water bottle. He buried the kit neatly in the summer grass "and went to sleep."

A French farmboy found him at dawn and took him home. Hartley told the family, "I am British airman." The farmer, despite obvious poverty, gave him his Sunday suit to replace his uniform. "I thought it best not to get these good people into trouble by hanging around," Hartley wrote. "So I headed for Gibraltar, a thousand miles away." He reached the Dieppe-Paris railway line, and was surrounded by the local constabulary with guns drawn. "Je suis Anglais," he said. Within seconds, the police were instructing him on how to reach Paris. "It is," said their chief, "the best way to Spain, even if indirect," and took Hartley to a small railway station. By midnight "Je suis Anglais" got him a room for the night in Paris with a friendly French couple. He spent the next day mingling with Germans, distinguishing between uniforms, as he'd been taught in groundschool. "I stopped at a bistro, thirsty and tired, and stupidly blurted out, 'Bière, please.' The proprietor whispered in English, 'Three francs.' He gave me a bed for the night, fed me, filled a bag with food for several days, and with his wife and kids took me to the railway station at Étampes as if on a family outing."

Hartley jumped from one train to walk along the river Cher. By Sunday, wistfully wishing he could keep his date with Vera, he limped along secondary roads and met a boy who was bartering homemade crystal sets for potatoes. He bartered for a piece of Hartley's gum. "The kid just assumed I was American," Hartley said. "I gave him my hot-water bottle. The crystal set was the kind I'd made as a kid, wire around a toilet roll's tube. With this one, you stroked the crystal with a bit of wire until you heard the BBC. The kid took me into a village where a grocer passed me to an escape line."

Hartley kept mental note of the cast of characters along a chain of civilians: "Butchers or bakers or lawyers or dentists or laborers or schoolkids. New identity papers were forged when my old ones got dirty or torn. When I had to leave a safehouse, someone would park me somewhere else as the 'body' to be collected by a courier from another circuit, each unknown to the next, usually a girl on her bicycle, one link in the chain. I could decide who to trust at each stopover. It was like a pilgrim's progress."

Plans to cross into Spain went awry, so he returned to Paris. The crowded city offered better means of escaping attention. Germans mostly relied on informants, and looked uncomfortable in the hostile streets. A French circuit-master told him to head for the Brittany coast where a group of civilians were assembling. He was horrified by their lack of caution. A Breton fishing smack arrived. Hartley quailed. "The water came up to the gunnels before we were beyond the reefs. It foundered. I scrambled over rocks and headed inland, alone." The others waded ashore in a tight bunch and were caught. He wandered around France, hoarding counterfeit currency from his escape kit, busily observing. He found "electric train services very reliable. German soldiers only boarded them while going on leave from barracks." He preferred walking. "I saw French secret-service officers, Dutchmen heading for England, Norwegians, Scots, English wives of Frenchmen, but I wanted no company." In Lyons, Virginia Hall was one stop on an escape line. She was also training French resistance forces. Hartley said her partisans needed more discipline. Anticipating his offer, she replied that he'd be executed as a spy if he was caught instructing them.

"I often had to retrace my footsteps, and surprised those who thought I was safe in England. They scrounged clothes to replace my rags and a fur greatcoat left by a government minister who had joined the Free French."

Hartley spent ten months looking for ways out. "It's safest to be a loner. I never again made the mistake of that 'Bière, please!' Each attempt to break through borders demands care. You can't guard against an escape line collapsing. When an exit is blocked, you look for another."

Hartley was a resourceful artful dodger by 1944 when he crossed the path of Chuck Yeager. By then, the Germans were shooting escapees.

Yeager's Mustang was shattered by a Focke-Wulf 190's 20-mm

cannons on Sunday, March 5, 1944. Suddenly the twenty-one-year-old pilot tumbled into farm country. He unholstered his pistol. As a boy, he had sniped squirrels for the pot. He could trap and hunt. One thing bothered him: U.S. regulations would stop him flying more missions. The Germans kept tabs on Allied airmen. If he was shot down again, he'd be tortured for information about Resistance fighters. Bits of metal in his arms and legs began to hurt. He ate a chocolate bar, wrapped his parachute around himself, and slept.

An elderly woodcutter found him at dawn. Chuck waved his pistol and said: "Me American. Need help. Find Resistance." The Frenchman signaled Chuck to stay hidden, then left on the run. Chuck retreated into the trees, prepared for betrayal. An hour later he was pointing his .45 at two men. One whispered, "Listen, American. A friend is here." The friend was a middle-aged woman in bed. "You're just a boy!" she cried in perfect English when Chuck was escorted into her small farmhouse. "Has America run out of men already?"

She stored him in the hayloft. A local doctor patched him up and advised rest. Chuck got restless after several days, went outside to sit under a tree, and froze when heavily armed Germans marched past, close enough to spit on him. After this, he spent most of his time sleeping until a group of men in black berets and bandoliers arrived. They said it was too soon to cross into Spain. The mountain routes were blocked by persistent snow. He could stick around while they blew things up. "Then," said the commander of this maquis, a peacetime lawyer, "we'll get you to Spain."

Chuck used to help his father shoot gas wells with plastic explosives. So when the RAF dropped fifteen-hundred-pound canisters crammed with equipment including fuses and plastic explosives, he told the guerrilla commander, "I can help you fix this stuff." The canisters included bundles of money, Sten guns and detachable silencers, .38 Llama pistols, ammunition, tire bursters, cans of abrasive carborundum powder to sabotage machinery, tree spigots for screwing into wood or brickwork in order to launch bomblets. Another drop disgorged transceivers with power packs to replace cumbersome forty-pound wireless sets in suitcases; these had Eureka position-indicators and S-phones by which Resistance leaders could talk directly to the SOE planes called "clockwork mice" because of their regular round trips. A pilot unable to find his customers could now be redirected by

Eureka to a "depot ground" where a portable blacksmith's forge was pedaled to generate power for a transceiver. Clockwork mice also brought what looked like department-store catalogs. Chuck was reminded of sitting in the outhouse as a boy, with sales catalogs strung up for toilet paper, wishing he had the money to buy Christmas toys. Now toys were offered free. The most fanciful were MCRs, miniature communication receivers, to be fitted into everyday objects that came with the MCRs: German Bibles, antique clocks, brandy flasks—all fake. There were illustrations of door keys and finger rings and collar studs to hold microprints, and toiletries cunningly fashioned to hide screwed-up paper messages. Things could be ordered by number, transmitted by wireless. Each time there was a delivery, the huge canisters had to be buried and the contents hidden in horse wagons or stuffed into root cellars and haystacks.

The customers were new to much of the technology. Chuck took charge of explosive-fuse devices and showed how to set them for different timings. He explained the Sten: inaccurate beyond a couple of meters, liable to fire if jolted, made from metal bicycle tubing, and good only for ambuscades.

"I became a terrorist," recalled Chuck. "I needed these guys, so I shared their lives. A German Fiesler Storch would sometimes skim over, able to drop into a cowpat if the pilot spotted us. My comrades said little, tight-knit but friendly. They knew these deep forests like I know the woods back home. We never stopped long in one place, and we hid by day and hit at night."

There were dozens of such groups in the forests and mountains. Their spies in marshaling yards and train depots reported on troop movements and targets. The White Rabbit's plea to Churchill was finally showering the landscape with phony rocks to balance wireless transmitters in rough country; bundles of faggots designed to fit local forestry flora but stuffed with explosives; "timber logs" resembling those used in artificial fireplaces and primed to blow up if plugged into a socket; fountain pens that squirted death; milk bottles with correct French markings that burst when the tops were unscrewed; plastic loaves of bread that blew up if broken open; packages of lethal "cigarettes." Iron nuts and bolts were hollowed out so incendiaries could be inserted when left in railyards or factories. The instructions that went with these toys needed to be explained. Chuck had difficulty with tins of Zambuk. The ingredients were listed as eucalyptus oil, soft and hard paraffin, powdered pale resin, and chlorophyll. Then he recognized the concoction as ointment from his childhood, except that Zambuk was English and his American version included "a well-known Indian healing oil," great for cleaning up weeping wounds. He relished his life as both terrorist and medicine man, but he still kept asking when he was going to be guided through the Pyrenees.

One wet evening he was led to a truck. He scrambled into the back, a tarpaulin dropped down, and he was aware of other bodies as the truck corkscrewed through narrow twisting lanes. When the truck stopped, torchlight revealed a Frenchman crouching on the floor between two benches of men. He gave out hand-drawn maps. The Frenchman spoke precise English, "You'll head for a central ridge in the Pyrenees at a boundary line between France and Spain. We've sketched your best crossing. South is safer. Up north, the Spaniards will sell you for a few francs. It'll take you five days to cross if you don't hit blizzards. You're at the starting point. It's that shepherd's shed, a hundred yards from here. Stay until night — no fires, no talking."

There were thirty men crowded in the hut. None said a word.

Hartley Watlington had been led on foot to the hut by "a Dutchman working with the British secret service who bound my feet and ankles with elastic bandages, a godsend in the ordeal ahead," he told Vera. "I saw these other escapees come out, muffled up to the eyebrows against the awful cold." There were two maquis, fifteen Americans, twelve Dutchmen, three Frenchmen, and a Belgian pilot who had escaped after more than three years in a prison camp. "We climbed through the night. The snow was thick and if the crust broke, we sank to our hips. We reached the top of one mountain just as the sun hit my eyes, blinding me. We went to the bottom of a valley to rest until nightfall, and skirted a small village to start the really big climb."

One by one, men dropped out from exhaustion. Others drifted apart in pairs, Chuck Yeager with a B-24 navigator he knew only as Pat. Late into the fourth day Chuck saw an empty cabin, where the two men collapsed into an exhausted sleep. Suddenly German troops were shooting through the cabin door. Chuck and Pat dived through a back window onto a log slide. "We went spinning ass over teakettle," Chuck recalled. They slid a couple of miles and ended up in an ice-cold creek. Pat had been shot in the knee by a soft-nose bullet. Only a tendon attached his lower leg to the upper. Chuck sliced away the tendon and tied a tourniquet made from a torn shirt around the stump. Pat was unconscious, his face ghastly gray. Chuck resolved "to carry this bomber guy over the last mountain ridge and sledge him down to Spain."

Hartley, now far off, reached the point where "I was moving on hands and feet, and eating benzedrine go-pills like candy," he said. "They were in my escape kit, with a printed warning: 'Take every three to six hours but only in extremity.' I figured this was extremity. We were at twelve thousand feet when, at 0630 on Tuesday the twenty-eighth of March, just as the sun came up, the guide said we were at the Spanish border. I sat down with the others and we all had a good cry."

Hartley and Chuck had to slide a long way down separate paths. Chuck skated Pat down a slope, then followed, crouching with a branch between his bent knees "just like I'd roller-skate downhill behind our house as a kid, with a broomstick as a brake." Hartley "slid with a tree branch between my knees, and ripped the ex-minister's fur coat to tatters."

Chuck dragged Pat's body to a glazed snowfield. Pat looked as if he were dead. There was nothing to be done, other than leave him on the roadside, half a mile from where Hartley landed.

Hartley had nursed through all his wanderings the escapee's pipe: the stem held a tiny compass, and the bowl contained a tightly wadded silk map. He figured he was above a tributary of the Garonne River. If he turned right, he would reach the Spanish village of Viella. Other escapees were moving in small groups. Hartley "elected to go by myself." He came across Pat's abandoned body, and saw no signs of life. He kept walking and was picked up by a Spanish police car and taken in for questioning at the Viella police station.

"A German Wehrmacht officer arrived and got into deep conversation with the Spanish chief of police," said Hartley. "When they parted, they exchanged Nazi salutes. Spain was supposed to be neutral. I found it all very peculiar. Service personnel of a belligerent weren't supposed to enter neutral territory in service uniforms. The German and his driver carried sidearms. That's something you better remember about neutrals—you're never sure which side they'll take."

When he was questioned by the Spanish police, he said, "I made up the biggest pack of lies. Said I was captured by the Germans. I was classed an escaped war prisoner — not an invader, for which I'd be imprisoned for the rest of the war."

He got the police chief to retrieve Pat, who was not, after all, lifeless. Six weeks later, an American consul in Barcelona sent Pat home minus his leg. Chuck was picked up and put into a cell, but used a sawblade from his escape kit. "It was made from good old American steel that zapped through the brass window bars like butter." He holed up in a small Spanish *pensión* near the police station, and on March 30, 1944, the same U.S. consul arrived to arrange travel back to England for both Chuck and Hartley.

Chuck was told: "No more combat." He argued his way up the chain of command until he faced General Dwight D. Eisenhower, and pointed out that London newspapers were now reporting a Resistance fighting the Germans. "So the maquis are out in the open," said Chuck. "I can't blow them to the Gestapo if I'm shot down again, General." Eisenhower personally arranged for Chuck to fly again after the pilot's huge harvest of unique details had been poured into Vera's lap. Hartley kept a delayed date with her, his precise recollections opening an enormously wide window into a world otherwise glimpsed through narrow slits. The secret agency MI9 that dealt with escape-and-evasion, now joined by a new American MIS-X escape-and-evasion service, expanded the gathering of intelligence. Allied servicemen rescued from capture equaled three divisions, some 35,190 men, a pool of observers that Chuck later called "the college of life and death." As a maquisard, his unscheduled training in closework gave authority to his argument for more Anglo-American-French officers to boost Resistance morale and provide badly needed instruction. Three-man "Jedburgh teams" went into action. Communications were compacted inside a "Jedburgh station": a skullcap with low-impedance phones and a midget wireless set. American Jedburghs held at Milton Hall, a country house in the Fens seventy-five miles north of London, no longer had to wait. For use around D-day, BBC instructions were memorized: "Plan Vert" meant "attack railways"; "Plan Tortue," attack German reinforcements coming by road; "Plan Violet," dislocate telecommunications; "Plan Jaune," attack munition dumps; "Plan Rouge," attack fuel stores; "Plan Noir," attack enemy HQs; "Plan Grenouille," sabotage railway turntables.

Hartley later described the reception given to Vera by some

Jedburgh recruits when they first heard lectures on codes. Her use of escapees fascinated the future CIA chiefs Bill Colby and Bill Casey, then young Jedburghs. "Casey asked about difficult agents. Others gave Leo Marks a hard time when he mentioned FANYs. 'Fannies!' Leo said it stood for First Aid Nursing Yeomanry. Its girls hoped they could claim to be prisoners of war instead of being executed if caught. That sobered up the Americans."[1]

De Gaulle's representative, Colonel Passy, had always insisted that "networks of envoys need only collect information and organize communications between small groups who would snowball into a vast Resistance." The word "snowball" alerted Soviet agents in the SIS to a possible plan to put General de Gaulle into postwar power, and under this influence, opposition in Whitehall continued to thwart the quiet buildup. The escapees, though, portrayed Vera's "shitpile" as merely anti-Nazi groups whose lack of liaison permitted the burgeoning of mutual suspicion and misunderstanding. Seeing the situation through the eyes of objective, if unplanned, observers, she saw a place both for small and uncoordinated actions and for Passy's dream of the "gigantic guerrilla" conjured up by Churchill in the full flow of his 1940 rhetoric.

Nobody had foreseen the accidental creation of spy networks whose accumulated observations bridged a gap between local guerrilla forces and experts in skullduggery sent out from England to perform specific tasks within separate provincial — and therefore parochial — regions. The policy of sealing off SOE activities was designed to maintain security, but it limited Vera's freedom to instruct and question agents on broader matters. The sufferings of escapees yielded the unexpected gain of a priceless, gigantic spyglass into the enemy's backyard. It was all the more effective because Vera had learned a dozen years before how to peer through her Bucharest spyglass into the tiny target of Berlin and integrate the scraps of professional observations passed along by the ambassador, Old Fritz.

# Rolande

"Park! Show our visitor the way to the Number Fifty-three bus stop."

"Yes, ma'am." The commissionaire led the girl to a back staircase. She had come to Room Six by way of an ancient lift: a rope was yanked to make unseen pulleys raise or lower passengers. She left by the tradesman's entrance. A precaution, the girl thought wryly, against encountering some new recruit on the way to being terrorized by Miss Atkins. Park was studying her face. She felt she was being photographed through the lenses of his neutral eyes.[1]

She was Rolande Colas, back in London amid talk of Europe's invasion on some unspecified D-day date, perhaps by late spring or early summer of 1944. She had been coolly dismissed by Vera to preserve the fiction that they had not met before. Rolande took it in stride. Her own life, after all, had dangled on thin threads of falsehood since their first meeting in Paris. Rolande had described petty officials in her sectors who wooed local voters as if the Revolution of 1789 and the Bastille were yesterday. Leaks to the enemy were a by-product of squabbles at provincial levels. German proconsuls often sought to boost the voter appeal of docile mayors by helping them with everyday matters of sewage and municipal drains, but in other *départements*, German officers fought with priests and parishioners. The complications were difficult to comprehend from a distance. The girl who had been an innocent seventeen-year-old student in 1940 was so seasoned in closework she could always command Vera's attention.

Park's name and this address near Regent's Park were dropped into Gestapo interrogations, Rolande had already reported. Captured agents were told "cooperate, don't suffer torture, we know everything."

Vera was more familiar with enemy interrogation centers than her enemies were with these quarters. She continued to use the address for "housekeeping" to avoid tipping off the enemy that their deception was known. Rolande said the interrogators had somehow got information to speak of "Park, the butler" and drop the name "Orchard Court" to convey the Gestapo's omniscience. The address had a posh ring to it. Vera let her opponents imagine it as the heart of a richly financed enterprise. Actually, it was far enough from Whitehall for her to run loyal retainers as reverential as Park, who were far from being butlers. They included a captain in the Hussars who was clever at "winning" army stores and improvising imaginative ways of using them. When the inevitable Scarlet-Faced Senior Officer pounced on demure Miss Atkins, she would smile seraphically and say, "But it's too late now to undo things, isn't it?"

She was on guard against agents "turned" by the enemy and sent back to England. She would ask counterintelligence *bons viveurs* to suck any such suspect into a drinking binge. Drunk by dawn, the suspect might let slip a damning disclosure. Booze was in short supply, but SOE was never short of Haig whiskey. She was certain of Rolande's loyalty. A Students Assessment Board had been wished upon Vera, made up of what she called dismissively "the trick cyclists": the psychiatrists. She had to let the board screen Rolande. The chairman told her, "There's nothing wrong with you, except that nobody in their right mind would volunteer for your job."

Rolande's fieldwork had been limited to northern France. Vera echoed Hartley's warning: "In the Côte d'Azur and around Cannes, resisters bog off for a little pastis and get nailed by the Gestapo. The fleshpots tempt our own agents to swan around."

Vera took Rolande to a Special Air Service commando training estate. Targets popped up at all angles. "Faster, faster—two rounds into each man, another two rounds to be sure. Change mags until you can do it in your sleep," commanded Vera, introducing the girl to the improved silencer, the weapon of the assassin. The SAS had perfected techniques in silent killing and found new uses for PE, the yellow plastic explosive of cyclonite mixed with a plasticizing medium.

Down at The Shop, sixteen miles southeast of central London, production of new devices had reached great heights. The Shop was near the sheltered anchorage in the "green bay," *grene wic* in Old English, that gave the name to Greenwich, in whose chapel Admiral Nelson's body lay after the Battle of Trafalgar. Vera wanted the girl to feel the weight of centuries of resistance since the Roman age. Under Tudor monarchs, the long association with the navy began here. It was from here that Queen Elizabeth had sent her fleet against the Spanish Armada. Remembering how long it took her to really understand England, Vera wanted the girl to get the feel of historical memory that rejected defeat. One of Rolande's future tasks was to convince waverers in France that the approaching day of liberation would end in Allied victory. Poles now operated in France, and the abandonment of Poland was common gossip.

"One jump from a balloon and one drop from a Whitley bomber will do," Vera said, sending the girl for a refresher course at Ringway, where a Canadian veteran of three hundred parachute jumps took her through the drill. He said, "When Miss Atkins says 'You're late!' she scares the daylights out of me." Rolande jumped, but broke a tooth. Vera probed, and exclaimed, "Heavens! I should've known you'd had local fillings. Get them redone the French way. Go see this woman dentist on Maddox Street. Looks sadistic but I'll ask her not to hurt you. It'll still be hellish, but good practice for — well, whenever."

Rolande was to work with old equipment, a B Mark II transmitter and receiver weighing thirty pounds that fit into a two-foot-long suitcase. It required a seventy-foot aerial that had to be laced through trees. Frequency was set by removable crystals, one for day, one for night, with several spares. Vera had to use up old inventories, to justify the dispatch of the new gadgets for the underground armies that were forming spontaneously, though still little known outside. Rolande had learned to make the best of things. Batteries for the B Mark II ran down fast and were recharged with a hand-cranked "buzz-box." She knew better than to run a wireless transmitter off the mains. Germans were now efficient in locating an operator by shutting down electricity in subdistricts, one after another. By a process of elimination, D/F direction-finding vans slowly closed in on "the pianist," the wireless operator. Rolande had mastered the art of cutting down each transmission to less time than it took the D/F vans to figure her location. They could do this now even if batteries were used, but she preferred them anyway because they gave her greater flexibility. She never transmitted from the same place twice.

She was given the new one-time pad of "silks," each slip printed with columns of random letters or figures. For coding each message, she was to use the top slip, then tear it off and burn it. Home base would have the same pad. Each message must have double security checks: a bluff check and a true check, peculiar to the individual operator. An early form of microwave transmission by S-phone had been tried during her first mission four years ago. It was finally in operation, with a fifty-mile range by air, fifteen miles at sea. A staff officer on a Moonlight plane could talk to the ground in emergencies.

During these preparations, an operator was lost. He was attached to the Anvil network around Falaise. Rolande was asked to step in. She holed up in a grim Bayswater basement room during the holding period when agents were banned from popular haunts like the Free French Club in Cavendish Square, where there was too much loose talk.

"I've wangled you a Women's Auxiliary Air Force commission," said Vera. "You get flying officer's pay. It's still the case you've no family here?"

"None."

"Good. Usually I write families once a month."

"Why?"

"The chap who last asked me that had to be told, 'Because you can't write letters home from the field.' The idiot had to understand why nobody should know where he was. I said my letters would tell them he was in good fettle. 'Or dead!' he said plaintively. I told him not to pull out that stop!"

In a Moonlight Squadron hut, Rolande was searched by a man from Scotland Yard who then gave her a parachute, a Sorbo spine pad, a .38 Browning, a flick knife, and a wad of 50,000 French francs. All remaining English money, final personal effects, and a stray No. 25 bus ticket were stuffed into an envelope with her real name on it. Vera counted out some pills to the familiar litany. "This, if you've been a long time awake and need to keep going. This to knock out a German who pesters you. How you get it into him is up to you. These pills are for sleeping. And this one puts you to sleep for good." Then she shook her hand. Rolande thought for a moment that Vera really wanted to peck her on the cheek.

Over the drop zone, the jumping strap between her legs, Rolande stood by the open door of the twin-engine Whitley. She had the wireless-suitcase on the end of a long cord, which she would pay out during the tranquillity that follows the heart-stopping exit. The cord would go slack when her belongings touched the ground, giving her enough warning to prepare for a jolt like jumping from a high wall. She saw the Whitley crew release containers first, and thought, They've got the sequence wrong.

A stream of red tracer bullets rose lazily, then seemed suddenly to accelerate to dance along the starboard wing. An engine coughed. The Whitley banked steeply into a tight turn and raced for home.

Next day Vera said, "You should have been dropped *before* the containers. But if you'd gone out first last night . . ." She hesitated. "Sure you want to try again?"

"Mais naturellement."

Vera examined her nicotine-stained fingers. "Anvil's betrayed. We don't yet know how. We're sending you by sea to Brittany. You'll make your way by an established line to another *réseau*. It's big." Vera gave her Virginia Hall's latest code name. "Her only pianist was killed in an ambush."

Rolande was accustomed to aborted missions. Agents sometimes elected to drop blind rather than endure more suspense. A voyage by sea would make a nice change.

"Calvados est une liqueur tres forte." Rolande heard the BBC message the following evening in a safehouse at Falaise, in the Calvados region of Normandy, a very slow three-hour drive inland from the coast by farm tractor. The BBC was her slender thread to Vera. The feeling of contact was comforting. In a stranger's attic above a water mill, in a narrow cot under a window open to the predawn song of nightingales, Rolande turned over and went to sleep like a baby. She later told all this to Aaron Bank, creator of the U.S. Green Berets. "It was like a home from home," she said.

# 33

# Tangled Webs

Rolande had spoken of Gestapo interrogators referring to "a Jewish woman" at SOE, and Vera still stayed in the shadows to protect her identity. Enemy-run channels conveyed details of SOE's structure. Vera wanted nothing to provide ammunition to her other enemies in Whitehall, where she suspected a leak. "Uncle" Claude Dansey of SIS still wanted to rebuild SOE as his own. He ran NOCs—agents under Non-Official Cover—art dealers, travel reps, businessmen like Kavan Elliott, who was now underground in Yugoslavia. One NOC was Charles Andrew Buchanan King, who had represented himself as aide to the movie mogul Alexander Korda. "Never heard of him," Korda told Vera.

She found Andrew King in Switzerland. King was one of the prewar Cambridge students recruited by the Communist Party. Strange that he should be now in Bern, where Allen Dulles had a case file on King. It remained dormant until Dulles became director of the CIA in 1959. Then he began inquiries into the infiltration of the SIS by Soviet moles and concluded that their disclosure of Western secrets to Moscow not only prolonged the war at the cost of millions of lives but allowed Stalin to seize half of Europe.

Vera had to focus on the known and immediate danger that Berlin's Cipher Office was only pretending to believe Enigma was unbreakable. Gustave Bertrand, the French intelligence specialist who first hired the Cipher Office informer Hans-Thilo Schmidt, had been arrested in January 1944 and then released. Why? On May 31 the BBC called him in with the message "The white lilacs have flowered." Bertrand was prepared. He was anxious to clear his name, and to deny that Rodolphe Lemoine, or any missing Polish decoders, had disclosed what he called later "the greatest enigma of the war." He was picked up on time and delivered to Vera.[1]

The threat posed by ULTRA if the enemy knew it was breaking Enigma codes had been outlined on July 19, 1943, when Churchill told his chiefs of staff, "I do not believe twenty-seven Anglo-American divisions are sufficient for Overlord in view of the extraordinary fighting efficiency of the German army, and the much larger forces they could so readily bring to bear against our troops even if the landings were successfully accomplished." If Allied reading of Enigma was known, the Germans could mislead invasion planners to the wrong conclusions.[2]

In these tense months before D-day, Gustave Bertrand described how he had been released by the Germans because he undertook to inform on Resistance networks. The moment he was out on the street, he slipped away. Vera continued to broadcast BBC messages as if he were still in France. She was told that Bertrand had become a German-run double agent. She asked, "What's the source?"—the question so often heard after Churchill adopted the Bletchley analyst whose "intuitions" about the movement of enemy warships had initially been ignored.

The answer now, as it had been before, was "Hinsley."

Harry Hinsley's intuition this time involved Bertrand and also Antoni Palluth, whose AVA company had studied the Enigma machine sent to the German embassy in Warsaw in 1929. Palluth was said to have been hunted by German counterintelligence. Hinsley asked: Why were the Germans so keen to find him? Was he in cahoots with Bertrand to fool the British? Hinsley now handled cooperation with the Americans on Bletchley's ULTRA. Since undergraduate days, his waking hours had been spent brooding over disembodied signals. Vera felt this made him insensitive to the streetwise tactics of those forever outwitting a murderous enemy. Bertrand might have saved himself by a ruse, but he had not betrayed ULTRA. She established that Palluth was killed in an Allied bombing raid.[3]

Indications that the ULTRA secret was still safe came from intercepted enemy signals. FUSAG, a fictitious First U.S. Army Group, faked a large military buildup in Kent and Sussex, and drew the Germans into massing troops around the Pas-de-Calais on the opposite side. Field Marshal Gerd von Runstedt informed Berlin that the war

had reached "a serious turning point." Murders of German senior officers and sabotage would grow with the hiring of criminal gangs. The
field marshal's Enigma-coded signals for Hitler admitted that he could
not move in France without heavy protection. Von Runstedt made his
staff officers practice English manners to divorce themselves from
Hitler's "lowbrow Nazis." He would still stand and fight, but Vera put
him in the same category as Admiral Canaris, who had asked Roosevelt to help anti-Nazi Germans get rid of Hitler.

An army of Whitehall military bureaucrats descended upon
SOE's Baker Street offices. Gubbins, now a major general, recalled
that he was obliged "to cheat and crawl" to get what he needed. SOE
was variously called the Racket, Some Potty Outfit, Bedlam, and
Stately 'Omes of England. Bill Donovan spoke up from the OSS side
and said if SOE did nothing else, it justified its existence by the sabotage of Norsk Hydro, the source of heavy water that German scientists
might use to retard nuclear reaction and build the bomb.

There were unplanned anti-Nazi bombshells. One came from a
middle-aged French spinster, whose heroic acts inspired a powerful letter from her bishop denouncing the deportation of French Jews. Vera
first learned about it from Rolande, who reported from the field on
Marie-Rose Gineste, an unmarried French social worker. Between the
ages of forty-one and forty-four, she had pedaled hundreds of miles on
a bicycle she called Semper, pilfering food ration cards for a Jewish underground. Finally she got her bishop, Pierre-Marie Théas of Mon-
taubon Diocese, to write a pastoral letter "in an outraged protest of
Christian conscience over men and women treated like wild animals,"
and calling on all Catholics to protect Jews not yet deported. Bishop
Théas proposed to post his denunciation outside all churches. Marie-
Rose warned him that Vichy's pro-Nazi police would intercept the
distributors. She proposed an alternative: the BBC. Rolande wirelessed the entire text and it was broadcast in the BBC French service.
This marked a turning point. French families risked sheltering surviving Jews, while Marie-Rose continued her crusade in isolation, a self-
motivated, self-taught resister.[4]

By May 1944 Vera estimated 100,000 resisters in France needed a
systematic SOE effort to bring together solitaries like Marie-Rose.
"Uncle" Claude Dansey jeered that she multiplied the figure by fifty.
Vera listed fifty active and well-organized SOE-run circuits, from

*The Beaulieu estate near the English Channel, sometimes known as SOE "finishing school,"
where wartime agents trained commando-style or waited for missions.*
(Courtesy of UK National Motor Museum and Beaulieu SOE Collection)

*The Westland Lysander, an all-purpose aircraft used to insert SOE agents into Nazi-controlled territory*

*An agent parachuting into
occupied France.*
(Courtesy of Sonia d'Artois)

*U.S. Air Force B-17 bombers dropping supplies
into France in 1944.*
(Courtesy of of BSC Papers and E-Spread)

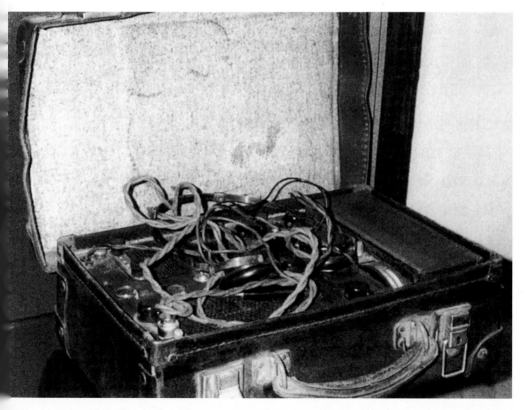

ABOVE: *False ID card for "Michel Pontlevé," real name Cyril Watney, a wireless operator involved in destroying French factories' capacity to produce propellers for German aircraft.* (Courtesy of Cyril Watney)

BELOW: *Suitcase wireless set carried by agents.*
(Courtesy of the Netherlands Institute for War Documentation)

ABOVE: *Agent gadgets and weapons.* (Courtesy of UK National Motor Museum and Beaulieu SOE Collection)

BELOW: *Agents packed dead rats with plastic explosives, then placed them near fires or furnaces in factories making products for the German forces. When guards found the rats and threw them into the fire, the resulting explosions caused a great deal of damage.*
(Courtesy of UK National Motor Museum and Beaulieu SOE Collection)

*Leo Marks, in 1998, displaying silk printed with SOE ciphers.* (Courtesy of *BBC History* magazine)

*One of countless rail lines sabotaged by SOE agents with the help of French rail workers to prevent German reinforcements from reaching D-day beaches.*
(Courtesy of the Office of the French Prime Minister and Commission d'Histoire de l'Occupation et de la Libération de la France, Ministère de l'Education Nationale)

*Vincent Doblin and his probability theory equation.*
(Courtesy of the Office of the French Prime Minister and Serge Louveau, Commission d'Histoire de l'Occupation et de la Libération de la France, Ministère de l'Education Nationale)

ABOVE: *Hugh Dalton with Władysław Raczkiewicz, president of the Government of the Polish Republic in Exile, and General Władysław Sikorski.* (Courtesy of BSC Papers and E-Spread)

BELOW: *Six female guards from the Ravensbrück concentration camp. Vera testified against these women at the British-controlled war crimes trials in Hamburg on December 10, 1946. Of the six pictured here, 1, 3, 4, and 5 were executed; 2 and 6 were imprisoned for ten years.* (Private collection)

*Vera and Colonel Maurice Buckmaster in East Sussex in 1988 or '89.*
(Courtesy of Michael Buckmaster)

Farmer in the north to Gardener in the south. These could be expanded to one hundred circuits with leadership from outside. Maquis commanders had 35,000 to 40,000 guerrillas, but only 10,000 were armed for more than a day's fighting. A Secret Army had a reserve of 350,000 youths. There were 500,000 railway men and 300,000 trade unionists ready to rise up. Much of the French workforce, about three million men and women, would help the Allies. SOE had to expand the training of agents to provide leadership, and this meant cutting down the time from two months to as little as two weeks.

There was always the threat of turncoats slipping into the ranks. Vera now had other ways to spot deceptive messages. The shabby old Denmark Hill Police Station in South London ran machines to intercept, record, and analyze high-speed transmissions from the field, and search for evidence of entrapment. At Beaumanor, Chicksands, near Bletchley, one of ULTRA's founding fathers, Gordon Welchman, reminded Vera that the ultramodern *Bismarck*'s fate was sealed when a high-ranking German officer sent a coded message to his son. The name matched one in Bletchley's files listing the crew of the battle cruiser, and this gave away its preparations to leave port. Since then, far larger files had been compiled so that enemy names, spotted in intercepted traffic, could be swiftly identified. In this way Welchman had independently come across incongruities to back Leo Marks's suspicion that the SOE network in Holland was under Gestapo control.

Vera ruled that "SOE messages should never contain true names that can be checked against a German list of serving officers and men." SOE stations were identified by letters of the alphabet and numbers. Propaganda officers at the Political Warfare Executive adopted the supersecret, ominous title London Control. Vera confided her misgivings about Control to a PWE officer, Vernon Bartlett, who wrote the prewar book *Nazi Germany Explained*. London Control was in fact near Bletchley, at Woburn Abbey on the Duke of Bedford's estate. Bored workers, transferred there from London, were compensated with French claret and gallons of gin and sherry. Little else amused them, other than skating on the duke's lake in winter or wandering through his zoo, where Bartlett liked to pretend "I was buggered by a llama and bitten by a rhea." In the chaos, he said, nobody oversaw Control's activities.

Kim Philby spun Control's broadcasts to Germany to serve

Moscow's aims. His exposure as a Soviet mole was twenty years away. Broadcasts named Vera's anti-Nazi friends, like the lovely Russian princess Marie "Missie" Vassiltchikov, who was in the German foreign office and protected by Vera's Ambassador Von der Schulenburg. Old Fritz's secret letters ended abruptly after his recall from Moscow. Vera tracked him to Krummhübel, a ski resort on the Czech border that now sheltered foreign office staff from SS sniffer dogs. Its new inhabitants called it Spies' Paradise because the servants were Czechs, the sawmills employed Serbs or disaffected Italians, and there was little supervision of labor imported from the sullen nearby lands where Vera's outstanding agent, the Polish countess Krystyna Skarbek, had slipped easily back and forth. Krystyna was still stuck in Cairo, but kept contacts along the Czech and Hungarian borders with Poland and reported that Schulenburg was making bold motoring trips to Budapest with Missie, who had been transferred from Berlin early in 1944. She had been met by Schulenburg when she arrived at the former resort on Monday, January 17. He wore a Russian fur hat acquired in Moscow and said jauntily that the staff lived in mountaintop cabins and slid on small sledges to his offices in the valley. Schulenburg, living in a wooden chalet without plumbing, was saved by Missie's poorer accommodation. At least it had a bath. He used it daily.

Vera cross-checked Krystyna's reports with other sources. One was Elizabeth Wiskemann, in neutral Switzerland, working for London Control and in touch with friends from her days in Berlin. Among her sources were anti-Nazi trade unionists, newsmen, and Geneva's Ecumenical Council of Churches, which helped escapees. Wiskemann's neighbors were the parents of Prince Heinrich zu Sayn-Wittgenstein, an ace night-fighter pilot who was credited with shooting down eighty-three Allied aircraft but who was a secret anti-Nazi. On the phone with Missie, he had spoken of blowing up Hitler and himself when next presented with more Oak Leaves to add to his Knight's Cross. Before that could happen, however, he was shot down.

For some mysterious reason Miss Wiskemann refused to deal with SOE. Vera wished she could talk with Schulenburg, who had mentioned the woman among visitors to Moscow. Old Fritz might become a target of Control's exposure of anti-Nazis. He had seen Stalin charm bigwigs like Sir Stafford Cripps, the British ambassador in Moscow until 1942, who was now in Churchill's War Cabinet and demanding that SOE secrets be shared with Moscow. How Schulenburg would laugh! He had motored with Missie into the Czech Protectorate, where he said to one of Krystyna's contacts that London broadcasts that named anti-Nazis might be calculated to undermine Hitler's morale.

Both sides were using deception to harm each other's self-confidence. There was the sudden revelation of a top-secret order from Hitler requiring "the extermination of enemy sabotage troops." A turncoat who broadcast from Berlin, Lord Haw-Haw, boasted that all was known about Bletchley: "The hands on the town hall clock are stuck at five minutes before noon!" This was true, but the story could have been planted by London Control. Vera questioned Sefton Delmer, the first reporter to interview Hitler and now running black propaganda. He said: "I can't say we planted the story and I can't say we didn't. My bosses don't like SOE. They don't mind sacrificing SOE *criminals*. You'll see. None of our files will survive the war."[5]

A criminal named Harold Cole saved British escapees but also worked with the Gestapo. "Worst traitor of the war," Scotland Yard's deputy commander Reginald Spooner called him. Vera had known he was a con artist, but recruited him to use his crooked talents in the cause. He was hosting a cocktail party in Paris and calling himself "Captain Mason, a British Secret Agent" when identified and shot down "while resisting arrest."

Vera recalled, "Other agents had criminal records, but they were 'gentleman-burglar' types, eager to serve in war. A billion francs or more were spread around to pay for SOE operations. Hardly a franc was unaccounted for." Currency was forged after SOE ran out of gold bars. OSS, the rich partner, made up for the drain on dwindling British finances. Bletchley needed four-wheel Enigma replicas to speed up code breaking. "Without charging a cent, National Cash Register of Dayton, Ohio, turned out seventy-five replicas in six months, more than the total British production for the entire war," Vera recalled. The U.S.-made bombes were stored at Mount Vernon School on Ne-braska Avenue in Washington, D.C., until brought to London by U.S. liaison officers attached to Bletchley. One was Lewis Powell, a future Supreme Court justice. "I acquired a taste for a local Bletchley news-paper, the *Leighton Buzzard Observer & North Bucks Times*," recalled Powell. "Just imagine! The geniuses who worked on the war's biggest secret relaxed with the weekly doings of the Ladies Bright Hour, published by Mister Midgeley."

London Control's flimflam disheartened local resisters, who could not investigate firsthand the integrity of SOE's policy makers. Resistance misgivings were conveyed through Vera's returning agents: If Germans were identified as secret opponents of Hitler, would London go on to name non-Germans now fighting the Nazi occupiers of their country? Lewis Powell saw that if Control or a Double Cross XX Committee tried to bamboozle the other side, it might also fool itself. He later turned down directorship of the postwar CIA. He never publicly discussed his wartime visits to Bletchley, nor to Woburn and London Control. In private, he confided his concern that Control harbored Russian-run English agents, and quoted Sir Walter Scott: "O what a tangled web we weave, / When first we practise to deceive!"[6]

# 34

# Deadly Mind and Wireless Games

"German Penetration of SOE," a postwar investigation, was never made public. Maurice Buckmaster had played wireless games of deception which he couldn't confide to Vera. Whitehall, with its old-school-tie mindset, preferred an Old Etonian like Buckmaster to take charge of F Section's bluffs. Agents were desperately needed in France before D-day, expected by mid-1944. Some were hastily dispatched to networks penetrated by the enemy. One was a shorthand typist from London's East End, Peggy Knight, dropped by parachute on May 5, 1944. She was given information she could reveal under Gestapo interrogation: that the Allied invasion would be launched against the Pas-de-Calais. Three of her colleagues, hurriedly trained like Peggy, were quickly caught and eventually executed.

Peggy Knight's instructors assessed her as "raw" and in need of more training, refusing to recommend that she be sent into the field. She had made one practice parachute jump instead of the normal three, but nevertheless was dropped with a wireless operator in the Côte d'Or at the wrong place, and was found by Casse-Cou, or Break-Neck, an inauspicious name matched by that of the Donkeyman circuit, penetrated already for two years since a courier lost his briefcase with details of two hundred members of the circuit. Donkeyman founder André Girard turned up in the United States, lecturing on secret operations, until Bill Stephenson had him gagged and questioned by the FBI. A warning to Vera arrived too late to repair any damage.

Sensing betrayal, Peggy Knight had joined forces with William Egan Colby, a twenty-three-year-old native of St. Paul, Minnesota, who would later become a CIA director. Colby dropped with a Jedburgh team and worked with a maquis that won spectacular gunfights. Peggy "blazed away at Germans hunting her down," Bill Simpson wrote later, "and fought with the ferocity you'd expect in a girl from the hardest hit part of London's blitzed slums."[1]

Bill Donovan had suggested that to ensure full use of SOE in the coming invasion, Vera should show General Dwight D. Eisenhower, the supreme commander, progress made in closework. This would off-set anti-SOE comments from senior British commanders and invigorate Donovan's campaign for OSS to play a major role. The dissecting rooms of the Natural History Museum in South Kensington were turned into a showcase for "wizard factories" making imaginative weapons that ranged from one-man submarines to *Sleeping Beauty*, a small battery-driven sailboat with saddlebags for waterproofed underwater charges.

The staid Victoria & Albert Museum displayed special devices made at the inn called the Thatched Barn. One specialty was a torch with an ultraviolet beam and a handkerchief concealing code keys that could be read only when the torch was switched on. Bill Pietsch of OSS said later, "Camel dung, horse manure, and the droppings of elephants had been studied at the London Zoo. Explosives were wrapped into whatever form of shit was native to its destination. Deadly devices were made in little Kensington factories. Film studios camouflaged everything and picked the brains of brilliant set designer Beverley Woodner, daughter of a Chicago Jewish rabbi, who was a cross between Merle Oberon and Vivien Leigh."

After working alongside Vera to make sure Ike also saw the SOE "finishing schools," Bill Pietsch was dropped with a Jedburgh team. Beverley Woodner recalled a poignant visit to one school, at Beaulieu, close to the family home of Edmund de Rothschild, now on active service as commander of an artillery battery and expecting to join a Jewish Brigade. Beaulieu was near enough to the English Channel to make France seem close. "Vera never showed me her feelings, but for this once," Beverley said. "She told me a cure for depression was the sound, color, and smells of the countryside . . . the miracle of the seasons . . . the healing powers of lapwings made of the same cells and tissues as ourselves but living in some invisible, unknowable place."

There were sound reasons for Vera's depression and her need to wander among a dozen country houses dotting the Beaulieu estate, where tidal saltings teemed with birdlife and offered the vitamin-rich samphire, a combination of asparagus and seaweed that compensated for the meagerness of the wartime diet. Edmund de Rothschild's adjacent property had been requisitioned by the Admiralty, and the Royal Navy's white ensign was surrounded by woodland paths, rhododendrons, streams and pools, ferns and water lilies, cedars and smooth grassy lawns that provided Vera with the "wilderness therapy" she craved, although this was not exactly a wilderness. Plant hunters of the Rothschild clan had brought exotic botanical specimens here from all over the world. A new member of the family had planned to study them, the agent Jean-Pierre Reinach, who had been captured and executed. His widow, Naomi of the Rothschild clan, eased her pain by working with refugee children and planning Jewish resettlement after the war. Meanwhile Vera was dealing with the loss of Noor Inayat Khan, descended from the last Mughal emperor.

As part of her training, Noor had been sent from Beaulieu on a grueling ninety-six-hour exercise to the Welsh border, to arrange live and dead letter boxes, and to find three separate locations for secret wireless transmissions, without arousing local suspicion and without maps. Noor accomplished these tasks brilliantly but was assessed by some instructors as too emotionally unstable for closework operations. Vera knew that Noor was now at 84 avenue Foch in Paris, in stark contrast to bucolic Beaulieu. Avenue Foch elegance had sunk into a dungeonlike twilight, where SS Sturmbannführer Hans Kieffer wormed his way into the minds of captured agents. The betrayal of the Prosper circuit, which became known a few days after Noor landed, prompted Vera to wireless Noor to return immediately aboard a pickup plane. Noor turned down the offer. An unusually strong-minded young woman, she was driven by principle to finish every task. Before she was caught, she had accomplished wonders, drawing on deep reservoirs of energy until, in a moment of exhausted carelessness, she forgot the one lesson Vera had drummed into her time and again. At Beaulieu, the last holding place before agents went into the field, one girl had been disqualified after she called out in English "Come in!" when instructors banged on her door in the middle of the night and shouted "Gestapo!" Noor's mistake was more dramatic.

Some sources insist that her fatal mistake was to leave one of her logbooks in a temporary safe house. Sonderführer Ernst Vogt testified in a postwar deposition that Noor had been denounced—and her network blown—on or about October 7. On October 13, Vogt trapped her when she returned to a temporary Paris apartment at 98 rue de la Faisenderie to pick up her wireless transmitter. She fought Vogt and bit through the hands of one of his German escorts, but was captured. She was held for several weeks at avenue Foch, managed to escape into the street, but was recaptured—destined for Dachau. If she did make mistakes, it was not from a lack of training.

Far from these requisitioned country houses, Lord Rothschild in London allowed his bank to be used as a testing ground for SOE. Precision armament parts and fuses were manufactured at the bank's facilities in the Royal Mint Refinery near the Tower of London, where before the war the Rothschilds had melted down and refined gold. SOE was the latest beneficiary of Rothschild skills. The N. M. Rothschild bank had provided the Duke of Wellington's armies in 1811 with gold coins and ingots to cover the costs of fighting Napoleon. A letter in the bank archives from the duke spoke of the need for gold, "having due consideration of the magnitude of the objectives in view, of the dispatch and secrecy it requires, and of the risk which may be incurred." In SOE closework, a major problem was financing agents and resistance groups; again, the Rothschilds were able to help. Victor de Rothschild, an expert in 1944 at defusing time bombs, was asked to test a lock that was impossible to pick. The prototype was put in a container with incendiary material that made it explode if anyone tried to cut through it, and The Shop sent it to the bank for testing. The Shop was telephoned next day. Rothschild's bank now had a large hole burned through one floor. Victor gently suggested they all go back to the drawing board.

Knowing the chances were now good for Edmund de Rothschild to join a British army Jewish Brigade, Vera recovered her normal buoyancy and drew comfort from discussing with Beverley Woodner another age in England when Jews were not "lesser breeds" but part of a thriving and tolerant society. Edmund's father, Lionel, was the eldest son of Leo, and was married at the Central Synagogue in London on January 19, 1881. Albert, Queen Victoria's consort, had signed the marriage contract, and omnibus drivers on the Piccadilly route had sported the Rothschild colors of blue and yellow on their horsewhips to mark the coming of age of Edmund's father in 1903.

"I need to go back to a time that seems enviably predictable," said Vera. "It helps deal with so much uncertainty."

# 35

# "The Life That I Have Is Yours"

Vera learned that in Paris she had been dealing with an antagonist who, while she knew him, appeared to know nothing about her: a formerly obscure small-town schoolteacher who had climbed in Hitler's esteem to become the SD wizard in mind games, Dr. Josef Goetz. The "Dr." was typical of German pretentiousness, she thought, adopted by Goetz in the same spirit as "Dr." Goebbels, to suggest academic superiorities that neither had.

Josef Goetz lurked at the Paris headquarters of Himmler's SD counterespionage service, west of the Arc de Triomphe, in two of the three houses at 82, 84, and 86 avenue Foch, where captured agents were interrogated. Vera knew the layout now, and that Goetz was also seen watching the Gestapo's torturers at 11 rue de Saussaies, behind the French Ministry of the Interior in charge of the pro-Nazi Vichy French police. Goetz used French police collaborators to pretend they were protecting SOE wireless operators held in custody. Vera reconstructed Goetz in her mind's eye: a well-fed, sedentary pen pusher with myopic blue eyes behind thick lenses, contentedly plotting to kill "subhumans" like her agents. She had to eliminate false information planted by the *milice*, the pro-Nazi police who had been seen in the immediate aftermath of the French surrender as Vichy's way to restore French honor. The *milice* now obeyed the violently pro-Nazi Joseph Darnand and mingled among resisters in the guise of French police "crossovers" to the Allied side. Vera cautioned her agents that local resisters talked too freely to "pseudo-crossovers." The Resistance was too trusting of volunteers who flaunted their patriotism, whereas communists ran a disciplined system of cells and silence, enforced by Soviet-trained experts. Henri Dericourt—a highly experienced prewar pilot and the French air movements officer for SOE flights into enemy territory—spoke of complicated traps hidden in a sinister world of uncertain loyalties. In answering Vera's carefully respectful questions, he let slip much about the fate of Noor Inayat Khan.

Arrogant in his belief that he was the indispensable traffic controller for her agents, Dericourt was not to know that Vera had growing numbers of experienced agents visiting her from the field by other routes than the ones he controlled. It gave her the power to cross-check information. Virginia Hall had been in London briefly for adjustments to Cuthbert, her artificial lower leg, and to consult her American compatriots at OSS headquarters. She was now back with Rolande Colas and the OSS in the Haute-Loire. Nearby was Pearl Witherington, aged seventeen when she first taught English in Paris. Now twenty-eight, she had sole command of an armed maquis of about 2,500 men and women. Violette Szabo had joined them before her capture, and was now in Fresnes Prison, ten miles outside Paris, historically the largest criminal facility in Europe.

The White Rabbit was also there when a sudden increase in BBC plain-language messages signaled the approach of D-day. French boys and girls bicycled around the prison and shouted BBC "stand by" messages for captured agents. On June 5, 1944, the BBC switched to "action." One boy on a bicycle, Jacques Deleporte, guessed D-day was imminent. He told Vera later that Fresnes was "a sprawling complex, a labyrinth of dungeons, high landings, endless corridors. The SS controlled it, helped by *les souris*, the ugly and stupid SS women in gray. Hundreds of thousand of prisoners had been held there since the Revolution, when many threw themselves from the upper levels rather than wait for the guillotine. In 1944 there was little the Germans could do to outwit us. We were street urchins whose strength was our contempt for adults and authority."[1]

Deception teams parachuted into the Pas-de-Calais to give the impression that this was the D-day target, using wind-up gramophones and the recorded sounds of armies. Ahead of the real invasion, too, landed twenty-two-year-old Charles Wheeler to scout behind enemy lines. He became the BBC's longest-serving foreign correspondent in postwar years. Another advance parachutist was George Millar, aged twenty-seven, former correspondent for the London *Sunday Express* in Paris, who in 1939 "reported how the French Army always ran away."

He joined the British Rifle Brigade, commanded a scout platoon, was captured, and jumped from a train to join Resistance groups that helped him cross the Pyrenees into Spain. From there he reached England, and laid the foundations of a lifelong friendship with Vera. By D-day, he was fighting alongside teenage resisters and had revised his views on the French fighting spirit. The French who "ran" in 1940, he now conceded, were tired old men afraid to repeat the 1914–18 carnage.[2]

In response to critics who smeared SOE as pro-Soviet, General Eisenhower declared his admiration for what SOE was accomplishing. Vera thought the Americans a godsend, free from rank-worship. This she had to tolerate with the influx of stiff-necked War Office disciplinarians at SOE headquarters. "I kept my head down, following the advice of an Australian, Richard 'Dikko' Hughes, who said 'I've signed nothing, you can prove nothing.'" Hughes's first wife was Jewish. A close friend of Ian Fleming, he later suggested that Fleming's 007 should run MOB, Miscellaneous Objectives Bureau, patterned on the thriller-writer's real-life Assault Unit intelligence-gathering command. Fleming, while still the star of naval intelligence, called it his Indecent Assault Unit.[3]

SAS teams advertised the fictional FUSAG or First U.S. Army Group and the Pas-de-Calais as their D-day target. This disinformation seemed to fool the Germans when a disconcerting enemy message boasted of fooling SOE. It came from a Prosper subcircuit, Butler, running since 1942 around Le Mans, southwest of Paris:

> We thank you for the large deliveries of arms and ammunition you
> have been kind enough to send us. We also appreciate the many
> tips you have given us regarding your plans.

Vera knew the Prosper master circuit was penetrated by Goetz, and that Buckmaster had pretended to take at face value messages dispatched by Prosper operators under German control. To maintain his counterdeception, he parachuted precious supplies to Prosper but did not receive the bluff-check warnings from his Gestapo-controlled agents. Leo Marks had tried to alert him to the betrayal of the master circuit after picking up signs that the Bulter subcircuit was *brulé*, blown. Now Vera discovered why Leo's warnings had been stifled.

Noor's presence in France had been known to Goetz. SOE agents had been dropped into the hands of three German-controlled circuits. Hitler, according to Goetz's later testimony, decided this was the best psychological moment to shake Allied confidence in the reliability of resistance movements. In SOE's counterplay, Goetz's attention was directed to circuits in a region well away from the D-day landings. Goetz received agents lured by his own game-playing and primed to distract his attention from the very big resistance networks still undetected.

Vera wondered if London Control had told Buckmaster to keep on dropping agents and supplies to fool the Germans in a double deception, stifling Leo's warnings. On the German side of Control's game was Josef Goetz; on the Allied side was Uncle Claude, whose real aim was to control SOE. Buckmaster was prepared to cooperate, but complained that the Secret Intelligence Service, he said, had "intruded on my turf."[4]

Prosper was allowed to grow too fast after a woman courier, Andrée Borrel, had been dropped near Paris on September 24–25, 1942. She was followed by Francis Suttill, who had the task of rebuilding a circuit around Paris. Suttill, a peacetime barrister aged thirty-two, was not as careful as he should have been about developing subagents and subcircuits. From the Ardennes to the Atlantic, the enterprise became too big to be supervised. Every Prosper agent save two had been betrayed, and executed after torture.

One missing agent was thirty-year-old Odette Sansom, married to a Combined Operations naval commander and mother of two daughters. On an autumn evening in 1942 she had wiped away her SOE number, S.23, chalked on a wall inside the Wimpole Street hideaway where agents memorized orders. In France she became entangled in the game run by Josef Goetz. Hugo Ernst Bleicher, aged forty-five and a member of Admiral Canaris's intelligence service, hooked her name out of SOE wireless traffic. Bleicher saw Odette after her arrest and said he would leave her free to negotiate peace terms on behalf of the German High Command. Odette was unsure if this was a ruse in order to have her lead his men to other SOE agents. A colleague, Peter Churchill, made a similar miscalculation, and both agents were now prisoners.

As far back as April 1943, Vera had urged Odette not to try to outwit the enemy. When she searched for lost agents later, she found

Maurice Southgate, one of three out of forty British agents still alive in Buchenwald. He said girls in captivity were sent to the ovens after telling him they tried to warn London of their capture. "The responsible SOE officer," he said, "should be court-martialed for causing the death of so many courageous women."

De Gaulle insisted that France was liberating itself, while in fact eighty-three Jedburgh teams, a score of American Operational Groups, the SAS, and the État-major des Forces Françaises de l'Interieur had been dropped behind the lines to join local French groups. The military wing of the Communist National Liberation Front, Francs-Tireurs et Partisans, worked with Gaullist Free French, pending a war within a war between de Gaulle and communist leaders. Yeo-Thomas, the White Rabbit, heard other voices coming through the air vents of his dungeon, singing "La Marseillaise." These were new prisoners who told of bitter fighting by French resisters. He had always put faith in a modernized form of guerrilla warfare and had talked so often with Vera about how "primitive" closework could empower impoverished victims of any tyranny, agreeing with her that if anyone should be part of SOE, it was the Jews whose only haven, Palestine, was denied them by both sides. Now he waited for his opportunity to get back into action.

Colin Gubbins wanted the Polish Home Army to be given unstinting help in defeating the German occupiers before Poland fell completely into the hands of the Russians. There had been only two successful SOE airdrops into Poland in four months. The Free Poles in London asked if four squadrons of a new Polish Air Force, made up from those who had flown with the RAF, could land at bases the Home Army had already recaptured from the Germans, ahead of the Russian advance into Poland. The request was rejected.

Jan Zurakowski went directly to Vera. "I'm sorry, Zura," she told him. "Something's going on at higher levels I don't understand."

"I'd never seen her show emotion," he said later. "She had tears in her eyes and bent forward and lit a cigarette. Then she turned icy cold and said, 'Our Foreign Office and Washington are obsessed with one thing: What will Stalin think if we help you?' I told her it was obvious the Soviet Union intended to run our guerrilla formations in Europe."[5]

With crisis piling upon crisis, to think ahead was difficult for SOE. Before the Operation Overlord landings, three battalions of British sappers went ashore at low tide to clear the mined beaches; three-quarters of the men were cut down by enemy machine guns. Such frightful losses were commonplace among French Resistance armies. SOE officers told of fierce battles to delay German reinforcements. French saboteurs cut telephone lines to force the Germans onto the airwaves for Bletchley to listen in. German reinforcements from the Eastern Front were attacked. In the agonizing weeks of uncertainty when, after D-day, the Allied advance stalled, Pimento's French railroad workers derailed 1,005 troop trains. Every German army train rushed up from the south was derailed by resisters. The German 11th Panzer Division, with the Tiger tanks that outgunned the Russians, took only a week to reach the Rhine from that front, but bogged down for another three weeks in French guerrilla quagmires. If it had reached Normandy sooner, it might have helped fling the Allies back into the sea. Montgomery's plans to quickly capture the strategic city of Caen were frighteningly delayed by the unsuspected presence of German forces within the ancient walls. Cadogan at the Foreign Office noted with studied insouciance on July 28, 1944, "We seem to be stuck against heavy opposition in Normandy." A secret Polish army in northern France, and a Polish Parachute Brigade reinforced by Polish workers who had escaped from German camps, managed to prevent a German counterattack that could have turned "stuck" into a total withdrawal of Allied invasion forces. Gubbins called SOE "a howling success." He had to beat the drum to break the silence of top commanders like Montgomery, who totally ignored the part SOE played and the clandestine forces it nurtured.[6]

Donovan, now better known as General William J., confirmed to Vera that the SS Panzer Division Das Reich was in southwest France when it should have been on the Russian front. Das Reich was reputedly one of the most formidable fighting units in the world. A French professional soldier, Jérôme Lescanne, posing as a farmer and watching the region between Bordeaux and Marseilles, had obtained the railway orders for Das Reich that would have landed the SS division at the Normandy bridgehead in time to defeat Overlord. Vera's agents worked with the French national railway to force trainloads of Das Reich men and equipment onto mined and booby-trapped roads.

Wheelwright, a large SOE-run circuit, waited until the Allied landings to blow up the division's fuel dumps. Two French schoolgirls, graduates of Pimento's impromptu training program, sabotaged axle boxes of transporter cars with abrasive powders. Chuck Yeager, after his escape, had told Vera that the powders were compact and easily hidden. "Even a schoolgirl could use them," he reported prophetically. After Das Reich panzers shook free at Toulouse, they ran another gauntlet of circuits: Digger, Fireman, the SAS team Bulbasket. What remained of the division then had to deal with Miss Pearl Witherington.

Miss Witherington's ancestor had fought on his knees after his legs were cut off at the battle of Chevy Chase. Her own early life was less spectacular. As a teenager, after her father left the family destitute, she had to find work in Paris to help her mother get by. When Paris fell, she escaped to London, became restless as a shorthand typist in Whitehall, and let it be known that she wanted to fight with the French underground. She was asked how she knew such a thing existed. "If it doesn't, it should," she replied. Vera dispatched her as a courier, but Miss Witherington took command of a guerrilla force when her organizer was killed. She had joined SOE in June 1943, parachuted into Maurice Southgate's circuit, and was reunited with her boyfriend, Henri Cornioley, a German prison camp escapee. Both were with Rolande Colas, making professional cuts to the strategically vital main rail line between Bordeaux and Paris, when a reward was put on Pearl Witherington's head. German placards displayed her photograph with offers of a million francs for anyone who turned her in.

"The Resistance liberated France south of the Loire, not the Allied armies," she said to Vera in a later debriefing. Sabotage, exploding fuel dumps, and twisted railway lines had forced German troops to use roads where guerrillas could further harrass them. There was no enemy opposition to Allied forces that landed on the Riviera two months after D-day. Their way was open along the lower Rhone valley all the way to Grenoble.

But a terrible price was paid by French civilians. Back in London after meetings with OSS representatives in North Africa in August 1944, Bill Donovan got detailed accounts from Allen Dulles in Bern. In Pearl Witherington's battleground was Limoges, the great porcelain and enamel center. It was in a virtual state of siege. Dulles reported:

Its barricades and block houses are held by Vichy's pro-Nazi security police and militia. Disorganized actions against the Germans by the citizenry result in reprisals that bathe the whole region in blood. The maquis were driven out of the city and attacked a German garrison, killing a colonel in a Das Reich SS regiment. In revenge, the SS moved into the neighboring village of Oradour-sur-Glane on June 10, where hundreds of children were on summer vacation. All the children were locked inside a church, which was then set on fire, and any child running out was machine-gunned to death. This savagery on the part of the Germans at Oradour is inexplicable. All the men were shut up in barns, women and children in a church among houses that were set on fire, the flames spreading to the barns and church. Some seven hundred innocents were killed, mostly burned alive. . . . The fate of Limoges and that of all the cities in the center of France is very much the same. . . . The only comfort in this frightful situation is to be found in the intense patriotism of these people.

German terrorist reprisals, Pearl Witherington argued, only inflamed civilian resistance. She weighed the cost against very heavy losses from conventional, and often unsuccessful, regular operations. A resister accomplished much more for much less. Within her region, a strategic French tunnel was plastered by RAF Squadron 617, using the biggest and costliest Tallboy bombs, just after D-day. This risked highly trained Pathfinder pilots but failed to close the tunnel. Miss Witherington did it with SOE explosives. No lives were lost. Armada, Vera's code name for a circuit of one chauffeur, a fireman, a garage hand, and a student, crippled a major arms factory and stopped canal traffic. A large force of regular troops would need to be diverted from hand-to-hand battles in Normandy to get the same results.

But reliance on individuals in covert action meant that the loss of one could have widespread, disastrous consequences. Das Reich panzers captured Violette Szabo after Vera dispatched her the night before D-day to the Limoges region. Violette was a crack shot. The Das Reich division was entangled in the brushwood of the maquisards three days after she arrived. She was sent in an old Renault on a liaison mission. A Das Reich patrol intercepted her car. She had a Sten gun and two magazines, each with thirty-two rounds. She took cover in a wheat field with her driver, and they crawled toward a wooded lot.

German armored cars circled the field, and the infantry closed in. Violette waved her driver to make a final dash for the trees while she held off the Germans. She was bleeding heavily and too weak to run. She was taken alive when she had nothing left to fight with except her bare hands, and dragged off to Limoges, where she was interrogated by the SS major who had hanged ninety-nine hostages the previous day in retaliation for a maquis attack that had killed forty German soldiers.

Some details reached Vera later, with a mutilated, undecipherable wireless signal. Leo Marks remembered standing in silence while Vera attacked it. She spotted *merde*. Shit. The letters were scattered. Then *Theo*. She heard again the voice of Rolande, when she was the pale-faced skinny medical student in Paris long ago, "Moi, je ne le laisserai plus m'emmerder" (As for me, I'm not going to put up with this shit any longer), meaning Hitler. Bit by bit, Vera broke the indecipherable. There was no triumph in her voice when she said to Leo: "Someone transmitted this for Rolande Colas. The Germans are 'sending our Joes up-the-chimney.' Trains are taking prisoners to crematoria in Germany. Violette Szabo's on the same transport, and so is Yeo-Thomas."

Rolande had provided a glimpse of the fate awaiting herself and Violette and the White Rabbit. Death-camp commanders were anxious to leave no living testimony and were incinerating prisoners of war, slave workers, and any other witnesses. Vera walked over to 70 Upper Grosvenor Street and the office of the OSS chief in Europe, David Bruce. Could someone at the very top warn that legal action would be taken against German executioners of prisoners? Within days, President Roosevelt told a press conference of the Oradour atrocities.

Still, as closework successes mounted, enemy fury increased against civilians. German lines of march were in chaos: divisions reached the bridgehead late, reduced often to mere companies and battalions. The 77th Infantry took thirteen days to make what should have been a two-day journey. The delays allowed the swelling tide of Allied power to sweep inland. SOE secrecy shrouded its own and other clandestine work. A prizewinning Normandy historian, Raymond Ruffin, waited thirty more years to write *La Résistance normande face à la Gestapo* after finally reconstructing the records of thirty-five groups of maquisards, *francs-tireurs*, and other irregulars within a single key target area—one hundred miles from Cherbourg to Dieppe, and inland by fifty miles to Domfront, with twenty-one German divisions within this tight space. Vengeful SS troops ravaged Domfront, the medieval town of misfortune where Vera had once noted the ancient warning: "Arrive at noon, hanged by one o'clock." Civilians were killed and raped on the pretext of flushing out terrorists. In Calvados country, *groupes de résistance* had held together despite months of German killings prior to D-day.

Vera worked under the physical stress of German V-1 missiles that began to hit London a week after D-day. One SOE agent located French quarries where the Germans had stored two thousand pilotless V-1 "buzz-bombs." Vera received a list of thirteen French cities where factories were making "flying bomb" parts. The BBC warned that the factories would be bombed, advising workers to stay home. She was leaving BBC headquarters at Bush House when a V-1 fell into Aldwych and killed everyone in a double-decker bus. The Guards' Chapel on Birdcage Walk was hit and sixty civilians were killed. This was the Sunday after Winston Churchill visited Normandy on June 12, 1944. London was undergoing another trial by fire. "London is full of people enjoying the sunshine," Churchill lied to Stalin. By July 6, Vera saw a three-week tally: 2,754 flying bombs killed 2,752 civilians: almost one for one. By August 30, 6,000 people had been killed and 750,000 houses hit. In the end, what Londoners called "doodlebugs" had struck 1,404,000 houses, 149 schools, 11 churches, and 95 hospitals. The high-flying V-2s, a prototype of ballistic missiles, killed 2,500 Londoners. The head of MI5's espionage B Branch, Guy Liddell, suggested using "the uranium bomb as a threat of retaliation." He was one of the few who knew about Allied development of an atomic bomb.

Despite all these losses, few tears were shed abroad for Londoners: all attention was on the desperate Allied struggle to break out of the heavily defended triangle extending inland from the Normandy beaches. Vera, knowing that agents and the maquis faced greater challenges ahead, had to pacify exiled secret-army chiefs like the Poles, who naturally thought they were solely responsible for anticipating the hailstorm of flying bombs and missiles. Their agents had retrieved an unexploded V-2 that fell in a swamp eighty miles east of Warsaw some two months before the attacks began. The Poles were unaware of earlier intelligence on the missiles from Norway in 1940. In June 1943, Scandinavian sources had identified the Baltic island of Peenemünde as the base for development of the FZG-76, the V-1, and the V-2. This prompted an attack by 330 heavy bombers on August 16–17, 1943, that set back Peenemünde's development program. For security reasons, one group could never be told of the successes of another country's agents.

The Polish underground's outstanding record in other fields should have helped Vera's efforts to meet urgent Polish requests for air backing. The Warsaw Uprising in August 1944, with the Red Army within a few miles, was a tragic example of unsupported gallantry: Stalin refused to let Allied aircraft refuel on landing fields under his control. Nazi death squads killed or captured nearly 200,000 Poles, one-fifth of Warsaw's population, during August and September 1944 while the West celebrated the final breakout of its forces in Normandy. The neglect of Central and East European "lesser breeds," Vera later wrote bitterly to Mary Stephenson, "lies behind indifference and prejudice, and still influences decision-makers at the top." SOE could no longer operate in Romania "because we are told that military operations are conducted there by the Russians and not by ourselves." The country of her birth was dismissed again as "a Balkan mess."

"She shared my faith in the superiority of individuals over machines, in thinking of the millions soon to face another tyrant's control," Bill Stephenson recalled. "Technical triumphs of the Berlin Cipher Office had been undercut by human intelligence. Hitler's new space-age weapons were foiled by the ingenuity of RAF pilots who invented a way to slide their wings under the fins of missiles and tip them away from their targets."

In the month following D-day, Hitler survived the thirty-first attempt on his life. It made Vera even more vigorous in championing SOE methods, but opponents who advocated mass bombing of German cities said the failure of the attempt proved them right. On July 20, 1944, a bomb had been planted next to Hitler by Lieutenant Colonel Claus von Stauffenberg in a briefing room in the Wolf's Lair in eastern Germany. It blew up beside Hitler, but a table leg saved him. "I am invulnerable!" he gloated. His supporters thought he must be right. His opponents were decimated in his revenge killings of the alleged plotters.

One was Otto John, who worked for the German airline Lufthansa. He flew to Madrid a few days later with lists of anti-Nazis and a warning that Vera saw: the names must never be used in propaganda.[7] Nonetheless, London Control broadcast the lists. There followed the execution of 4,980 German officers and civilians. Admiral Canaris was publicly strangled. Count von der Schulenburg, named as a future foreign minister in a post-Hitler government, was filmed, on Hitler's orders, hanging with a wire noose around his neck.

The ambassador's horrible end hit Vera hard. Since their times together, Old Fritz had tried to steer Germany back to sanity. She felt the awful indifference of the SIS after it infiltrated Ronald Thornley into her administration. Ten days after Stauffenberg's attempt on Hitler's life, Thornley memoed: "I have no doubt von T will be pleasantly arrested and fed on bacon and eggs for a month or two in order to improve his position." The "von T" stood for Adam von Trott zu Solz, the anti-Nazi named in Control's broadcasts. Bill Donovan urged a more "subtle psychological approach" to win over such anti-Nazi German officers, but Roosevelt refused to soften the demand for unconditional surrender. Thornley, appointed to run SOE's German section, opposed covert action that might install an anti-Nazi German government to join the Allies against Stalin.[8]

Vera had known Stauffenberg was in touch with German generals who had been captured by the Russians and were persuaded that Stalin was ready to make a separate peace without disarming German armed forces. This offer was communicated through a "Seydlitz Committee" named after General Walter von Seydlitz, who was taken prisoner at Stalingrad. Since the first Control broadcasts, the Nazis had published claims that 7,000 Germans had been arrested, 5,764 executed, and another 5,684 later killed. The dead included twenty-one generals, thirty-three colonels, two ambassadors, seven senior diplomats, a minister of state, three secretaries of state, the chief of the Criminal Police, provincial governors, leading police chiefs, and high officials. It seemed that Thornley, whose communist loyalties were known, rejoiced that if Stalin could not command Hitler-free German armies against the West in his plan to rule Europe, the West at least was prevented from using anti-Nazi troops against Stalin.[9]

Thornley was replaced by Gerald Templer, later chief of the Imperial General Staff, Field Marshal Lord Templer. As the new chief of

SOE/Germany, he approved Periwig, an operation to give Germans the impression of a domestic revolt backed by the Allies. Superimposed on the Allied-controlled *Soldatensender* music programs were Morse signals sent by German volunteers recruited from prisoner-of-war camps. In March 1945, Otto Heinrich and Franz Langmere were dropped west of the Chiemsee with paraphernalia suggesting they were to meet anti-Nazi Germans in Bavaria. Shortly after, Hans Bienecke and Josef Kick were parachuted into the Bremen area with similar "evidence." Their SOE instructors had not been told that the Germans would carry fake "proof" of a vast resistance movement, designed to fall into Gestapo hands. The appearance of growing public resistance to Hitler might make the lies come true.

Vera thought more about the mystery of Schulenburg's exposure by London Control. She was haunted by the specter of that amusing and intelligent man strung up by Hitler's hangmen. Camp 020 had persuaded another German army prisoner, recorded only as "Schmidt," to become a double agent. He was dropped into Germany with a parachute that would never open. Coded messages were wirelessed to his nonexistent network, using codes the enemy would find on his body, as if London were unaware of his death and kept in contact with his anti-Nazi network and German resisters. To reinforce such illusions, a German briefcase with incriminating documents was dropped by a low-flying Mosquito, and carrier pigeons were released with messages that indicated links between anti-Nazis and Allied intelligence. The Frankfurt radio wavelength was commandeered and bogus orders were issued, as if from officials in German cities telling the populace to leave threatened areas. Reports that Hitler had boltholes for Nazi leaders in Argentina were planted in Latin American newspapers. This ran counter to Anglo-American propaganda that Hitler would let the Third Reich crash down upon him, and the German people should dump him at once. Vera said later, "There was a danger we'd confuse only ourselves." SOE/Germany's Periwig went against common sense and was abandoned.

Aaron Bank was to lead an OSS mission to capture Hitler if he retreated to his Alpine hideout as Nazi Germany collapsed. Bank, the future initiator of U.S. Special Forces, was offered the thick file compiled by the British that by now contained details of Hitler's movements to the last detail. The offer was never taken up, because Bill

Donovan withdrew his OSS/Germany liaison officer with SOE. The move was intended to demonstrate that OSS was not a tool of the British secret services, a suspicion held by Cordell Hull at the U.S. State Department, whose foremost foreign policy aim was to end British imperial financial power. Gubbins hoped for the postwar continuation of special operations that would defend British imperial interests against the OSS, one of whose senior officers had said, "If OSS believes its own propaganda, it should declare war on the British, for they have set themselves up as the master race in India."

Gubby wrote indignantly to Lord Selborne that "the OSS embraces so many facets of secret work that it can be likened to the NKVD, the Russian secret service." The OSS was "used by the American government as an instrument of policy" to dismantle British economic interests.

SOE owed an enormous debt to Donovan. Now, to save the OSS, he seemed to cater to Roosevelt's urge to dismantle the British Empire. One of Churchill's staff, Sir Ronald Wingate, wrote irritably, "We had been at war with Germany longer than any other power, we had suffered more, we had sacrificed more, and in the end we would lose more than any other power. Yet here were these God-awful American OSS academics rushing about, talking about the four freedoms and the Atlantic Charter."

SOE successes were out of proportion to its few agents. No more than nine thousand, they counted for nothing among vast armies whose career-minded generals played to the gallery. Montgomery's 21st Army Group finally held Caen and Falaise, and provided the secure hub around which U.S. troops under General Omar Bradley could rotate to advance. Now Montgomery and Bradley tried to upstage each other. Was this the end of Anglo-American cooperation? Clement Attlee, the socialist leader preparing to take Churchill's place, planned to discontinue SOE, about which he knew nothing, calling it "a British Comintern" (Communist International). The curtain of silence on covert operations also endangered British Security Coordination, and Bill Stephenson flew from New York to discuss strategies. "Yes," he told Vera and Gubby, "Donovan's politically obliged to separate himself from us. But we need to cooperate against the Soviets. People don't want to think of another conflict. They only see Russia winning against Hitler."

Gubby agreed to overlook differences to save hard-won Anglo-American experience in closework. He wrote to Lord Selborne defending SOE and operations run by Stephenson "in view of his unique relationship with the Americans and in particular General Donovan."[10]

Meanwhile, Nazi Germany was fighting back ferociously and resorting to greater atrocities. Vera needed more closework successes, though hampered by secrecy, to ensure SOE's survival. The White Rabbit, on a death-camp train, was saved by Violette Szabo, the former London shop assistant. She had crawled through crowded prisoner wagons, hands and feet manacled, to bring water to Yeo-Thomas, whose prewar Paris fashion house had sold her "my first and only decent dress." Violette was caught and executed. The White Rabbit would later escape to report the girl's heroism. Vera regained one of her best agents but lost the other.

In Leo Marks's den at Norgeby House, she read what he had finally composed for Violette in place of *Three Blind Mice* as a poem-code. He had first written his poignantly personal poem for a girl he loved, Ruth, the half-Jewish goddaughter of SOE's onetime executive council chief Sir Charles Hambro. Ruth had been killed when her plane crashed. Leo had decided that the dead girl would not mind if he assigned the poem to Violette and pulled a copy from the "ditty box" in which he kept coding materials. He told Vera: "When I gave her these lines, Violette asked me who wrote it. I told her she'd find out when she came back. She never did. I shall carry the sadness with me for the rest of my life."

> The life that I have
> Is all that I have
> And the life that I have is yours.
> The love that I have
> Of the life that I have
> Is yours and yours and yours.
> A sleep I shall have,
> A rest I shall have,
> Yet death will be but a pause.
> For the peace of my years
> In the long green grass
> Will be yours and yours and yours.

# 36

# "My Uncle Is Lord Vansittart"

The train carrying Violette had left Paris for the Buchenwald concentration camp, with forty agents classified as "Nacht und Nebel, Rückkehr Ungewünscht" (night and fog, return not required).

Bits of folded paper with handwritten messages were first thrown into the streets around Fresnes Prison, some scribbled by sixty-five-year-old General Charles Delestraint, chief of the Armée Secrète, destined to be hanged by the Germans. He named imprisoned agents: one was Squadron Leader Dodkin, the cover name for Yeo-Thomas, who had learned from Delestraint of the death of Commandant Pierre Brossolette, the French Resistance hero that Tommy had come to save. Despite his assumed RAF rank and POW status, the White Rabbit had been labeled "a terrorist to be exterminated."[1]

The "terrorists" had begun their final journey in German trucks to the Gare de l'Est in central Paris. Amond them was Diana Hope Rowden, transferred on December 5, 1943, to Fresnes, from where she was taken for regular Gestapo interrogation at the rue des Saussaies. Others who were trucked back and forth between jail and the Gestapo included Peter Churchill and Odette Sansom, captured in the Haute-Savoie in April 1943. They had fallen in love. Diana knew the story. She bravely put herself between indifferent French guards and Peter and Odette, to allow them to talk before boarding the death-train. Peter glanced quickly at Diana and asked who this refined creature was. Odette said softly, "One of us."

The Buchenwald shipment also included Maurice Southgate, whose maquisards were now commanded by Pearl Witherington.

Rolande Colas counted some thirty-seven agents tossing notes into the streets. One message began Chez Amis, mentioned "Barbara" three times in forty words, promised "Je reviendrai bientôt," and had been dropped by Yeo-Thomas. His promise to return was picked up in time for the next Moonlight flight to London, and miraculously reached his wife within days. Barbara confided it only to Vera.

Vera's Mossad spies reported that the prisoners were on a train for Verdun, delayed at Châlons-sur-Marne for questioning by another Gestapo group competing against SS Captain Theodor Dannecker, head of "Jewish matters" in Paris. The Mossad had tracked thousands of Jews piled into deportation wagons since February 1941. In July 1944, a month before Free French troops liberated Paris, more Jewish prisoners were delayed at Châlons-sur-Marne, piled into huts, and incinerated by flamethrowers.

The Mossad passed on pleas from Jews in Auschwitz for the Allies to bomb the camp. Even if the inmates were killed, at least the facilities would be destroyed. The Mossad was told Auschwitz was beyond range, yet U.S. bombers attacked IG Farben installations adjacent to it. "Allied warlords wanted to lay waste cities," André Malraux wrote later. "We were unheard at daily conferences on the massive movement of huge armies and fleets of bombers."

Vera badgered those who trusted her. She knew from Chuck Yeager about new young pilots who freelanced, "hitting fast and getting the hell out." He had just flown what he called "a hush-hush mission for the Brits," extracting an agent who sat on Chuck's knees in his single-seat Mustang fighter. Chuck had an admirer and ally in David Bruce of OSS, who backed Vera's request for train busters to "freelance" against the delayed prison train. By now Vera knew its exact location.

On August 8, ten days before the last deportation of Jews from Paris and seventeen days before de Gaulle arrived, the White Rabbit heard the roar of fighter-bombers and the chatter of 20 mm airborne cannon. Guards locked carriage doors. Prisoners were tossed into a heap from wagons. Vera had calculated that sabotaging the train would give the prisoners a chance to escape, but German guards were frightened of the punishment they would suffer for losing even one prisoner. Rolande reported later, "They manacled us in pairs. I had my identification as a Red Cross ambulance driver. Violette could not claim POW status. We were trucked into Verdun and slept in horse stables. Armed guards stopped us from crossing a rope separating the sexes. We whispered across the rope. Escape is possible if you stick to a bloody-minded resolve. If I should escape, I was to let Vera know Violette was alive by quoting, 'The life that I have is yours . . .'"

Early next day, loaded onto trucks, the prisoners dropped more notes as their convoy passed through sunlit villages, where people boldly gave the V-for-Victory sign. Yeo-Thomas escaped during a transfer of prisoners amid the chaos of a brief Allied air-to-ground attack. He was the only prisoner to escape unseen. By the time he began to look for Violette, he was caught again. The convoy rattled into Germany, and, at the camp, Rolande had to walk between *les souris*, who made the chained and handcuffed women defecate naked under the leering gaze of male guards. Rolande reckoned later that there were certainly forty SOE prisoners. Only she and three others were destined to come out alive.

Vera had to piece together an increasingly chaotic picture of events, the reports often out of sequence, so that the chronology had to sort itself out later. Her old ally Gardyne de Chastelain had parachuted back into Romania on Christmas Day. The following August 1944, King Michael deposed the dictator, Marshal Antonescu. Gardyne was arrested as a spy, then treated as an unofficial envoy, then rearrested, and finally consulted as "His Majesty's representative from Great Britain." An official SOE historian, William Mackenzie, confessed: "It is unfortunate that this cannot be made fully intelligible without a detailed study of Romanian politics." His voluminous study was published only in 2000, with chunks of detail missing. Gardyne's account for Vera disclosed that King Michael wanted to escape the Russian advance but had no wish to become Germany's slave. He had lost confidence in British promises and flew out of Bucharest on a German transport plane, hoping Berlin would preserve the monarchy.[2] Russia intended to install a Soviet government. Gardyne's proposals for preventing this were based on SOE plans that Whitehall refused to sanction. The Moscow conference of Allies in October 1944 gave the Soviet Union a "ratio of interest of 80 percent" in Romania, virtually the West's surrender to Stalin's aims.

Gardyne returned to his SOE/Cairo base to find that Krystyna was in France. On the night of July 7, 1944, Krystyna parachuted into the Vercors, the maquis mountain fortress southwest of Grenoble. The Battle of Vercors stopped German reinforcements from helping to stem the D-day tide of Allied forces in Normandy. By August the Allies had broken out to sweep inland. But the enemy still held the Vercors region.

Krystyna replaced an aide to twenty-eight-year-old Francis Cammaerts, son of the poet Émile Cammaerts, who had taken over an SOE circuit from Peter Churchill. Returning from a briefing in England in February 1944, Cammaerts's Lysander had caught fire. He parachuted from a high altitude and survived. He told Krystyna that he had been a convinced pacifist until his brother, who was in the RAF, had been killed. The beautiful Polish countess and the sensitive veteran of closework became battlefield lovers. "We are tied by the stupidity of others," he told her. "Allied commanders ignore us, and Miss Atkins is without the proper English background to make a lot of noise. It is better that way! She is more effective, fighting as we do, making the best of hidden resources."

Krystyna herself had been injured when she landed that night. The French commando who had jumped ahead of her fractured his skull. Her pilot had continued circling, worried about the high winds, until Krystyna lost patience and dropped also from too great a height. She was blown far from the reception committee. It was likely her hip was dislocated. "It's only bruised," she told her OSS wireless operator, André Paray. They were part of an inter-Allied enterprise with Polish forces and a maquis of five hundred armed men, another five hundred partisans drawn from villages and farms on the plateau, and two thousand ordinary French people, mostly housewives, who provided the backbone of Resistance by continuing a normal life, while in the hills and mountains assembled the better-trained maquisards.

"After an attack on a German convoy on Route Nationale 75, killing up to sixty of the enemy, the Germans bombed and strafed communities along the edges of the Vercors to stop supplies being sent into the forest hideouts," Krystyna wirelessed Vera. "A French boy caught after the attack on an enemy convoy was paraded in the village of Lalley. The locals were told they would all suffer his fate as a terrorist. He claimed POW status because he was with an American commando unit, but his tongue and eyes were torn out in front of villagers, who were forced to watch him finally being bayonetted to death."

On Bastille Day 1944, U.S. Air Force Flying Fortresses flew to the Vercors from Algeria, where Donovan had established his OSS headquarters to escape the cramping effect of Whitehall. Eighty-five bombers dropped gay Fourth-of-July celebration colors attached to parachutes, but the containers lacked what was really needed: mortars and heavy machine guns. The mission chiefs in the Vercors asked for the appropriate arms. They were answered by fatuous radio warnings about nonexistent German troop movements, ending "Love to P." P was Pauline, the code name for Krystyna.

"Why did Algiers disregard the call for proper arms?" Krystyna asked Cammaerts. He said Americans had planned to invade the south of France from Algiers. Churchill objected: invading southern France would divert forces from Field Marshal Harold Alexander's drive to knock Italy out of the war, a plan that followed ULTRA's decoding of Hitler's order that Italy "must be the final line blocking [Allied] entry into [Italy], which would have incalculable military and political consequences for Germany." Roosevelt stuck to his plan to invade southern France. Churchill gave way, but said this dashed all hope for a swift victory in Italy. He was astonished when U.S. General George Marshall said that, if absolute weight had been given to these ULTRA insights, Overlord and the D-day landings might never have been necessary.[3]

Cammaerts believed it had now been downgraded by all Allied commanders. Krystyna feared that Vera's organization was also being treated with near contempt. "Power is as power does," Krystyna told Cammaerts. Recalling her words later, he said, "Krystyna was not intimidated by the thunder and lightning of mighty armies but believed in improvisation. If the Alpine passes were vital to Hitler, she'd subvert German satellite soldiers guarding those passes. I followed her for days while she spoke with Eastern European conscripts. She was sure they would throw away their weapons, especially the Poles. But when we returned, the Germans had blockaded all eight roads into the Vercors."

Hostages were taken and brutalized before being shot. Peasants were forced to walk ahead of German troops to set off landmines. Others were made to bring up ammunition and then were shot in the back as they walked away. The maquis, horrified by the savagery, collapsed. Krystyna saw five children buried under one destroyed house. "Only eleven-year-old Arlette Blanc remained alive but for five days lay trapped, pleading for water from German soldiers who passed by her, laughing. Arlette died from gangrene. One woman was raped by seventeen men. A German army doctor checked her pulse in case she fainted before the next soldier's turn. Another woman's stomach was slit open and her guts strung around her neck," Krystyna wirelessed Vera.[4]

Cammaerts and two companions were caught and taken to the Vichy French militia and Gestapo facility at Digne. Krystyna decided that if she tried an armed rescue, Cammaerts would be killed. Instead, she walked into the Gestapo-militia office. Cammaerts himself later told Vera: "She said she was General Montgomery's niece and his armies were just around the corner. She would save the jailers if they released her friends. A Gestapo interpreter, Max Waem, had to listen for three hours to all of this. She knew we were to be shot that evening and warned Waem the Gestapo would pay a frightful price. Then she declared, 'Lord Vansittart is my uncle.'"

The veteran diplomat's hatred of Nazis was well known, and Krystyna said she would radio His Lordship and get him to pardon Waem if the prisoners were freed. Waem hurriedly advised the Vichy-run militia to free the prisoners. At SOE/Cairo, General W. A. M. Stawell recommended that Krystyna receive the George Cross, the highest civilian award, "for one of the most remarkable personal exploits of the war." But what Krystyna wanted was British citizenship. A French hero tried to help. General de Lattre de Tassigny, who commanded the First French Army of 250,000 men, testified to her "good character and superior judgment in war." De Lattre had fought with inferior arms against General Heinz Guderian's panzers, and then escaped to North Africa.[5] His word carried weight everywhere but in Whitehall. MI5's B Branch espionage section's officers, who had never heard a shot fired in anger, questioned Krystyna's loyalties even as Vera endorsed what General Stawell called, "Krystyna's hairiest mission yet."[6]

# 37

## "But If the Cause Be Not Good . . ."

Vera moved with the self-assurance of a pilot officer. She commandeered a Stinson Reliant monoplane to shuttle between London and liberated Paris. She became ever more acutely aware of the daily tensions within the Allied camp.

England was tired. London suffered more destruction: the homeless burrowed like troglodytes into the London Underground. Housewives queued for whale meat, a substitute for normal fare, and claimed their egg-per-person-per-month, if lucky. The movie house near Trafalgar Square screened newsreels of heavy fighting, but the main attraction was escape from the depressing sight of rats and rubble. To feed the demands of war, every domestic need was in short supply.

Vera flew unchallenged within the unbroken stream of uniforms and machines pouring out of the island kingdom to prosecute a war that in Paris was regarded as over by Charles de Gaulle. He now demanded respect as head of a provisional government of France. When he entered Paris on foot on August 25, 1944, Vera was there to meet Resistance leaders from the two largest quarreling factions: Gaullists and communists. "You see in Paris the romantic tension that surrounds great events," said Henri Tanguy, and recalled that lovemaking had been the chief diversion of ladies fleeing the parochialism of prewar Romania. "Hop into bed" was the answer to all stress. She just smiled; she needed his full report on the fruits of the financing sent to fuel insurrection in Paris. The results were not bad: rail and police strikes had begun two weeks before de Gaulle arrived. But that was after he had a disastrous quarrel with Churchill on the eve of D-day. She had read the reports.

Henri Tanguy's posters called for revolutionary action. The tricolor on Notre Dame spurred on Resistance fighters in gun battles against German military units still holding out in city blocks even as de Gaulle came down the Champs Elysées with his long stride and his sour expression. Vera knew the foibles that made him awkward, but she was not in a forgiving mood. In London, civilians endured the absence of every necessity, while in Paris many had lived well off the occupiers, while supplies were showered upon a Resistance now fighting itself.

André Malraux, a future minister of culture under de Gaulle, told her, "The partisan forces held together only to get the Germans out of France." At age forty-three, Malraux boasted of his brave record in the Resistance. Vera said resisters could prevent entire German divisions from reaching the Fatherland. Malraux predicted, accurately as it turned out, that one in a thousand of his countrymen would be killed in battles between Gaullist administrators, anti-Gaullists, and communists.

Vera's Paris base was Special Forces Advanced Headquarters. She had offices in the Hotel Cecil and at 37 boulevard des Capucines. The latest Gestapo Enigma, known as TGD, remained unbroken, and she needed to crack it as one way to learn the fate of missing agents, some perhaps betrayed by French collaborators in the dispatch of Jews. She had to know who, where, and why. Her Mossad sources were helpful, but the Jewish Agency and the chief rabbi of London, J. N. Hertz, reminded her that many soldiers in the new Jewish Brigade felt bitter about British policy in Palestine. To offset this, Rabbi Hertz publicly applauded British formation of a Jewish Brigade within the British army. Privately, he worried about "a splinter off a splinter" off the mainstream Zionist movement using terror to protest the British ban on migration to Palestine.

The Jewish Brigade had a covert command to salvage what was left of European Jewry, and it welcomed Vera's unmatched experience. But SOE came first. London's sensibilities had been dulled, and few there questioned the cost in British overseas territories and long-term loans for U.S. heavy arms and aircraft. SOE had to struggle. Harold Macmillan, a future prime minister, was the influential minister-resident in Algiers when he rejected SIS/Foreign Office condemnation of SOE as "disobedient, ungovernable, unpredictable, and dangerous."

The critics were conditioned by traditional, tidy routine. SOE was anything but tidily regulated. "That," said Macmillan," is its strength."

Vera had hoped for support from General de Gaulle for SOE's extension into an inter-Allied agency. SOE had lost only one hundred aircraft, while its 507 experts had trained and armed more than 50,000 maquisards. "They were the equivalent of fifteen divisions, and shortened the war by months in facilitating the rapidity of our advance across France," Eisenhower told de Gaulle.[1] But the Frenchman had been visibly upset two days before D-day when he went to Churchill's temporary quarters in a train near Portsmouth and said he wanted to lead France, not have it taken over by the Americans. Churchill urged him to speak about this with Roosevelt. De Gaulle bristled. Was he supposed to submit his candidacy to the U.S. president? Churchill burst out: "We are going to liberate Europe because the Americans are with us to do it. . . . Every time I have to choose between you and Roosevelt, I shall choose Roosevelt."[2]

Now de Gaulle wanted SOE out of France. Vera had hoped for a reprieve after his exchange with SOE's George Starr. On September 18, 1944, de Gaulle accused Starr of being sent behind the lines to undercut Gaullist administrators. Starr shouted back that he was loyal to his French superior officers. He had been parachuted in November 1942 to take over the large Toulouse circuit whose leader, Philippe de Vomécourt, and all wireless operators had been killed or captured. Starr had fought long and fierce battles against German reinforcements before and after D-day. De Gaulle accused Starr of meddling in French affairs by continuing to fight. Starr replied, "The situation is like that of feudal baronetcies: local commanders are taking advantage of lawlessness and confusion. . . . You are full of shit, *merde!*" De Gaulle ordered him to leave France at once, and then suddenly shook his hand and said there was one thing Starr got right: "You know how to say *merde*."

Months of fighting in Germany still lay ahead, from which de Gaulle appeared detached. This endangered Vera's long-term aims. She impressed upon Malraux the need to rescue Jewish survivors in the camps and to look for agents who might yet be saved from execution. Thirty-two of her young women had been inserted into occupied France since the start of the year, nine of them after D-day. Malraux was sympathetic and said de Gaulle was flexible after having his distrust of covert action confirmed by Arthur Stratton. Stratton, who was recruiting for the U.S. Seventh Army, wrote to Bill Donovan that French women agents were, more often than not, prostitutes: Madame X "enjoyed danger, enjoyed the spotlight of being a spy, and enjoyed all the men she could. . . . her method of getting information was that she stole, she lied, she cheated." Stratton denigrated another woman "who could not bring herself to jump from the plane." The ultimate insult was Stratton's afterthought: "Her name I forget."[3]

Malraux said later this helped Vera to continue without de Gaulle's approval. There were still pockets of pro-Nazi resistance. She was trusted as a spymistress by the Jewish Brigade's covert-action specialists, who had nurtured the Mossad escape lines. Now hundreds of thousands of homeless refugees were being labeled DPs, displaced persons, and Allied commanders were herding them into camps pending an accommodation of Stalin's demand of May 31, 1944, for the return to Soviet control of "Russian prisoners," of whom Vera reckoned only 10 percent were Russian. The rest had lived in eastern European countries where Stalin would have them enslaved if they reappeared in territories where he took control with tacit Allied approval.

Vera had always marveled at Shakespeare's understanding of war. The lines from *King Henry V*, spoken by a soldier on the eve of battle in France, now haunted her:

> But if the cause be not good, the king himself hath a heavy reckoning to make; when all those legs and arms and heads, chopped off in battle, shall join together at the latter day, and cry all, "We died at such a place" . . .

The Western cause was no good, Vera wrote angrily to Gubbins, if "those we professed to fight for are abandoned." He had to watch his beloved Poland disappear into Stalin's pocket, and discovered an unpublicized finding by the legal adviser to the British Foreign Office, drafted on June 24, 1944, but kept secret: "This [surrender of prisoners and DPs] is purely a question for the Soviet authorities and does not concern His Majesty's Government. . . . all those with whom the Soviet authorities desire to deal must be handed over to them, and we are not concerned with the fact that they may be shot."

# 38

## "If These Do Not Die Well, It Will Be a Black Matter"

Vera was afraid for agents held in camps overrun by Russian armies. Eisenhower had said he would not race the Russians for Berlin. What did this mean for millions of innocents drifting between the armies? She made Leo Marks comb through old transmissions of agents. At twenty-four he still had a boyish quality, although he was at last recognized as a genius in cryptography even at Bletchley, where he said later, "I was originally rejected because I was a Yid of the shopkeeper class. Did they fear a Jew might use Bletchley to create *Eretz-Israel*, Land of Israel? Stalin by 1945 was conspiring to shovel homeless Jews into Palestine, and the Nazis did, to ignite Arab violence against the British."

In Paris, Vera heard more about Henri Dericourt, the air movements officer linked to the fate of Princess Noor Inayat Khan. There was talk that some of his curious behavior indicated that he was a Russian mole when communists and Gaullists worked together. Noor was born in the Kremlin. Vera reviewed the missing agent's file and Leo's recollections.

Noor had stunned Leo by saying her father taught her never to lie.

"Her life depends on telling lies!" Leo had said in anguish to Vera in 1943. "Her father heads a sect that says anyone who lies is damned."

Noor was directly descended from Tipu Sultan, the last Muslim leader of southern India, the Tiger of Mysore. Her father, Hasra Inayat Khan, was teaching Sufism in New York when he married a niece of Mary Baker Eddy, the founder of Christian Science. Noor was born in

1914 when her father taught at the Conservatoire in Moscow, and she was thirteen when he died.

Leo had shown Noor how to insert "bluff security checks" if she was caught and forced to send radio messages under German control. "That would be telling lies!" she exclaimed. Leo quoted her own words to her from a prewar storybook she had written and published, *Twenty Jataka Tales*.[1] In it, monkeys reach safety when a prince who becomes the Buddha makes his body into a bridge for them to cross a canyon. Leo said that each time Noor encoded, she must see the letters as monkeys making a bridge to London. "When there's a truth to be passed on, don't let your code tell lies."

Leo's mystic interpretation satisfied the girl. Her astonishing beauty, he had concluded, grew out of inner tranquillity. But it was hard to take seriously a girl so gorgeous. A commando instructor reported that "a sudden pistol shot during an exercise startled her into a Sufi-like trance lasting several hours." She had been known to prewar French radio listeners for her readings of children's stories, and this put her on the German *Sonderpfändungsliste*, the Wanted List of persons to be arrested in occupied countries. Nonetheless, she was flown by Lysander to France in June 1943. The promised Resistance reception committee was missing. She flew back to England and waited patiently until the moonlit night of June 16, when she arrived with Diana Hope Rowden and was met by Henri Dericourt. Noor made her own way to Paris. Within days her Resistance contacts were blown or under scrutiny. She worked with other French resisters, constantly changing her address after leaving the first apartment near the Bois de Boulogne, where she first learned of the collapse of three subcircuits of the sprawling Prosper network. Vera recalled telling Noor to return to England. She had refused "until a replacement can be found."

Vera now knew the Germans were always aware of Noor's activities. They intercepted messages but found it hard to catch her. How had she lasted four months? She was arrested on October 13, 1943. She escaped twice, and was recaptured. She had apparently given away nothing, despite the cunning of her captors, but might have unwittingly led the Germans to her contacts.

Vera explored the possibiity that the French secret service officers who first worked with the German Enigma spy, Hans-Thilo

Schmidt, might shed light on the strange coincidences surrounding Noor's capture. She concluded that Schmidt's early French contacts had disclosed SOE methods. Months before D-day, ten SOE dropping grounds were in German hands. Vera turned to Paul Mellon, an oil tycoon from Pittsburgh, who was working with the OSS in London. He shot holes in a theory that Schmidt was still alive. Mellon said there was no doubt that Schmidt had died from self-administered potassium cyanide in a Gestapo jail in September 1943. His brother, General Rudolf Schmidt, had arranged the burial because neither the Catholic Church nor the state would take responsibility. Rudolf, "one of the Führer's favorite generals," had been discharged from the army during the inquiry into his brother's activities, and yet he remained free. Was it the Russians who were now playing mind games?

Pierre Raynaud, the young Free French officer who joined Cammaerts's original circuit, met Vera at 37 boulevard des Capucines in Paris to claim that the two SOE Canadians dispatched with other agents from Fresnes Prison, Frank Pickersgill and John Macalister, had incriminating evidence planted on them by London Control before they left England. When they were captured — two brave and doomed men — the planted evidence could have helped the Gestapo to draw a net around other SOE agents and subagents. Raynaud himself had escaped to take charge of the Third Battalion of the French Forces of the Interior (FFI). He had been with Noor when both were waiting to leave on different missions. In a Moonlight Squadron hut, he was astounded to see her studying a prewar French railway timetable. He thought then she was out of her depth. Now he believed she was meant to be caught. Raynaud later deposited with the National Archives in Paris a dossier that he said contained proof that Noor and other agents were used by London Control. He quoted a French girl, a cellmate of Noor at Fresnes Prison, Alix d'Unienville. She had worked at General de Gaulle's headquarters in London before Vera parachuted her in, at the end of March 1944, with 40 million francs for distribution by the Gaullist delegate-general in Paris. On D-day, Alix was caught in a German roundup. While in prison, she was told by Noor that the Germans knew about the *parachutage* in the Vercors. Alix herself made a death-defying escape when the train carrying prisoners destined for Buchenwald was bombed.[2]

Pierre Raynaud's version of events was not supported by any records that the British released. After the war he claimed that SOE records were destroyed to save reputations. But France itself had a great deal to hide. The comte de Marenches, who served with Alix d'Unienville at de Gaulle's intelligence center in London, wrote of returning to France just after D-day to find "forty-two million people had fought for the Resistance!" He called those who joined the Resistance at the last minute *naphtalines* or mothballs. One hundred eighteen thousand prosecutions for collaboration were announced. Fewer than fifty thousand of the accused went on trial; 791 were executed. French archives have since recorded that one in two French women agents were executed by the Germans. The SD interrogation files in Paris listed informers drawn from criminal elements in Paris like the notorious Bony-Lafont gang. Pro-Nazi Pierre Bony worked for German counterintelligence with a criminal he had once hunted, Henri Lafont. Bony-Lafont and other gangsters were used by Goetz's SD colleagues to watch Noor and her companions. Bony told Vera that Noor escaped a third time, and was in an apartment when she was caught again.

Another four women agents were murdered even while de Gaulle was preparing his triumphal walk through Paris. One was Squadron Leader Diana Rowden, whose free spirit impressed the disfigured RAF fighter pilot, Bill Simpson. Another was Andrée Borrel, sent in September 1942 to liaise with the betrayed Prosper network. A third was Sonia Olschanezky, barely twenty years old and living at 72 rue du Faubourg Poissonière in Paris when she became a courier in March 1942. She had evaded discovery until late January 1944. The fourth was Vera Leigh, a dress designer who had helped downed Allied airmen escape before she herself escaped from France in 1942. After three months of SOE training she returned and became a friend of Julienne Aisner, ex-mistress of Henri Dericourt, the air movements officer in France.

Dericourt's questioning had been left to Harry Sporborg, adviser on SOE affairs to Lord Selborne. Vera wondered why the SIS deputy chief "Uncle Claude" Dansey intruded and insisted that Dericourt was "clean." Was Uncle Claude using Dericourt to extract information from within the German secret services? The agent Vera Leigh had herself suggested that Dericourt colluded to get rid of a Gestapo agent disliked by the rival Abwehr. Just before her arrest in October 1943, French agents had said Vera Leigh was in danger for saying Dericourt served his own interests. Was Dericourt protected at high levels in games of deception? To the extent that Vera Leigh was a sacrificial lamb?[3]

Vera Atkins reconstructed the fate of Vera Leigh, Sonia Olschanezky, Andrée Borrel, and Diana Hope Rowden, all of whom were held at Karlsruhe with common criminals. Noor was imprisoned separately, hands and feet manacled, in November 1943. A woman jailkeeper objected that the four other girls had not been brought before a court, and were held as convicts when they were clearly spies. SS General Ernst Kaltenbrunner, later hanged as a war criminal at Nuremberg, agreed with the busybody jailkeeper, and in July 1944 he dispatched the four girls to a German death camp on French soil, Natzweiler-Struthof, near Strasbourg in Alsace, just west of the Rhine.

If de Gaulle had been less preoccupied in Paris with asserting his supreme authority, Free French paratroopers could have seized Struthof-Natzweiler. Instead, this camp, now within French jurisdiction, continued to go about its ghastly duties. The staff found time to inflict upon the four girls the worst of many crimes recorded by Maurice Southgate, the twenty-year-old artist whose SOE circuit was taken over by Pearl Witherington. A prisoner himself at Natzweiler, he recognized Diana Hope Rowden when she was brought in. He survived to sketch for Vera the faces of all the women he saw at Natzweiler in July 1944. Southgate also wrote for Vera a formal accusation that girls like Diana were trained by incompetent instructors or used as decoys. Bureaucrats in London said his long incarceration had unbalanced his mind. When Vera found him, she invited him to his first home-cooked meal. Southgate fled, sickened by the smell of roasting flesh.

He showed Vera the camp after its staff had melted away. It stood at the end of what was called the Road of Despair by prisoners forced to build it. In August 1943 eighty-seven Jewish men and women had been dragged to an adjoining facility for "medical experiments." Competitors were invited from German industry to build "processing units." The contract for disposing of two thousand bodies every twelve hours went to Topt & Company of Thuringia. The German Armaments

Corporation put in the winning bid to produce "corpse cellars and gas-proof doors with rubber surround and observation post of double 8-millimetre glass, type 100/192." Manicured lawns covered the cellars, and "sanitary orderlies" dropped Zyklon-B crystal-blue crystals down shafts under concrete mushrooms in a gardenlike setting. The bodies, preserved in tanks, were sent to Strasbourg University's Institute of Anatomy.[4]

After the four SOE women arrived, other prisoners were confined to quarters. Southgate at first thought the four were given injections "against typhus." To save money, it had become customary to use only enough of the expensive gas to stun victims. This time, injections were used. He said, "I think they were alive when thrown into the ovens."[5]

Noor and three other missing SOE women agents were in a German military train from Karlsruhe in the Rhine Valley. Vera had supposed that they had perished at Natzweiler, but found to her horror that they, too, might have been condemned to death at another camp. On September 12, 1944, U.S. and British war planners, at a second Quebec conference, agreed that they should concentrate on Japan because Germany's defeat was certain. Noor's group was passing through the Swabian mountains on a death-train.

The countryside was ablaze with autumnal colors. Two of the girls were FANYs, two were WAAFs. Their instructors had said that, if they were caught, they should try and hold out for forty-eight hours, giving their associates time to scatter. Noor had been offered the usual cyanide capsule provided for departing agents. Vera had told her, "It must be quickly crushed between the teeth and swallowed. The smell is known to German interrogators. They'll try to make you vomit." Noor had refused to take the L-pill. The others would have long since disposed of the pills, knowing possession identified them as spies to the Gestapo. They must have been dazzled by the autumnal sunshine after so long a confinement in dank cells. Each girl was trained to seize and use a German weapon separately, but would they know how to act in concert against their three armed but dozing Gestapo escorts? Probably it had seemed wiser to assume that, as officers, they would be treated as POWs. They were so close to freedom.

Vera imagined the train puffing serenely along what could have been some local line in England. Three of the agents had been in school when the war began. Eliane Plewman, née Browne-Bartrolli, was a strikingly beautiful girl whose brother was also a secret agent. After parachuting into the Jura on the night of August 13–14, 1943, she had worked with a small circuit around Marseilles. Her training in sabotage helped close the main railway to Toulon. She showed her French comrades how to block tunnels by derailing trains, then destroying the trains that piled up behind. By early March 1944 her group had damaged sixty locomotives, putting most of them out of commission. A German "mousetrap" caught her, and the bait was said to have been Jack Sinclair, aged twenty-two, who joined her on March 6–7, 1944. French Resistance investigators would later say that incriminating documents were planted on him. The official Whitehall response was that he had been wrongly dispatched because of a "staff muddle." The details were conveniently "lost."

Another of the four girls, Madeleine Damerment, had parachuted in late February 1944, straight into the hands of a Gestapo reception committee imitating all the correct signals. This sort of thing had happened to eighteen agents in her section. None survived.

The third on the train, Yolande Beekman, came from neutral Switzerland. Moral convictions had made her volunteer.

Noor and her companions arrived at a railroad station near Munich and with their guards stumbled through the midnight darkness to a camp with a name they did not recognize: Dachau. After that one splendid day of sunshine, a Stygian gloom descended. They were locked in cells without food or water and taken next morning into a yard where they were lined up before a drab brick wall.

Noor reached out to touch another hand. Soon all the girls were holding hands. It was the last autumn of World War II. No guard bothered to stop Noor when she began the linking of hands. The gesture made the task easier. Each girl received a bullet in the back of the head. The sudden pistol shot was not the first Noor had heard at close quarters. Years before, during her training, an SOE instructor was so alarmed by Noor's dreamlike reaction to his gunshot that he had told Vera the girl was too emotional for fieldwork. Now, before the wall, she withdrew into a state of meditation. A British War Office report in June 1947 described the executions. Noor was posthumously awarded the George Cross for conspicuous courage, moral and physical, during prolonged clandestine operations.

Of such as these, Churchill spoke in Westminster Abbey: "Nothing of which we have any knowledge or record has ever been done by mortal men which surpasses the splendour and daring of their feats of arms." His tribute was delayed until May 21, 1948. Secrecy still prevailed.

The White Rabbit had been caught yet again while trying to engineer the escape of a French colleague. At Buchenwald, he found a member of the German medical team administering "experimental" injections. Yeo-Thomas promised the man that if he cooperated, he could be saved from war-crime charges. Tommy was not sent to the crematorium. He broke out of the prison and made his way along the escape routes, but was caught, tortured, and slipped his captors again. He found his father in Paris on May 8, 1945, celebrating VE-day.

Vera found in Yeo-Thomas the qualities of the naval pilot she had loved and lost, but she could never say so. Leo Marks adored Noor, but could never say so. Emotional entanglement with an agent endangered everyone. When Leo wrote code-poems, though, his feelings often shone through. He composed one for a member of a Jedburgh team parachuted near Dachau with the goal of breaking into the camp, but the team arrived just too late to save Noor and her companions. The OSS officer for whom the poem was written was dropped in September 1944, about the time Noor linked hands with the others. He was himself captured and executed.

Leo's code-poem, given to the doomed American, was composed with Noor in mind:

> Want to say so
> Don't know how
> Want to hug you
> Don't know if I should
> Hope you understand
> I'd take your place if I could.

# A Terrible Irony

*It seems appropriate that a special Jewish unit of that race
which has suffered indescribable torments from the Nazis,
should be represented as a distinct formation
amongst the forces gathered for their overthrow.*

—Winston Churchill, addressing Parliament, September 1944

"The Jews you wanted are finally yours,"
Billy Stephenson wrote to Vera before he was dubbed Sir William for
his work as Coordinator of British Security. "But it's almost five years
late! Those with every motive to hit back at the enemy, who spoke the
languages and had the skills, were locked away in camps." Vera had
been wise to shed her Jewish family name when she left Romania
ahead of Heinrich Himmler's order to SS generals "to exterminate the
Jewish race."

Twelve years later, as the Allies were closing in, Himmler told his
Gauleiters, "I think we had better take this secret with us to our
graves."

"Everyone connected with it will be hunted down and put to
death," Churchill promised Parliament on July 11, 1944. The secret
was so well buried that few non-Jews responded. Within a year, he was
ousted as prime minister. But he had launched the Jewish Fighting
Brigade.

No voice was raised for Diana Hope Rowden. No flag-draped coffin carried her body between honor guards. "Are Jews to vanish into

the same silence?" Vera asked Chaim Weizmann as France spoke of the "Day of Liberation" and reports came in of twelve thousand Jews incinerated daily in Hungary alone. Weizmann gave the estimated figures to Churchill, who requested "action at any cost." Nothing happened. His Foreign Office chief, Anthony Eden, was described by Eden's secretary: "A. E. loves Arabs and hates Jews." A copy of the memo reached Vera. She told Stephenson, "There are towns in France yet to be liberated where Vichy officials obey German regulations, and exercise meticulous care in separating Jewish parents from their children so there's less to offend the public eye."[1]

President Roosevelt said that he did not want a flood of Jewish survivors entering the United States. Whitehall opposed Jewish "displaced persons" settling in Palestine, antagonizing Arabs, endangering Saudi oil interests, and, more importantly, the lifeline to half the empire, the Suez Canal, which ran through Egypt. Churchill described as a "gross breach of faith" the repudiation of the Balfour Declaration with its conditional recognition of Palestine as a Jewish homeland. Many shared his feelings that the new Jewish Brigade Group had a moral right to use irregular warfare specialists trained by Orde Wingate. These included the Haganah underground and Irgun, organizations that were originally set up to resist the Arabs and now stood increasingly at odds with the local British army command.

Edmund de Rothschild, whose family estates provided training facilities for SOE, was too well known to take command of the brigade. The War Office insisted that it "should *not* serve in Palestine or be sent there for disbandment or demobilization." The order added that the Jewish Agency, representing Jews in Palestine, "have not been told of this nor is it intended they should be," because the Agency was "using this opportunity to have their men trained in active operations at our expense."

Vera saw a mirror image of Whitehall's fear of SOE's unconventional methods. She also recognized that nothing would stop Jews now that, after years of silence, newspaper reports began to reveal the Holocaust. On July 8, 1944, the *Times* of London provided eyewitness accounts of sixty-two railway cars entering Auschwitz, each wagon crammed with children under eight. While investigating the fate of missing agents, Vera now had a new resource. She got little help from French collaborators. Decades would pass before the subtleties of behavior under enemy rule were fully explored. The opposition of Allied commanders to closework missions and the Jewish Brigade was hidden until January 1, 2005, when the British Freedom of Information Act (FOIA) became law. "But before this date," said Richard Smith, the FOIA director assisting the deputy prime minister, "directives from secret departments were coming down to us to throw away certain papers." The Campaign for Freedom of Information alleged the papers were destroyed "in anticipation of the Act coming into force." Geoffrey Elliott, the banker who tried to unearth secrets about his father's service in SOE, wrote: "If files should miraculously surface, they'd bear the message seen on toilets in American motels: Sanitised For Your Protection."[2]

The only Jewish unit in Allied forces, the brigade both gave and received scraps of intelligence on the concentration camps, but there was no concerted Allied effort to investigate these. On Christmas Eve 1944, Krystyna, whose Jewish mother had vanished in Warsaw, was almost captured trying to learn the worst. She had sent a small special-operations team from Italy to Poland and was to follow by parachute. Before she could leave Bari, however, the team wirelessed: "Russians wiping out . . . all seen as subverting Stalin." Her colleagues were arrested by Red Army intelligence and disappeared forever.

Edmund de Rothschild, wounded in the May 1944 battle of Monte Cassino, transferred into the Jewish Infantry Brigade Group. On November 8, 1944, the chief rabbi of London wrote: "This would mean a great deal to Jews everywhere." It would also mean a lot to Jews if Krystyna could execute another plan: parachuting agents into the concentration camps. She discussed logistics with the SOE controlling officer in Rome. He had heard so many stories about her — that she wore Leo Marks's coding silks around her neck like a scarf while scrutinized at a German checkpoint; that she silenced a Gestapo Alsatian "sniffer" by hugging the dog to death; that she held up her hands in mock surrender when confronted by a trio of enemy soldiers, then disclosed a grenade in each hand and said if they shot her, they would all be blown away. "She's completely without nerves," the rabbi wrote. "Once, she waited to jump, but the aircraft took so long surveying the dropping zone, she fell asleep."

Her agents, dressed as slave workers, were to be dropped near concentration camps to join the daily entry of foreign workers and help inmates break out while Allied planes strafed the area. Vera wanted no delay. She had heard of behavior among the exterminators that was "madly insane." The wife of a German officer boarded a death train by mistake, saw the ovens when she arrived, and was cremated to stop her talking about them.

Baron Philippe de Vomécourt proposed a similar scheme, but both he and Krystyna ran into fierce opposition. Some governments-in-exile were infected with the old anti-Semitism, and Whitehall was afraid of letting loose Jewish survivors in their liberated lands.[3] In Washington, James Forrestal, the U.S. secretary of defense, said, "The Jewish lobby influences U.S. policy and endangers national security." Oilman Max Thornburg of Caltex feared the U.S. would extinguish Arab faith in American ideals if it backed Palestine for the Jews.[4]

As the Jews became a political time bomb, Vera watched SOE's fortunes decline. The Canadian Army's Brigadier Ernest Benjamin, with twenty-five years of military service, took command of the Jewish Brigade to meet the War Office requirement that whoever was appointed "should not have an aversion to Jews." He was a Jew. He wanted to blow open a camp but Whitehall rejected the plan, recalling Himmler's endorsement in 1943 of His Eminence the Grossmufti, Mohammed Amin al-Husseini, a dedicated terrorist in Palestine, which led to irregular warfare between Arabs and Jews. "We could have done it," Brigadier Benjamin told Vera. "Now I look the other way while my men do what they can."

Benjamin's 5,500 men wore the yellow Star of David on their battledress. "So many millions were condemned to death after being forced to wear it," said one soldier, Maxim Kahan. Another, Ted Arison, said, "The first time we took German prisoners, it was unbelievable." At Passover on March 26, 1945, refugees were astounded to see Jews bearing arms. Rothschild noted that camp survivors told him, "The message for us is: Don't go east, they don't like us. Don't go west, they don't like us. There's no place to go."

A brigade closework specialist, Chanan Greenwald, confirmed Vera's lifelong fear: "Every refugee needs a country of origin. Allied commanders say, 'You don't appear on our books. You are not a nation.'"

Vera recalled, "Balfour hoped Arabs would not 'begrudge that small notch . . . being given to the people who for all these centuries have been separated from it.' But Arabs did begrudge the small notch in Palestine. Old hatreds festered everywhere. Hitler's SS had 150,000 volunteers from non-German Europe helping run the death camps." She wanted SOE to speak for Jews on an Allied armistice commission. In reply, she received copies of a memo by a Foreign Office official, A. J. Dew: "A disproportionate amount of the time of the Office is wasted on dealing with these wailing Jews."[5]

At Mannheim the Jewish Brigade sped "through an archway which still bore the repulsive legend *Judenrein* (Cleansed of Jews)," said Edmund de Rothschild, commanding 604 P battery of the 200 Field Regiment. Jewish soldiers reacted violently. Rothschild's own men were forced to dispatch Uzbek soldiers across a bridge with the Hammer and Sickle at the far end. Rothschild heard shots. All the Uzbeks were murdered. Hundreds of thousands of "displaced" soldiers under Allied command were handed over to certain death. When fifty thousand Cossacks resisted, British soldiers used bayonets to force weeping families into Red Army hands. The West was keeping its agreement with the Soviet Union to surrender everyone Stalin deemed to be Russian.

To avoid ugly scenes, the War Office ordered the brigade to leave German soil. It moved to Belgium to guard military dumps. This proved a better base for closework. There were fifty-four nationalities represented on the brigade rolls, and those searching for their families could reach anywhere in Europe in a day's Jeep ride, weaving through Soviet controls. Rothschild sent his men off on forty-eight-hour "leaves to Paris." They never saw Paris. When the British army conducted an inspection, Rothschild had his remaining soldiers wear forage caps on one side, and then reappear with forage caps tipped to the other side after nipping down the line, out of sight, giving an impression that the entire battery was all present and correct. An inspecting general said to Sergeant Heller, "I've seen you before, haven't I?" Heller replied with great presence of mind, "Sir, you saw my twin brother."[6]

Vera's ally David Bruce, now OSS chief for Europe, was always clashing with the British SIS. He dismissed misgivings about the ethics of such brigade actions: power dictated morality. After President Roosevelt's death in April 1945, Harry S. Truman as the 33rd U.S. president rejected on moral grounds Bill Donovan's plan to turn the OSS into America's first centralized intelligence agency. Then OSS agents began chronicling Stalin's ambitions. American envoy Arthur Schoenfeld cabled an account of communist dictatorship imposed on Hungary. U.S. proconsul Ellery Stone in Rome reported plans for a communist takeover of Italy. Donovan's plan to create the CIA was saved by Truman's decision to confront Stalin. "The Jews," concluded Bruce, "will get moral support when they display power as a nation."

Vera got Lord Selborne to argue for SOE's survival in spite of clandestine cooperation with Jewish agencies. "It would be madness to allow SOE to be stifled," Selborne wrote. "It is a highly specialized weapon." But Churchill, its inspiration, met Truman and Stalin at Potsdam on July 25, 1945, and said he must leave early to fight an election. Stalin glanced at the mousey leader of the opposition, Clement Attlee, and growled, "Mr. Attlee does not look to me like a man who is hungry for power." Next day Britain voted for the Labour Party and Attlee replaced Churchill.

Gubby, as SOE's titular director of operations, wrote again to Lord Selborne: "British Security Coordination (BSC) comprises SIS, SOE, and security and secret-communications sections. . . . It should continue." On October 16, 1945, Gubbins was told his services were no longer required. Stephenson defiantly continued BSC operations and arranged for Vera to be paid out of the Secret Fund. "BSC and SOE had tentacles that were impossible to disentangle," noted William Mackenzie in his highly classified SOE history, kept secret for fifty-five years. With undercover Jewish help, Vera crossed into Russian zones, wearing a squadron leader's uniform, changing into civilian clothes when neccessary. She was helped by twenty-one-year-old Captain Yurka Galitzine, the English-born son of a Russian nobleman. She talked her way past the Russians at Auschwitz, and told the commandant, Rudolf Hoess, she would not leave his detention cell until he told her everything.

She suggested that 1.5 million prisoners had been killed at Auschwitz.

"No! No!" Hoess's professional pride was hurt. "It was 2,345,001."[7]

"Anything is in order that helps Jewish victims move from Y to Z," said an enraged Jewish Brigade aide. "We call it 'up-my-arse' business. . . . TTG stands for the Hebrew version of up-my-arse. We write TTG on forms to shift army lorries around Europe to collect refugees. We ask British officers at checkpoints, 'You mean you don't know what TTG means?' and they say, 'Why, yes, of course!' and wave us on." Jewish Brigade agents stole weapons from storage dumps, and filled out British army forms to cover the disappearance of blankets, milk, chocolate, even airplanes. Shaul Ramat, a Gordon Highlander attached to the brigade, showed Vera how "we make two sets of papers and license plates for each British army lorry." In this way Yerucham Amitai, later deputy commander of the Israeli Air Force, escaped from Warsaw. "Thousands of us were picked up in thirty-four double-licensed trucks. Convoys delivered us to brigade camps and sped back to rescue more. I was shunted to Rome to join a 'flying club.'"[8]

After Churchill's downfall, Krystyna was stuck in Cairo. She was given "a special Middle East movement job" looking for rusting cargo ships whose owners would run the British naval blockade to deliver refugees to Palestine. From Poland, she received reports of Soviet Russian propaganda that Jews were again engaged in the ritual killing of Gentile children, inciting fresh atrocities. Clearly the war against the Jews continued. Forgers in the Jewish Brigade gave "official authorization" for refugees to get military training. Discarded aircraft were flown into Palestine by veteran airmen like Ezer Weizman, the RAF Spitfire pilot who became president of Israel. These actions could never be made public, and Vera, her Jewish background still hidden, stuck to her British vow of lifelong silence.

But while Edmund de Rothschild was still fighting in Italy, he received a large buff envelope from London bearing the seal of the Secretary of State for War, marked "MOST IMMEDIATE." Inside was another sealed envelope marked "PRIME MINISTER." At the time, Winston Churchill was still in office. Inside the innermost envelope, heavily sealed, was a note to be read on the battlefield. "Thank you," wrote Churchill.

# Unsolved Mysteries

At Ravensbrück, fifty miles north of Berlin, once the weekend vacation spot for city dwellers, some 100,000 women prisoners had died since the start of the war. When the Red Army liberated the camp in 1945, there were only 12,000 women still alive. The SS camp overseer, Obersturmführer Johann Schwarzhuber, sat in a vacant cell under Vera's steely gaze. Yes, he said, it was in January 1945 that Violette Szabo, Lilian Rolfe, and Danielle Williams (Denise Bloch) were brought from the satellite camp at Königsberg to Ravensbrück. At the time, the mechanisms for mass murder were not running efficiently. Poison gas was in short supply, so each girl was shot in the back of the head by Corporal Schenk, then shoved into the ovens.

"Corporal Schenk? What was his full name? What unit did he belong to?" Vera asked.

The camp overseer scratched his chin. "We kept good records," he said, and winced. The Russian barbarians had smashed into his office and burned all his papers. Illiterate, dirty scum!

Vera heard another version. An English woman, Mary Lindell, who was also a prisoner, an escape-line organizer, survived. She said Violette and the other girls were hanged, and their stained clothes handed to the camp storekeepers to be laundered.

In Berlin, Vera sought answers to one of the greatest mysteries: Why did the Cipher Office never discover the ULTRA secret? The most significant spy of the era, Hans-Thilo Schmidt, made ULTRA possible by delivering German Enigma machines to the Allies. His brother Rudolf Schmidt, the panzer general, had been taken away by the Russians. Rodolphe Lemoine, who hired Hans-Thilo in 1931 for the French Secret Service, was never seen again after his arrest by the Germans. Did Admiral Canaris hide leaking the Enigma coding system to the Allies? His first wartime secretary, Inga Haag, was now in England, where David Bruce, OSS chief for all Europe, confirmed that she and Admiral Canaris had helped the Allies. Because of OSS skirmishes with Stewart Menzies, head of the SIS, Bruce had kept this information to himself. Menzies took credit for ULTRA, but his service was penetrated by Soviet agents. Bruce, the supreme diplomat, deemed it wise to say nothing of Inga Haag's part in protecting the secret. Lewis F. Powell, who "accepted" ULTRA intelligence for the U.S. Strategic Air Force, recalled after he became a U.S. Supreme Court justice that the Allies never shared ULTRA information with the Soviet Union—but the KGB had a dedicated communist at Bletchley who did.[1]

After escaping from Romania in August 1944, a step ahead of the Russians, Inga Haag worked for David Bruce. Inga lived at 1 Upper Wimpole Street, an upscale London address. She said Canaris ran the November 6, 1937, investigation to cover up the leak of information on Enigma. Those around Canaris were "amateur spymasters," World War I officers with no illusions about Hitler. "We had to have agents, but they were very inefficient, and the best spies worked for both sides," she said. SOE agents who fell into the hands of Canaris's officers in Paris, when Inga served there, were treated "honorably" as prisoners-of-war.

Missie Vassiltchikov escaped to Austria and married Peter Harnden of U.S. Army Intelligence in September 1945. Missie said Ambassador von der Schulenburg, her lover and Vera's, was condemned by the "hanging judge," Roland Freisler of the People's Court, after being named by London Control as foreign minister in a future anti-Nazi German government. Also named was Fabian von Schlabrendorff, who plotted to kill Hitler. The judge, a showman who always tormented the accused with manic speeches about cleansing the world of Jews, forced the defendant to listen for hours to his ranting. Schlabrendorff was close to fainting when an Allied bomb hit the courthouse and killed the judge. The prisoner in the dock escaped.

Hasso von Etzdorf, Vera's friend from her Berlin days, became consul general in Genoa ahead of the roundup of plotters. He was highly regarded in London and became the postwar German ambassador there. Vera no longer had any doubt that London Control's naming of such men as part of the 1944 plot was deliberate: a campaign to get rid of Germans who might have formed an anti-Nazi government against Russia. Stalin's intent, to wipe out all possible opposition to Soviet expansion, was reflected in the way he rebuffed an appeal from Churchill and Roosevelt on August 22, 1944, "to drop immediate supplies and munitions to the patriot Poles of Warsaw." The exchange was recorded by Roosevelt's ULTRA briefing officer, Admiral Bill Mott, who told Vera of Stalin's negative response, condemning the Polish underground as "power-seeking criminals." Stalin had promised that "the Red Army will stint no effort to crush the Germans at Warsaw." He meant, of course, that the Red Army would henceforth control Poland.[2]

Krystyna could never return to Poland. She applied to join the UN's British Section at Geneva but was told, "You are not British at all. You're a foreigner with a British passport." She settled in London, taking any job she could: shop assistant at Harrod's, tearoom waitress, second-class stewardess on a down-at-heel cruise ship. There was no trace of her husband. She was thirty-seven when she was stabbed and killed at her shabby London lodgings one midsummer night in 1952. A spurned suitor, George Muldowney, was convicted of her murder.

Pearl Witherington, who joined the Stationer circuit when she was twenty-five, joked about turning "into a matron" in her two years underground. She took the surrender of eighteen thousand Germans, after expanding her circuit from 20 to 3,500 resisters who, she said with all due modesty, "killed about a thousand Germans...their wounded were counted in thousands." She married her second-in-command, Henri Cornioley, and settled in France after writing citations and recommending the highest awards for gallantry.

SOE agents were not recognized until May 6, 1991, when the widow of King George VI, the Queen Mother, finally laid a wreath at Valençay, in the Loire valley, beneath a monument in the shape of an elongated Byzantine cross. Above it, a glowing white moon signified air drops timed by phases of the moon. The costs were shouldered by old partisans brought together by the Fédération Nationale de Libre

Résistance. The sculptress was secretary of the RAF Escaping Society, Elizabeth Lucas Harrison. The names of unrecognized agents were finally disclosed. The London *Daily Telegraph* asked, "Why did their memorial take 40 years to build?"

The delay had been longer. On December 5, 1946, Vera faced seven German women guards from Ravensbrück at a War Crimes Court in Hamburg. Odette Marie Sansom told how, while waiting to follow other women into the ovens, she was suddenly taken for a drive in a shiny new Mercedes-Benz by the camp commandant, Fritz Suhren, to meet an advance patrol of U.S. infantry. He was proud to announce safe delivery of "a relation to Winston Churchill, the prime minister of England." He was later tried, convicted, and executed, as were some of the female guards.

"L'affaire Odette" caused eventual unease. On February 12, 1959, *L'Express* reported that Baron Henri de Malaval, president of an association of those imprisoned at Fresnes, had been arrested after the Gestapo saw a note left by Peter Churchill, directing Odette and other SOE agents to the baron's villa. It cost the baron his freedom and the lives of others. Accusations were made public that agents were sacrificed to plant false information. Dame Irene Ward tabled a motion in the House of Commons on November 13, 1958, headed "Special Operations Executive and Official Secrets," calling for an inquiry into charges of German penetration of SOE. The motion was never called, and there was no debate. Instead, Prime Minister Harold Macmillan promised that an official history would be published, but Lord John Hope of the Foreign Office warned, "We are bound to bear security in mind first and foremost." There had been "an accidental fire." The SOE Liquidation Section chief, Norman Mott, said records on women agents were destroyed, together with the contents of his own office, where he kept operational files. Briefs from SOE country sections relating to investigations into the blown *réseaux* or circuits were gone. The English-born chief of the Polish section of SOE, known as Colonel Harry Perkins and addressed by Krystyna as "Perks Kochay" or "Darling Perks," said his essential records had been "destroyed by fire."

In 1995, in his last months in office, French president François Mitterrand appointed Vera Atkins commander of the Légion d'Honneur. "A particularly significant decoration," editorialized the *Times* of

London. It looked to her like a last-minute atonement. "The deathbed revelations of President François Mitterrand concerning his indifference toward Vichy's anti-Jewish policies during the war . . . shocked most French men and women," wrote Walter Laqueur.[3] Mitterrand had been a close friend of René Bousquet, head of Vichy French police affairs, a man congratulated by Hitler on joint French-German operations against the maquis.

SS Brigadeführer Franz Six was "recuperated" by the U.S. Army's counterintelligence corps. Six, described by Adolf Eichmann at his Jerusalem trial in 1962 as a man who descended to the depravity of mass murder from his pedestal of "intellectual," had been tried in a case against the Einsatzkommando mass murderers and sentenced to twenty years in prison. He was out within four years to join old colleagues in the postwar German intelligence service run by General Reinhard Gehlen, Hitler's intelligence expert on the Soviet Union.[4]

The Polish code breakers in France met different fates. Those who escaped to England were not allowed to work at Bletchley. Their different paths remained secret until Hugh Sebag-Montefiore documented their stories in *Enigma: The Battle for the Code*, recalling the shabby treatment awarded them by British authorities. The Poles received no public honors or praise. Henryk Zygalski, who had solved the code with Marian Rejewski, took a modest teaching post in an English Children's school. Marian returned to Poland, where the communist regime put him to work in a Soviet-style factory. Maksymilian Ciezki died in obscurity in England in 1951, his huge contribution to ULTRA unacknowledged because of the Official Secrets Act.

Two years after the war ended, Vera estimated that 250,000 Jewish "displaced persons" were adrift in Germany. Shiploads of Jews trying to reach Palestine had been turned back by the British navy and redirected to the scene of the crimes against them. Aloisius Cardinal Muench, Vatican liaison with Germany from 1946 to 1959, recorded a return to anti-Semitism: Germans blamed Jews for delaying American reconstruction.

Vera felt she had been lucky to learn in childhood the consequences of never being able to answer the question "What's your country of origin?" And so Vera Maria Rosenberg was forever buried. As Vera Atkins, she simply asked that, when she died, her body be cremated and her ashes scattered over the English Channel.

# The American Connection

"Moneypenny?"

"Yes," Vera said into the phone at her home in Winchelsea.

"Is this a good connection?"

"I hear you very well," she replied.

"Can you come over for dinner?"

"Where?"

"New York." Bill Casey, then director of the CIA, mumbled a date. The Artful Mumble, she called it—"used by those who guard secrets."

The name Moneypenny was a joke between them. Ian Fleming had tried out other names for the submissive secretary of James Bond —Miss Pettavel, Flissity Brown, and Dominique Domino—then borrowed Moneypenny from *The Sett*, an unfinished novel by his older brother Peter. These were in keeping with the use of cover names, real names, and code names. It seemed to Casey that this suited a woman with several identities. Her present identity fit her life on the Sussex coast. She was now seventy-five and well able to jet across the Atlantic for dinner at short notice.

Winchelsea folk also called her Miss Moneypenny for fun. They live with a history that is in many ways so French, and yet also so English. Their local government is the only one of its kind left in England: a *jurat* appointed by the mayor and parish church councillors after the fashion of medieval Norman France, which once ruled here.

Vera soaked herself in the town's history and the significance of events surrounding the Church of St. Thomas the Martyr. She was there in 1988 on the seven-hundredth anniversary of its foundation, when the Queen Mother planted a chestnut tree in the churchyard. Royalty's interest was more than ceremonial. Winchelsea was part of a confederation of the Cinque Ports, five towns formed to defend part of the east coast against foreign invaders.

Vera reached New York in good time for dinner with Casey on September 22, 1983. It was far more elaborate than she expected. CIA chiefs and veterans of the OSS welcomed her aboard the U.S. aircraft carrier *Intrepid*, berthed at Pier 86, at 46th Street and 12th Avenue. In the hangar deck, cleared of warplanes, a giant portrait of General William J. Donovan loomed over guests in evening gowns and dinner jackets. She heard U.S. president Ronald Reagan's tribute to Sir William Stephenson, recipient of the William J. Donovan Award. "As long as Americans value courage and freedom," said President Reagan, "there will be a special place in our hearts, our minds, and our history books for the man called Intrepid." Stephenson thought Vera Atkins deserved the Donovan Award, but London and Washington had agreed that neither would declassify secrets the other wished to keep. Margaret Thatcher was the previous recipient of the award as the British prime minister who received clandestine U.S. help in the Falklands War.

"Closework was a weapon forged in the Second World War," Stephenson told *Intrepid* guests, "terrible as the atomic bomb. All the world knows about the bomb. Secrecy makes it hard to debate publicly how to handle this other weapon with integrity and prevent its use against us."

After the dinner, Vera paraphrased Russian poet Yevgeny Yevtushenko: "How sharply our children will be ashamed . . . remembering so strange a time when common integrity should look like courage." With us was Beverley Woodner, the Jewish Hollywood set designer whose make-believe skills deceived the Nazis. She said, "If veterans of OSS publicly honored Miss Atkins, even now, we'd upset London. She always had to keep out of sight." Beverley had been an intimate friend of the novelist Graham Greene, a wartime intelligence officer. "He said everyone was so secretive, nobody knew who did what."

"Vera chose obscurity," said a prominent New York businessman, John M. Shaheen. "Men didn't like the idea of a spymistress." In 1943

Shaheen was chief of special projects, and Bill Casey was chief of the OSS Intelligence Service in General Dwight D. Eisenhower's command. Shaheen headed a team that penetrated the Italian Supreme Command, using motor torpedo boats and new signal systems to get through and kidnap an Italian admiral. With the admiral came samples of new Italian naval weapons.

Peter Sichel joined us. He had been a Jedburgh parachuted behind the lines. Now a leading wine merchant, he was with the CIA in Hong Kong, where I had known him. He joked about a small crisis on *Intrepid*. He had whispered in Stephenson's ear, "What wine do you prefer with dinner?" Stephenson replied, "Niersteiner," as he welcomed aboard another colleague, Ernie Cuneo, a wartime adviser to Roosevelt. Peter dashed ashore with Vera. He had arranged the best wines for dinner—but not Niersteiner. They smuggled it aboard in brown paper bags. "It had to do with U.S. Navy and New York City liquor laws," she said. "He used me for cover. An old lady with an English accent. *That* foxed the customs men."

She had foxed many for longer than was realized outside the distinguished group on *Intrepid*. They included those whose careers in OSS extended into the CIA. They remembered how Chamberlain's spirit of appeasement almost let Hitler get away with taking over Europe, and how Roosevelt's yearning for peace led to appeasing Stalin. In December 1945 President Harry Truman's secretary of state James Byrnes, back from Moscow, reported that Stalin "is trying to do in a slick-dip way what Hitler tried to do." The following March, Churchill delivered his famous Iron Curtain speech in Fulton, Missouri: "From Stettin in the Baltic to Trieste in the Adriatic, an iron curtain has descended across the continent. Beyond that line lie all the capitals of the ancient states of Central and Eastern Europe . . ."[1]

Vera was drawn into a postwar Anglo-American intelligence alliance. She was only in her late thirties, with unrivaled experience. Stephenson had written in a foreword to *Top Secret*, an account compiled in 1946 but not made public until fifty years later: "The only hope for democracy's survival is to be forewarned—and to be forewarned clearly necessitates a worldwide Intelligence Service of maximum effectiveness."

A final chapter opened for Vera in the story she could never tell.

In a graduation address at the U.S. Military Academy at West Point in June 1962, President John F. Kennedy said, "This is another type of war, new in its intensity . . . war by guerrillas, subversives, insurgents, assassins; war by ambush instead of combat; by infiltration instead of aggression . . ."

In April 1987 Judge William H. Webster, the former FBI director, testifying before the U.S. Senate Intelligence Committee as the next CIA director, quoted Stephenson when he said, "Secrecy demands integrity. I can't put it better than that."

From time to time, Vera would disappear on unexplained journeys abroad. She was said to be "awesome" and "austere" by those who saw her at the RAF Club in Piccadilly. She preferred it to what was first called the SOE Club to keep together experts in case of future need. It took in the SAS, and became the Special Forces Club. As she aged, she invited her Winchelsea neighbors in for evening drinks, ending at eight o'clock on the dot. The last of her successive homes, Chapel Plat, meaning Place of the Chapel, was the site of a Wesleyan chapel built in 1800. On her ninetieth birthday, the townsfolk presented her with a collage of a succession of modest Winchelsea homes she had occupied when dividing herself between the pressures of work and rural quietude. The town museum also honored a St. Thomas choirboy who had become one of her agents, Major Henri Peuleve. He was a BBC cameraman in the early days of television, and then volunteered to parachute into France in July 1942. He broke a leg, was hunted by the Gestapo, and escaped home through Spain. He was twenty-seven years old when he again parachuted into France and built one of the best SOE circuits, until he was captured in March 1944 and dispatched to Buchenwald. The memorial plaque says: "The rest of his network owed its survival to his fortitude."

Behind Winchelsea's sleepy façade are clues to the duality of Miss Moneypenny-Atkins. There is a house called Moneysellers. It seems close to the name of Moneypenny, as Ian Fleming noted. Moneysellers is a reminder that in 1333 Winchelsea was one of only twenty towns in England where foreign money could be exchanged. Mulberry trees date from when Winchelsea provided these resources to the Third Battalion of the Cinque Ports Volunteers for the Revolutionary and Napoleonic Wars. Caen stone from France was used to build gothic arches and ribs for forty cellars where wines were stored, 120 hogsheads (6,300 gallons) to a cellar. The town attracted artists and writers: Turner, Thackeray, Conrad. Edward Lear, the author of nonsense rhymes, lived nearby. So did three members of the Pre-Raphaelite Brotherhood: Dante Gabriel Rossetti, John Everett Millais, and William Holman Hunt. And here Beatrix Potter dedicated Peter Rabbit to her nephew. Ellen Terry, one of the greatest English actresses, lived in Tower Cottage "on the ivied wall of the ancient Town Gate" and drove visitors around the countryside in a nineteenth-century governess cart. Ford Madox Ford lived on Friar's Road. Winchelsea was the perfect setting for Agatha Christie's Miss Marple, and some who visited Vera thought she suited the part.

In its October 1998 issue, the parish magazine reported that Vera Atkins, at one of the Second Wednesday Society meetings, finally broke silence about her wartime work. Still, she disclosed very little. "Her wry sense of humor demonstrated how she was able to cope with a most demanding and harrowing task," wrote Daphne B. Robertson. "She pointed out that she only agreed to talk because she'd been promised cucumber sandwiches for tea."

This was the same person who had memorized the instruction "There is required . . . an element of legerdemain, an original and sinister touch, which leaves the enemy puzzled as well as beaten." SOE was to represent "tangle within tangle, plot and counter-plot, ruse and treachery, cross and double-cross, true agent, false agent, double agent." Ian Fleming had quoted Winston Churchill in creating James Bond as "a blunt instrument" outside the law. Vera had reminded Fleming that Bond and blunt instruments were the weapons of the weak. She said that Bond was popular because he was human; his devices were inspired by SOE "toys" that sprang from resources so limited that only paupers would bother to turn them into deadly weapons, which was why it was dangerous to talk about them.

In mid-2000, when Vera fell seriously ill, George Millar raced across half of England from Dorset, but arrived too late. "I spent so many years with her," he told me. "When I proposed writing my first book, Maquis, she remonstrated, 'How can you make money out of all this?' But she forgave me, and I enjoyed expensive dinners in London she gave me, and her quick wit. Yet, until the day she died, I never knew she had a Jewish background."

Vera died on June 24, 2000. Her obituary in the Times gave her name as Vera Maria Rosenberg, "intelligence agent." A memorial service was held at the Church of St. Thomas the Martyr. "Grant unto her eternal rest," intoned the preacher. "And let perpetual light shine upon her," responded the congregation. They had long ago welcomed as one of them the girl born a Romanian Jew.

# Notes

CHAPTER 1: MAX'S DAUGHTER

1. Kenneth Rose, *Elusive Rothschild: The Life of Victor, Third Baron* (London: Weidenfeld and Nicolson, 2003), records efforts by Soviet agents in British intelligence services to smear Victor de Rothschild as a communist mole. The book's flap copy notes that Victor, a public-spirited patriot, endured much public humiliation before Margaret Thatcher cleared him of spying for Russia.

2. Vera's recollections, shared with Sir William Stephenson, Lady Mary Stephenson, and Sonia d'Artois, and in David K. E. Bruce, letters to author, 1975–76.

3. Formerly the Public Record Office, the National Archives recorded the existence of the Committee for Imperial Defence, but details were still treated as secret. National Archives documents are otherwise open for research. However, a loophole in the UK's Freedom of Information Act (FOIA) of January 1, 2005, was noted by *BBC History* magazine in October 2004 under the headline, "Legal loophole 'could spell doom for historic research.'" "There is nothing to stop records being destroyed prior to a request," noted the Institute of Historical Research. Prior to enforcement of the act, information deemed to impinge on national security was destroyed or concealed. The UK's notorious obsession with secrecy had already obscured World War II SOE records. Katherine Gunderson of the Campaign for Freedom of Information was quoted in the same issue of *BBC History*: "We are concerned that information could be destroyed in anticipation of the act." Richard Smith in the Office of the Deputy Prime Minister disclosed that "initiatives are coming down to us to whittle away our records" before the FOIA was enforced. Scholars protested that secret wartime documents dating back sixty years and more were "weeded" during this period. The earlier thirty-year rule should have opened documents filed during SOE's operations between 1940 and 1945, but important SOE files were burned in 1945, and no official record of Vera Maria Rosenberg's early life is to be found in these archives.

4. *BBC History*, October 2004.

5. Vera entrusted these and the following details to Lady Stephenson, who shared them with the author.

6. Lady Stephenson's recollections to the author.

7. Identity not made public.

8. Vera's response to queries about her time in Germany from notes kept by Sir William Stephenson.

9. See Walter Laqueur, ed., *The Holocaust Encyclopedia* (New Haven, Conn.: Yale University Press, 2001).

10. Robert Mendelsohn, British author and publisher of Prion Books, is a widely traveled entrepreneur whose businesses range from gold mining in Central Europe to exporting Scotch whiskey to Japan. An amiable and acute observer of these times, Mendelsohn with his generosity in sharing research and firsthand knowledge greatly assisted the author.

11. Quoted in the author's *A Man Called Intrepid* (New York: Harcourt Brace Jovanovich, 1976).

12. Margaret MacMillan, *Paris 1919* (New York: Random House, 2001).

13. Srinagarindra, Princess Mother of Thailand, interview by author; the author's *The Revolutionary King* (London: Constable, 1998).

CHAPTER 2: MUTUAL FRIENDS VS. GUILTY MEN

1. Elena Marks, interview by author.

2. Frank Whittle, interview by author.

3. Ian Kershaw, "Making Friends with Hitler," *BBC History*, November 2004.

4. Vera was so impressed by this Churchillian statement that many years later she told the youngest female agent in SOE, Sonia d'Artois, that she had tried but failed to trace its origin. Sonia became a close companion to Vera in later years, and I am indebted to her for many anecdotes repeated here. Her husband, Guy d'Artois, immediately followed Sonia's insertion into France. Both are better honored in Canadian military records than British, although France recognized their gallantry and awarded Guy the Legion of Honor. Sonia's feats appeared in Sebastian Faulks's novel, *Charlotte Gray*, and in the 2005 movie of same.

CHAPTER 3: KILL HITLER?

1. MacMillan, *Paris 1919*.

2. From notes kept by Mary Stephenson, and her later observations to the author.

3. Menachem Begin, *The Revolt: Story of the Irgun*, trans. Samuel Katz (London: W. H. Allen, 1951); Begin, televised interview by author, 1977.

4. Begin, *The Revolt*.

5. Laqueur, *The Holocaust Encyclopedia*; also Walter Laqueur, *A World of Secrets: The Uses and Limits of Intelligence* (New York: Basic Books, 1985).

6. Rose, *Elusive Rothschild*.

7. W. J. M. Mackenzie, *The Secret History of SOE: Special Operations Executive, 1940–1945* (London: St. Ermin's Press, 2000). Though it was written immediately after the war at the suggestion of General Sir Colin Gubbins, executive head of SOE, publication was delayed until 2000, when an edited version became available in the Public Record Office.

8. Hugh Dalton, *The Second World War Diary: 1940–1945* (London: Jonathan Cape, 1986).

9. From notes of Vera's conversations with Mary Stephenson.

CHAPTER 4: RETURN TO BERLIN

1. *Parliamentary Debates Hansard*, November 1935.

2. John Weitz, *Hitler's Diplomat* (New York: Ticknor and Fields, 1992), an authoritative account of the social and political basis of Nazi Germany, and the first full-length biography of Joachim von Ribbentrop, Hitler's notorious foreign minister.

3. Charles Williams, *The Last Great Frenchman* (London: Little, Brown, 1993). This biography of Charles de Gaulle by a former British ambassador in Paris is an indispensable, objective record of French history of this period and how it shaped the determination of General de Gaulle as leader of the Free French.

4. John Costello, *Mask of Treachery* (New York: William Morrow, 1988). Costello shared his extensive research and notes from the Cadogan diaries with Monika Jensen, then staff producer at CBS's *60 Minutes*, who was preparing the segment "The Last Nazi."

CHAPTER 5: CROWN OR COMMONER: WHERE LIES THE TREACHERY?

1. Fritz Hesse, *Hitler and the English*, trans. F. A. Voigt (London: Wingate, 1954).

2. David K. E. Bruce, conversations with and letters to author, 1975–76.

3. Colin Gubbins, interviews with and letters to author, 1970s, when the Official Secrets Act still applied.

4. Paul Schmidt, *Hitler's Interpreter* (New York: Macmillan, 1951), quoted by Ian Kershaw, one of the world's leading authorities on Hitler and a professor of modern history at the University of Sheffield, in "Making Friends with Hitler," *BBC History Magazine*, November 2004.

CHAPTER 6: "ENGLAND CUT OFF"

1. Paul Johnson, *Modern Times: The World from the Twenties to the Eighties* (New York: Harper and Row, 1983). Johnson had been editor of the left-wing *New Statesman* but became increasingly critical of Lloyd George's pacifist followers.

2. Winterbotham had to wait thirty-five years to disclose Poland's role in the ULTRA saga that was later considered a key to Britain's survival. Winterbotham's book *The Ultra Secret* (New York: Harper and Row, 1974) was published in defiance of British government attempts to suppress it. Until then, the story of brilliant academics working round the clock in dreary conditions to break the constantly changing Enigma codes had been such a closely guarded secret that even Bletchley townsfolk had never talked about it. The *Daily Mirror* quoted Winterbotham's account of how he was punished for breaking the silence: "I never ranked higher than a group captain." Winterbotham was employed by the RAF and by the Secret Intelligence Service, but was left without a pension from either.

3. Chandos Brudenell-Bruce, Earl of Cardigan, *I Walked Alone* (London: Routledge and K. Paul, 1950).

4. Quoted in E. H. Cookridge, *Inside SOE: The First Full Story of Special Operations Executive in Western Europe 1940–45* (London: Arthur Baker, 1966).

5. Among those who said Vera talked informally with Churchill and provided him with one-sheet reports on resistance in wartime Europe were the Stephensons; Bill Casey, who became CIA director; and news correspondents who later served as agents in occupied France.

6. Ian Fleming, conversation with author, 1956.

7. Geoffrey Cox, conversation with author, who worked with him at Independent Television News. Cox ran ITN in the 1960s and 1970s.

CHAPTER 7: CONNECTIONS

1. Nadya Letteney, interview by author. She later became a buyer at Macy's on Broadway after serving in Stephenson's wartime operations in New York.

2. Irina von Meyendorff, conversations with author. On widespread suspicions about British "black propaganda" see Marie Vassiltchikov, *Berlin Diaries: 1940–1945* (New York: Knopf, 1987).

3. Goerdeler was not hanged until February 2 because Himmler hoped Goerdeler's contacts with the West might save Himmler's neck if things collapsed.

4. Stanley A. Blumberg and Gwinn Owens, *The Survival Factor: Israeli Intelligence from World War I to the Present* (New York: Putnam, 1981).

5. C. H. Ellis, *The Transcaspian Episode: 1918–1919* (London: Hutchinson, 1963).

CHAPTER 8: SPATTERING BRAINS WITH A KNOBKERRIE

1. The full extent of his influence was finally laid out in Amanda Smith, ed., *Hostage to Fortune: The Letters of Joseph P. Kennedy* (New York: Viking, 2001).

2. Weitz, *Hitler's Diplomat.*

3. William L. Shirer, *The Rise and Fall of the Third Reich: A History of Nazi Germany* (New York: Simon and Schuster, 1960).

4. Richard Hughes, interview by author. Hughes interviewed Burgess in 1957 in Moscow. See also Peter Wright, *Spycatcher: The Candid Autobiography of a Senior Intelligence Officer* (New York: Viking, 1987).

CHAPTER 9: POLAND BREAKS THE FIRST ENIGMA

1. Malcolm MacDonald, interview by author; Yehuda Bauer, *From Diplomacy to Resistance: A History of Jewish Palestine, 1939–45*, trans. Alton M. Winters (Philadelphia: Jewish Publication Society of America, 1970); minutes taken at the Weizmann-MacDonald conference. See also Bernard Wasserstein, *Britain and the Jews of Europe, 1939–1945* (New York: Oxford University Press, 1979); and Cordell Hull, *Memoirs of Cordell Hull* (New York: Macmillan, 1948).

2. Anthony Cavendish, interview by author. See also *Inside Intelligence*

by Anthony Cavendish, first privately printed in 1987. The British government tried to silence him by claiming there was a lifelong duty of confidentiality that was understood by secret service officers. A more circumspect version was later published (London: Collins, 1990).

3. *The Diaries of Sir Alexander Cadogan, O.M., 1938–1945*, were censored even when published a quarter century later (New York: Putnam, 1972), although they were billed as "Secret Diaries Reveal Countless Hitherto Unknown Facts."

4. Colin Gubbins, interview by and letters to author.

CHAPTER 10: BETRAYALS ALL AROUND

1. Paul Paillole, *Notre espion chez Hitler* (Paris: Robert Laffont, 1985).

2. Gordon Welchman, interviews by and letters to author. For a thorough description, see the most authoritative work: Hugh Sebag-Montefiore, *Enigma: The Battle for the Code* (New York: John Wiley, 2000).

3. Stalin's sources included the spy network Rote Kapelle, a cryptonym coined by the German central security office, the Reichssicherheitshauptamt or RSHA. London acknowledged later that messages exchanged with the British ambassador in Berlin, Sir Neville Henderson, were intercepted by Germany and passed on to Moscow. See also *The Diaries of Sir Alexander Cadogan*.

CHAPTER 11: VERA'S FIRST MISSION IN AN OPEN WAR

1. *The Diaries of Sir Alexander Cadogan*.

2. See minutes of the British Foreign Office quoted in Blumberg and Owens, *The Survival Factor*, and Wasserstein, *Britain and the Jews of Europe*.

3. Rev. Charles E. Coughlin, *A Series of Lectures on Social Justice* (Royal Oak, Mich.: Radio League of the Little Flower, 1935). Father Coughlin was notoriously pro-Nazi. Philip Johnson's record as a fascist ran from 1932 to 1940, between the ages of twenty-six and thirty-four. This was later overshadowed by his reputation in the architectural world after he joined the Museum of Modern Art in New York. He died in January 2005, and the *New York Times* obituary barely mentioned his "brief involvement in right-wing politics." Other reports have also played down his involvement with the Nazi cause. Franz Schulze's authoritative biography, *Philip Johnson: Life and Work* (New York: Knopf, 1994), chronicles his period of dedication to the Nazi cause, his efforts to start an American fascist party, and his virulent anti-Semitism. Johnson later publicly apologized for his "utter, unbelievable stupidity" after it was fully documented by William L. Shirer in *Berlin Diary* (New York: Knopf, 1941).

4. Stanley Orlowski and Jan Zurakowski, interviews by author.

5. Joseph Goebbels, *The Goebbels Diaries: 1939–1941*, trans. and ed. Fred Taylor (New York: Putnam, 1983).

6. Simon papers and Hebrew University of Jerusalem.

7. Hugh Dalton, *The Fateful Years: Memoirs, 1931–1945* (London: Muller, 1957).

CHAPTER 12: KBO: KEEP BUGGERING ON

1. National Archives (London), Prem 3/22/44, July 10, 1941.

2. *War Cabinet Minutes 1939–45* (London: Her Majesty's Stationery Office, 1989), 22: September 21, 1939, 11 A.M.

3. Martin Gilbert, *Finest Hour: Winston S. Churchill, 1939–1941* (London: Heinemann, 1983).

4. *British Security Coordination: The Secret History of British Intelligence in the Americas, 1940–1945* (New York: Fromm International, 1999), first compiled for BSC in New York by William Stephenson in 1945; Joseph E. Persico, *Roosevelt's Secret War* (New York: Random House, 2001); Harold Nicolson, *Diaries and Letters, 1939–1945* (London: Collins, 1967).

5. Made public only many years later in *The Diaries of Sir Alexander Cadogan*.

CHAPTER 13: YOUR AFFECTIONATE OPPOSITION: THE GESTAPO

1. Goebbels, *Diaries*.

2. Schellenberg later appeared at the Nuremberg war crimes trials and denied knowledge of Nazi atrocities. Before Berlin fell, he was in Sweden, he said, "to negotiate an end to the war." In January 1948 he faced an American military tribunal that sentenced him to six years in prison. He said he always helped prisoners in concentration camps. He didn't serve his full sentence, as the Allies used such "experts" to help fight communism.

3. See U.S. intelligence analysis of captured Nazi records: Thomas Troy, CIA historian, and his account, "The Coordinator of Information and British Intelligence," classified secret and circulated within the CIA, 1970, and published in *Studies in Intelligence* (Washington, D.C.: U.S. Central Intelligence Agency, 1974). See also Walter Schellenberg, *The Labyrinth: Memoirs*, trans. Louis Hagen (New York: Harper, 1956).

4. Goebbels, *Diaries*.

CHAPTER 14: THE PHONY WAR ENDS

1. Noel Coward, interview by author, 1973.

CHAPTER 15: "A GIGANTIC GUERRILLA"

1. Dalton, *Second World War Diary*.

2. Quoted in Hugh Cudlipp, *Publish and Be Damned!: The Astonishing Story of the Daily Mirror* (London: Andrew Dakers, 1953).

3. John Colville, *The Fringes of Power: 10 Downing Street Diaries, 1939–1955* (New York: W. W. Norton, 1986); John Lukacs, *Five Days in London: May 1940* (New Haven, Conn.: Yale University Press, 1999).

4. From the account written by Nadya Letteney for the author.

5. Richard J. Whalen, *The Founding Father: The Story of Joseph P. Kennedy* (New York: New American Library, 1964); Persico, *Roosevelt's Secret War*; Randolph Churchill, personal account to author and Vera in Cairo, 1956.

6. *War Cabinet Minutes* 155: June 5, 1940, 12:30 P.M.

CHAPTER 16: THE LIPS OF A STRANGE WOMAN

1. Winston Churchill, *The World Crisis* (New York: Scribner, 1949); Ian Fleming's letter to Sir William Stephenson.

2. Winston Churchill, *Their Finest Hour*, vol. 2 of *The Second World War* (Boston: Houghton Mifflin, 1949).

3. Quoted by Lukacs in *Five Days in London*; Andrew Roberts, *Eminent Churchillians* (New York: Simon and Schuster, 1994). In July 1938 Halifax received Wiedemann in London.

CHAPTER 17: SABOTAGE ETCETERA ETCETERA

1. It would be another sixty years before official records of Stephenson's wartime directorship of British Security Coordination, labeled "top secret" and from which these details originate, became available. BSC papers make clear why he became the first foreigner to receive the highest U.S. civilian decoration, the Presidential Medal for Merit, for "invaluable assistance . . . in the fields of intelligence and special operations."

2. Douglas Dodds-Parker, *Setting Europe Ablaze: Some Accounts of Ungentlemanly Warfare* (Windlesham, Surrey: Springwood Books, 1983).

3. Publicly acknowledged at the end of 2001 with the declassification of British government documents on the Political Warfare Executive.

4. John Morton Blum, *From the Morgenthau Diaries*, vol. 2, *Years of Urgency, 1938–1941* (Boston: Houghton Mifflin, 1965).

5. *History of the Second World War* (London: Her Majesty's Stationery Office).

CHAPTER 18: A YEAR ALONE

1. From Portal's memo, *Secret and Personal, February 1, 1941: An Official Document* (London: Her Majesty's Stationery Office, 1966).

CHAPTER 19: A CIVIL WAR ENDS, A NIGHTMARE BEGINS

1. *House of Commons Hansard*, November 12, 1940.

2. National Archives, CAB 80/56.

3. Just before Leo Marks died at the end of the century, he used the line as the title of a book that finally broke a British government ban, *Between Silk and Cyanide: A Codemaker's War, 1941–1945* (New York: Free Press, 1998).

CHAPTER 20: "SPECIALLY EMPLOYED AND NOT PAID FROM ARMY FUNDS"

1. Ben Levy, interview by author.

CHAPTER 21: "SHE COULD DO ANYTHING WITH DYNAMITE EXCEPT EAT IT"

1. Arthur Koestler, *The Invisible Writing: An Autobiography* (Boston: Beacon Press, 1955).

CHAPTER 22: THE BLACK CHAMBER

1. National Archives, UKRO HW 14/7, letter, October 21, 1940.

CHAPTER 23: "SHE HAS TO BELIEVE IN WHAT SHE IS DOING OR GO MAD"

1. His name was blackened in secret MI5 reports that smoldered until forcibly made public early in the twenty-first century. Bodington was portrayed in the MI5 reports as a traitor, but was never given the opportunity to clear his name. Once again secrecy falsified history. Vera lived in the same constant danger of unsupportable accusations that, being secret, could never be refuted.

2. Daniel Cordier, *Jean Moulin*, 3 vols. (Paris: Lattès, 1989–93); Douglas Porch, *The French Secret Services* (London: Macmillan, 1996). Porch draws on numerous memoirs by French agents of World War II, and his objective survey is useful as an antidote to more exaggerated anecdotal histories.

3. The poem "The Life That I Have" was destined to become one of

Britain's most popular love poems after a ban was finally lifted by the British government in 1998 and Marks was able to publish his memoirs, which told how Violette saved the life of the White Rabbit and lost her own; see Marks, *Between Silk and Cyanide*.

CHAPTER 24: THE FLYING VISIT

1. Charles Fraser-Smith, interviews by and correspondence with author, 1981–83.

2. Fraser-Smith and Hugh Thomas, interviews with author, 1981 (Thomas was the British Army surgeon who examined Hess in Spandau jail, Berlin); Hess's keepers at Spandau, interviews by author; research for William Stevenson, *Eclipse* (New York: Doubleday, 1986).

3. Rudolf Hess and Ilse Hess, *Prisoner of Peace* (Torrance: Institute for Historical Review, 1954), in which Oddie writes: "Secrecy has never been and never will be a weapon of Good while more often than not it is the distinguishing mark of Evil." See also Winston Churchill, *The Second World War*, vol. 3, *The Grand Alliance* (Boston: Houghton Mifflin, 1950), in which he comments: "Reflecting upon the whole of this story, I am glad not to be responsible for the way in which Hess has been and is being treated."

4. Quoted in Vassiltchikov, *Berlin Diaries*; Missie's postwar conversations with Vera.

5. Wright, *Spycatcher*. Wright was said to have spent twenty-five years inside the highest echelons of British intelligence. He accused the Crown of suppressing the truth about SIS traitors from the privileged upper class by misusing the Official Secrets Act. The British government suppressed the publication of the book and launched lawsuits throughout the world as Wright tried to find a country where he could publish his findings. Finally, in Australia in 1986–87, the Crown sent its most senior security adviser, Cabinet Secretary Sir Robert (later Lord) Armstrong, to seek an injunction in the Supreme Court of New South Wales. Armstrong was famously committed to ancient doctrines of official secrecy. Peter Wright's lawyer was an Australian who tore into the English guardian of secrecy with all the ferocity of the New World confronting the Old. *Spycatcher* was eventually published everywhere except in Britain. U.S. editions were smuggled into London. The establishment took revenge, using its well-worn tools for character assassination. MI5 director general Stella Rimington, after her retirement in 2000, still kept up the barrage of attacks on Wright, who by then was dead, and told the press, "He was self-important. He had an overdeveloped imagination and an obsessive personality which turned to paranoia."

CHAPTER 26: "WE ARE IN THE PRESENCE OF A CRIME WITHOUT A NAME"

1. Jan Zurakowski, interview by author. "Zura" told me the entire story while testing a prototype long-range fighter, the Avro CF-100. He was demonstrating his new aerobatic, the first to be invented in years, when we had an emergency after pulling out of his "Zurabatic." I was in the rear cockpit of the two-seater jet when he told me quietly that we'd have to bail out. Later, back on the ground, we had to spend the night in a form of quarantine because the CF-100 was still secret. World War II had ended some ten years earlier. He no longer needed to worry about *that* secrecy.

2. Diane T. Putney, ed., *ULTRA and the Army Air Forces in World War II: An Interview with Associate Justice of the U.S. Supreme Court Lewis F. Powell, Jr.* (Washington, D.C.: Office of Air Force History, 1987); and Admiral William C. Mott, *Intelligence Report* (the newsletter for the American Bar Association's Standing Committee on Law and National Security), August 1988.

3. Schellenberg, *The Labyrinth*.

4. John Raymond Godley Baron Kilbracken, *Bring Back My Stringbag: Swordfish Pilot at War, 1940–45* (London: Peter Davis, 1979); Lord Kilbracken, correspondence with author.

5. Ezer Weizman, interview by author. Ezer Weizman dropped the final "n" from his name, not wishing to ride on Chaim's coattails.

6. Bill Mott and CBS *60 Minutes* producer Monika Jensen, interviews by author, 1983–85. Supreme Court Justice Powell said in parallel interviews that he kept his own role secret for another thirty years, even from his wife.

CHAPTER 27: "THIN RED LINE"

1. Baron Rüdiger von Etzdorf took British nationality at the war's end, dropped his titles, and died in London in May 1967 "unknown and unsung," commented the *Times*. He had helped the escape of an untold number of Allied soldiers and airmen, and civilian refugees. His brother in 1967 was German ambassador to Britain.

2. Colonel Passy, *Deuxième Bureau Londres* and *10 Duke Street, Londres* (Monte Carlo: Raoul Solar, 1947) and *Missions secrètes en France: novembre 1942–juin 1943* (Paris: Plon, 1951). A fourth volume was not published.

CHAPTER 28: FULLY OCCUPIED

1. Prince Bisadej, conversations with author, 1992. This former SOE Siam Section agent provided vivid accounts of hard training after King

Bhumibol, the Ninth Rama, agreed there was no further need for secrecy. Bisadej is a phonetic rendering of the single name by which Thais are customarily known.

2. Bickham Sweet-Escott, interviews by author, 1974; Sweet-Escott, *Baker Street Irregular* (London: Methuen, 1965).

3. Obituary of Hermione, Countess of Ranfurly, *Daily Telegraph*, February 13, 2001. She was eighty-seven.

4. Randolph Churchill, his Yugoslav translator in Zagreb and Cairo, Mrdjn Lenka, and Ted Howe, interviews by author. Ted Howe parachuted into Yugoslavia and floated down a German searchlight beam. He sideslipped into the darkness and spent what he called "hideous months trekking through mountains on horseback, gradually eating the horses as we ran out of food."

5. Roy Jenkins, *Churchill: A Biography* (New York: Farrar, Straus and Giroux, 2001).

6. Mackenzie, *Secret History of SOE*. Although it was written immediately after the war at the suggestion of General Sir Colin Gubbins, executive head of SOE, publication was delayed until 2000, when an edited version became available in the Public Record Office.

7. Benjamin Cowburn, *No Cloak, No Dagger* (London: Jarrolds, 1960).

8. Jozef Cyrankiewicz, interview by author; reports in the London *Daily Express*, 1953; reports in the Toronto *Daily Star*, 1953.

9. W. J. West, ed., *Orwell: The War Commentaries* (New York: Pantheon, 1985).

10. Jan Nowak, interviews by author; Nowak, *Courier from Warsaw* (Detroit: Wayne State University Press, 1982).

CHAPTER 29: BLUFF AND COUNTERBLUFF

1. Raymond Ruffin, *La Résistance normande face à la Gestapo* (Paris: Presses de la Cité, 1977).

2. From Carleton Coon's report to Sir William Stephenson, found among top secret papers for Intrepid's postwar official history.

3. David Bruce, interviews by and correspondence with author.

4. Reinhard Gehlen, interviews by author, conducted in 1972 at Gehlen's home after he retired as chief of West Germany's first spy agency; Gehlen, *The Service*, trans. David Irving (New York: World, 1972).

5. Charles Webster and Noble Frankland, *The Strategic Air Offensive Against Germany 1939–1945* (London: Her Majesty's Stationery Office, 1961).

6. Goebbels, *Diaries*; Roger Manvel and Heinrich Fraenkel, *The Canaris Conspiracy: The Secret Resistance to Hitler in the German Army* (New York: McKay, 1969).

7. Terence O'Brien, *The Moonlight War: The Story of Clandestine Operations in South-East Asia, 1944–5* (London: Collins, 1987); Charles Dunne, conversations with author. Charles Dunne was O'Brien's fellow pilot.

8. Dunne and Bill Simpson, conversations with author; Prince Svasti's intelligence reports in author's files.

CHAPTER 30: THE WHITE RABBIT HOPS INTO THE "GOVERNOR'S" DEN

1. Inga was honored for her heroic work only after controls over "non-existent" SOE records were partly relaxed. Conversations and correspondence with the author.

2. The full Churchill interview was recounted by Yeo-Thomas to Vera Atkins. See Bruce Marshall, *The White Rabbit*, from the story told to him by F. F. E. Yeo-Thomas (Boston: Houghton Mifflin, 1952); Leo Marks and Wing Commander F. F. E. Yeo-Thomas, GC, MC, interviews by author.

CHAPTER 31: AN UNPLANNED AND GIGANTIC SPYGLASS

1. The French side of the stories of Watlington and Yeager is given in the *Bulletin de l'Amicale des Maquis et des Anciens Réfractaires et Résistants A.S. de la Haute-Corrèze*, 1992, published regularly under UNESCO Classification 34/ Dossier de déclaration annuelle. After the war, Hartley Watlington dictated an account to his wife, Faith. His memoir was approved by security officials after he left out details of unconventional warfare that might help future postwar enemies, and this was published in the *Bermuda Historical Quarterly* in 1949. See also Chuck Yeager and Leo Janos, *Yeager: An Autobiography* (New York: Bantam Books, 1985). Yeager shot down a dozen enemy aircraft after Eisenhower agreed he could resume flying combat operations. He made a dramatic leap into supersonic aviation as a test pilot, and later flew tactical bombers in Asia and supervised military defenses in Pakistan and Afghanistan.

CHAPTER 32: ROLANDE

1. She recalled all this years later when she was being honored at the U.S. Special Forces base at Fort Bragg, North Carolina.

CHAPTER 33: TANGLED WEBS

1. Gustave Bertrand, *Enigma, ou La plus grande énigme de la guerre 1939–1945* (Paris: Plon, 1973).

2. Martin Gilbert, *Winston S. Churchill*, vol. 7, *Road to Victory* (Boston: Houghton Mifflin, 1966) and *The Second World War: A Complete History* (New York: Henry Holt, 1989).

3. Bertrand in fact kept the ULTRA secret from the public until 1973, then published his version, *Enigma, ou La plus grande énigme de la guerre*. It was a break in the silence. Twenty years later, code breaker Hinsley was allowed to disclose that early reading of the German army and air force Enigma traffic staved off Britain's defeat in 1940. Paul Paillole in *Notre espion chez Hitler* described Hans-Thilo Schmidt as "our spy" but did not mention his contribution to successes that were made clear in F. H. Hinsley and Alan Stripp, eds., *Codebreakers: The Inside Story of Bletchley Park* (New York: Oxford University Press, 1994), a compilation of essays by those who worked at Bletchley. See also Paul Paillole, *L'homme des services secrets: Entretiens avec Alain-Gilles Minella* (Paris: Julliard, 1995).

4. The bicycle Semper is now in Israel's Holocaust Memorial Center. Marie-Rose donated it in 2000, when she was eighty-nine, fifteen years after Israel made her one of the Righteous Among Nations.

5. Sefton Delmer, *Black Boomerang* (New York: Viking, 1962); Delmer, interviews by author. Delmer said incriminating Political Warfare Executive documents were officially "destroyed" after 1945, adding, "These things don't happen by mistake."

6. Justice Powell and Justice William Brennan, conversations and correspondence with author, 1984. The conversations took place at the U.S. Supreme Court.

CHAPTER 34: DEADLY MIND AND WIRELESS GAMES

1. Colby became a director of the CIA; Peggy Knight sank into obscurity, with no pension, as a London suburban housewife.

CHAPTER 35: "THE LIFE THAT I HAVE IS YOURS"

1. Jacques Deleporte, conversations with the author, 1945.

2. George Millar, interviews with author. See also Millar, *Maquis* (London: Heinemann, 1945). Somerset Maugham called him "the man of the future."

3. Richard Hughes, conversations with the author. Hughes was memo-

rialized in a spy novel by John le Carré, *The Honourable Schoolboy* (New York: Knopf, 1977).

4. Maurice J. Buckmaster, *Specially Employed: The Story of British Aid to French Patriots of the Resistance* (London: Batchworth, 1952) and *They Fought Alone: The Story of British Agents in France* (New York: W. W. Norton, 1958).

5. Jan Zurakowski and Colin Gubbins, conversations with author. See also Peter Wilkinson and Joan Bright Astley, *Gubbins and SOE* (London: Leo Cooper, 1993).

6. M. R. D. Foot, *SOE in France*, rev. ed. (Portland, Ore.: Frank Cass, 2003).

7. Otto John, televised interview with author, 1973.

8. Thornley's letter to Peter Wilkinson of SOE was not made public until the Gubbins biography *Gubbins and SOE*, heavily screened by the Foreign Office, was published in 1993.

9. After the war, Missie tried to obtain information about these broadcasts. According to her *Berlin Diaries*, all those responsible "denied any knowledge" of the broadcasts. The existence of a Controlling Officer of Deception and the London Control Directorate had not yet been disclosed. Even in 2002 the disclosure of a report written in 1947 for the British government on the Political Warfare Executive sheds no light on the mystery.

10. Gubbins, conversations and correspondence with author. See also *Gubbins and SOE*.

CHAPTER 36: "MY UNCLE IS LORD VANSITTART"

1. See *Bulletin de l'Amicale des Maquis et des Anciens Réfractaires et Résistants A.S. de la Haute-Corrèze*, 1992.

2. The German pilot's logbook is in the author's files.

3. Gilbert, *Winston S. Churchill*, vol. 7.

4. See also Pierre Tanant, *Vercors, haut-lieu de France: Souvenirs* (Grenoble: Arthaud, 1947), a detailed account by the maquis chief of staff.

5. General de Lattre de Tassigny signed the German surrender documents on behalf of France on May 8, 1945. He later commanded the French forces in Indochina, 1950–52, and after his death in 1952 was posthumously made a marshal of France.

6. General Stawell to Gubbins, quoted in M. J. Nurenberger, *The Scared and the Doomed* (Oakville, N.Y.: Mosaic Press, 1985).

CHAPTER 37: "BUT IF THE CAUSE BE NOT GOOD . . ."

1. See Carlo D'Este, *Eisenhower: A Soldier's Life* (New York: Henry Holt, 2002).

2. See Williams, *The Last Great Frenchman*. This is a sympathetic biography by Lord Williams of Elvel, the deputy leader of the opposition in Britain's House of Lords.

3. A copy of Stratton's note to Donovan survived among Sir William Stephenson's papers.

4. William Shakespeare, *Henry V*, Act IV, Scene I.

CHAPTER 38: "IF THESE DO NOT DIE WELL, IT WILL BE A BLACK MATTER"

1. Noor Inayat Khan, *Twenty Jataka Tales* (London: George G. Harrap, 1939).

2. Alix d'Unienville wrote her recollections for her family.

3. Suspicions that Dericourt was a Soviet double agent had been nurtured by London Control. Yet later he was to fly in French Indochina for Aigle Azure, an airline also used for delivering Laotian paratroopers during the first Vietnam war. He later joined the CIA proprietory airline Air America, and was killed in Laos on November 20, 1962.

4. Martin Gilbert, *Final Journey: The Fate of the Jews in Nazi Europe* (London: Allen and Unwin, 1979); Johnson, *Modern Times*.

5. See *The Natzweiler Trial*, ed. Anthony M. Webb (London: Hodge, 1949). On the third week of June each year, there is a vigil held at the camp. *Libre Résistance*, published by an association of French survivors who worked with SOE networks, contains information "lost" in London files, including those for eighty SOE circuits.

CHAPTER 39: A TERRIBLE IRONY

1. Sir William Stephenson, interviews with author. See Laquer, *The Holocaust Encyclopedia*.

2. Geoffrey Elliott, *I Spy: The Secret Life of a British Agent* (London: Little, Brown, 1998).

3. Philippe de Vomécourt, *Who Lived to See the Day: France in Arms, 1940–1945* (London: Hutchinson, 1961).

4. Quoted in Alfred Steinberg, *The Man from Missouri: The Life and Times of Harry S. Truman* (New York: Putnam, 1962).

5. Yitshaq Ben-Ami, *Years of Wrath, Days of Glory: Memoirs from the Irgun* (New York: Robert Speller, 1982); Brigadier Ernest Benjamin, interviews by author.

6. Edmund de Rothschild, *A Gilt-Edged Life: Memoir* (London: John Murray, 1998); Rothschild's conversations with author, 2001; Jewish Brigade survivors, interviews by author.

7. *Gubbins and SOE*; Gubbins, correspondence with Sir William Stephenson and author; Mackenzie, *The Secret History of SOE*, which noted subterranean links between nine U.K. secret services.

8. Yerucham Amitai, conversations with author.

CHAPTER 40: UNSOLVED MYSTERIES

1. Putney, *ULTRA and the Army Air Forces in World War II*.

2. Mott, *Intelligence Report*, August 1988; Mott, interviews by author.

3. *Holocaust Encyclopedia*.

4. Gehlen, interview by author; Tom Bower, *The Pledge Betrayed: America and Britain and the Denazification of Postwar Germany* (New York: Doubleday, 1982).

CHAPTER 41: THE AMERICAN CONNECTION

1. Patricia Dawson Ward, *The Threat of Peace: James F. Byrnes and the Council of Foreign Ministers, 1945–1946* (Kent, Ohio: Kent State University Press, 1979).

# INDEX